READER'S REVIEW
(June-2012 edition)

"Thanks for the book you shared, it's very informative and very well organized. Sure it will help me as I am preparing to join back to work after a gap of 2 years." *By a Software professional with 2+ years of experience in software industry (Java Programmer)*

"First half is very good for beginner and middle level professional like me. In the second half I found it become very specific for professional software engineers even I skipped some pages specially which explains code and issues related answers. I think the one who works in the similar field can get it completely. The book fulfils your purpose to guide the software professionals for their job interviews, if possible try to put some more material for beginners it depends on your objective of writing the book." *By a Software professional with 5+ years of experience in software industry(Device Drivers, Embedded Programming)*

"When I first received it, I had quickly glanced through your book as I could not get time during my transition. But yesterday I read it in detail and could cover around 35-40% of it. This is definitely a very valuable resource for someone who's sincerely preparing for job. If the person has got some work experience, your book provides excellent guidance to articulate his/her experience and profile. Your book is a very realistic read…while reading I myself could co-relate so many of my experiences with what you have described in your book. Your writing style is also very interesting and keeps one engaged. Keep it up buddy! You're doing the real kind & great work by spreading the light…sharing your experiences for the betterment of others." *By a Software professional with 10+ years of experience in software industry (Network Security)*

"Today I got chance to go through the book (Haven't finished it yet), it is a "Masterpiece" that is what I can say. I took printout of the book and started reading, it came to me like the most needed question-answers set which we never prepare before interview or simply ignore it, but those questions has a big impact on interview. Some of the questions were from frequently asked one, but the way you explained the alternate answers is amazing. It actually gives us pointers to frame our answers for interviews, also helps us in understanding the intention / mind set of interviewer. Author have caught it well. All I can say …The most needed and less cared segment of technical interviews can now easily be prepared using this book.

It's really a great effort & hard work done in compiling questions, and on top of that giving alternate answers to those questions." *By a Software professional with 8+ years of experience in software industry (VOIP, Telecom, Datacom)*

"The book was sufficient for me to prepare for the interview I was preparing for. Thanks for writing it." *By a final year B. Tech Student from a top Indian engineering college*

"Its very good to prepare general question such as why you want to change etc. On Algorithm side, I couldn't find it very deep. May be this could be good if someone is just starting, overall good work." *By a software professional with 4+ years of experience and working for a branded company in United States*

"I would say that your idea of bringing such book was really great and you did a fantastic job pal." *By software professional with 4+ years of experience*

"The book is really good.. But I thought it was better if u had provided more examples in the technical questions. Like some good questions asked in some famous companies or so.. The book has very useful info.. Feels happy to read the book." *By a final year B. Tech Student from a top Indian engineering college*

"Well this book helped me a lot to improve myself as I am organizing training sessions for freshers and experienced guys for." *By software professional with 4+ years of experience, and currently serving as a IT head for his own start-up in India.*

"I have gone through the open ended questions and they were very helpful. I am a fresher, so the starting chapters were more for experienced persons, rather than me. Overall, the book is very good." *By a final year B. Tech Student from a top Indian engineering college*

"Thanks for your great effort in helping people to get best job.

This book gives a structured way for interview preparation and focuses on every possible areas." *By a final year B. Tech Student from a top Indian engineering college*

"Thank you for allowing me to download your book. There is a shortage of information of this type in one place. I volunteer with a job seekers group and many of them would appreciate a book of this type. It is a great topic, and obviously well researched.

I've only had time to skim through it, although I hope to sit down and read it in detail soon. The information seems very solid; however, I have been very pleased with the book." *By a Business operation manager from United States*

Execute
the Job Interview

SUMIT ARORA

EXECUTE THE JOB INTERVIEW

April-2013 Second Edition Published by Sumit Arora

RC GRID: RC-01-LIZ0000001464-7

ISBN-13: 978-0615797830
ISBN-10: 0615797830

www.thecareertools.com

Limit of Liability/Disclaimer of Warranty: EXECUTE THE JOB INTERVIEW doesn't provide detailed knowledge or concepts of any technical items. It's assumes that a candidate will refer to appropriate text books based perception. Moreover, this book explains the thought process, reasoning with job Interviews and provides several types of examples, which helps a candidate prepare for Job Interviews, especially in regards to technical companies.

EXECUTE THE JOB INTERVIEW frequently uses Job Interview related terms such as Interviewer (employer), interviewing (process) an interviewee (candidate).

EXECUTE THE JOB INTERVIEW only provides guidelines, as the author acquired valuable years of experience in the job interviews area.

You agree that the use of EXECUTE THE JOB INTERVIEW contents are entirely at your own risk and without any warranties of any kind. The author cannot guarantee the accuracy, security or quality of these contents.

The publisher /author makes no representations or warranties with respect to the accuracy or completeness of the contents of this work and specifically disclaims all warranties, including without limitation warranties of fitness for a particular purpose. The fact that an organization or web site is referred to in this work as a citation and/or a potential source of further information does not mean that the author endorses the information the organization or web site may provide or the recommendations it may make. Furthermore, readers should be aware that Internet web sites listed in this work may have changed or disappeared between when this work was written and when it is read.

ABOUT THE AUTHOR

Originally from Roorkee (Uttranchal), North India, Sumit Arora now lives in Seoul, South Korea.

Sumit is an experienced software professional with more than 10 years of experience in the development of convergent network application technologies. He graduated from Madan Mohan Malviya Engineering College, Gorakhpur, India (www.mmmec.ac.in), and has worked for Telecom, Datacom, and Embedded software development domains with an exposure in web-domain.

Sumit has always been interested in the appropriate technical solutions which can change the human's thought-process, adopting a creative way of doing things for self development, and which should reflect an appropriate contribution to society.

Sumit's career updates are available at:
http://www.linkedin.com/in/sumitarora

Sumit's personal Facebook page can be accessed at:
http://www.facebook.com/esumit.arora

TABLE OF CONTENTS

③ PAST PROJECT AREAS

4 PROGRAMMING SKILLS 191

5 TEST AREAS 579

6 THOUGHT PROCESS 605

7 TECHNICAL AREAS 627

8 HOW TO'S 653

9 MISC 659

APPENDIX 663

Preface

When candidates apply for jobs or are directly approached by a company /recruiter /hiring manager, the desired end result is to receive a call for a job interview.

- This could be a telephone/written/face-to-face interview, or based on any type of communication, but all interviewers are generally looking for ideal candidates, and interviewees are looking for an ideal job.

- Both are in a process of evaluating the other, e.g. candidates are in a process to identify a good job, and employers are in a process to select the best candidate for their job.

- It is common for a candidate to be concerned about the interview, even if experienced. In order to prepare candidates might try to refer to several sources of information, including interview question/answers.

- However, most of the times finding the answers to standard interview questions doesn't really help because each interview is different. From employer side e.g. job title, responsibility, department, project type, technology type, skills type, years of experience, mind set of interviewer/interviewers. From candidate side e.g. the way CV (resume) was presented, the way the candidate carried the technical/non-technical discussion.

- Employers and candidates have an equal stake in the employment process. Employers look for the best candidate in terms of several productivity related parameters, while the candidate is looking for the best of his career-related parameters.

- It has been observed that referring to several random sources doesn't provide an organized approach to prepare for job interviews.

- It has been also observed that in many situations the candidate is very good on his technical knowledge and several other skill related parameters, but he lacks expressing the answers the way he should be.

  [++The very important thing in a job interview is the communication, how the views towards the questions asked by the interviewer are expressed e.g. the approach to solve the coding problem, providing strategic answers for common questions, how to frame to the point or strategic technical answers, a creative way to present your career profile (in a form of CV), how you carry forward a technical discussion and many other communication related parameters.]

This book has been organized with a philosophy to provide a clear and clean guidance to the readers. This book provides enough examples, guidance and clear steps so the candidates can organize themselves for the technical job interview. It provides detailed and professional answers of various frequently asked interview questions, so that it can improve the reader's communication skills. It also explains

a systematic approach to answering the technical/coding/skills/past experience related questions and once that approach will be taken into account then throughout the career journey it is not needed to prepare it again.

This book also helps (not limited to):

- Hiring managers/recruiters/interviewers to organize a systematic and effective job interview.
- Recruitment/placement/consultant companies to screen/interview the candidates based on the requirement.

*Lecturers/training and placement officers/professors/career counsellors for their career guidance lectures to their students.

EXECUTE THE JOB INTERVIEW's intention is to make a *reader able to tackle the interview with interesting and strong communication.

*reader – employer/candidate/ hiring manager/recruiters/interviewers/ recruitment/placement/consultant/ lecturer/training and placement officer/professors/ career counsellors

ACKNOWLEDGEMENTS

A big thank you goes to Mircea-Gabriel Suciu, Csernik Előd.

Thanks to Krystal Yates, Niladri Mukherjee, Naren Alam, Ankit Bhandari, Rishikul, Amit Singhai, Davinder Pal Singh, Ravindra Kumar and the other readers of the first release of this book who provided their comments as feedback, critiques, reviews.

WHY DID I WRITE THIS?

University students are involved in miscellaneous activities, e.g. dissertation, university events, writing summer training reports, classes, course work and finally job interviews.

To prepare for job interviews, university students consult their seniors, friends, search the web and look for other sources of information.

This is an ongoing process, because even after getting the job, we encounter changes or shifting in our career.

We can also find ourselves in a position to interview candidates. Every time, we need to prepare ourselves as an interviewee or as an interviewer. This book is meant as a reference to provide some practical thoughts about interviews, e.g.

question/answers related to general areas, past project areas, skills areas, thought process and how to's.

While interviewing candidates for a job, an interviewer is looking for specific information. There are many different reasons that the interviewers are unable to attain that information, for example the candidate may not have organized their answers in a way to convey the information properly to the interviewer, or, maybe the interviewer did not ask the relevant information from the candidate.

It doesn't mean that if the candidate didn't convince to the interviewer, then he lacks skills or something else, as sooner or later surely he will get a decent job.

This is the same from the employer's side. It doesn't mean that if the employer didn't hire this candidate then he will not hire anyone, sooner or later surely the employer will find the candidate.

RESULTS: A lengthy process for the candidate to get the right job or employer to select the right candidate.

With such thoughts in mind, I wrote this Execute the Job Interview, in order to help both interviewers and interviewee as a reference to plan their Interview.

IS THIS BOOK FOR YOU?

Generally there are four types of candidate categories, by considering experience levels, in consulting and IT services based companies (Wipro, Infosys, TCS, CTS, Mahindra Satyam etc.).

1. Freshers–College pass-outs
2. 2-5–(Jr.developers)
3. 5-9–(Sr. Developers, Team Leads)
4. 9+ (Tech Leads, Managers, Project leads & SMEs and Gurus).

There are four types in product companies, again there are strategies, but based on their extreme hands on and innovative-research and creative skills.

1. Interns,
2. SDE, SDE II, Lead Engineers
3. Program Managers
4. R&D Engineers and Scientists

This book has been organized in a way so that it can appeal to a varieties of candidates.

If you are a computer science professional preparing for job interviews, e.g.; you may be anyone from following(but not limited to):

- Students are in their final /pre-final year of graduation or post graduation and preparing for job interviews.
- Professionals have just graduated college and are job hunting.
- Entry level candidates (2-5 yrs) who want to change jobs.
- Senior candidates (5+) who might need a quick jump-start to prepare themselves for upcoming job interview.
- Employers: Project Managers/Leaders, HR Managers, Hiring Managers / Professionals dealing with job interviews for hiring.
- Candidates who have been absent from work for 1-2 years e.g. house-wives, hello world entrepreneurs and would like to back on work with a jump-start from this book.
- Placement/Recruitment agencies who support the hiring.
- Training Institute/Universities/engineering colleges professors, lecturers, training and placement officers, who would like to provide an organized idea about the job interviews to their students.

GETTING THE MOST OUT OF THIS BOOK

You might be a hiring manager/HR manager/professional/candidate/fresher with a clear objectives related to the job interviews.

There could be multiple rounds of interviews e.g. including anything from general questions to past project experience, discussion related with basic technical building blocks to problem-solving techniques, attitude towards answering the question, approach while algorithm solving, concepts of programming language.

To get the most from this book you should know the following:

- This book explains a few important areas related to a well planned job interview. By studying the content explained in this book, the interviewee/ interviewers can prepare and plan job interviews q/a which best suits to their profile.
- You should complete the exercises mentioned in the book!. Remember, practice makes perfect!

[! based on your self-defined capabilities (background, experiences), objectives (for what objectives you are reading this book), parameters (job, company, career, skills, CV, technologies exposures, thoughts process)]

CONVENTIONS

BEGINNER: It means that given sample answer from a beginner point of view, who has just started his career or about to start.

BEGINNER+: It means that given sample answer can be from a beginner or can be from a professional.

PROFESSIONAL: A Professional who acquired a reasonable experience to gain the maturity on his career ladder.

CONTACT US/ FEEDBACK

Because we value our readers greatly, we would be grateful if you could provide us with your thoughts on the book. Let us know what you enjoyed and what we could improve, or suggestions with respect to other areas you would like to see us publish in.

However, because of the high volume of mail we receive regularly, we cannot guarantee an immediate answer to all queries. Furthermore, we may sometimes be unable to help with a technical problem, in case it is beyond our control.

What we do promise, however, is to do our best and review every comment, trying to come up with an answer within 24-48 hours. We will also do our best to incorporate any changes that we believe are appropriate in the future releases of the book.

When contacting us, the subject line of the e-mail must start with EXECUTE THE JOB INTERVIEW or EJI

*For writing to the author:	sumit@thecareertools.com
*For errata:	errata@thecareertools.com
*For feedback	feedback@thecareertools.com
*For suggestions	suggestions@thecareertools.com
*For misc	contact@thecareertools.com
*Subject line must start with: EXECUTE THE JOB INTERVIEW or EJI	
Web presence	www.thecareertools.com
Linkedin presence	http://www.linkedin.com/groups/thecareer-tools-4472804/about
Facebook	http://www.facebook.com/groups/451185014894729/
Twitter	www.twitter.com/thecareertools

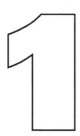

Introduction

There is no standard process for what type of Q/A would be discussed in a Job Interview. Some of the Q/A can be common for a specific type of job profile and some of the Q/A can be the standard one e.g. past experiences, general areas.

So who defines this process? Is it the employers or the candidates? The employer's responsibility is to create the type of job profile, though candidate's responsibility is to prepare his career profile. The candidate reads the given job description from various sources. If there is a match between this job description and the candidate's career profile then he forward his CV to the concerned employer. The employer reviews the candidate's profile and if applicable then an invitation is sent to the candidate for the job interview discussion. It is the candidate's responsibility to prepare well for what he or she defined on his CV and then It is the employer's responsibility to review and verify the profile based on the set of relevant Q/As during the discussion.

It all depends on how a candidate presents his career details into a word/pdf/html/text format profile.

E.g. "Skills (C++/Linux›s OS›s API) " vs. "Technologies Used (Apache Web Server)"

Different professionals can have different skills e.g. for someone who just used the apache SOLR search as a technology and someone who has worked for years on Apache Solr with JAVA, someone writing the C++ based apps on Linux by using Linux IPC, Posix threads, sockets, file system APIs/C++ though he would have only used the technologies of the Apache Web Server.

Various technologies exist, as well as various types of job titles too, such as C# developer or software engineer for C# related project development, in various companies.

In a situation when the candidate is ready for an in-person interview with a company, he is required to present his skills, capabilities, and especially the strongest skills from his perspective.

Companies arranging three to seven or more rounds of interviews would really like to confirm whether the candidate is really good. These companies would normally want to check this by arranging interviews with 4-5 different people, so they can have a clear matrix of who to hire.

Execute the job Interview is organized mainly on the four sections below:

GENERAL AREAS

It talks about the standard questions, but such questions are least prepared, and that also play an important role during job interviews.

*Most of the standard questions, e.g. Please tell me about yourself?, What is your positive skills? What is your negative skills? What type of job you like? How do you feel that such job fits to you? Why did you opt for this job? Why you are looking for a job?

The objective of this section, so that the candidate must know these answers from his perspective, is to provide several example answers from well established professionals.

PAST EXPERIENCE AREAS

This section talks about the past experience areas relevant to the job applied to e.g. you might be a professional who worked on various companies, or you might be a beginner who learned several technologies while in college.

Its really required to frame your answers the way you have described or explained your experience on your CV/resume.

The objective of this section is to explain how a candidate can prepare a self-technical questionnaire, and understand the complete pattern.

He can formally write his own answers, based on his personality and various other parameters. Several examples answers, and type of questions are explained to provide an approach to prepare well for job interviews.

SKILLS AREAS

Programming Skills are those areas which remain with you, even when you change projects . May be one project you have worked on X technologies or business case, On another project Y technological area or business case, but basic skills remain the same.

You might be working for a telecom company, on which for 2 years you worked on a project which extensively uses SS7 technologies, and next project uses cloud computing related technologies.

However basic skills, e.g. algorithms, coding, programming languages, operating system, computer network concepts will remain same. Many times that happened

to be common between you and the interviewer e.g. may be you have worked on SS7 (switch singnaling-7 in telecom area) but it doesn't mean that the interviewer knows much about that, so the basics comes into the pictures.

This section tries its best to let a candidate prepare his skill table and make it grow based on the updates happening all around, from books, from mentors, from self-exercise, until you feel to be satisfy from yourself.

Various examples and solutions are given, and an exercise is given that will help to handle the overall skill things.

THOUGHT PROCESS

The interviewer will try to judge the thought process of a candidate by asking certain standard/non-standard questions, but their answers vary based on the type of candidate. e.g.

How a individual usually thinks, how it approaches problems, how he actually understands the situation and reacts accordingly, how he measures the complexity of the problem, how he reacts on open-ended scenarios, how he or she handles a raw concept to its feasibility analysis.

On every company such as Microsoft /Google /Apple/ Amazon these guys will surely ask some open ended questions too, such as 'How would you design a new browser?'or 'How will you design a new operating system?' or even 'How would you design a railway track?'.

Several other example answers- and an overall approach has been explained to help produce such type of answers.

THIS BOOK DEFINES THE STEPS BELOW TO FRAME THE JOB INTERVIEW IN A WAY THAT SUITS THE CANDIDATE.

[Step-1]: Prepare a package of the skill items related to general areas, past experience areas, skills areas, thought process and other parameters.

[Step-2]: Frame your package to a closely matching job title.

[Step-3]: Present your package(CV, e-mail, way of talking and many more) based on the type of company, job title and execute the job interview.

IN THE OTHER WAY THE EMPLOYER FRAMES BELOW STEPS FOR THE INTENDED JOB INTERVIEW.

[Step-1]: Review the receive package (CV,email,way of talking and many more) based on the type of company, job title and several other job related parameters.

[Step-2]: Compare this package to a closely matching job title.

[Step-3]: Prepare a set of question related to general areas, past experience areas, skills areas, thought process and other relevent parameters.

 ✔$¢£¥€₠✔ ☺ ♫♪ ☺ ✔$¢£¥€₠✔

NINTENDO, COMPUTER ASSOCIATES, ORACLE, HEWLETT PACKARD, SYMANTEC, ACTIVISION BLIZZARD, EMC

MICROSOFT,
IBM,
SAP,
ERICSSON

JobInterview.exe

ADOBE,
ELECTRONIC ARTS,
APPLE,
GOOGLE

CISCO, SONY, ALCATEL-LUCENT, HITACHI, DASSAULT SYSTEMS, SALESFORCE, TCS, INFOSYS, HCL, SAMSUNG, ARICENT

SOFTWARE QUALITY ASSURANCE (ANALYST, ENGINEER, LEAD, LEAD TESTER, SPECIALIST), SOFTWARE ENGINEER / DEVELOPER / PROGRAMMER (CLIENT/SERVER, CLIENT APPLICATIONS, DATA WAREHOUSE, EMBEDDED DEVICES, GAMES, OPERATING SYSTEMS, SAP, WEB APPLICATIONS), SOFTWARE DEVELOPER ENGINEER IN TEST, SOFTWARE APPLICATIONS ENGINEER, SOFTWARE APPLICATIONS DEVELOPER, SOFTWARE ARCHITECT, SECURITY ARCHITECT, NETWORK ENGINEER, NETWORK ADMINISTRATOR, DATABASE ANALYST, C++/C#/ JAVA SOFTWARE ENGINEER, SOFTWARE RESEARCH ENGINEER, SOFTWARE SOLUTIONS MAKER,

SOFTWARE DEVELOPER
ENGINEER IN TEST,
SOFTWARE APPLICATIONS
ENGINEER,
SOFTWARE APPLICATIONS
DEVELOPER

JobInterview.Ink

SOFTWARE DEVELOPER
ENGINEER IN TEST,
SOFTWARE APPLICATIONS
ENGINEER, SOFTWARE
APPLICATIONS
DEVELOPER

SOFTWARE QUALITY ASSURANCE (ANALYST, ENGINEER, LEAD, LEAD TESTER, SPECIALIST), SOFTWARE ENGINEER / DEVELOPER / PROGRAMMER (CLIENT/SERVER, CLIENT APPLICATIONS, DATA WAREHOUSE, EMBEDDED DEVICES, GAMES, OPERATING SYSTEMS, SAP, WEB APPLICATIONS), SOFTWARE DEVELOPER ENGINEER IN TEST

GeneralAreas.Obj	**PastExperience.Obj**	**Skills.Obj**	**ThoughtProcess.Obj**
/* Parameter */	/* Parameter */	/* Parameter */	/* Parameter */
IndividualEfforts *	IndividualEfforts *	IndividualEfforts *	IndividualEfforts *
/* Functions */	/* Functions */	/* Functions */	/* Functions */
Academic_Background{ }	Code_Design{ }	ProgrammingLanguages{	TechnologySelection{ }
Career_Aspirations{ }	Current_Company{ }	}	Scenarios{ }
Career_Negotiation{ }	Managerial_Skills{ }	Coding{ }	OpenEndedQuestions{ }
Indvidual_Capablities{ }	Past_Projects{ }	OS_Multithreading{ }	Algorithims{ }
Job_Fit{ }	Group_Collobaration{ }	OS_Sockets{ }	LogicalQuestions{ }
Work_Attitude{ }	Documentation{ }	OS_Events{ }	AnalyticalProblems{ }
.....	Technical_Domain{ }	OS_CriticalSection{ }	.....
	Technologies{ }	.....	
	Domain{ }		
	.....		

Execute the job Interview

JOB INTERVIEWS WITH MICROSOFT, GOOGLE, AMAZON, APPLE

The job interviews with Microsoft, Google, Amazon, Apple are different. Most of the jobs which are available in these companies are software development and software development in test. Usually in Microsoft there are four types of hiring jobs:

1. Software development engineer [e.g. Software Development]
2. Software development engineer in Test [e.g. Test tool development]
3. Software Test Engineer [e.g. Mostly test case executions, manual testing]
4. Program Managers [e.g. Managing development schedules]

Now this is a known buzzword that all these companies are founded by the highly technical founders.

If we take the example of Microsoft and if you take the example of Bill Gates, who actually made the technologies and the operating system, you will see why.

If we take the example of Google and if you take the example of Sarje Bin, Larry Page, they actually made the technologies, they made the search engine, which is appreciated and used by everyone around the globe.

All the products designed by these companies are highly technical and their future products would be technical too, and they need the best technical people.

Since the first day, these companies started hiring the most technical people, or in other ways the people who solidly understood the most needed concepts of computer science subjects.

Now if you happen to have good computer science education/past experience, and you want to work in any one of the companies and you also know that getting on this company is harder than some other company.

It's not exactly possible to define the definition of " hard". Let's say if you talk about Microsoft. There are plenty of groups, such as Windows group, Visual Studio group, SQL Server Group, MS Office group.

And then these groups have sub-groups and further each team has different roles to serve on the product. There are other groups as well e.g. research, business, marketing, support.

Few groups are really the core of the business and they really need people who are the best around the globe, but most of the groups require software professionals who understand and have good hands–on the most needed concepts of computer science subjects.

But yes, in Microsoft the interviewer people are trained for job interviews, they are trained for how to take interviews. Each and every employee who is going to conduct interviews is actually trained.

BEFORE THE INTERVIEW

1. Interviewer has already read your CV
2. Interviewer is very clear about the decision process for "Hire" or "No Hire"
3. Interviewer is already prepared with the questions he might ask, and he already knows what type of discussion would be carried forward
4. Interviewer already framed the set of questions he going to ask, and subsequent questions based on the progress of the interview.

Interviewers truly understands that the candidate might /from Interviewer to Interviewers come from a different technical background and may possess different skills, so they are after the most needed computer science skills and problem solving abilities.

Interviewers from Microsoft or Google come up with general technical problems every day, because software developers involved in software development are required to design the logic and code of efficient programs. This also involves certain other direct/non-direct concepts e.g. coding require a decent knowledge about the working of compilers but may not require in-depth knowledge.

So a typical job interview in these companies consists of four to six in-person interview rounds.

Prior to that you might have a phone-screening, or informational interview.

[Informational – usually if candidate would like to know more about the job before filing his application or hiring manager would like to understand the candidate a bit before going for a formal discussion]

Most of the interviews test the candidate's problem solving skills. That problem can be a logical problem, but most of the time those problems used to be coding problems. The solutions of those problems carry a why, what, how discussion.

INTERVIEWER TRIES TO TEST

- How well you can write code
- How well you understood the problem.
- How well you optimize the solution e.g. logn vs n2 vs nlogn.
- Do you really understand the problem before jumping to the solution?
- Do you ask valid questions to clarify the problem?

- Do you actually have an approach to solve the problem first or just directly write the solution?
- Are you doing loud thinking while writing the solutions?
- Do you understand the direct/in-direct technical concepts related to the coding problems? (E.g. limitations of memory, CPU usage, design patterns, sockets, memory leaks, garbage collection, do and don'ts)

MOST OF THE TIMES YOU ARE REQUIRED TO WRITE THE CODE ON WHITE-BOARD, AND YOU HAVE 30 MINUTES (USUAL INTERVIEW DURATION IS 45 MINUTES)

- Do you really organize the space on board?
- Do you use standard approach to solve the problem?

  [E.g. understand the problem, understand what type of solutions this problem required, write a design of this problem as a approach which will lead to optimal solution, actual data structures to be used and why?]
- Did you consider most error/logical/solution cases before writing the solution?
- Are you using the right data structure to solve the problem?
- Are you using the right algorithm to solve the problem?

AFTER WRITING THE SOLUTION

- Do you really trace the solution for applicable test cases or not?
- The solution is the same as designed?
- Is it the only approach or certain other approaches are also possible?
- Do you write efficient code?
- Do you really understand the meaning of n2 vs nlogn?
- Do you really know the concepts of different available data structures and tricks/tips/creativity of coding?
- How well you wrote the name of the functions, and variable names?
- How well code has been organized in functions and sub-functions?

The software development items are common in Software Development engineer and Software Development engineer in test e.g. data structures, coding, multi-threading, algorithms, operating system APIs, socket programming, Events, programming language concepts, file systems.

But the SDET(Software development engineer in test) interviews test the test automation/testing skills as well.

SAMPLE INTERVIEW LOOP: AT MICROSOFT, GOOGLE, AMAZON, GOOGLE

May you please explain a sample interview loop at Microsoft, Amazon, Google, Apple?

RATIONALE: *Professionals apply at Apple, Microsoft, Amazon, Google for a job, based on various job related parameters.*

Job-title e.g. Software Development engineer in Test at Microsoft, Software Engineer in test at Google, Software Development Engineer at Amazon, Software Development Engineer at Microsoft, Program Manager at Microsoft.

The requisite skills e.g. programming language skills, development skills, program management skills, test automation skills, problem solving skills, strong communication and collaboration skills, academic degree, most needed/frequently used computer science/technologies concepts.

SAMPLE INTERVIEW LOOP

If applied for Software Test Engineer positions, then interviewee may expect nearly all test related questions, other than relevant questions from general areas, past experience areas, skills areas, thought process.

If applied for Software Development Engineer in Test, Software engineer in test, Software Quality engineer in test positions, then the interviewee may expect test automation, test tools related questions, relevant questions from general areas, past experience areas, skills areas, thought process.

If applied for Software Development Engineer, then the most relevant questions come from the software development items e.g. data structures, coding, multithreading, operating system APIs, socket programming, events, programming language concepts, data structures, queues, file systems.

If applied for a Program Manager position, then interviewee may expect program management related questions, relevant questions from general areas, past experience areas, skills areas, thought process.

SAMPLE INTERVIEW FLOW

HR CALL

Duration – 30 to 45 Minutes | Number of rounds: 1 or 2 based on situation

HR or Recruiter may call a candidate and ask the following types of Q/A for 30 to 45 minutes:

- Misc Q/A e.g. to understand candidate's background in more detail, why he or she looking for a job, his or her goals.
- Logical and open-ended q/a e.g. designing a traffic light system, design escalator system
- Understand his presence of mind, way of talking, candidate's preferences
- Recruiter may explain more about the job description to candidate and to make clear his objectives and interest towards the job.
- Recruiter may check his or her eligibility for the company e.g.; visa status (If a foreign candidate), references, and background check
- Recruiter may ask some basic programming languages related questions e.g. difference between private and public inheritance in C++.

TECHNICAL TELEPHONE INTERVIEW

Duration – 30 to 60 Minutes: Number of round: 1 or 2 based on situation

One of the team member from hiring team or hiring manager or anyone else who made responsible to screen candidate's technical skills

- Basic questions from core subjects of computer science e.g. operating system, database, computer networking, software engineering, algorithms
- Questions related with from general areas, past experience areas, skills areas, thought process and others
- Coding problem

FACE-TO-FACE

[5 to 7 rounds]

- Basic questions from the core subjects of computer science e.g. operating system, database, networking, software engineering, algorithms and others.
- Questions related to general areas, past project areas, test areas, technical areas, scenarios, coding areas, algorithms and others.

SAMPLE HIRING MANAGER Q/AS

- How was your interview day? What prompted you to apply for this position, How did you prepare for this Interview?
- Scenarios e.g. If you are supposed to test a CD-ROM device, if you are supposed to develop a x project.

SAMPLE Q/A FROM DIRECTOR OR ABOVE THAN HIRING MANAGER

- Situation based–e.g. tell me a situation when you had a hard time working with your teammates?
- Position Based – e.g. why do you like development? What have you done in development? Why do you like the program manager role?

[Solutions of all the above problems are available on applicable places e.g. General Areas, Past Experience Areas, Skills Areas, Thought Process]

SAMPLE SDET INTERVIEW: AT MICROSOFT GOOGLE

May you please explain a sample Software Development Engineer in Test or Software Engineer in Test Interview loop at Microsoft, Google?

RATIONALE: *Job-title e.g. Software Development engineer in Test at Microsoft, Software Engineer in Test at Google, Software Quality Engineer in test concentrate on*

*Testing methodologies and techniques, test automation and test tools development by using advanced development (e.g. C, C++, C#) and debugging skills

*Excellent problem solving skills, strong communication and collaboration skills, product development and testing experience

SAMPLE INTERVIEW LOOP

STEP-1: E-MAIL SCREENING

Sample Questions:

- **Q-** Given a singly linked list of integers, write a function to remove all nodes with even values,
- **Q-** Provide a set of test cases against that function "removeAllNodesWithEvenValues".
- **Q-** What kinds of testing have you done in the past?
- **Q-** What kinds of testing have you done in the past?
- **Q-** What are your 3 strongest technical and/ or functional skills?
- **Q-** What is your areas for Improvement?
- **Q-** Have you ever created your own automation for testing purposes?

[E-MAIL SCREENING – coding questions would be emailed to you, and you are suppose to provide answers within two hours or couple of hours or some other time limit]

STEP-2: HR CALL

Duration – 30 to 45 Minutes | Number of round: 1 or 2 based on situation

HR or Recruiter may call a candidate and ask following types of Q/A for 30 to 45 minutes:

- Misc Q/A e.g. to understand candidate's background in more detail, Why he or she looking for a job, his or her goals,
- Logical and open-ended Q/A e.g. designing a traffic light system, design escalator system
- Understand his presence of mind, way of talking, candidate's preferences
- Recruiter may explain more about the job description to candidate and to make clear his objectives and interest towards the job.
- Recruiter may check his or her eligibility for the company e.g.; visa status (if a foreign candidate), references, background check.
- Recruiter may ask some basic programming languages related questions e.g. difference between private and public inheritance in C++.

STEP-3: TECHNICAL TELEPHONIC

BASIC QUESTIONS FROM CORE SUBJECTS OF COMPUTER SCIENCE

- **Q-** Please explain your understanding related to Polymorphism?
- **Q-** Write a program to reverse a string and then explain appropriate test cases to test your function?

TEST SCENARIO

Please test following web screen:

```
..[Path]..............[Browse]
..[Path]..............[Browse]
[+Add]
[Upload]   [Cancel]
```

- **Q-** On click to browse one can select a file and its file appear in path text box
- **Q-** On clicking to Add, it will create another path and Browse Button
- **Q-** On click to upload, select files start uploading to a designated server.
- **Q-** On click to cancel it cancel uploading.

Please explain all functionality of the above write down various test strategies and test cases.

STEP-4: FACE-TO-FACE-1

- **Q-** Given two singly linked lists, you have to write a function which can take two individual linked list as input, and find out If at any point these link list are merging together?
- **Q-** Write down various test strategies, test cases to test this function.

STEP-5: FACE-TO-FACE-2

- **Q-** Write a program which can reverse the digits of a given integer.
- **Q-** Write down various test strategies, test cases to test this function.

STEP-6: FACE-TO-FACE-3

[E.g. Lunch Interview]

- **Q-** How you will test Connection Manager on a Mobile phone (It was just opted as a module for a Q/A round, not belong to specific OS)
- **Q-** Please explain your past experience on Wi-Fi device driver testing.
- **Q-** What do you understand from a Test Tool?

STEP-7: FACE-TO-FACE-4

- **Q-** Imagine a note that is constructed using words cut out from a book (e.g. If the book was "I am a very short and useless book" then "very useless" and "I am a book" can be constructed using words from the book while "and books" cannot). Implement the following function in C# (if you know it, C/C++ otherwise) [e.g. boolCanConstructNote(string note , string book)]

  ```
  /* bool CanConstructNote( string note, string book) */
  ```

  The function returns true if the note can be constructed using words from the book and false otherwise.

  - ▷ What assumptions did you make when writing the function?
  - ▷ Provide as few test cases, as you need to completely test the sanity of the function. For each test case state specifically what condition it tests.

STEP-8: FACE-TO-FACE-5

[Usually Hiring Manager]

- **Q-** How do you feel about your interview day?

- **Q-** What would your ideal job be? What product/technology/application do you want to work on?
- **Q-** You are supposed to test a CD-ROM device, Please explain various test strategies, test cases.

SAMPLE Q/A FROM DIRECTOR OR ABOVE THAN HIRING MANAGER

- **Q-** Tell me a situation when you had hard time to work with your team mates
- **Q-** Why you like development? What you have done in development?
- **Q-** What do you know about a commercial product?

MISC POINTS

- If Interviewee will not perform well during first three interviews, then it might be possible that he or she will not proceed for a 4th and 5th round of Interviews
- On some cases a Director (senior hiring manager) might interview a candidate

[Solutions of all the above problems are available on applicable places e.g. General Areas, Past Experience Areas, Skills Areas, Thought Process]

SAMPLE SDE INTERVIEW:
AT MICROSOFT, GOOGLE, AMAZON

May you please explain a Sample Software Development Engineer or Software Engineer Interview Loop at Microsoft, Amazon, and Google?

RATIONALE: *Software Development Engineers or Software Engineers are responsible for design, development, writing unit tests for multiple components.*

SAMPLE INTERVIEW LOOP

STEP-1:E-MAIL SCREENING

Sample Questions:

- **Q-** You have a tape with all but one of the integers between 1 and 1,000,000. No duplicates. You can read it once, after which it will self-destruct.

    ▷ Implement the code to find the missing integer

    ▷ Outline why you selected your approach to solving the problem

    ▷ Document any assumptions that you make

- **Q-** Write a function that detects whether a linked list has circular reference or not.

STEP-2: HR CALL

Duration – 30 to 45 Minutes

Number of round: 1 or 2 based on situation

HR or Recruiter may call a candidate and ask following types of Q/A for 30 to 45 minutes:

- Misc Q/A e.g. To Understand candidate's background in more detail, Why he or she looking for a job, his or her goals,

- Logical and open ended Q/A e.g. designing a traffic light system, design escalator system

- Understand his presence of mind, way of talking, candidate's preferences

- Recruiter may explain more about the job description to candidate and to make clear his objectives and interest towards the job.
- Recruiter may check his or her eligibility for the company e.g.; Visa status (If a foreign candidate), references, background check
- Recruiter may ask some basic programming languages related questions e.g. difference between private and public inheritance in C++.

STEP-3: TECHNICAL TELEPHONIC

- Q- Please explain the complete process, when a user enters a URL to the browser and then browser shows a web page.
- Q- Please explain the complete process, when a user enters type from a standard input e.g. keyboard and standard output e.g. monitor display typed input.
- Q- What are race conditions?
- Q- Write a memcpy function?
- Q- Write a strcmp function?
- Q- Write a strcat function?

[If asked memcpy then subsequent discussion may lead to memory management. If asked strcmp then subsequent discussion may lead to string things.]

STEP-4:FACE-TO-FACE-1

- Q- Find the kth largest value in the array efficiently. You may assume that k is much smaller than n

STEP-5: FACE-TO-FACE-2

- Q- Function to convert an integer n into its ASCII string representation for a given base?

STEP-6: FACE-TO-FACE-3

- Q- Implement the following function, FindSortedArrayRotation, which takes as its input an array of unique integers that has been sorted in ascending order, then rotated by an unknown amount X where 0 <= X <= (arrayLength−1). An array rotation by amount X moves every element array[i] to array[(i + X) % arrayLength]. FindSortedArray-Rotation discovers and returns X by examining the array. Consider performance, memory utilization and code clarity and elegance of the solution when implementing the function

STEP-7: FACE-TO-FACE-4

- **Q-** Write your design to implement single link list and its functions by using OOPS

STEP-8: FACE-TO-FACE-5

- **Q-** Write a Program to get the stack functioning from two queues?

[Solutions of all the above problems are available on applicable places e.g. General Areas, Past Experience Areas, Skills Areas, Thought Process]

SAMPLE SQET INTERVIEW: AT AMAZON

May you please explain a Sample Quality engineer in Test at Amazon?

RATIONALE: *Software Quality Engineers in Test concentrate in Test Areas.*

SAMPLE INTERVIEW LOOP

STEP-1: HR INTERVIEW

- **Q-** Why you interested to work in Amazon?
- **Q-** Explain your capabilities regarding SDET Job Position?

STEP-2: TELEPHONIC INTERVIEW-1

- **Q-** C++ related questions e.g.; what is Object Slicing in C++?
- **Q-** Design Patterns: explain types, and your experience using them in past why go for OOPS?
- **Q-** Discussion on Inheritance, ISA, HASA types

STEP-3: TELEPHONIC INTERVIEW-2

- **Q-** How you will test Connection Manager on a mobile phone (It was just opted as a module for a Q/A round, not belong to specific OS)
- **Q-** Please explain your past experience on *Wi-Fi Testing
- **Q-** What are different *SIP methods?

*[*Interviewer find few technical keywords from an interviewee's CV, in your case it would be different or same]*

STEP-4: FACE-TO-FACE-1

- **Q-** What are the directories on Linux, Why is that for, explain file systems, directory structures?
- **Q-** What happens when you type "PS –A" as a command in linux command shell?

STEP-5: FACE-TO-FACE-2

- **Q-** Did you use IPC Before? Explain that? And discussion about shared memory and messages queues?

- **Q-** Explain the use pthread condition variable?

STEP-6: FACE-TO-FACE-3

- **Q-** Write a program to get the stack functioning from two queues?

STEP-7: FACE-TO-FACE-4

- **Q-** Discussion about the test tool design?

STEP-8: FACE-TO-FACE-5

- **Q-** Write a Program to Create 01234567890 123456789001234567890.... kind of series based on some set of rules, and discussion on it.

  E.g.; If given input say 11–It should create a series: 01234567890 Or If given input is 5 it should create series: 01234 or given input is 77 then (0123456789 ..(10 times) 0123456)

STEP-9: FACE-TO-FACE-6

- **Q-** Write your design to implement single link list and its functions by using OOPS

STEP-10: FACE-TO-FACE-7

- **Q-** How you define a best team?
- **Q-** What recently new you studied? Did that help you on your current project?
- **Q-** What you want to achieve from this job

[Solutions of all the above problems are available on applicable places e.g. General Areas, Past Experience Areas, Programming Skills Areas, Thought Process]

PHONE INTERVIEW INSTRUCTION FROM AMAZON

[Received by a candidate for his interview at Amazon]

Since the interview may include basic coding, algorithms, data structures, problem solving, and/or design questions, please consider the following five (5) interview tips:

1. Be in a quiet place where you are comfortable and there are no distractions.

2. Have a copy of your resume available just in case you are questioned on it.

3. Have paper and pen ready to use.

4. Have any questions you have for the interviewer ready.

5. You might also want a glass of water nearby.

HELPFUL RESOURCES FROM MICROSOFT

[Received by a candidate for his interview at Microsoft]

These resources come highly recommended from engineers across Microsoft. Although we cannot guarantee a positive interview result, please feel free to utilize the resources below to explore the SDET position and broaden the base of your technical skills.

Binder, Robert V., Testing Object-Oriented Systems: Models, Patterns, and Tools, Chapter 3: Testing: A Brief Introduction, (Addison-Wesley, 1999)   Provides a concise description of testing very much in alignment with how Microsoft approaches testing. We have attached this chapter, with permission, for your edification. We hope that by reading this chapter you will better appreciate the types of activities you may be involved with, as well as a rudimentary testing vocabulary (for example, "partition testing").

SOFTWARE DEVELOPMENT RESOURCES RECOMMENDATIONS

Box, Don. Essential.NET, Volume I: The Common Language Runtime. Addison-Wesley Professional, 2003.

Brooks, Fredrick. The Mythical Man-Month: Essays on Software Engineering. Addison-Wesley Professional, 1995.

Cormen, T.H., Leiserson, C.E., Reivert, R.L., Stein, Cliff, eds. Introduction to Algorithms. McGraw-Hill, 1990.

Howard, Michael, LeBlanc, David, eds. Writing Secure Code. Microsoft Press, 2001.

Maguire, Steve. Writing Solid Code: Microsoft's Techniques for Developing Bug-Free C Programs. Microsoft Press, 1993.

McConnell, Steve. Code Complete: A Practical Handbook of Software Construction. Microsoft Press, 1993.

McConnell, Steve. Rapid Development: Taming Wild Software Schedules. Microsoft Press, 1996.

Tanenbaum, Andrew. Modern Operating Systems. second edition. Prentice Hall, 2001.

TESTING RECOMMENDATIONS

Black, Rex. Managing the Testing Process: Practical Tools and Techniques for Managing Hardware and Software Testing, second edition. John Wiley and Sons, 2002.

Myers, Glenford. The Art of Software Testing. John Wiley and Sons, 1979.

Patton, Ron. Software Testing. SAMS Publishing, 2000.

Whittaker, James. How to Break Software. Addison-Wesley, 2002.

Viega, John, McGraw, Gary, eds. Building Secure Software: How to Avoid Security Problems the Right Way. Addison-Wesley, 2001.

ONLINE TESTING RESOURCES

Software Testers Make the Grade, Charles Waltner, Information Week:
http://www.informationweek.com/756/testers.htm

Visual Studio Testing, MSDN
http://msdn.microsoft.com/library/default.asp?url=/library/en-us/vsent7/html/vxoritestingoptimizing.asp

Testing .NET Application Blocks—Version 1.0, MSDN
http://msdn.microsoft.com/library/default.asp?url=/library/en-us/dnpag2/html/MTF.asp

LogiGear Software Testing site
http://www.qacity.com/

Software QA/Test Resource Center Question: What steps are needed to develop and run software tests?
http://www.softwareqatest.com/qatfaq2.html

Teaching Domain Testing: A Status Report, Cem Kaner, J.D., PhD
http://www.testingeducation.org/articles/domain_testing_cseet.rtf

An Introduction to Scenario Testing, Cem Kaner, J.D., PhD
http://www.testingeducation.org/articles/scenario_intro_ver4.doc

A Course in Blackbox Software Testing, Center for Software Testing Education and Research
http://www.testingeducation.org/coursenotes/kaner_cem/ac_200108_blackbox-testing/

The Grand Index of Techniques, Brian Marick, Testing Foundations
http://www.testingcraft.com/techniques.html

Technical/Software Testing, Microsoft Careers
http://members.microsoft.com/careers/careerpath/technical/softwaretesting.mspx

ADDITIONAL HELPFUL LINKS

Microsoft's Jobsblog
http://blogs.msdn.com/jobsblog

Channel 9 Segment: What's it like to interview at Microsoft
http://channel9.msdn.com/ShowPost.aspx?PostID=18472

Channel 9 Segment: Mock White boarding problem
http://channel9.msdn.com/ShowPost.aspx?PostID=19171

Channel 9 Segment: Riding the recruiter shuttle
http://channel9.msdn.com/ShowPost.aspx?PostID=18718

General Areas

General Areas are those areas, which are very common to ask an interviewee about, regardless of their domain. There is always a general set of questions to ask a candidate.

Areas where interviewee talks about, e.g. candidate thought process related with their experience, candidates goals and way to achieve that goals, evaluating his or her academic profile, evaluating his or her career curve and see how much candidate is actively involved to accelerate his or her career.

Actually it talks about the standard questions, but such questions are least prepared, and that also play an important role during job interviews.

Those questions are something like:

Please tell me about yourself?, What are your biggest strengths? What are your biggest weaknesses? What type of job would you like? Why do you feel that such a job fits to you? Why did you opt for this job? Why are you looking for a job?

In general in life we always interact with people, in many situation.

EXAMPLE

Sometimes it happens, let's say you are meeting with a friend, and then that friend introduces you to another friend.

And then what happens, you try to ask the basic questions from him, example, what you did, what your hobbies are, etc.

Based on his answer, you understand the type of education he has or personality types or something else.

But on this side, this is on the job perspectives so it would be suggested that on this situation the candidate need to answer those type of answers which are really aligned with the applied job type.

EXAMPLE

Please tell me about yourself.

Please tell me about yourself is a very basic question. You can expect to hear it almost everywhere, but if you have to provide an answer to it during a job interview then the answer must be delivered according to the type of job applied for.

Your answers must carry some connection with the applied job type, it must have the connection with your qualities (e.g. skills, positives) and why you are a good fit to the job.

So these answers are very important, but usually what happens, when somebody asks such kind of questions, many times we are not prepared well for these answers.

Now the problem is how one can define himself. You need to re-ask yourself and you need to have your own way of framing the answers.

But yes you need some references, you need some examples, you need the guidance from professionals.

In these general areas chapter, most of the common questions are taken and answered from a beginner/professional point of view.

It would be great if you could prepare a table or an Excel Sheet with applicable number of rows and columns. You can define the most common questions you feel that those are the perfect matches with your career-profile, and another side you can write the answers based on your career-profile.

So every time you can ask from yourself, is that the answers you really think that suit to your personality and satisfy you the way you answered or going to answer?

Definitely over the time you can change the answers or modify them. If you will add more creativity and clarity to those answers and later use those on a job-interview then it will greatly help to an interviewer to understand your insights. At the same time, it will satisfy you as well.

NINTENDO, COMPUTER ASSOCIATES, ORACLE, HEWLETT PACKARD, SYMANTEC, ACTIVISION BLIZZARD, EMC MICROSOFT, IBM, SAP, ERICSSON, ADOBE, ELECTRONIC ARTS, APPLE, GOOGLE CISCO, SONY, ALCATEL-LUCENT, HITACHI, DASSAULT SYSTEMS, SALESFORCE, TCS, INFOSYS, HCL, SAMSUNG, ARICENT

Software Development Engineer, Test (SDET), Test / Quality Assurance (QA) Engineer (Computer Software), Test / Quality Assurance (QA) Engineer (Integrated Circuit), **Test / Quality Assurance (QA) Engineer**, (Computer Networking), Test Analyst, Test Engineer (Automation), Test Engineer, Automation, Test Engineer, Computer Hardware, Test Engineer, **Test Engineering Manager**, Test Manager, **Software Lead Tester**, Software Quality Analyst, Software Quality Assurance (SQA) Analyst, **Software Quality Assurance (SQA) Engineer**, Software Quality Assurance (SQA) Lead, **Software Quality Assurance (SQA) Lead Tester**, Software Quality Assurance (SQA) Manager, Software Quality Assurance (SQA) Specialist, **Software Quality Assurance (SQA) Supervisor**, Software Quality Control (QC) Analyst, Software Quality Control (QC) Manager, **Software Quality Engineer Manager, Software Quality Tester**, Software Team Leader, **Software Technical Training Coordinator**, Software Test Analyst, Software Test Associate, **Software Test Engineer (STE), Four Year B.Tech Degree**, P.hD (Computer Science), **Masters in Computer Applications**, B.E, M.S

CAREER SUMMARY

Since 12 years working in software industry, primarily worked in data/telecom/web/embedded domain, achieved various work related accomplishment, coded several features/modules in C/C++/C#/Java/Linux/Windows, designed/developed various solutions from test tools to technology related, worked with cross-cultural teams e.g. Alcatel France (Paris), Freescale China (Shanghai), Aricent India (Gurgaon), Microsoft United States (Redmond) and now in Samsung South Korea (Suwon)....

Apart from my IT career, done masters in computers applications from MMMEC, India, attended technical forums, delivered weekend lectures on Software Quality Assurance, Software Requirement Engineering, Software Testing at Fudan, Shanghai- Jia Tong Univ, Shanghai, China, Open talks in various Indian engineering colleges, Volunteer English speaking mentorship in South Korea, Founded startup AppScaleOut Technologies to transform traditional web solution to cloud based solution, Created professional groups e.g. Seoul Professional Group, Organized professionals meetups, Wrote/reviewed a Technical Careers book and maintaining my blog: www.thecareertools.com

CAREER SUMMARY

I am in the final year of Bachelor of engineering course. Since last 4 years I studied the varied subjects of computer sciences. Operating systems and computer networks became the most interesting ones. Other than studying the theoretical topics of Operating system, I performed various practical as well. e.g.

Downloaded the Linux Kernel source code from Linux Website, Understood how Linux boots, Bought XYZ Linux related books to understand its internals and practically watched the code as well for Important data structure of Linux and file system.

Most of the programming I did in C Language, I also made a project to demonstrate my knowledge on these areas....

Or

Since last 4 Years, I am developing, designing, supporting Java, Objective-C based mobile applications

CAREER SUMMARY

A seasoned hands-on Technical Lead with 5+ years of experience in designing, developing enterprise scale business applications for financial industry.

I position myself as a well-rounded A Technical Architect who understands the business problems holistically and provides technology solutions to enable success of my employer and my clients. I want a job where I am accountable to provide end-to-end solutions to clients. My interest is just to solve problems for my clients, and help them succeed, and I see technology as just one of the vehicles to solve those problems.

I'm a professional developer specialized in Microsoft Technologies (.NET) with 4 years of experience in development and leadership. I have thorough understanding of current and emerging Microsoft technologies and Development Lifecycle...

ACADEMIC BACKGROUND: ABOUT YOURSELF

Please tell me about yourself?

RATIONALE: *On every job interview there is a first question to be asked: "Please tell me about yourself", and surprisingly, this is one of the questions least prepared by the candidates. If it's not prepared well or not well thought of, then it creates some stuttering that makes the beginning of a interview more nervous and uncomfortable. At the same time, this question is often a chance for an interviewee to make a great first impression, so it would be best to prepare it in advance.*

But is there really a standard pattern for answering this question?

Actually there is no standard answer template, it all depends on the situation.

One of your friends introduced you to another friend on some casual meeting, and It usually happens that after some "Hi, Hello" – you usually want to know more about the guy who was just introduced to you e.g. you ask – Hey, What do you do? ", "Where are you from? " and after a while you become more comfortable as you know about him e.g. His Job, where he is from, maybe his work, his hobbies etc. and then you do next level communication.

Same with dating – If you date someone, it happens that you explain about your hobbies, the way you live life, the food you like, the entertainment activities you like, means to find the common activities in between so that you can find a topic to talk further.

To tell about yourself can be customized based on the job type e.g. a little customization can be applied based on the job type and minimum skills required for that job.

SAMPLE ANSWER FROM A PROFESSIONAL POINT OF VIEW

[A professional who has 12 years of experience in software development has made below one of his standard templates to explain about himself while producing an answer for "Please tell me about yourself". You can change few key words based on the applied job type e.g. If applied for embedded domain then you can stress more about your embedded experience]

Since 12 years I have been working in software industry, primarily worked in data/telecom/web/embedded domain, achieved various work related accomplishment, coded several features/modules in C/C++/C#/Java/Linux/Windows, designed/developed various solutions from test tools to technology related, worked with cross-cultural teams e.g. Alcatel France (Paris), Freescale China (Shanghai), Aricent India (Gurgaon), Microsoft United States (Redmond) and now in Samsung South Korea (Suwon).

Apart from my IT career, done masters in computers applications from MMMEC, India, attended technical forums, delivered weekend lectures on Software Quality Assurance, Software Requirement Engineering, Software Testing at Fudan, Shanghai- Jia Tong Univ, Shanghai, China, Open talks in various Indian engineering colleges, Volunteer English speaking mentorship in South Korea, Founded startup AppScaleOut Technologies to transform traditional web solution to cloud based solution, Created professional groups e.g. Seoul Professional Group, Organized professionals meet ups, Wrote/reviewed a Technical Careers book and maintaining my blog: www.thecareertools.com

I have strong interest to do the things in an organized way, approach to make things perfect e.g. from documentation to running technology. I also would like to work in a place where independence is given to individuals, so I can apply my creativity.

SAMPLE ANSWER FROM A BEGINNER POINT OF VIEW

Since last four years I studied the varied subjects of computer sciences. Operating systems and computer networks became the most interesting ones. Other than studying the theoretical topics of Operating system, I performed various practical as well. e.g.

Downloaded the Linux Kernel source code from Linux Website, understood how Linux boots, bought XYZ Linux related books to understand its internals and practically watched the code as well for important data structure of Linux and file system.

Most of the programming I did in C Language, I also made a project to demonstrate my knowledge on these areas

#The project involves the creation of a virtual file system. The project would require the creation and manipulation of various data structures to store the contents of the file system. There should be a programmer-level library of functions (API) like my_create, my_delete, my_open, my_close, my_read, my_write, etc to simulate file system operations. The APIs will work on this simulated file system. The file system can model an existing system such as Unix/Windows or you can invent your own.

[#reference: https://www.classle.net/projects/project_ideas/file-system-simulation]

Other than that, I like swimming as much I can, and I am quite flexible of doing freestyle and breast-stroke swimming.

Please feel free let me know If you would like to know some specific about myself to understand me more?

Exercise:	Q:	Please tell me about yourself?

[Am I going to answer this question now? And adding the notes on my career note book?]

(a).[Yes] (b).[No] (c).[Later] (d).[Its not relevant to my career] (e) [I framed this question on other way]

Date and Time:

ACADEMIC BACKGROUND: YOUR PROFESSIONAL KNOWLEDGE

What exactly you have done academically to improve your professional knowledge?

RATIONALE: *Everyone sees his career in a different way, and prepares himself to be the best professional for job market . On the other hand, the educational institutes compiles their lectures, learning system, based on a defined syllabus.*

The interviewer want to understand how a candidate has prepared himself to reduce that gap.

Students might have joined extra training programs, learned foreign Languages, participated in tech-fests, or developed something related to their individual creativity and analyzed the proof of his or her capabilities.

SAMPLE ANSWER FROM A BEGINNER+ POINT OF VIEW-1

I don't understand properly about the business models, business case and solutions made by the companies and how professionals works on this. But I tried my best to involve on the computer science study very efficiently, and did following activities.

Studied /implemented data structures and seriously followed the exercise defined on the relevant book, especially for well know data structures [e.g. Introduction to algorithms from corman]

Studied seriously about computer networks, downloaded the linux source code, bought linux network internals book, and tried to understand the mapping between theory and practicals.

Studied C++ languages from relevant book to implement the basic well know FTP, TFTP things by using best of my creativity and thoughts

And for other activities: I was involved in the following:

- Participated in cultural events, e.g.; dumb shared extempore, debates to improve my communication skills.
- Did summer internship to better understand the industry
- Spent extra time in laboratories to work on various subjects related practical, It helped me to learn subjects to advanced level

SAMPLE ANSWER FROM A BEGINNER POINT OF VIEW − 2

Found a mentor in the software industry thereby learning industry patterns, industry projects, contribution of an engineer, why different technologies exist, what an engineer does with specific technologies, why different types of engineers exist, how the career relates to the industry, and all together how to become more industry oriented than academic study oriented.

And started thinking on a direction to become the expert for web applications solutions area by studying /experimenting the below technologies.

EXAMPLE: LEARNT

- To prepare a base platform, e.g. Windows, Linux areas,
- To prepare technologies on that platform e.g. Middle-ware Java component and various Frameworks -Java, EJB3 (Stateful/Stateless Session Bean, Entity Bean), Connection Pooling, Instance Pooling, Transactions, J2EE Design Patterns...etc. JBoss Seam Framework, ORM(object relational mapping)
- To prepare a industry solution domain e.g. data communication with http://www.ietf.org/rfc.html

Exercise:	Q:	**What I am doing to improve my professional studies/expertise?**

[Am I going to answer this question now? And adding the notes on my career note book?]

(a).[Yes] (b).[No] (c).[Later] (d).[Its not relevant to my career] (e) [I framed this question on other way]

Date and Time:

CAREER ASPIRATIONS: GOALS FOR THE FUTURE

What are your goals for the future of your career?

RATIONALE: *Career goals are depended on individual situations and relate to skill, study, research or job profile takes you to the next step. It may be " by this time, I will be very experienced in XYZ technologies", or "I will finish part of my project work", which will help me to promote on the next level.*

It up to an individual to define their career goals, whether pursuing a management program or learning a different skill or role and following through until that is achieved.

Interviewer wants to understand how organized and disciplined you are with your career.

POSSIBLE ANSWER FROM A BEGINNER+ POINT OF VIEW

I made goals in previous years and have done well achieving those. Two years ago I made a goal to obtain a masters degree in XYZ area as you can see from my resume, I have achieved that goal. At this time, I am working on one of my short-term goals to find successful career based on XYZ parameters.

(XYZ parameters: may relate with work type, company's project background, learning curve, job responsibilities)

Computer networking is my chosen area. To understand the linux's internals of network programming and make my career in this area, I made several short terms goals including,

- TO UNDERSTAND THE NETWORK PROTOCOLS INTERNALS AND EXERCISE SOCKET PROGRAMMING

    I also wrote a FTP(file transfer protocol) with a clear user Interface for windows/linux platforms.

- TO KEEP MYSELF UPDATED ON THE AREA OF LINUX

    I am a regular follower/member/ attendee /learner of http://www.linuxfoundation.org/, http://lwn.net/

- TO KEEP MY HANDS ON UP TO DATE

    I do various experiments on my linux box, by having a reference of the book: Understanding Linux Network Internals, Christian Benvenuti

Exercise:	Q:	**What are my goals for the future of my career?**

Am I going to answer this question now? And adding the notes on my career note book?

(a).[Yes] (b).[No] (c).[Later] (d).[Its not relevant to my career] (e) [I framed this question on other way]

Date and Time:

CAREER ASPIRATIONS: FIRST JOB

How did you find your first job? What did you consider most when coming out of College?

RATIONALE: *To get a job and plan a career, university students define the career parameters, e.g. job type, company, technologies to work on .Everyone has his or her own means to get a job, e.g.; campus interview, self-search, professor/friend/senior's recommendation, etc.*

Interviewer wants to understand interviewee career-related parameters while selecting his or her first job.

SAMPLE ANSWER FROM A BEGINNER POINT OF VIEW-1

I mainly considered my skills, and tried to understand the gap, what exactly needed and what I have, and that gave a me a clear understanding.

So during my academic career/ while undergoing masters degree, I concentrated on data-communication domain. I studied TCP/IP protocol stack and wrote sample projects on the same while obtaining knowledge about working methodologies in Telecom/ Network companies.

I did my internship at Cisco. While an intern Cisco offered me a full time position.

I concentrated more and was particularly interested in data communication domain area and never bothered much about the company name, salary or work location. My priority was always to work in the data communication area.

SAMPLE ANSWER FROM A BEGINNER POINT OF VIEW-2

(I knew that campus visit will never happens to my college), I made a plan, and that made my self strict into.

I planned to present my self as a C++ developer on windows platform, so during my most year of education, I studied C++ thoroughly.

Studied /practiced the basics of game programming from: Beginning C++ Through Game Programming by Michael Dawson, wrote some programs, projects and reflected that on my CV. I approached several companies based on my reference list (company list on basis of job advertisements), and that gave me a job the way I needed that.

Am I going to answer this question now? And adding the notes on my career note book?

(a).[Yes] (b).[No] (c).[Later] (d).[Its not relevant to my career] (e) [I framed this question on other way]

Date and Time:

CAREER ASPIRATIONS: INTERESTS IN PROJECTS

What exactly interests you while working on a project?

RATIONALE: *Professionals/beginners work in their respective organization based on their job profile, attitude, etc. usually something related to a particular job that interests its professionals.*

The interviewer wants to know which parts of the job you find most interesting.

SAMPLE ANSWER FROM A BEGINNER+ POINT OF VIEW -1

- Working with a team, being able to learn from the other members of the team and but also being able to make a valuable contribution.
- Working in a progressive environment, because in many cases projects get scraped.
- Happy to have involvement in a project from conceptual proof to production.
- Working on a job which involves moving to a different location every three months, because I enjoy travel.
- Working on a job where my ideas and creativity are recognized.

SAMPLE ANSWER FROM A PROFESSIONAL POINT OF VIEW -2

At this time I am seriously looking to work in a environment where all people are motivated, aggressive for creativity, interested to do something, always with active ideas and passion to achieve the functionality.

Team which like to track the progress, understand the challenges, have closed discussion and language is not the barrier.

Team or individual work continuously to achieve the goals.

Support from team to make every moment productive.

Working on something which can activate the individual's passion so that an individual can use all of his capabilities.

Very Important: I am looking something to be focus on one area for next few years.

| Exercise: | Q: | **What exactly interests you while working on a project?** |

Am I going to answer this question now? And adding the notes on my career note book?

(a).[Yes] (b).[No] (c).[Later] (d).[Its not relevant to my career] (e) [I framed this question on other way]

Date and Time:

CAREER ASPIRATIONS: YOUR DREAM COMPANY?

How did you determine your dream company?

RATIONALE: *Companies exist all around the world in different domains, products, services, cultures, etc. University students, professionals learnt about the company based on Individual research.*

Interviewer wants to understand Interviewee's belief and deciding factors to mark a company to his or her dream company.

SAMPLE ANSWER FROM A PROFESSIONAL POINT OF VIEW -1

I didn't consider company as such, more I considered what exactly I really like, and I was very much interested on research activities, that made me explore more around research areas.

During my work days in India, I found that most companies are services based companies that follow a top to bottom approach, e.g. company receives pre-defined and planned work items from customers. I became excited about working in the USA to understand work origination, and dreamt of working at a products based company in the USA.

SAMPLE ANSWER FROM A PROFESSIONAL POINT OF VIEW -2

I didn't know much about the industry, While in school, I sincerely interacted with many professionals and friends who worked for companies such as, e.g. NetApp, Cisco, Infosys, Freescale etc. After having a series of discussion in about things such as type of work, opportunities to introduce creativity, career path, work environment, type of management, type of people, products they worked on, technologies they use, etc. I compared that information with my capabilities.

Based on such analysis, I decided that A, B, C was my dream company and joined A to start my career.

Exercise:	Q:	How did you determine your dream company?

Am I going to answer this question now? And adding the notes on my career note book?

(a).[Yes] (b).[No] (c).[Later] (d).[Its not relevant to my career] (e) [I framed this question on other way]

Date and Time:

CAREER ASPIRATIONS: WORKING FOR XYZ COMPANY?

Why are you interested in working for XYZ Company?

RATIONALE: *Each company has his own business model, products, technologies, services, policy, pay scale, benefits, location, people, and many more. Interviewer wants to see why this candidate selected XYZ Company for a job as many other companies exist.*

Beginners/professionals generates their interest to work in another company because of several parameters –research, understood parameters such as location, position, responsibility, technology, work environment.

The interviewer wants to understand why the interviewee decided to work in XYZ company?

SAMPLE ANSWER FROM A PROFESSIONAL POINT OF VIEW -1

- XYZ builds up creative products with inventive pool of engineers; it would be very interesting, exciting and career oriented feature to work with smart and intelligent people of XYZ.

- Technologies, concepts used in XYZ are related with experience of mine, so by providing my continuous contribution and getting great learning back, will add more values to my career and company both.

- Looking for a long-term vision with a stable company which XYZ is.

SAMPLE ANSWER FROM A PROFESSIONAL POINT OF VIEW -2

[Individuals might have generalized idea or may be specific interest to work in xyz company. Somebody is just looking a job, and somebody has clear idea about the why?]

1. I was interested to involve in research activities on xyz area, and that company has specific edge on it, and my core area lies on it, that is the first thing I have interest.

2. As I heard most of the people are technical and research oriented people. If somebody is senior than he is a senior researcher, Its not like a non-technical guy involved on technical item, especially on that situation when its irrelevant. Such thoughts made me to choose such companies [research on xyz area].

[xyz can be anything e.g. How memory management works from end to end?, A customized operating system for TVs?, Am automated system to clean the home efficiently, an automated security locks.

(If beginner) "This xyz works on Imaging Area, especially on Image Processors and while in school I studied digital Image processing that was a major subject of mine, I want to continue my career on this area".

(If experienced person), "I worked on Imaging area, and now wanted to do more, as XYZ pioneer on Digital Imaging area and I got amazed for A-Pix, Dr-ix technology"]

Exercise:	Q:	**Why are you interested in working for xyz company?**

Am I going to answer this question now? And adding the notes on my career note book?

(a).[Yes] (b).[No] (c).[Later] (d).[Its not relevant to my career] (e) [I framed this question on other way]

Date and Time:

CAREER ASPIRATIONS: RECENTLY STUDIED OR RESEARCHED?

What have you recently studied or researched?

RATIONALE: *Professionals/beginners perform variety of study based on their mind set*

> ** Somebody research about historical things e.g. Adolf Hitler*
>
> ** Somebody watching a science drama or action series e.g. Spartacus*
>
> ** Somebody researching on 3-D printer e.g. to make very basic common hardware items for Indian households.*
>
> *Interviewee is intended to know, when Interviewee understand the professionalism, what he did to improve his profession.*

SAMPLE ANSWER FROM A BEGINNER POINT OF VIEW -1

I am too much passionate about the work I am doing, and that require to interact with man technologies directly or in-directly. So since last few months I studied the following to improve my hands on.

- Design Patterns in C++,: Wrote Test Tool based on Factory Design Pattern
- Record and Play Back Frameworks,: To automate GUI related testing
- Libcurl Libraries,: command line tool to transferring data via various protocols
- Shuffle Algorithms: Shuffling Cards
- Parsing Algorithms: Parsing Strings etc
- TUX Frameworks: 32 bit client/server test harness, which executes test files as DLLs, especially to test device driver related things.
- Multi-Threading: pthreads

SAMPLE ANSWER FROM A BEGINNER POINT OF VIEW -2

Actually I grown up in India, and I observed, how housewives actually cleans the house. They actually required to use various traditional tools to clean the house. But as a lot of modernization came, new technologies came, but still I feel that a lot of things are still missing in the area of cleaning.

When I travelled to China, France, United States and some other countries. I observed in most of the common homes they have a separate area to keep the cleaning tools such as broom or piece of clothes which can clean the floors, various wet tissues and several other cleaning items which are required on different situations.

At this point of time and researching a way so that I can make a box, which can be designed in a way, so that it can accommodate most of the cleaning tools e.g. floor mops, floor wipers, brooms, kitchen–scourers & wipes, toilet brushes, cloth brushes, floor, scrubbing brushes and these all should be designed the way of a Indian house-hold needs.

So I am studying about autocad, 3d printers, material concepts and various other related items.

Exercise:	Q:	**What have you recently studied or researched?**

Am I going to answer this question now? And adding the notes on my career note book?

(a).[Yes] (b).[No] (c).[Later] (d).[Its not relevant to my career] (e) [I framed this question on other way]

Date and Time:

INDIVIDUAL CAPABILITIES: POSITIVE QUALITIES

Are you really in a situation where you can recognize your positive qualities?

RATIONALE: *A positive quality accelerates the individuals' productivity and professional experiences. Such qualities include attitude, skills, personality type, self-development, etc.*

The interviewer wants to listen to the interviewee's positive qualities based on his or her self-evaluation.

SAMPLE ANSWER FROM A BEGINNER POINT OF VIEW -1

I recognized my networking skills; I keep a pleasant attitude with people and always try to respect people on every situation. Try to keep in touch with people as and when required such as casual eye-touch, hellos, listens from people during lunch/dinner and attends seminar, product's exhibitions, etc.

Getting various types of work done require good relationships with people, such as I might need to decide which technology to use on a situation and need to have expert's comments

SAMPLE ANSWER FROM A BEGINNER POINT OF VIEW -2

Since last five years I have been working in C++. I have in-depth experience related to C++. I can code any business requirement in C++ by using expert level OOP concepts and Design Patterns.

SAMPLE ANSWER FROM A BEGINNER POINT OF VIEW -3

Since last three years I have been working on the development of an iPhone app and practically experienced all iMAC Internals.

SAMPLE ANSWER FROM A BEGINNER POINT OF VIEW -4

- I know how to work in a team, which includes how to be a good mentor, because that will give you a long-lasting relationship with your juniors, they will become a next hand for you.

- I prepare a very disciplined and organized plan to perform any activity, whether related with a professional or personal subject.

Exercise:	Q:	**Are you really in a situation where you can recognize your positive qualities?**

Am I going to answer this question now? And adding the notes on my career note book?

(a).[Yes] (b).[No] (c).[Later] (d).[Its not relevant to my career] (e) [I framed this question on other way]

Date and Time:

INDIVIDUAL CAPABILITIES: NEGATIVE QUALITIES

Are you really in a situation where you can recognize your negative qualities?

RATIONALE: *A professional may refer to some situation, which didn't work well, based on his or her personality type or work style or something lacking in a specific skill or something else.*

Interviewer wants to know whether there is anything which may affect to your performance and If yes they will look for what you have learned from this experience.

SAMPLE ANSWER FROM A BEGINNER POINT OF VIEW -1

I might not be able to make good relationships where people keep high attitude and proudness such as people not providing the right answer, pretending to be busy, not available for help on urgent cases promptly. Such types of situations affect my work, and until now I don't have a better solution to manage such people.

SAMPLE ANSWER FROM A BEGINNER POINT OF VIEW -2

Sometime I receive little or almost no information about work, and the work provider is reluctant to provide detailed information and shows total unwillingness when asked to get some details. Such situations affect my work, and I try to get such details from other sources.

SAMPLE ANSWER FROM A BEGINNER POINT OF VIEW -3

I observed that my communication skills especially to represent my ideas or views on some complex technical situation aren't up to the mark, means I am not very satisfied by myself.

I am working on X, Y, Z things to make it better, so that I can be adjusted well to this professional world.

Exercise:	Q:	**Are you really in a situation where you can recognize your negative qualities?**

Am I going to answer this question now? And adding the notes on my career note book?

(a).[Yes] (b).[No] (c).[Later] (d).[Its not relevant to my career] (e) [I framed this question on other way]

Date and Time:

How do you feel about your interview day?

RATIONALE: *The interview process might involve rounds of interviews; on one side interviewers evaluate interviewee's performance, and on the other side the interviewee also has his self-evaluation.*

After a few rounds of interview, the Interviewer would like to understand the interviewee's feelings towards his performance on this interview.

SAMPLE ANSWER FROM A BEGINNER POINT OF VIEW -1

It was a good discussion with all interviewers, those discussed about my past product development experience, coding skills, problem solving skills.

While solving Problem 'A' I didn't design optimized solution initially, but I corrected immediately while I applied "XYZ" thoughts.

Actually during interview with "Mr. X", I was stuck while solving one "undirected graph" problem, and on second interview with "Mr. Y", It went well, but there was slight mistakes in the solution which I gave.

And at last I didn't ask any question from "Mr. Z", it might be that my questions were already answered.

Exercise:	Q:	How did you feel about your interview day recently/earlier?

Am I going to answer this question now? And adding the notes on my career note book?

(a).[Yes] (b).[No] (c).[Later] (d).[Its not relevant to my career] (e) [I framed this question on other way]

Date and Time:

INDIVIDUAL CAPABILITIES: STRONGEST TECHNICAL SKILLS

What are your 3 strongest technical skills?

RATIONALE: *It might be possible, candidate would have shown various technologies and skills on his CV, and few might be relevant to the applied job type and few might be not.*

So the interviewer asked from the candidate, which are the three main technologies you are highly skilled in.

In that situation it is recommended, that a candidate need to answer those relevant skills, which are closely relevant to the applied job type.

SAMPLE ANSWER FROM A BEGINNER+ POINT OF VIEW

Concept of CMS: I totally understand the concept of CMS (content management system), the applicable business use cases to use such type of CMS. So I have very good experience to design a CMS based on the applicable business use cases.

Technical architecture of a CMS: I had already designed/implemented various CMS with the use of WordPress/Joomla. I practically understand the overall internals of WordPress/Joomla. Example, it's architecture, its internal coding, its functions, databases. I totally understand all the in and out of WordPress/Joomla.

Design/Implementation in Joomla/Wordpress: In most of the business use cases it required to implement the themes, plug-in so I can write professional themes and plug-ins in WordPress/Joomla.

Based on this I can define myself a software professional who can design and delivered a WordPress/Joomla based CMS for complex business requirements.

SAMPLE ANSWER FROM A PROFESSIONAL POINT OF VIEW

I have worked on several big projects, so I can easily understand the whole system, its components, even it uses whatever the technology and whatever the software program tools, technology, design pattern, development environment, including the role of hardware.

I have very good technical knowledge about the C++ Language, as well as Linux Operating Systems, Network Programming (protocols, socket programming), which really increase my software development and debugging skills.

I am very good while writing the design of a software tasks or making some chang-es on the existing, and later how to transform it to real optimal logic.

Exercise:	Q:	What are your 3 strongest technical skills?

Am I going to answer this question now? And adding the notes on my career note book?

(a).[Yes] (b).[No] (c).[Later] (d).[Its not relevant to my career] (e) [I framed this question on other way]

Date and Time:

INDIVIDUAL CAPABILITIES: AREAS FOR IMPROVEMENT

What are your areas for Improvement?

RATIONALE: *From time to time and based on the situation individuals try to improve their professional skills.*

Actually at various points of time, individuals come across with various new technical concepts, technologies and the nature of problems to be solved by that. Individuals refers various source of information, and self –defined learning program to keep themselves up to date, so that they can bring the best expertise to their profession.

Because professionals are ahead from beginners, as they have worked on business areas, worked on those problems which society needs, so they understand more the area of improvement better.

Interview would like to understand whether such practices followed by this individual, if yes then on which are his interest lies, and how he is trying to improve it .

[However it would be great if the answer can have a connection with the applied job type.]

SAMPLE ANSWER FROM A BEGINNER POINT OF VIEW

I am a beginner, in the final year for my education. Since last four years I'm improving my hands-on skills with programming and the use of operating system.

I'm trying my best to understand the different modules, application programming interfaces provided by the operating system and how I can use those with programming to make a business solution.

Because currently I am involved in study, so my major objective to have a reasonable level of expertise in the area of programming with the decent working knowledge with operating system API. In my case it is C++ and Linux operating system. So I keep improving my expertise based on these areas.

SAMPLE ANSWER FROM A PROFESSIONAL POINT OF VIEW

Recently the cloud computing technology has been introduced to the information technology world. This technology provides various platforms so those can serve to the relevant customer base. It solves various business problems by providing an organized virtual computing machine as big as it needs to be.

Because this technology is new, only a few solutions addressed in the market based on the various concepts and the use of network virtualization. Different industries are building their solutions, private cloud computing for the in-house enterprise demands and public cloud computing as a service to the customers.

As a professional and working on this area since last one year:

I am improving my understanding of network virtualization, concepts of cloud computing, scaling.

I am improving my hands-on in the automation of computing resources, their monitoring and build a profile so that a specific type cloud computing solution can solve a specific type of business problem e.g. It can scale it automatically based on the business needs.

Exercise:	Q:	What are your areas of improvement?

Am I going to answer this question now? And adding the notes on my career note book?

(a).[Yes] (b).[No] (c).[Later] (d).[Its not relevant to my career] (e) [I framed this question on other way]

Date and Time:

JOB FIT: WHY ARE YOU LOOKING FOR A JOB?

Why are you looking for a Job at this time?

RATIONALE: *The interviewer totally understands the hiring process to hire a candidate based on the company or individual job needs. Interviewer would like to understand the candidate towards the job-fit, e.g. his or her interest, belief towards this applied job, an adequate reason why he or she looking for a job at this time.*

Beginners also have options to study further.

There could be many reasons from straightforward to situation specific, e.g. this is my career move, i want to relocate to XYZ area because of XYZ reasons, my company is going to shut down its business so, i would like to understand the business concepts and industry before I make another move for study or research.

SAMPLE ANSWER FROM A PROFESSIONAL POINT OF VIEW

At this time, I am not exactly changing my job; I am exploring what other options are available at the job market, because this job is not providing the interest which I have a passion to do. Yes, I have handsome money, and designation, but my work—is just XYZ and since last two year I am doing that.

In this company, it appeared that I have very few chances to join any prominent work. I need a place to learn and only on this X technological or solution domain area with preferred xyz parameters e.g. location, job-profile, if I get those I may choose. At this time I couldn't actually sit or wait for something which I really need for the advancement of my career.

So I have planned to get the right job based on my interest and belief, and because of that effort I am here.

SAMPLE ANSWER FROM A BEGINNER POINT OF VIEW

At this time, I have finished my education, and as a next step of my career, I would like to join a job by keeping following objective in mind:

- Job which offers me at least a standard pay-cheque
- My preferred location is X
- My preferred technology/domain area of work is A
- Etc.

And I have already evaluated my options, which are giving a good match for this Job.

Exercise:	Q:	Are you looking a job at this time, If yes then why?

Am I going to answer this question now? And adding the notes on my career note book?

(a).[Yes] (b).[No] (c).[Later] (d).[Its not relevant to my career] (e) [I framed this question on other way]

Date and Time:

JOB FIT: WHAT DO YOU KNOW ABOUT THIS JOB?

What do you know about this Job?

RATIONALE: *Employer advertises jobs with required job description. It doesn't tell all 'in and out' e.g.; product to work on, technologies, career path, team size, what day to day activities would be to work on, length of the project, type of work, what made an employer to hire a candidate.*

This situation comes when you have already received the telephone call from HR or someone else, who explained you about the job, and you understood about the job or this is the first interviewer who asked about this.

On each case, your response will be different, imagine, you read job description, matched your skills and capabilities with this job, and submitted your CV for next steps. Afterwards, you got the telephonic call from the company for interview, and this is just a first question you get? On that case, your best answer, something where you have made your research to know about this job already.

Usually candidates didn't know much about the specifics. Such answers shows, how much careful a candidate is, for choosing his or her career.

SAMPLE ANSWER FROM A BEGINNER+ POINT OF VIEW

Thanks for asking such a type of question; actually I didn't get the chance to talk in detail. I referred the XYZ job-site or careers section of the company, and only know about the job description, skills required.

I have various questions to understand my professional life while doing this job e.g.

I have questions to understand deeply about the career path?

- How much importance of this job role to this project?
- What is the stage of this project?
- If this project is long terms or short term?
- What type of work i would be doing?,
- This is a R&D project or related to a product or service project?
- How old the team is, how many members in that?

- Is this group for commercial products?

- It's a kind of support group or It's a team to develop/maintenance the inhouse work?

- Is that a serious hire means you need a person soon? Or you expecting a work to come? Or It's a project which has been just started?

- May you provide me some example careers of people who are already in this project since last few years e.g. how well they grown on that career, technology and position?

- I really would like to understand the work environment of the team, and would like to know about the relationship with boss and team-mates?

- What kind of career programs this company offer to a candidate while in work e.g. trainings, devices, books?

- Any recent or memorable accomplishment by the hiring team towards the contribution to company?

[It depends on the situation and type of information an individual might need. It may be possible that a lot of information he or she has already collected from the websites or friends. But yes, the questions still remains, and that is a good opportunity to get the answers from interviewer.]

Exercise:	Q:	**What do you know about the applied job or expected to apply?**

Am I going to answer this question now? And adding the notes on my career note book?

(a).[Yes] (b).[No] (c).[Later] (d).[Its not relevant to my career] (e) [I framed this question on other way]

Date and Time:

JOB FIT: WHY SHOULD I HIRE YOU?

Why should I hire you?

RATIONALE: *Employers use this criteria to short list a candidate for an open position and call that candidate for a job interview. The interviewer wants to understand the candidate's confidence related to this job opportunity.*

A candidate can answer case by case if he or she should have done his research and clearly understood the advertised job requirements and also have confidence on his capabilities.

SAMPLE ANSWER FROM A PROFESSIONAL POINT OF VIEW

This job demands a professional software-development engineer in test areas. As I have mentioned on my profile, I wrote requisite test tools for mobile client applications to perform automated functional/non-functional /stress /performance /reliability /regression testing for Apple-Mac platform.

I can write very efficient test cases, automation and do well in all test engineering areas, If requirement, test environment, time line, project phase, my role, resources, dependency, customer, end user (different age group, or different profession), targeted industry, interoperability, conformance product specification, requirement use cases(not limited to) clear to me.

SAMPLE ANSWER FROM A BEGINNER POINT OF VIEW

I totally understand, that this job require S1, S2, S3 skills and definitely it would be good for an organization that a new joinee can ramp up with the work as fast as possible. But If I evaluate this job's requirement and my capabilities, then I would like to say that:

- Have seriously studied the most needed subjects of the computer science, have very good hands-on in C++ programming and operating system APIs (especially sockets, events, threads).
- Understand the concept of a project, it's development stages, it's complexities, designs and various other work related parameters.
- Have developed project 'P' with my college team that demonstrates the proof of my C1, C2, C3 capabilities.

So I can confidently say that I am a perfect fit for this job.

Am I going to answer this question now? And adding the notes on my career note book?

(a).[Yes] (b).[No] (c).[Later] (d).[Its not relevant to my career] (e) [I framed this question on other way]

Date and Time:

JOB FIT: JOB INTERVIEW PREPARATION

What kind of preparation did you do before this job interview?

RATIONALE: *Jobs required skills from beginner to advanced level. Most of the employers advertise a job opportunity in that much detail where an applicant can understand the job's requirements.*

Interviewer wants to see whether a candidate has reviewed advertised job requirements and prepared himself for an interview discussion.

POSSIBLE ANSWER FROM A PROFESSIONAL **POINT OF VIEW**

Below are the major requirements asked in advertised job description:

- Expert knowledge about SIP(Session Initiation Protocol for Signalling)
- Expert knowledge about Network Protocols based solutions
- Expert C/C++ skills on Linux platform.

To have a good technical discussion with Interviewers and Hiring Manager, I studied following things before the interview:

- RFC3261 Session Initiation Protocol
- RFC3264 an Offer/Answer Model with the Session Description Protocol (SDP)
- Network Protocols (TCP/IP)
- RFC3489 Simple Traversal of UDP through NAT (STUN)
- Programming with C, C++, Data Structures, Objected Oriented Analysis (OOA), Object Oriented Design (OOD), Multithreading, Network Programming, Algorithms
- Misc: General Areas, Past Project Areas, Skills Areas, Thought Process

POSSIBLE ANSWER FROM A BEGINNER **POINT OF VIEW**

This job requires a working knowledge in the web development area. In terms of skills it talks about Java programming, databases and the requisite tools to develop the business solution.

So I welcome an opportunity to discuss my skills as requested by the job, with the interviewers and that's what I am prepared for.

[Misc: General Areas, Past Project Areas, Skills Areas, Thought Process]

| Exercise: | Q: | **What is your way to prepare for job interview?** |

Am I going to answer this question now? And adding the notes on my career note book?

(a).[Yes] (b).[No] (c).[Later] (d).[Its not relevant to my career] (e) [I framed this question on other way]

Date and Time:

JOB FIT:
DECIDING FACTOR TO CHOOSE THE JOB PROFILE

How did you decide which job profile fits you?

RATIONALE: *Professionals change or start their career in a particular job profile, e.g. Software Quality Engineer, Software Designer, software Architect, Program Manager, Software Developer in Test, Software Developer, Project Manager, Software Engineering Manager.*

There is always a gap between professional's self-evaluation before to join a job-profile, and while in that job-profile. Professional understand that gap once he or she joins that job-profile.

The Interviewer wants to understand e.g. what made an interviewee to apply for a program manager or software engineering manager or why he selected that specific role.

POSSIBLE ANSWER FROM A PROFESSIONAL POINT OF VIEW

These situations when a professional actually decides his career, it all depends on various parameters, e.g. from where he started his career, type of people he was involved, type of project he did, type of tool he learned, types of methodologies he learned, type of projects he interacted, and many more.

I have five years of experience, and I have worked in 2-3 different roles, and that doesn't mean–that I did more specifics related to my official designation.

Because before joining my first company, I knew about industry but not much, so Initially I joined in a role of a software engineer, that meant for that company was: e.g. to engineer anything in software, it can be a development job; it can test tool job; it can be anything related to software.

Even I am serving in a role of a senior software engineer since last three years in my current organization, but my current role actually related to managing a software project.

My actual role is:

- **Understanding the needs of the project:** because I am working in a product based company, and I need to involve myself in product development, e.g. by having series of discussion with related people, findings by self-evaluation, studying market trends, its enhancement. All together to form its need into a requirement that can be turned to as a project

feature or a module or enhancement or performance test or prototype of something, it can be anything.

- **Understanding those requirements in detail:** in terms of its significance, and then come up with a clear design, e.g. for what use cases we are going to apply in our project because of these additional requirements.

- **Move to design phase:** Once those use cases are approved via having closed discussion with dependent people, and with several other analysis parameters.

- **Development consideration:** I talk to my team, and I divide the work, e.g. how many people will involve into development, testing, documents writings and many other areas.

- **Work progress:** Involve thoroughly what we have done, what could be changed, who should know about this update, difference between exact deliverable vs the developed items, and decide a deadline.

- **Establish a way to monitor the progress:** In terms of quality standards, in terms of the use case thought about, in terms of the environment to deployment and many more.

- **At the end, a deliverable:** which is production ready, clean, with all sorts of documents, source code with comments, releases, builds.

Since last three years I am doing this, so I have defined my role as a *Software Engineering Manager* rather a *Senior Engineer,* hence at this time I am specifically looking at a job position where I can utilize my acquired capabilities in a bigger level and by having a specific job title.

Exercise:	Q:	**What type of job profile suits to your career?**

Am I going to answer this question now? And adding the notes on my career note book?

(a).[Yes] (b).[No] (c).[Later] (d).[Its not relevant to my career] (e) [I framed this question on other way]

Date and Time:

JOB FIT:
EXPECTATION FROM THE JOB YOU APPLIED FOR

What would you like to achieve from this job?

RATIONALE: *It is perfectly fine that each work is associated with a salary. But other than that, each professional has his own career path. Professional starts his career on a beginner level job and then intermediate level job and then advanced level responsibilities. So when professional join the job, he always carry a set of expectations e.g. he might carries the work environment expectation where he can utilize his internal creativity or something else which triggered him to change the job.*

Professional might have an expectation that he would be using his existing skill on the applied job, and then while working on that job he would be improving his skills to the next level or professional might be assuming that he would meet with his career expectation. It's a kind of hint to the professional from interviewer;it's a reminder to the professional whether he really knows his existing capabilities and the expected career this job might offer.

Example: Interviewer has applied SDET(software developer engineer in test), or SQET(Software quality engineer in test) or SET(software engineer in test). So Interviewer would like to know whether interviewee know about this job profile?

POSSIBLE ANSWER FROM A PROFESSIONAL POINT OF VIEW

This job related with test things, means software development engineer in test, so I want to achieve software development experience in the field of test and this position excites me because:

- It excites about product's actual requirement, which will base for the test.

- It excites to write test-plan and consider all factors of testing, e.g. regarding my role in testing, available resources, the situation of the product in project development, globalization, targeted user, consider slowly about functional aspects, subsequently move to non-functional and next work about various advanced techniques for specific use cases and scenarios.

- It excites about my interaction with various other internal/cross-cultural /across teams, e.g.; PM, Team Members, Devs, Test Manager, Test Lead, Technical Program Manager.

- It excites to use my past experience and current capabilities to write very efficient test cases, automation and do well in all test engineering stuff. It require to have the clear requirement understanding, test environment, time line, project phase, my role, resources, dependency, targeted customer, end user (different age group, or different profession), targeted industry, interoperability, conformance product specification, requirement use cases.

Exercise:	Q:	**What you want to achieve from your expected or current job?**

Am I going to answer this question now? And adding the notes on my career note book?

(a).[Yes] (b).[No] (c).[Later] (d).[Its not relevant to my career] (e) [I framed this question on other way]

Date and Time:

JOB FIT:
PRODUCT/TECHNOLOGY/APPLICATION YOU WANT

What product/technology/application do you want to work on?

RATIONALE: *Professional has applied for a job in the company and that company's products are very much known in industry.*

The Interviewer wants to understand the Interviewee's opinion related to its products, and on which product he wanted to work for any specific contribution.

POSSIBLE ANSWER FROM A BEGINNER POINT OF VIEW

I would like to work for 'ABC' product, because it excites me, e.g. ABC's products team, great learning opportunities, I can feel proud to work in such a product, which later will spread out to rest of the world. I would like to add following functionalities to improve it:

- I have used 'ABC' product, I really want to add more user friendly functionalities in ABC test tool kit e.g. as currently it can just parse one log file at a time; I want to introduce a feature so that it can parse multiple log files at one time, and can show various other log manipulation features, perform parallel testing.

- Develop small-2 footprint devices with full documentation, which provide step-by step guidance for the development, and later it could be part of the next ABC release, as same way ABC Test tool kit is part of release.

Exercise:	Q:	What product /technology/ application do you want to work on?

Am I going to answer this question now? And adding the notes on my career note book?

(a).[Yes] (b).[No] (c).[Later] (d).[Its not relevant to my career] (e) [I framed this question on other way]

Date and Time:

SITUATION MANAGEMENT: NON TECHNICAL BOSS

How would you explain a technical situation to a non-technical boss?

RATIONALE: *People or teams carry work related individual responsibility while working in an organization. On many situations, these people or teams share information for obvious reasons. Consider this Situation:*

Example: "You are working on an issue, which is taking more time than as usual. Your supervisor or any other team member has no Idea about the internals of that technology or work, and those people don›t know why it's taking a long time.

On another way, you are doing your best to get the things done? And struggling to get things done, but your supervisor or customer or somebody else has a dependency on you. How you will explain issue›s situation?

Because whenever you›re stuck, and somebody asks–«What is the problem and why?". You are trying to explain the situation, and in parallel you›re struggling to solve the issue, because solving the issue isn›t straight forward as other feels yes it is. Above situation is very common, and Its assumed that interviewee would have experienced this. Even technical people, who are in significantly different field or responsibility, they least understand someone else's work. Interviewer wanted to understand the best practices or approaches made by interviewee to handle such situations.

POSSIBLE ANSWER FROM A BEGINNER+ POINT OF VIEW

Updating the status of 'X' to concern people depends on the issue's nature. If I know "that I am working more than as usual to find out the solution on X". First, I try to use common means, e.g. depends on the easiest communication medium, If possible talking in person with concerned people directly, or via IM or phone call Or e-mail with high level information and specific low level information e.g. what I have done to fix this issue and what more need to be done. Let me explain you a simple Issue:

Once I was assigned to modify Android based application screens (views), and one of my senior manager asked me why it's taking a long time:

I explained Android application screens need to be modified for all four types of devices (15-screen*8 layouts = 120 screens), horizontal and vertical both, and it requires to test these views, change the business logic, database part and testing.

[On this case I didn't explained the actual technicality but explained the measured work items. Later he asked some specific questions related to the actual technicality, and that I explained to him. So It was a discussion from high level to low level, or sometime just supervisor or dependent people would like to hear the progress.]

Exercise:	Q:	**What is your style to explain the technical things to non-technical people?**

Am I going to answer this question now? And adding the notes on my career note book?

(a).[Yes] (b).[No] (c).[Later] (d).[Its not relevant to my career] (e) [I framed this question on other way]

Date and Time:

TEAM MATCHING: THE BEST TEAM

How would you define the best team?

RATIONALE: *Each individual has his own way of doing things. He does things individually by applying his thoughts, knowledge, creativity and various other skill related parameters to get the things done.*

Usually the team consists of 3+ people and team members can have different thoughts and skills, but the goal used to be same. So it happens that most of the team members aligned their thoughts, creativity, knowledge and several other skills related parameters based on the defined task for that team.

It happens, that individuals would like to do something different, or something, which can satisfy his professional needs e.g. only research oriented team, aggressive start-ups. But it also happens that the team members might not be the same the way individual thinks. Then such individuals keep an ideal structure of the team.

Interviewer would like to understand from the interviewee, what type of belief he carries towards the expected team, which can be the best based on his view.

SAMPLE ANSWER FROM A BEGINNER+ POINT OF VIEW

- Highly active Manager and dynamic people.
- Effective collaboration within the team, e.g.; though we might not be efficient enough in terms of knowledge about any functionality of ongoing project/product, but effective collaboration will make everything possible and great.
- Manager or responsible person should clear the objective of work to the team with the inclusion of short-term and long-term vision.
- Manager should provide timely update/status to team member based on the situation to situation.
- Team should jointly work to achieve the goals.

SAMPLE ANSWER FROM A PROFESSIONAL POINT OF VIEW

The team should have following minimum properties: great in terms of working together, close working on problems, bringing ideas, very careful with the milestones, like to grow, serious with the learning and career, punctual with timings, no useless time wastage, very focus towards the work, spend time in healthy discussions, create an environment so that everybody is comfortable to work with any individual, overall and the main objective is project and professional career.

Exercise:	Q:	**What type of team work you really like?**

Am I going to answer this question now? And adding the notes on my career note book?

(a).[Yes] (b).[No] (c).[Later] (d).[Its not relevant to my career] (e) [I framed this question on other way]

Date and Time:

Further reads:

Eat That Frog!: 21 Great Ways to Stop Procrastinating and Get More Done in Less Time	Brian Tracy
You've Only Got Three Seconds	Camille Lavington
Patent It Yourself: Your Step-by-Step Guide to Filing at the U.S. Patent Office	David Pressman Attorney
How to Write and Publish a Scientific Paper	Robert A. Day, Barbara Gastel
The Architecture Of Open Source Applications	Amy Brown, Greg Wilson
Code Complete: A Practical Handbook of Software Construction, Second Edition	Steve McConnell

Past Project Areas

Candidates come up with past projects that would be treated as samples of their creativity. These projects become important evaluation points for the interviewer e.g.; to check candidate's competency, their role, technologies used, time taken to develop the project, the logical functionality achieved and, last but not least, what exactly they learnt from these past projects by evaluating their technical attitude.

NINTENDO, COMPUTER ASSOCIATES, ORACLE, HEWLETT PACKARD, SYMANTEC, ACTIVISION BLIZZARD, EMC
MICROSOFT, IBM, SAP, ERICSSON, ADOBE, ELECTRONIC ARTS, APPLE, GOOGLE
CISCO, SONY, ALCATEL-LUCENT, HITACHI, DASSAULT SYSTEMS, SALESFORCE, TCS, INFOSYS, HCL, SAMSUNG, ARICENT

Software Development Engineer, Test (SDET), Test / Quality Assurance (QA) Engineer (Computer Software), Test / Quality Assurance (QA) Engineer (Integrated Circuit), **Test / Quality Assurance (QA) Engineer**, (Computer Networking), Test Analyst, Test Engineer (Automation), Test Engineer, Automation, Test Engineer, Computer Hardware, Test Engineer, **Test Engineering Manager**, Test Manager, **Software Lead Tester**, Software Quality Analyst, Software Quality Assurance (SQA) Analyst, **Software Quality Assurance (SQA) Engineer**, Software Quality Assurance (SQA) Lead, **Software Quality Assurance (SQA) Lead Tester**, Software Quality Assurance (SQA) Manager, Software Quality Assurance (SQA) Specialist, **Software Quality Assurance (SQA) Supervisor**, Software Quality Control (QC) Analyst, Software Quality Control (QC) Manager, **Software Quality Engineer Manager, Software Quality Tester**, Software Team Leader, **Software Technical Training Coordinator**, Software Test Analyst, Software Test Associate, **Software Test Engineer (STE)**

RESPONSIBILITY

Responsible for investigating poorly performing web based applications to increase their throughput and migrating them into high performance infrastructure and application servers.
Responsible for conceptualizing design methodologies and tool sets, and conducting tests.
Responsible to involve in planning to implementation including user (client) acceptance testing for each product.
Responsible to Handle all kind of support/requirements/bugs request from APAC customers, especially for the ongoing/proposed product projects/development e.g.; series of Application Processor, by becoming the interface from Application engineers/Field Application engineers / Sales Team /Business Development Team/ Marketing Team spread all over the ASIA.
Responsible to setup the processes for first-line and second-line customer support;
Responsible to work with Sales team to identify the services that xyz could provide along with the product.

ACCOMPLISHMENTS

Wrote Patent: System and method for creating well-connected device groups for distributed devices with heterogeneous Protocols.
Founded seed funded start-up for small business erp application to transform traditional web based solutions to cloud based.
Developed a low latency, highly scalable large scale distributed business enterprise application using Oracle Coherence and weblogic application server;
Developed a real-time, automated research distribution process, called Straight Through Process(STP), using Core Java, Multithreading, XML and JavaEE framework;
Prestigious award given on complition of few SIP related features delivered in very short time and worked as a individual contributor in that project. Also contributed in Innovative ideas on different CM products.
Publication: Rate monotonic schedulability tests using period-dependent conditions
Publication: Symbolic quality control for multimedia applications
Publication: Improved multiprocessor global schedulability analysis
Publication: FireFly: a cross-layer platform for real-time embedded wireless networks

TECHNICAL ENVIRONMENT

Java v1.5 (JDBC, Multithreading and Concurrency), PL/SQL, UML v2
JavaEE v6, JSP, Servlet, **EJB**, XML, Spring v3.1, Hibernate v3.0, Oracle Coherence v3.5, JMS v1.0
Sun Solaris v10, SUSE Linux v11.3 Sybase ASE v12, Oracle v10g
Oracle **WebLogic Application** Servers v10.3,
IBM WebSphere Application Servers v8.5, WebSphere MQ v7.5
Apache Subversion v1.7, SmartSVN v7.5, **Concurrent Versions System** (CVS) v1.11, WinCvs v2.1
Eclipse, DBArtisan v8.5, SQL Developer v3.2, Rational Rose, Microsoft Visio v2010, Astah UML v6.2, JUnit v4.0, **JMock v2.0**, JProfiler v7.2, Apache JMeter v2.8, Samurai
Open Source: Apache Solr, Google's **libJingle**, OpenVPN, **libupnp**, Linux Kernel, Netty, Node.Js, MongoDB
Languages: C, C++, C#, Java
Embedded/Device Drivers: CD-ROM, Storage, FM-Radio, i.MX Series Freescale Processors, Board Support Packages
Platforms: **Windows/Linux/Mac/WinCE**/MS-Auto
Web/Databases: **wordpress**/php/css/javascript/mysql/lamp
Tools: Code optimization to testing, packets captures, simulators, wrote customized tools.
Documentation: MS-Office/Latex/Adobe Tools

BEST PRACTICES – EFFECTIVE WHILE AT WORK

Is there any best practice you have, which you feel to be effective while at work?

RATIONALE: *Everyone may define types of best practices, which suit and fit to him or her and that depends on individual's situation, e.g. background, work styles, type of work. Interviewer wants to listen to some of the best practices which interviewee might have realized based on his or her work experience.*

SAMPLE ANSWER FROM A PROFESSIONAL POINT OF VIEW:

- Understand given task very well, follow best communication and get the things done.
- Be active in the workplace, rather than waiting for something to happen, stand up and get the things.
- Take initiative e.g.; don't wait if X will organize a discussion, rather you may actively stand up and organize the discussion.
- Define every work-day's short goal.
- Based on your work situation, make your focus hours [working hours] to be productive.
- Maintain status for all ongoing tasks given to you or around you.

Exercise:	Q:	Is there any best practice you have, which you feel to be effective while in Work?

Am I going to answer this question now? And adding the notes on my career note book?

(a).[Yes] (b).[No] (c).[Later] (d).[Its not relevant to my career] (e) [I framed this question on other way]

Date and Time:

BEST PRACTICES –
JOB-FIT WITH YOUR CAPABILITIES OR ASPIRATIONS

Why does this job looks like a match to you?

RATIONALE: *Company advertises job position, which comes with job description, require specific skills, academic qualification and some nice to have.*

Interviewer wants to verify if a candidate had studied all jobs related information before actually applying.

SAMPLE ANSWER FROM A PROFESSIONAL **POINT OF VIEW**

How my software design, development and maintenance capabilities matches.

Regarding software design capabilities: Either to design a software component/project/feature/enhancement from scratch or making changes on existing, I have worked practically on scenarios, where I have practically considered compatibility, extensibility, fault-tolerance, maintainability, modularity, packaging, reliability, re-usability, robustness, security, and usability for software design.

Regarding software development capabilities: I am experienced in programming with C, C++, C# .NET, Data Structures, Objected Oriented Analysis(OOA), Object Oriented Design(OOD), Multithreading, Network Programming, Algorithms, Client/Server, Device Driver, System Programming, Application Development in UNIX, Embedded /LINUX, Embedded WinCE OS, and Windows operating System.

Regarding software maintenance capabilities: Maintenance of a software product after delivery to correct discovered problems, I am experience with a software product usable in a changed or changing environment, e.g. improve performance, maintainability, detect and correct latent issues.

Exercise:	Q:	**What type of job profile you feel to be a fit with your capabilities or aspirations?**

Am I going to answer this question now? And adding the notes on my career note book?

(a).[Yes] (b).[No] (c).[Later] (d).[Its not relevant to my career] (e) [I framed this question on other way]

Date and Time:

CAREER ASPIRATIONS: EXPECTATIONS FROM WORK

What are your expectations from work?

RATIONALE: *After certain years of work experience, professionals may become specific with work items, especially those who are involved in specific areas e.g. technology domain, solution domain.*

Interviewer wanted to understand Interviewee's expectation towards this applied job, because interviewee has some key criteria in his or her mind.

SAMPLE ANSWER FROM A PROFESSIONAL POINT OF VIEW

Candidate applied for X opportunity in YZ division, his sample answer:

Working with 'A' type of team and project must use A/B/C, because that is my capabilities and skill-set, and I want to continue to apply it in various types of business use cases around X solution domain projects. As I have already fixed my skill set direction to A, B, C area. That is also one of the reason that I have applied this job.

[X – e.g. healthcare or retail or telecom or mobile or cloud computing]

[A, B, C – C++/Linux or C++/Windows or Java area]

Furthermore, looking close involvement in team work, individual responsibility and environment where I can utilize my capabilities, creativity, share my ideas, learn extensively and receive feedback from the team.

Exercise:	Q:	What are your expectations from work?

Am I going to answer this question now? And adding the notes on my career note book?

(a).[Yes] (b).[No] (c).[Later] (d).[Its not relevant to my career] (e) [I framed this question on other way]

Date and Time:

CAREER ASPIRATIONS: IDEAS FOR SUCCESS

Please explain a situation when you had a good idea towards the benefit of a project, initially nobody listened to it, and later the responsible person accepted your idea?

RATIONALE: *Interviewer wanted to understand your deep thinking about work, have you thought other than given work, means did you bring any creative idea or something, which was supposed to be of reasonable benefit, e.g.; you would have recommended a Test-tool, which could reduce a lot of manual test efforts, or you would have provided some designed alternatives, something, which has a direct impact to project.*

Interviewer wanted to understand whether interviewee actively participate in work related discussions, and what Interviewee feel the weight-age of his or her ideas

If yes, then what actually happened when you gave ideas, It's your call to say what exactly happened when you got an idea, was it ignored by the team? Or accepted?

SAMPLE ANSWER FROM A PROFESSIONAL POINT OF VIEW

It was happened with me while I worked on XYZ project. There was a development of various modules of XYZ Project, It was basically very big client/Server architecture, and that require immense test activities for project development. Initially, most of the test activities planned manually. I studied test situation thoroughly and did many R&D. After careful considerations, I proposed automation for few core test functionalities.

I gave the actual reason with theoretical and practical proof to my team members and other responsible people.

Yes, I proposed my idea; my idea listened out well, and not got ignored.

Other than that, I actively participate in work related discussion and wherever appropriate I provide my suggestion, ideas, and critical comments as and when required. Example: my team member started thinking towards forming a team in the area of Network Virtualization without concentrating on actual work items, my team member defined set of test cases of a software product without aiming certain test objective, critical and reasonable comments on a certain type of software design.

| Exercise: | Q: | **Please list out all the ideas you ever proposed, and later how many were accepted/ignored?** |

Am I going to answer this question now? And adding the notes on my career note book?

(a).[Yes] (b).[No] (c).[Later] (d).[Its not relevant to my career] (e) [I framed this question on other way]

Date and Time:

CAREER ASPIRATIONS: PROMOTIONS

When did you get your first promotion? How much do you care about promotions or your role within the company?

RATIONALE: *Professionals joined a role in company and afterwards, there are series of next level roles and people get promotions based on their work styles, achievements, company policies and several other parameters, e.g. time lines or grading.*

If promotion is delayed, then the professional might feel a peer pressure. Interviewer wants to understand interviewee views related with promotions.

SAMPLE ANSWER FROM A PROFESSIONAL POINT OF VIEW

I don't care about promotions or such kind of activities. I care about the work I supposed to do. I understand my work. I try to understand concerned team members. I try understanding that is doing what? How things work? Who is doing what kind of jobs?

I try to understand more internals of work, try to keep ownership so what deliverables I have to make. I understand my responsibility even more than that; I try to keep my ethics high on work in every case, especially on my focus hours. So promotion for me just kind of activity which should happen based on situation, and I truly understand when it is right.

SAMPLE ANSWER FROM A PROFESSIONAL POINT OF VIEW

I really care about promotion, because I wanted to grow in company as well as to my career. I try learn the competition, my capabilities, and how senior people are doing their work on that position where I would like to be.

I tried to analyze the gap between my current situation and the qualities I need to acquire to reach to next step. Wherever I will be, on whichever company I will be. I will surely follow the same path to increase my role and responsibility, and receive a next level promotion as a reward of my efforts.

| Exercise: | Q: | **How much do you care about promotions or your role?** |

Am I going to answer this question now? And adding the notes on my career note book?

(a).[Yes] (b).[No] (c).[Later] (d).[Its not relevant to my career] (e) [I framed this question on other way]

Date and Time:

CAREER CAUTIOUS: SPENDING NON-WORK HOURS

Did you find any situation when you didn't have any official work? Means work was very low, and you need to spend official hours in Office?

RATIONALE: *Everyday work routine doesn't require being busy constantly. It sometime works load go high or low and professional understand the nature of their work. Interviewer wanted to understand, How as a professional, Interviewee utilizes his or her non-work official hours?*

SAMPLE ANSWER FROM A PROFESSIONAL POINT OF VIEW

My non-work official hours:

Though I really get little, I try to review what I did in my last months or week, reorganize my work habits with objectives such as how I can make it more productive, time management.

- I also read XYZ based on my interest and related with work requirements. Listen to appropriate video, which helps to make me productive.
- I do visit to the gym more than as usual and try to study IEEE articles to see what research going on XYZ based on my project requirements and interest. All together, together I try to utilize my focus work hours to be productive.

SAMPLE ANSWER FROM A PROFESSIONAL POINT OF VIEW

My objective while in work is to do the work. Yes it happens that many times I don't have any officially assigned work. But it does not mean that I have nothing to do, it's my usual habit or it's my career need that I used to be busy to sharpen my skills if I'm not doing any official task.

Example: I'm very much skilled in C++ language, I can fulfill my job based on the knowledge I have, but still whenever I get the time I tried to study the C++ standards, the new updates related to C++ standards, updates on STL, updates on the boost library which I am fond to use on my various work related activities.

If still I have time then I try to write papers on a specific topic of mine and most importantly I keep my work hours for work.

Exercise:	Q:	**How you spend your free office hours?**

Am I going to answer this question now? And adding the notes on my career note book?

(a).[Yes] (b).[No] (c).[Later] (d).[Its not relevant to my career] (e) [I framed this question on other way]

Date and Time:

CAREER CHANGE:
WHY DID YOU LEAVE YOUR LAST JOB?

Why did you leave your last job?

RATIONALE: *As professionals grows, they understand the concept of the career. The best they can do, their strengths, their qualities and most importantly "what should be the right ladder for their career".And because of such understanding they move ahead if the current career not providing the expected career aspects.*

Interviewer wants to understand the reasons, why you left your last job for the current job. If in past then you might have changed your career either twice or more than twice

POSSIBLE ANSWER FROM A PROFESSIONAL POINT OF VIEW

It was my professional reason to leave that job. I didn't find career growth in terms of my work. Assigned work was related with a maintenance project, and we were involved in bug fixing. I was in the same role for two years, though I got the promotion in terms of designation, but work life was same. I didn't find any other interesting project around that company, so I left that job.

POSSIBLE ANSWER FROM A PROFESSIONAL POINT OF VIEW

It was my personal reason to leave that job: My work, team and company, everything was good. However, the location of the company was very far from my home. I used to travel almost four hours every day.

It was a waste of my time, energy and health. So I left the job and joined XYZ company.

POSSIBLE ANSWER FROM A PROFESSIONAL POINT OF VIEW

The main situation on my current job is the work environment that is very much casual. It does not bring any motivation. It's so chaotic, so boring. It does not provide any opportunity so that I can use any of my real technical skills. It pushes more towards the random work, the work is not streamlined with any objective, the small tasks appear randomly and that has minimal or no association with the next or previous task. It's a so-called support activity for the already developed product.

I'm very serious with my career, it's my responsibility for myself to understand the situation and try to find the best, which can fulfil my career aspirations. This is the reason that I'm here to understand your offerings and see how it matches with my career aspirations.

Exercise:	Q:	**Why did you leave your last jobs or planning to leave current job?**

Am I going to answer this question now? And adding the notes on my career note book?

(a).[Yes] (b).[No] (c).[Later] (d).[Its not relevant to my career] (e) [I framed this question on other way]

Date and Time:

CAREER MOVEMENT:
DECISION TO LEAVE CURRENT JOB

In what situation you feel that yes, this is time to leave the current job and find another one?

RATIONALE: *Starting years of career gives different job experience to professionals, e.g. work practices, work type, association with a team and several external factors create career related psychological pressure to professionals, e.g. friends, job market, next step in the career ladder. Professionals do not leave jobs just because of only issues; people leave jobs on career advancement in general. It depends on individual's mind set, e.g. may be salary, may be location or may be work, may be designation or may be any issue with company or may be interest to pursue another education program or pursue some self-defined research or focus on self-capabilities to bring a creative solution in the business market.*

Interviewer wants to understand, whether the interviewee has ever experienced any specific situation on which you surely leave your job.

SAMPLE ANSWER FROM A PROFESSIONAL POINT OF VIEW

I always would like to be better in terms of my career, I may look for better opportunity inside or outside the company, if

- If a professional like me doesn't feel to be proud to the work based on self-evaluation

- If my work would be increasingly becoming monotonous with not much excitement left based on self evaluation.

- May be I would like to go back to university for further education e.g. Ph.D, MBA

- I might opt entirely different role e.g. research on something.

Exercise:	Q:	**In What Situation you feel that Yes, this is time to leave current job and find another?**

Am I going to answer this question now? And adding the notes on my career note book?

(a).[Yes] (b).[No] (c).[Later] (d).[Its not relevant to my career] (e) [I framed this question on other way]

Date and Time:

CAREER MOVEMENT: PAST WORK EXPERIENCE

How was your work experience while working in your last job?

RATIONALE: *Each company provides standard items to its employees, e.g.; products, services, policies, work style, work type, technologies, work situations, work environments, business parameters, and various other professional skill related parameters. Though a professional might have generic job title, e.g.; "Member of Technical Staff," but nearly everyone will have his or her own perception related with such standard items and everyone uses those standard items to transform in a defined work accomplishment. Interviewer would like to understand your greatest accomplishment you might made in your last job e.g. in terms of learning, in terms of implementation.*

SAMPLE ANSWER FROM A PROFESSIONAL POINT OF VIEW

- Learnt technologies, e.g.; A, B, C, interacted with business development people and learnt in and out related with product's requirements.

- Learnt how to select the right pair of technologies, e.g.; SIP signalling vs XMPP signalling.

- Learnt how to work with cross-cultural teams and gained certain practical experience, e.g.; my Chinese team more comfortable to talk on instant messenger rather on phone.

- Learnt to set up a test lab for company's products and its newly developed items.

- In terms of my managerial skills: mentored three new comers, and assigned task to them, that gave me a bigger accomplishment, because I made a big deliverable than just owned by myself.

SAMPLE ANSWER FROM A PROFESSIONAL POINT OF VIEW

I would like to express my proud on writing a patent as one of the job accomplishment, which was a result of working on the use case of "convergence network platforms" for "mobile data sharing applications". It was "System and method for creating well-connected device groups for distributed devices with heterogeneous Protocols."

Its Summary is: "Many applications and services are built to synchronize several users connected to the same networking subnet (same wi-fi router or same lan subnet) A good example is the PC-Mobile synchronization applications in which one end which wish to connect the other should set the other side explicit IP address. In addition there are many games on the Android market that enable several users play together on a server less setup in the same method. The system and methods for creating well connected device groups for distributed devices with heterogeneous protocols is planned to enable these existing applications that are not aware of the limitless of networks such as 3G, different lan networks."

Exercise:	Q:	How was your work experience while working in your last job?

Am I going to answer this question now? And adding the notes on my career note book?

(a).[Yes] (b).[No] (c).[Later] (d).[Its not relevant to my career] (e) [I framed this question on other way]

Date and Time:

CAREER MOVEMENT: TOO MANY CHANGES

Why did you shift to many companies?

RATIONALE: *Professionals start their career from a company, and they work there for some period, and get experience with work, projects, policies, benefits, work environment, teamwork, supervisor behavior, learning, career growth and many other things.*

During that period, they also see what's happening in the job market, latest technologies from friends, news and some other individual-based efforts. Based on self-decision if they feel something else best for their career, they make a career move. The interviewer wants to understand what made an interviewee to change his or her job so many times or an interviewee worked on a company for a very small duration.

SAMPLE ANSWER FROM A PROFESSIONAL POINT OF VIEW

I worked for a year in 'X'; there I worked on 'A' Project with a team of four people. 'X' was a small company with strength of 90 people. That company only executes such type of projects, which requires less than a year of time line and three to four people in the team.

After six months of working in X, I evaluated my career and found I should move to Y company. Because 'Y' company was pioneered on tele/data communication domain and executes any size projects e.g.; development of base station controller software, mobile switching station software, switch signalling seven stacks.

To accustom myself with big projects, teams, working with varieties of people who are sitting in the different time zone, I decided to move my career from company X to company Y.

Exercise:	Q:	Why you shifted to many companies or planning to move from the current one?

Am I going to answer this question now? And adding the notes on my career note book?

(a).[Yes] (b).[No] (c).[Later] (d).[Its not relevant to my career] (e) [I framed this question on other way]

Date and Time:

CAREER NEGOTIATION: JOB OFFERS

Do you have any other Offer in your hand? Then why did you choose to be here?

RATIONALE: *Recruiter or HR might ask such questions from a candidate before proceeding to in person interview, If a candidate really has any offer in hand, then why he or she still coming for a job interview.*

A candidate or experienced professional would have evaluated his prospective job based on his past academic or professional experience. It happens that a candidate interacting with more than one company for job opportunities, and he or she received one job offer but he or she still evaluating the best.

SAMPLE ANSWER FROM A PROFESSIONAL **POINT OF VIEW**

I have one offer already in my hand, e.g.; I got the offer to work for Amazon (Retail Customer Experience group) as Software Design Engineer in Test to join its Quality Assurance team at Amazon, Seattle and that required years of development experience in Java/C++/Ruby, for both web applications and back end services, [mainly my C++ experience got convinced by Amazon to extend the offer].

However, I have years of C++ experience in the embedded area, I didn't decide yet to change my career to web area, so I am interested to explore this embedded opportunity as Technical manager for Telephony & Messaging software team.

Exercise:	Q:	What is your criteria to evaluate a job offer?

Am I going to answer this question now? And adding the notes on my career note book?

(a).[Yes] (b).[No] (c).[Later] (d).[Its not relevant to my career] (e) [I framed this question on other way]

Date and Time:

CAREER OBJECTIVES: GRATIFYING ABOUT YOUR ROLE

What do you find gratifying about your role in the development of software?

RATIONALE: *Professional will have his own view based on his or her software-development experience and situation, e.g. a professional may say, "my role in the development of software provides me a great experience in test automation, using algorithmic logic, write optimized code and believe in the completeness of solution."*

SAMPLE ANSWER FROM A PROFESSIONAL **POINT OF VIEW**

Developing software means, developing a product or service which helps to automate a manual solution belong to a specific domain, e.g.

An online bank-service in the banking-domain has automated most of the bank-related service, for its end customer.

- Either someone keeps calling to a vehicle's driver to understand the vehicle location or vehicle is equipped with GPS machine, which is sending its location update to a server, mobile app client fetching those updates and user happily can see a vehicle's geographical location.

In terms what is exactly gratifying to me during my software development is:

Software development experience gratify me to write such type of automated solution

- By writing algorithmic logic
- Getting the help from a intelligent but mechanical robot (computer), explaining what specifically I want to the computer, and computer let given algorithmic logic to turn out an automated solution.
- It gratifies me to operate my real-life activities more logically and automated way e.g.
- I have to send verities of wish messages to my friend's e-mail id, e.g. Christmas message, birthday message
  - ▷ Configured an e-mail client in such a way, so that it linked with the calendar's date, type of message and designated contact.
  - ▷ Programmed so it automatically send appropriate message to set of contacts, based on the date and time.

Other than that, If any time I feel to develop a business solution or something to be contributed to the society or something related to research. In each and every case the computer will help, and that give me strength to perform a bigger task by using the computational power of computer.

Exercise:	Q:	**What do you find gratifying about your role in the development of software?**

Am I going to answer this question now? And adding the notes on my career note book?

(a).[Yes] (b).[No] (c).[Later] (d).[Its not relevant to my career] (e) [I framed this question on other way]

Date and Time:

CODING: LARGEST CODE PROJECT

What is the largest code project you've been involved in? How many people were part of it? What was your role in it?

RATIONALE: *Interviewer is interested to find interviewee coding capabilities, because in all of these software's, ultimate thing is the code.*

SAMPLE ANSWER FROM A PROFESSIONAL **POINT OF VIEW**

Largest Code Project I have involved until the date was that of coding for Base Station Controller (GSM), it had all software components written for Base Station Controller. Code was of millions lines. Because this BSC was architecture based on distributed computing in which various hardware and software architectures were used. At a lower level, these products interconnected with multiple CPUs with some sort of network, regardless of whether that network is printed onto a circuit board or made up of loosely-coupled devices and cables. At a higher level, these products interconnect processes running on those CPUs with some sort of communication system. It was around 40 different teams (sitting on various geographical locations), around 800 people worked on that project. I worked for three years on this Project, and I was involved on following activities:

- Design/Development of the Fault management modules of Base Station Controller, specifically for Alarm Handling (Design, coding, testing aspects)

- Release Testing, Test Plan, Test Cases Development/Execution, automation, Test Case Execution for e.g. Performance management, Software Replacement, System start UP, HDLC management (High Level Data Link Control, LAPD), SS7 management, TDM Switching management (Time Division Multiplexing), Qmux management, R/W (Read Write bit Management), MLPPP management (Multilink Point-to-Point Protocol), E1 alarm management, TPGSM (Transmission Processing for GSM) synchronization management, Transmission local and maintenance terminal (LMT).

- Prepare the Test setup, which includes the BSC Installation, Connection with E1s, and Connection with BTS, MSC Simulators.

SAMPLE ANSWER FROM A PROFESSIONAL **POINT OF VIEW**

I developed a VOIP Test-Tool[150,000+ lines of Code- Without using any open source or any kind of library, From SIP parser to string comparison, etc., everything was written by us in a team of three people. All code was written from scratch, and I was the main person, who started this work and later two more people joined the team. **My exact role was:** Design and coding of Test Tool for VOIP communication protocol stack (UDP, IP, ARP, ICMP, TCP must and must not requirement), SDP, SIP, and Offer/Answer Model-rfc-3264).

Exercise:	Q:	**What is the largest code project you've been involved in? How many people were part of it? What was your role in it?**

Am I going to answer this question now? And adding the notes on my career note book?

(a).[Yes] (b).[No] (c).[Later] (d).[Its not relevant to my career] (e) [I framed this question on other way]

Date and Time:

COMMERCIAL PRODUCTS:
INVOLVED WITH DEVELOPING COMMERCIAL
PRODUCTS

Have you been involved with developing commercial products that have been taken through a full product life cycle? If so, what type of product was it and what was your role? What were your key learnings from this experience?

RATIONALE: *Commercial product, something which is available in the market, e.g. Microsoft's Windows Mobile, Adobe's Products, Google Nexus, Apple's iCloud Service, Test Tools, Web Services, Libraries, Frameworks as a whole or part of the project.*

Interviewer wants to understand whether the interviewee was involved in any kind of project as a whole or part of it, from scratch to shipment.

SAMPLE ANSWER FROM A PROFESSIONAL POINT OF VIEW

I worked for a product from scratch; where I wrote requirement specs, overall flow and everything for it for development and marketing strategy. Everything, means from the end to end, from the concept to tangible entity.

Type of product was: Android Application.

My role was: Overall Individual Contributor to let it develop from scratch to shipment.

Learned on various key areas:

Performed/Designed functional/non-functional end-to-end testing, fixed and debugged functional Issues, managed requirement changes, server-setup, code versioning, timely–code backup, wrote pseudo code stubs, wrote overall code, code-reviews, help-text, user-interface forms, user experience texts, test driven development approach.

Furthermore, learned how market works, converting the ideas into tangible entity.

SAMPLE ANSWER FROM A PROFESSIONAL POINT OF VIEW

Product: V2IP (Video and Voice over IP) middleware for XYZ product

Duration: 1 Year 3 Months

Percentage of involvement in the major product development activities:

1) Specifications (20%) 2) Design (30%) 3) Development (40%) 4) Testing (10%)

This project was not so big, and team was around12 engineers, but the development of this project was from scratch.

We bought the SIP stack/Video/Audio Codec from third party, and rest of the development was done by the team.

Key learning from this experience with my role as a senior software engineer

- Participated in the management meeting for the use/analysis/growth/future of this project.
- Learnt to involve in writing the requirements and specification of this project.
- Learnt to involve in recruiting/interviewing other candidates into this team.
- Learnt to involve in task assignment.
- Learnt to Involve in the integration of SIP (Session Initiation protocol)/ STUN (Simple Traversal of UDP over NAT) and reviewing the whole project.
- Learnt to exercise every phase of software engineering on this project and delivered the release on given time.

Exercise:	Q:	Have you been involved with developing commercial products that have been taken through a full product life cycle? If so, what type of product and what was your role? What were your key learnings from this experience?

Am I going to answer this question now? And adding the notes on my career note book?

(a).[Yes] (b).[No] (c).[Later] (d).[Its not relevant to my career] (e) [I framed this question on other way]

Date and Time:

COMMUNICATION STYLE – EMAIL/PHONE/ COMMUNICATOR

What suits your personality best while communicating with the team located in different geographical location or with a team with which in person communication is not easily possible? Do you prefer email, phone conversations or instant messaging software?

RATIONALE: *Interviewer wants to understand interviewee experience and effective mode of communication with the team members located in different geographical location.*

SAMPLE ANSWER FROM A PROFESSIONAL POINT OF VIEW

It all depends on situation to situation. All tools exist (messenger, e-mail or phone or face-to-face), It depends, which could be best on certain situation.

- IM works well e.g. discussion on a very short type of Q/A, people who are not good in spoken English but writing works (e.g. Chinese, Japanese, etc.), random communication, a silent way of communication

- E-mail works, e.g. when it requires keeping many people in the loop, things are in little detail and must be in records

- Phone works e.g. to avoid e-mail or IM, rather having back and forth many mails; you can just have phoned.

If there is a big discussion, e.g. reviewing documents, or understand requirements or something, which takes days to work out, better to have a in-person discussion.

These are all just my view, someone's view might be different, but it automatically happens what works best, and usually we try phone, e-mail, IM first or Cisco Web-Ex types of solutions and In person on some important situations only.

Exercise:	Q:	Which mode of communication best suits to your personality?

Am I going to answer this question now? And adding the notes on my career note book?

(a).[Yes] (b).[No] (c).[Later] (d).[Its not relevant to my career] (e) [I framed this question on other way]

Date and Time:

CONTRIBUTION: ROLE ON XYZ PROJECT

May you please describe your exact role on this "XYZ" project?

RATIONALE: *Professionals usually associated with a designation, e.g. developer, software test engineer, project manager, technical lead, etc. and perform projects based duties.*

Interviewer wants to understand duties performed by interviewee while working in XYZ project. It's good to provide a bird's eye view of job duties to a reasonable level and then based on a type of interviewer's question interviewee may answer next level of question, which might be derived from the given answer.

SAMPLE ANSWER FROM A PROFESSIONAL **POINT OF VIEW**

On this "XYZ" project my official designation was senior software engineer, but In terms of exact job duties which I did:

- Ramped up on XMPP (Extensible Messaging and Presence Protocol) standards and related technologies, e.g. Clients, Servers for Messaging

- Designed/developed/coded and unit tested Client Application based on XMPP Standards for Linux/windows/Android platforms, and Implemented features, e.g. Multi-User Chat, Client Login/Logout, File Transfer across Clients, Presence, and Rosters.

SAMPLE ANSWER FROM A PROFESSIONAL **POINT OF VIEW**

During my work on XYZ project, I have worked mostly in Bluetooth Application Development e.g. development of new profiles, features, interfaces and participated for Bluetooth qualification related testing activities.

Exercise:	Q:	May you please describe your role for the defined projects on your CV/ resume?

Am I going to answer this question now? And adding the notes on my career note book?

(a).[Yes] (b).[No] (c).[Later] (d).[Its not relevant to my career] (e) [I framed this question on other way]

Date and Time:

CURRENT COMPANY: BUSINESS LINE

Describe the current or most recent company you worked for/what is the line of business/who are the customers?

RATIONALE: *Interviewer is interested to find out Interviewee's knowledge about the company, its business and customers, for he or she is currently working.*

Interviewee might not need to tell anything related with trade secret or sensitive information, e.g. he or she can answer only that information which is openly available in the company's website.

SAMPLE ANSWER FROM A PROFESSIONAL **POINT OF VIEW**

I am employed in X Imaging corporation in his San Jose (California) office. X works on CMOS Imaging Technology and solutions that enabled high-quality imaging for Automotive, DSLR, Medical, Mobile, PC Camera, Surveillance solutions.

Lines of business are: Image Sensors, Image Processors, and Wafer-Level Cameras, etc.

Our customers are from small business start-up to high-end technological companies throughout the globe.

Exercise:	Q:	Describe your current or most recent company/what is the line of business/who are the customers?

Am I going to answer this question now? And adding the notes on my career note book?

(a).[Yes] (b).[No] (c).[Later] (d).[Its not relevant to my career] (e) [I framed this question on other way]

Date and Time:

CURRENT WORK ITEM: DESCRIBE YOUR PART

Describe what part of the product and product development you work on and what percentage you own?

RATIONALE: *The Process of product development involved various activities depending on its stage, e.g.*

Which already exist in market or likely to be in the market.

Test Tool for a software product (somehow that is a part of software, but it will not ship to market in return of some commerce).

The exact product (core part) developed in XYZ's company, and some work outsourced to another company may be as a part of the product.

Interviewer wanted to analyze on what part Interviewee worked or working on, and what percentage he or she own. It really difficult to measure, but yes there could be an ideal or reasonable guess could be made.

SAMPLE ANSWER FROM A PROFESSIONAL **POINT OF VIEW**

For product X, I was involved in test part, e.g.

Tool development,

- Reviewing/improving the test process, test specification,
- Coding, execution, writing, and maintenance of test cases for various device drivers/system application/working scenarios.

What percentage you own:

- Total 14 people belong to the team, who are responsible to perform complete testing for this product.
- Team comprises one main leader, two team leaders, and 11 engineers. I was responsible for 50% of the test work with five engineers out of 11 engineers for test-related work; not any people management just worked related management with people.

Exercise:	Q:	**Describe what part of the product and product development you work on and what percentage you own?**

Am I going to answer this question now? And adding the notes on my career note book?

(a).[Yes] (b).[No] (c).[Later] (d).[Its not relevant to my career] (e) [I framed this question on other way]

Date and Time:

CURRENT WORK ITEM: DESCRIBE YOUR TEAM

How many people are you working with on your current project? What are their roles?

RATIONALE: *Interviewer wanted to understand the organization of Interviewee's current project team, e.g. how the big team is, individual roles, and how much interviewee knows about them.*

SAMPLE ANSWER FROM A PROFESSIONAL **POINT OF VIEW**

Total 14 people are working on my team, here is the breakdown:

Project Leader–1:

- Manages manpower by interacting daily with Team Leaders, understand work progress and share such progress with his superiors.
- Receive work from US Office counterparts, understand the work, once overall understanding cleared, talk with other two team leaders for next steps.
- Perform the evaluation of these two team leaders; also interact with other teams for several meeting to review and other work-related possessions.
- Understand work-related requirement with help of Team Leaders and write complete work structure.
- Interact with Application Engineers (connected with customers) who assign some of the additional requirements to the engineering team (having said Project Leader is a part of engineering team)

Team Leader (Me) + Six Development Engineers = 7: [Development Team]

- Manage six developers in respect to work.
- Understand team activities, define work priorities.
- Each team member owns one or more feature of ongoing project, e.g.; one team member responsible to develop the X drivers for an embedded software work

1- Team Leader + Five Team Members = 6 [Test Team]

- Team Members write overall test specifications, test strategy, test cases, test tool, study assigned feature, standards.
- Execute tests based on the requirements, based on the received bugs,
- Perform various types of testing from functional to stress testing and from regression to non-regression testing.

Exercise:	Q:	How many people are you working with on your current project? What are their roles?

Am I going to answer this question now? And adding the notes on my career note book?

(a).[Yes] (b).[No] (c).[Later] (d).[Its not relevant to my career] (e) [I framed this question on other way]

Date and Time:

CURRENT WORK ITEM: PRODUCT YOU WORK ON

Describe the product you work on – what does it do and who is the end user for the product?

RATIONALE: *This question is related with the use-case, which means on whatever product a professional have worked or have been working, were they associated with any end user.*

SAMPLE ANSWER FROM A PROFESSIONAL POINT OF VIEW

Product I worked on: I am currently working on a product named–Windows Phone–OS (7.5 -"Mango") which is a successor of Windows Mobile (base is Windows CE) targeted for competitive smart phone market. One of the commercial Windows-Phone OS based smart-phone recently launched from HTC.

What it does: It has most of the common features e.g.; Internet Explorer, contacts, e-mail, multimedia, games, search, microsoft office suite with entirely different stream of UI (different from Apple, Symbian, Android etc). It has most of comfortable set of functionalities e.g.; user can manually enter contacts names but he can also import contacts from facebook or Windows Live, or Linked In Or Twitter etc.

End users: It is targeted to skilled professionals, who use Smartphone for several other purposes rather just for call and message.

SAMPLE ANSWER FROM A PROFESSIONAL POINT OF VIEW

Product I worked on: It's a Interview Exact App on android Platform. Interview Exact App provides highly practical answers which helps job-seekers (means those are dedicatedly looking for job or already in job and looking for a shift, but all together looking for a job). It has been included answers from right professionals, and given these answers as sample answers, complete answers not only guidelines.

What it does: It provides list of question/answers from XYZ topics. It also provide a best way to store user's own comments as notes while user read question/answer, user can add his thoughts by having his own view on that, so on that case he can keep notes.

End users: Students who are in their final /pre-final year of graduation or post graduation preparing for technical interviews. University graduates who came out from college and looking at a job. Professionals who have 0-1 years of experience and trying to get ready for branded companies. Professionals who wanted to switch their jobs and preparing for job interviews. Project Managers/Leaders, HR Managers, Hiring Managers effectively dealing with job interviews. Companies that wanted to have a reference to write a question-paper for job interviews. HR Managers/Hiring-Team Members who are visiting campuses and wanted to test candidate's skills.

Am I going to answer this question now? And adding the notes on my career note book?

(a).[Yes] (b).[No] (c).[Later] (d).[Its not relevant to my career] (e) [I framed this question on other way]

Date and Time:

CURRENT WORK ITEM:
STAGE OF THE CURRENT WORK ITEM

What is the stage of your current project at present?

RATIONALE: *Projects start from scratch and over a period of time, it expands. When a project expands, it also incorporates more people, and after that people join projects with different types of job roles, e.g. a software developer for the enhancement of an existing feature on a maintenance project, a software test engineer to test certain functional test cases to provide for project support.*

Interviewer wants to know the stage of interviewee's current project, and being as a developer how he or she contributing in the different phase of a project, other than development, e.g. testing, support.

SAMPLE ANSWER FROM A PROFESSIONAL POINT OF VIEW

I am involved in a maintenance type of a project as a software developer. We are currently involved in the optimization of the feature which we wrote earlier, and performing high end testing for that. Test professionals performing their tests, and logging bugs under my name if that supposed to be fixed by myself.

SAMPLE ANSWER FROM A PROFESSIONAL POINT OF VIEW

I am a software developer and working in a support team. Customer of our xyz product requested the customization on xyz e.g. extra feature development, changes in existing feature. Being as a software developer my contribution it to provide development support for XYZ product.

Exercise:	Q:	What is the stage of your current project at present?

Am I going to answer this question now? And adding the notes on my career note book?

(a).[Yes] (b).[No] (c).[Later] (d).[Its not relevant to my career] (e) [I framed this question on other way]

Date and Time:

CURRENT WORK ITEM:
LIST OF BUGS ON YOUR CURRENT PROJECT

May you please explain a list of bugs on your current project? Or any specific bug?

RATIONALE: *Projects starts from a scratch at some point of time, and evolve for later releases, e.g. software in its first phase of development, software in its subsequent phase of development, software has been developed but its performance was not up to the mark. Software requires to add certain extra features because of XYZ, software already in use by its end-users and current development is based on user's feedback.*

Project always keeps going, and that also associated with several types of bugs, with diverse status, e.g. open, in progress, solved but not reviewed.

Interviewer is looking to the dynamics of the work being done on this project, means in whatever stage current project would be, and it might be associated with some bugs. Are you aware of those?

Interviewer understands, that it's all depends on what your role is (other than marketing, or sales person), but if somehow the interviewee has linked with development area, then.

SAMPLE ANSWER FROM A PROFESSIONAL POINT OF VIEW

We are working in the development of an application, which has set of functionality associated with its modules, e.g.

- Business logic to process the received input from user interface or received input from the server while a user login into the server.
- Front end User Interface which let a user to perform several action, e.g. login to the server to retrieve a user specific data.
- It was started three month ago, and now we have reached to its finish date. It has few small minor to major bugs.

Minor bugs related to User Interface, e.g.; addition of XYZ view or adding of a field, On A, B, C cases it doesn't work.

Major bugs related to User's Login to Server, e.g.; related with its authorization module because its development still in process and developer working on to get it fix.

Open issues related to user's authorization while login to the server, e.g. exact design and flow while a user login to the server with appropriate authorization mechanism still has not been finalized.

Exercise:	Q:	May you please explain a list of bugs on your current project? Or any specific bug?

Am I going to answer this question now? And adding the notes on my career note book?

(a).[Yes] (b).[No] (c).[Later] (d).[Its not relevant to my career] (e) [I framed this question on other way]

Date and Time:

CURRENT WORK ITEM: TEAM SIZE INFORMATION

Is your current project managed by just one team or are there other teams also involved in it? If there are other teams then how many of them are involved? How do you manage the overall collaboration between the teams during the project development?

RATIONALE: *Interviewer wants to understand how big your team is, and is there many teams working together? If yes how the interviewee manages (based on his or her role) collaboration across a team.*

Interviewee might not be a that type of team member who supposed to interact with others, but still. If several teams work together, then the interviewee must be affected via some means.

SAMPLE ANSWER FROM A PROFESSIONAL POINT OF VIEW

This project involves several other teams; people are even sitting in different countries.

I interact with three other teams and those sits in entirely different geographical locations.

Work has been already divided and respective accountable people also. We used to have collaboration via e-mail, phone, video conferencing, face-to-face visit meetings and we have defined scheduled for weekly report, milestone to track the progress.

Exercise:	Q:	How do you manage the overall collaboration between the teams during the project development?

Am I going to answer this question now? And adding the notes on my career note book?

(a).[Yes] (b).[No] (c).[Later] (d).[Its not relevant to my career] (e) [I framed this question on other way]

Date and Time:

DEBUGGING:
PAST DEBUGGING EXPERIENCE OF YOURS

Can you please provide or describe any past experience of yours which can describe your proficiency in debugging.

RATIONALE: *Interviewer wants to understand interviewee experience in debugging e.g. how well the interviewee can use GDB or some other debuggers, skill related with tracing the code, situation when a debugger cannot be used.*

SAMPLE ANSWER FROM A PROFESSIONAL POINT OF VIEW

Debugger I use when I need to see the code flow against the already found/to fix bug or to test/debug/trace code, e.g.; GDB, Visual C++ Debugger.

However, I also solve many complex issues where it's not easy or applicable to use a debugger, which could be done with the help of various projects related items and tools, e.g. analyze system behavior, remember past steps which are performed for a specific execution/operation, understand the code flow, check design documentation, discuss with other developers, analyze third party libraries, recent changes.

Exercise:	Q:	Can you please provide or describe any past experience of yours which can describe your proficiency in debugging.?

Am I going to answer this question now? And adding the notes on my career note book?

(a).[Yes] (b).[No] (c).[Later] (d).[Its not relevant to my career] (e) [I framed this question on other way]

Date and Time:

DECISION MAKING – PROJECT'S PROGRESS

Is there any situation when you made a mistake that made a huge impact on the progress of your project?

RATIONALE: *There might be a situation during your work, on which you made a mistake which affected to project e.g. used A approach to design the work-item though approach B was more appropriate, used C technology for a project though D was more appropriate. Though rarely it would have happened, because most of the organization made the system which avoids any mistake to happen. But still Interviewer wants to see on any case, if something happened, which let you feel a mistake made from your side.*

SAMPLE ANSWER FROM A PROFESSIONAL **POINT OF VIEW**

Nopes, in my whole professional experience, I didn't make any kind of mistake Or something else which made me feel like a mistake happened or something which got affected to project as detraction, because whatever decisions were made that made after series of review and situation by that time and I didn't feel something happened like that which tells any mistake.

SAMPLE ANSWER FROM A PROFESSIONAL **POINT OF VIEW**

There was a situation where initially we decided to use one open source framework for a solution. But while actually working on that solution we found, that is not right solution for that project(that made around one month delay in project). But it was reasonable because nobody had such experience e.g.; kind of hands-on to that work. We did our effort on first month to find out right way, whether we are going towards right directions or not. That was not a mistake, that was a time to confirm the decision made for development.

[Difference between UDT [UDP Level Data Transport Protocol] and LWIP[A Light Weight TCP/IP stack]]:

UDT is a reliable transport over UDP. It is designed to overcome the TCP slow window increments and provide fast reliable throughput in HPC[High Performance Computing] which is characterized by low latency and high bandwidth. But our solution was supposed to be running in internet environment (high latency and low bandwidth). Also our integration with UDT was not simple. We had to create a complicated mapping between UNIX sockets and our sockets.

We received a recommendation to evaluate the lwip library. Lwip is a TCP/IP stack implementation. It was designed to be integrated by embedded applications. It also has a UNIX, Win32 and Mac porting in the contrib files. We didn't have to make any changes to the library. We only implemented a driver layer providing read and write functionality over the socket.

Exercise:	Q:	**Situations where you made any mistake that made a huge impact on the progress of project?**

Am I going to answer this question now? And adding the notes on my career note book?

(a).[Yes] (b).[No] (c).[Later] (d).[Its not relevant to my career] (e) [I framed this question on other way]

Date and Time:

DECISION MAKING – SUGGESTION/OWNERSHIP

Is there any situation when you made great suggestion/ownerships that made a huge Impact on the progress of your project?

RATIONALE: *In many situations it happens, that people perform the task the way it assigned to, they might not come up with there own thoughts, creativity or something which can make that task better than the way it planned. Interviewer would like to know from interviewee that how he reacted when he received a task, and later he found that something could be done in a different way than what actually suggested(especially when that impacted to the progress of the project).*

SAMPLE ANSWER FROM A PROFESSIONAL POINT OF VIEW

I worked on a network software product which supposed to deploy on various types of network topologies, but to define its stability it was required to test this product on many different scenarios. Rather than using all such hardware computers simulate types of network topologies, I suggested and implemented the simulation of "Real Network Topologies" with user mode-Linux/VDE/QEMU Virtual Machines/Open vSwitch/Bridge/ip-tables/lvs-director. That impacted on the project's development progress.

SAMPLE ANSWER FROM A PROFESSIONAL POINT OF VIEW

I suggested to use XMPP Jingle signalling than to us SIP signalling on XYZ project because of XYZ reason

SAMPLE ANSWER FROM A PROFESSIONAL POINT OF VIEW

I suggested to implement part of a mobile application in native Code [C, C++], so it could be portable easily to different mobile platforms.

SAMPLE ANSWER FROM A PROFESSIONAL POINT OF VIEW

I suggested to perform scalability testing on some product before to move to next step.

SAMPLE ANSWER FROM A PROFESSIONAL POINT OF VIEW

I changed the process or setup some policy because of XYZ reason that made huge impact. Because I learned or did R&D on XYZ stuff during my education/past-project/self-research. So my work was exactly related to that work and then I gave various suggestion to customer regarding his approach, gap in deliverables and where we can make some more changes to get solid solution.

Exercise:	Q:	Situations when you made great suggestions/ownerships that made a huge impact on the progress of project?

Am I going to answer this question now? And adding the notes on my career note book?

(a).[Yes] (b).[No] (c).[Later] (d).[Its not relevant to my career] (e) [I framed this question on other way]

Date and Time:

DESIGN SKILLS: APPROACH WHILE DESIGNING THE X

Please explain to me your complete approach while designing the X feature on the Y Project? How did you optimize the code?

RATIONALE: *Interviewer is interested to understand interviewee approach while designing X Feature on Y project as that was mentioned on his resume.*

SAMPLE ANSWER FROM A PROFESSIONAL POINT OF VIEW

TASK

*Integration of third party SIP-Stack into the V2IP Middleware, Design, Development and Testing of the Call Features of V2IP (Video and Voice Over IP) e.g.; Basic Call, Call Hold, Call Forward, Call Waiting, API Testing

TASK DEFINITION

*Call Control Adapters are the wrapper function to access the Call Signalling stacks. As per the design of V2IP, it can have the access of both H.323 and SIP stack for Call Signalling.

*Call control Adapters provide the common set of API which in front of the Call Manager are same API, which do not depicts that which stack they are going to use for signalling, its depends on the configuration of the V2IP, configuration can be changeable dynamically.

*There was not much documentation was available to study this SIP Stack, it was time consuming to understand implementation of this SIP Stack, and how to transform the top layers, call signalling of this SIP Stack into Call Control API e.g. CCA_CM_INIT_FUN(), CCA_CM_START_FUN(), CCA_CM_EXIT_FUN(), CCA_CM_CALLMAKE_FUN(), CCA_CM_CALLACCEPT_FUN(), CCA_CM_CALLREJECT_FUN(), CCA_CM_CALLDROP_FUN()

#CCA (Call Control Adapter), CM (Call Manager)

METHODOLOGY USED TO ADDRESS PROBLEM

Following methodology has been followed:

1. Collected as much documentation of this third part stack.
2. Tried to understand the approach, coding styles, data structures and flow of various functions

3. Studied make files, configuration settings, and found, what are the minimal changes are required to run this SIP Stack, and what kind of environment required.

4. Made possible changes, possible configuration setting, code changes, and changes in make files and executed the SIP Stack.

5. Made various scenarios, based on the settings in configuration files, and used GDB to study the flow of Sip call signalling for both incoming and outgoing.

6. After having detailed analysis, the possible integration of top layer functions has been finalized, and practiced.

STEPS/SPECIFIC TASKS THAT I HAVE PERFORMED

The tasks that I have performed are as follows:

1. Integrated all the initialization process on one Init function

2. Integrated all the Exit process on one Exit function

3. Wrote a new call-back, which can interact with the SIP Stack Call back Function.

4. Integrated various function specific functionalities into one Call Control Adapter API e. g.; Call Make Functions, Call Create Function, Call Hold Functions, Call Accept Functions etc

5. Made possible interaction with Call Control Adapter Call Back, which was interacting with Sip Call Back Functions.

6. Wrote various test stubs to test the developed API, Used ethereal and Client/Server tools to test the developed features

HOW CODE WAS IMPLEMENTED

Code was implemented and tested in C on Linux environment.

FINAL RESULT

API was developed as per the requirement and delivered to the customers with possible releases of V2IP Middleware.

Exercise:	Q:	**Please explain to me your complete approach while designing the X feature on Y Project?, How did you optimize the code (X Feature and Y Project from Your CV)?**

Am I going to answer this question now? And adding the notes on my career note book?

(a).[Yes] (b).[No] (c).[Later] (d).[Its not relevant to my career] (e) [I framed this question on other way]

Date and Time:

WORK INTEREST: NEXT WORK LEVEL ACTIVITIES

What are the main features planned for the next release of your current project?

RATIONALE: *Projects are associated with many ongoing activities and plan to do next, e.g. its incremental releases with add on features, bug fixes, vision, objectives and it all depends on the project situation.*

Interviewer wants to know Interviewee's understanding related with the project understanding in large, mentioned as a current project on his or her resume.

SAMPLE ANSWER FROM A PROFESSIONAL POINT OF VIEW

My role on this project as an engineer and I am more involved in technology, e.g. Implementation of a set of functionality in a specific time schedule.

I try to be more skilled and up to date in the technological area, e.g. new released features on X technology.

SAMPLE ANSWER FROM A PROFESSIONAL POINT OF VIEW

My role on this project as an engineer and I keep high interest on my work, and always curious to know more about the project, so that I can efficiently choose an interesting project items for implementation and learning.

Next release of X project has been planned around M month and that is after N month of now. That time it has planned to implement A, B and C.

Next release which is due after three months, and it has planned with few features, e.g. Sugar-Sync integration for connected data backup, Google Docs Integration for on-line document view.

Next release feature also depends on some other parameters as well e.g. customer feedback, management decision.

Exercise:	Q:	**What are the main features planned for next release of your current Project?**

Am I going to answer this question now? And adding the notes on my career note book?

(a).[Yes] (b).[No] (c).[Later] (d).[Its not relevant to my career] (e) [I framed this question on other way]

Date and Time:

DOCUMENTATION: ARCHITECTURE, SPECIFICATIONS

Have you ever written specifications, architecture, wiki pages, user manuals and other design documents?

RATIONALE: *Documentation really required on several stages of the work, some of the document directly related to the work e.g., designing the concept, writing the product requirements. Some of them are not a part of the work or not directly related to the work, but it creates a great value to the product e.g. wiki-pages. It's a professional skills that he or she organise the information in such document so that it can fulfil the purpose.*

Example: person 'A' working on 'X' thing, and 'X' has some information which required by person 'B', 'C', 'D', 'E'. Rather every time 'B', 'C', 'D', 'E' approach to 'A' to get the information. 'A' can create a wiki page for such type of information. Every time when 'A' feels that 'abc' information related to 'X' must be conveyed to 'B', 'C', 'D', 'E' then he can add such information to the corresponding wiki page and notification should move to 'B', 'C', 'D', 'E'. Interviewer wants to see what type of documentation interviewee wrote in experience, what is the interviewee opinion on the importance of documentation?

SAMPLE ANSWER FROM A PROFESSIONAL POINT OF VIEW

Certainly, I wrote a lot of documentation based on case by case, e.g.; user manual to requirement document, from high level design to low level design document, test plans, test design documents, wiki-pages (e.g. setted up a wordpress based server, and team can write supportive documents/contents for others). Recently I wrote one test plan document by considering following factors:

Writing a test plan it's not straight forward and has pre-defined set of items to write, Its all depends upon what kind of testing it is, various other parameters, e.g.; clearing requirement, test environment, timeline, project phase, my role, resources, dependency, targeted customer, end user(different age group, or different profession), targeted industry, interoperability, conformance product specification, requirement use cases.

Altogether following test plan elements considered in a test plan, but again, its description would be different based on the individual project needs and may be some other additional items:

Scope, what to test what not to be test, References to various other artefacts, e.g.; requirements considered. Test Area Breakdown(if that is a module or integrations of various modules), What kind of testing going to perform, Possible Functional Testing – Which again divided in Positive and Negative testing, Non-Functional Testing – e.g.; Performance, Stress, Globalization Testing, Accessibility Testing, Open Points if Any, TimeLine, List of Test Cases, Automation Criteria, Test Case Classifications, Test Time Line, Test Environments…

Exercise:	Q:	**Have you ever written specifications, architecture, wiki pages, user manuals and other design documents?**

Am I going to answer this question now? And adding the notes on my career note book?

(a).[Yes] (b).[No] (c).[Later] (d).[Its not relevant to my career] (e) [I framed this question on other way]

Date and Time:

GROUP COLLABORATION: LANGUAGE BARRIER

There are many situations when your counter-part may not be very good in English. How do you manage such situations?

RATIONALE: *Working in China/Korea/Japan is completely different than working in USA/Australia/UK. The major concepts lies with the language, and the cultural philosophy at work.*

Interviewer wants to understand interviewee's view and experience, while working with cross-cultural teams, e.g. Chinese people prefer to talk in Chinese language than English, Korean/ Japanese people prefer to talk in their language than English. Interviewer also would like to see, have you learnt any foreign language, did you travel by yourself to expand your horizon, have you ever experienced with such environment, do you really keep an inclination to mix with different cultures/ background?

SAMPLE ANSWER FROM A PROFESSIONAL POINT OF VIEW

I am from Indian origin, and my English level is above average in terms of writing, listening and speaking. I have worked mostly in US, and interacted with people who were from diverse culture and countries, but didn't face any issue.

SAMPLE ANSWER FROM A PROFESSIONAL POINT OF VIEW

It happened to work myself in China for long times, yes I had a very hard time to talk with my Chinese co-workers in English, because of their native phonetics. It was very nervous time while communicating in English, though I tried to learn mandarin but that was not enough to discuss difficult issues. So to let myself adjust on their culture took some time, e.g.; to understand their ways of talking, understand their frequently used words and its intentional meaning.

To manage such situation, I used to write more than speaking, I used to speak slow, I used to use simple words, I used short sentences, I used to keep in touch with an at-least one viable individual who is conversant with English language.

| Exercise: | Q: | **Do you really keep an inclination to mix with different cultures/ background?** |

Am I going to answer this question now? And adding the notes on my career note book?

(a).[Yes] (b).[No] (c).[Later] (d).[Its not relevant to my career] (e) [I framed this question on other way]

Date and Time:

CAREER ASPIRATIONS:
NOT ENJOYING THE WORK ASSIGNED

Was there any situation when you didn't like the work given to you? What did you do? Why exactly didn't you like the given work?

RATIONALE: *Professionals can be flexible or very specific with given work items.*

Interviewer wants to understand your experience related with your job profile, were you assigned to any work which you didn't like, if yes, then how did you manage such a type of situation.

SAMPLE ANSWER FROM A PROFESSIONAL POINT OF VIEW

Work is very important part of my daily life, because I learn from my work, and clearly understand my job responsibility. Based on my job responsibility I work effectively on given, assigned work items with appropriate dedication.

SAMPLE ANSWER FROM A PROFESSIONAL POINT OF VIEW

I got into a situation where I was assigned to work on test areas. I am a software developer, and my productivity and contribution work better on the development side. I explained my situation to concerned person and assigned to development work.

SAMPLE ANSWER FROM A PROFESSIONAL POINT OF VIEW

Didn't like to work maybe an irrelevant term. It happens that on some situation when you get a work which has no mean. You are not very clear what you are doing, and why you are doing. Many things you are doing because of company policies, or the concerned boss has his on ego or on many situation happens that we are working for a person than working for a project.

Such kind of work environment made the work non-interesting and trigger a thought to comment for " like" Or "not-like".

I didn't face such type of situations much, as I am very clear with my profile and before joining a job-position. I follow an ethical standard for my work, and happily perform the best which I have already convinced to offer.

Exercise:	Q:	**List the situation and type of work you don't like?**

Am I going to answer this question now? And adding the notes on my career note book?

(a).[Yes] (b).[No] (c).[Later] (d).[Its not relevant to my career] (e) [I framed this question on other way]

Date and Time:

GROUP COLLABORATION: SHARE YOUR EXPERIENCE

How much experience do you have in cross group collaboration? Please describe a specific example when you had to exercise your collaboration skills. [Beginner+]

RATIONALE: *It's possible that in an organization, teams geographically non-geographically located in different areas, e.g. test team located at location 'A', development team located at location 'B'.*

Keeping a right attitude while communicating with peers or members of other teams has been believed a professional practice, e.g. to improve relationships and effective communication inside/across groups.

SAMPLE ANSWER FROM A PROFESSIONAL **POINT OF VIEW**

In terms of my understanding related with cross group collaboration, e.g. working with several teams, interacting with those teams who are partly or because of some reasons connected with my team to achieve the mutual goals.

I truly understand, as cross communications go a long way for the success of the project. My work required me to interact with multiple teams and work at different locations, e.g. support team, marketing team, engineering team, HR team, team across geographical location, multi-cultural team (worked in Japan for two years).

On my case other than the official work, I used to keep a flexible attitude towards work, e.g. having lunch with the team, actively interacting on team-building sessions (officially organized events) especially for cross group communication.

One simple example: There was a team which was associated with my team, but In terms of work, I didn't interact with that team because I didn't have any direct work with them.

On one instance, I was working on my work, and I required some set of embedded devices with some customization in software. Somehow idea got clicked to reach that intended team from my built-up relationship with other teams (that team sits entirely in different building).

I requested help from them, all done very effectively and promptly, and my team members so surprised and saying, "Hey, how you made this," because by keeping such interaction across groups, It provides you more ways around, because all are professionals and yes–we need to get success in terms of work and project."

Am I going to answer this question now? And adding the notes on my career note book?

(a).[Yes] (b).[No] (c).[Later] (d).[Its not relevant to my career] (e) [I framed this question on other way]

Date and Time:

INDIVIDUAL PERSPECTIVE: A WELL DESIGNED PRODUCT

What is your definition of a well-designed product? Can you provide any Specific Example?

RATIONALE: *Defining something, which is perfect on every single sense–may not bet right, because products keep evolving with time and with various issues getting fixed–over a period. E.g. reusability was not considered during the design phase, scalability while building client/server based applications, performance for real time products, storage while handling large amount of data, crashes with data structures, memory issues for system specific product.*

Example – Design Challenges

- *On a client/server based product, where a client would be served by the server, faces design challenges, e.g.*

- *Scalability: If servers are supposed to serve millions of users across geography,*

  ▷ *Performance: If users are supposed to share data with other users,*

  ▷ *Request handling: millions of updates sent to the server for presence as status.*

- *Writing a TCP/IP stack for low cost embedded devices, e.g.*

  ▷ *Optimize Linux's TCP/IP stack for a low-cost network device.*

However, there is a concept of well designed product and Interviewer wants to understand interviewee designing skill in terms of its definition defined by him.

SAMPLE ANSWER FROM A PROFESSIONAL POINT OF VIEW

In definition, well design product should have A, B, C, D…endless things. According to me, a well design product should do for what it was indented for e.g. If a product has targeted to handle millions of client requests in an hour, it should do this. If a product has targeted for blind people for X purpose, it should serve that purpose rightly.

A well design product should serve its intended purpose based on the available resources, timeline, schedule, budget and able to cope with requisite changes over time for its subsequent releases.

Exercise:	Q:	What is your definition of a well-designed product? Can you provide Any Specific Example?

Am I going to answer this question now? And adding the notes on my career note book?

(a).[Yes] (b).[No] (c).[Later] (d).[Its not relevant to my career] (e) [I framed this question on other way]

Date and Time:

LEADERSHIP: GOALS/OBJECTIVES OF YOUR POSITION

What are the goals/objectives of your position? How do you measure your success/know if you are doing a good job?

RATIONALE: *Professionals organize their professional life by defining job position based on goals, e.g. skills enhancement, delivering a work-item, filing a patent, learning foreign language. Other than this, some obvious goals are associated with a professional's job position. Something which job positions have an intention to achieve at some point of time, Interviewer wants to see whether the interviewee understands his or her job position based goals.*

SAMPLE ANSWER FROM A PROFESSIONAL **POINT OF VIEW**

Certain goals and objectives seems to be fixed based on my official designation as software engineer but many got changes based on time and schedule.

RELATIVELY FIXED OR PREDEFINED GOALS: I am working for a product 'A', and I have complete ownership of its XYZ area, so some of my work-related goals:

- Work on XYZ from end-to-end means e.g.; get clear understanding of the requirements. What has to be developed, how it has to be designed, business logic, user interfaces, etc.?

- As of now I have the time line to develop a XYZ feature in three months, with extra months for testing. Afterwards, there are succeeding planned work items for this, which would be included on subsequent round.

SELF DEFINED GOALS TO MAKE JOB MORE EFFICIENT: Since I am involved in a project where I require interacting more with Japanese colleagues and CDN (Content Delivery Network) Technology, following are my goals to make myself more efficient e.g. In terms of communication, In terms of technology

Learning Japanese language by having two classes every week for six month.

- Enrolled myself to a course of *Content delivery Network, Once a week for 3 months.

WHETHER I AM DOING A GOOD JOB?: My job position is attached with some set of contribution to the company, because company have set of business requirements based on his customers, and business requirements travelled to me in terms of my work environment. Following are few points which help me to measure my job success:

- Performing job duties on time with efficiency and quality.

- Showing more creativity, increasing job responsibility, adding extra contribution in terms of work

- Getting appreciation, reorganization either by myself or from company.

- Feeling a important part of the team and company

Exercise:	Q:	What are the goals/objectives of your position? How do you measure your success/know if you are doing a good job?

Am I going to answer this question now? And adding the notes on my career note book?

(a).[Yes] (b).[No] (c).[Later] (d).[Its not relevant to my career] (e) [I framed this question on other way]

Date and Time:

LEADERSHIP: IF YOU WERE LEADING THE TEAM

If you were leading the team how would you define specific roles of your team members?

RATIONALE: *It's a kind of open ended question, which require a lot of other information e.g. project's objective, project requirement, business requirements, who will be the intended users, Its use cases. Interviewer wants to know Interviewee's thought process while handling an open ended situation.*

> **SAMPLE PROJECT:** *Interviewer says "This Project is a Software Purchase' application" with following information:*
>
> - *This application will allow users to buy software products online.*
>
> - *The new website will be based on client/server architecture.*
>
> - *Customers will also be able to access the website via a mobile device or a PC based internet browser.*
>
> - *Company has a database system which tracks customer data after a purchase is made.*
>
> - *This data may be updated by customers (e.g. a customer may change their address or phone number).*

SAMPLE ANSWER FROM A PROFESSIONAL **POINT OF VIEW**

HOW I WILL DEFINE THE ROLES OF TEAM MEMBERS?: First I will see my role in this project and what type of activity I will be doing on this project. Let's say my role on this project is to lead test activities of this Software Purchase Application, and then I might have several questions before actually decide the roles of my team members:

- What are the detailed requirement and specifications of this Software Purchase Application?
- What is the time line of the testing?
- How many resources do I have to test it?
- Who are the targeted customers?
- What are the deliverables of test execution?
- What process we are using to develop the test automation?

- What is the application development plan, and on which phase of the development plan, such test assignment has handed over to me.

- Is it to be tested for physically challenged people (example: blind)?

- Is it to be tested on different localizations (English) or only in English?

- Any applicable geographic location to access this application.

- At what stage I will get the resources e.g.; different mobile devices, PCs and other teams

- Architecture of this application and other design documents

- Is this application ban to use by specific set of users?

- After having such answers I will surely able to define roles of my team members e.g.; based on the individual set of functionalities (client side or server side or security)

Once the above and other related information will come to me, then I might design the overall plan, then I might schedule more discussion with myself and related people, then I will plan the specific roles, and then after having a discussion with team I will assign the roles.

Exercise:	Q:	If you were leading the team how would you define specific roles of your team members?

Am I going to answer this question now? And adding the notes on my career note book?

(a).[Yes] (b).[No] (c).[Later] (d).[Its not relevant to my career] (e) [I framed this question on other way]

Date and Time:

LEADERSHIP: TEAM LEADING

Do you now (or have you previously) had direct reports? If so, how many and what were their roles?

RATIONALE: *Nearly all professionals work in a hierarchical and pyramidical team structure, which involves team members and their leaders. Interviewer wanted to understand whether interviewee carrying a lead role, e.g. Mentor, Project Leader, Team Leader, Manager, Part Leader.*

SAMPLE ANSWER FROM A PROFESSIONAL POINT OF VIEW

I have work-related direct reports, and my responsibility includes e.g. Team comprises: myself, one team leader – three developers, a SQA, a User Interface Developer, one for misc activities e.g.; SCM = Eight Team Members. Myself:

- Understand business requirements and transform into product requirements
- Write specifications and design document for product requirements
- Estimate Work, and divide the work and review it from end to end.
- Interact with my superiors and other dependent groups

Team Leader – Closely Interacting with Developers, UI Developer, SQA

Developers – Writing C/C++ based code for ongoing project, porting libraries (C Language) for other platforms. Writing JNI Layer, JAVA type of APIs corresponding to C Language Native API, writing product related additional features

UI Developer – Writing UI on top of it based on several use cases (User Interface Developer)

SQA+ Misc Activities – Test Bed setup, SQE, Reference App, SCM, Software Engineering Work, Software Library's API, User Manual, Documentation etc

SAMPLE ANSWER FROM A PROFESSIONAL POINT OF VIEW

My project has a complete plan, and activities are based on its schedule and deliverables, hence time to time work activities and individual's responsibility changes. I have two direct reports as developers, who work based on the schedule and defined responsibilities by that time.

Work consist of a web-based application, and currently we are involved to develop the core parts, e.g. data-base design, front end's look and feel, business logic, design patterns, technologies, frameworks, libraries, architecture and design. I look after the complete web app, related with all aspects from the requirement to its end. A developer working on front end activities, e.g. user interface, forms design and another developer working on business logic and database design area.

Exercise:	Q:	Do you now (or have you previously) had direct reports? If so, how many and what were their roles?

Am I going to answer this question now? And adding the notes on my career note book?

(a).[Yes] (b).[No] (c).[Later] (d).[Its not relevant to my career] (e) [I framed this question on other way]

Date and Time:

MENTORING – TO JUNIORS OR TEAM MEMBERS

Explain how you formally or non-formally did mentoring on your juniors or other team members?

RATIONALE: *Professionals may work in same team for a long time, and team grows or replaces with different people. New people to the project or team or company may require types of help from the existing people. It might be possible that you are formally assigned to mentor someone or non-formally mentor or help someone. Interviewer would like to understand your mentoring/leadership capabilities and any best practices you might comment.*

SAMPLE ANSWER FROM A PROFESSIONAL POINT OF VIEW

I was working on a project from the day-1, so I got complete knowledge, e.g. why those changes are made, why requirements got made, why UX experience got used, why things got integrated and being an old team member on a project. I used to attend most of the meetings. In my time span–many members joined the team, and on many situations, I guided right requirements to team members/new joinees/project trainees that greatly helped to let them understand requirement, complete vision and deliverables.

Here are the common list of activities which I did as a mentor for mentee:

SUPPORTED FOR DAY-TO-DAY NON-OFFICIAL ACTIVITIES

- How company intranet can help on various situations,
- How to book the meeting room via intranet,
- Mentee's may be new to the city so: Where is downtown, Best way to go to downtown,
- Best economic places for shopping (Uniquolo for economic level, Land-rover for best shoes, SPAO for another economic level, Thermal Inner-wear's are different in the current location than your home location)
- Encourage him to understand the new location e.g. its weather.

ALWAYS WILLING TO LISTEN (SILENTLY/NON-SILENTLY) ABOUT THE CURIOSITY AND PROVIDE THE ANSWER BY SAME TIME OR AS AND WHEN APPLICABLE

- Suddenly few people shifted to another floor for Task Force (What is this Task force?, What is that's Objective, why those people shifted?),
- We have to work hard for what?,

- How a promotion happens in this company?
- What is the career curve?
- How he should provide his contribution to the project?
- Explanation about the career related training offered by company for mentee's career aspirations. If mentee has any specific skills then how he or she can help to make the knowledge transfer for the success of project.

ALWAYS WILLING TO PROVIDE AS A TEAM MEMBER FEELING TO THE MENTEE THAN JUST A ISOLATED STAFF MEMBER

- Involving the mentee to the most of the project related meetings and activities,
- Encouraged other team members to mix with the new member
- Learn mentee's past experience skills and creativity,
- Encourage team to work together for better output, takes suggestions from mentee as and when required to let him understand as a part of the team always

SOFT AND PROFESSIONAL TASK MONITORING

- Weekly meeting with task's progress and encouraging him to bring his creativity to make the ongoing work items more professional and productive.

ENFORCE PRODUCTIVENESS BY REDUCING THE REPEATABLE ACTIVITIES

One person John started acclivity A and then another person Bob joined the same team and started his work from the understanding of the activity A, then another person Mike joined the team he also started the activity –A. To make the things productive, John gave a very good knowledge transfer to Bob, when mike joined then John and Bob together gave a good knowledge transfer understanding to Mike (Mentee), by this means the work happened faster, rather Mike (Mentee) spent time to understand same technical/project philosophy just by randomly working by himself(means by having random assumptions), he interacted with Bob. John etc, and understood most of the things, and extra time he spent to make the other things better.

CLOSENESS TO DEPICT THAT TOGETHER WE ARE WORKING FOR THE PROJECT AND SUCCESS

Time to time mentor updated to mentee e.g. related to the work objective (as objective changes time to time) and very important about the definition of success.

MENTOR MADE HIMSELF TO BE EASILY ACCESSIBLE FOR WORK RELATED TASK FOR MENTEE

- Mentee wasn't able to understand the project related documents, he spends time to understand all, but that didn't help, Mentor was available to support on this time to time and that made mentee's task easier and productive.

- Willingly invited to Team's lunches and other get-together e.g. On every dinner and get-together mentor helped to mentee to adapt the new environment, encouraged team members to talk with mentee, explained mentee about the get-together objective, involved him to causal games and made him a friend during non-official activities.

CASUALLY HAVING A COFFEE TIME AT-LEAST ONCE IN TWO WEEKS

- Talks about Mentee's experience e.g. project, career aspirations and project objectives

- Talks how Mentee can improve himself on some rough areas

Exercise:	Q:	Explain how you formally or non-formally did mentoring on your juniors or team members?

Am I going to answer this question now? And adding the notes on my career note book?

(a).[Yes] (b).[No] (c).[Later] (d).[Its not relevent to my career] (e) [I framed this question on other way]

Date and Time:

MOTIVATION FACTOR – APPRAISAL/FEEDBACK

Have you ever experienced appraisal for your work?
Were you really satisfied with the feedback given to you?

RATIONALE: *Nearly all corporate companies follow a standard system which performs HR activities, e.g.; appraisal of employees in a certain time interval. Interviewer wants to understand Interviewee's experience and comments on that.*

SAMPLE ANSWER FROM A PROFESSIONAL POINT OF VIEW

I have experienced appraisals and I define appraisal as following:

It's a kind of feedback from a system for which I work for. Actually it's a cycle.

An individual work on certain work items, and on a regular interval those work items reviewed by his or her supervisor and some other evaluators, e.g. for what he is good, for what he needs to improve, creatively he or she introduced while delivering xyz work items, ownership he or she had shown on X and may be many more. From the system point of view, this feedback should satisfy for work needs and individual's growth e.g. if a person is new to the work, if a person spent one year to the same work.

Another side an individual also maintains his or her own self-evaluation, if the given feedback and individual's self –evaluation has a reasonable or no gap then this cycle continues in terms of company's and individual's productivity.

Regarding the received feedback and my satisfaction:

I couldn't say when I was satisfied from my appraisal and when I was not, but I keep following view:

With that appraisal actually an individual may receive some other things as well e.g. remuneration, promotion, more challenging work items. Usually somebody looking on me out of the box, and I am viewing myself inside a box. I have self-evaluation, and the evaluator has his own view. If I totally understand the gap between my evaluation and evaluator's evaluation then I usually get satisfied. If not then I might write my critical comments on that e.g. to either explain to reviewer or any other appropriate means, and I keep continue with my things.

Because I feel appraisal is a part of the process. I also feel if it requires introducing my comments on some appropriate situation, then I will do, if it fits.

| Exercise: | Q: | **Have you ever experienced for your appraisal? Were you really satisfied with the given feedback to you?** |

Am I going to answer this question now? And adding the notes on my career note book?

(a).[Yes] (b).[No] (c).[Later] (d).[Its not relevant to my career] (e) [I framed this question on other way]

Date and Time:

PAST EXPERIENCE: PAST WORK ITEMS

Can you describe various projects on which you have worked in the past which required you to develop a product from scratch?

RATIONALE: *Interviewer doesn't mean that interviewee has developed a complete project from scratch; rather the interviewee must have received a task that supposed to be done from scratch, e.g. development of a library, feature, and module of a project.*

SAMPLE ANSWER FROM A PROFESSIONAL POINT OF VIEW

* Have designed from scratch to a fully functional VOIP Test Tool, for VOIP communication protocol stack (UDP, IP, ARP, ICMP, TCP SDP, SIP, and Offer/Answer Model-rfc-3264(must and must not requirement)) in C++.

* Key member in the design of V2OIP Middleware: Design of STUN Client, Call Manager, Call Control Functions, Call Control Adapter API, Call Features in C/C++.

* Designed for Global Title Translation features on SCCP (Signal Connection Control Port) for X-Signal Transfer Point Product in C Language.

* Designed and Coded Encoder/Decoder Library for Interconnect User Part (IUP) Protocol Messages in C++.

Exercise:	Q:	Can you describe various projects on which you have worked in the past which required you to develop a product from scratch?

Am I going to answer this question now? And adding the notes on my career note book?

(a).[Yes] (b).[No] (c).[Later] (d).[Its not relevant to my career] (e) [I framed this question on other way]

Date and Time:

PAST PROJECTS:
BUSINESS REQUIREMENTS OF XYZ PROJECT

What are the main business requirements of XYZ project?

RATIONALE: *Interviewer might concentrate on any project which interviewee has specified in his or her resume.*

Definitely, if a professional working in a company that most likely to be related with some business, and here interviewer is interested in knowing the major requirements of work the interviewee has done or has been doing. For sure, the answer will be different based on the situation as people are working on varied roles based on their experience and project requirements.

SAMPLE ANSWER FROM A PROFESSIONAL POINT OF VIEW

This project has a long history. It's a product developed by 'A' company, and we are preferred vendor to that company for our "Test-Tool" development.

Because of its B features, we got its functional test requirements, and those test requirements act as a business requirement for this project, where four Developers and a Technical Leader were involved to finish that task in a specific time frame.

In terms of exact business requirements of this project, we were supposed to test the SIP (RFC-3261) protocol functionality on a developed VOIP product.

Functional requirements took from RFC-3261 (Must and Must-Not requirement" e.g. The Request-URI MUST NOT contain un-escaped spaces or control characters and MUST NOT be enclosed within "<>".

SAMPLE ANSWER FROM A PROFESSIONAL POINT OF VIEW

This Project was related with 'A' product of this company, which is one of the most saleable products, So for its next release; Company defined a set of its functional and non-functional requirements, e.g.; Google's docs integration to view stored documents online, Sugar-Sync integration to backup data.

This product was kind of web product, and I was involved in the implementation of Google docs integration feature.

| Exercise: | Q: | **What are the main business requirements of the project you mentioned on your CV/resume?** |

Am I going to answer this question now? And adding the notes on my career note book?

(a).[Yes] (b).[No] (c).[Later] (d).[Its not relevant to my career] (e) [I framed this question on other way]

Date and Time:

PRIORITIES CLASHES – PERSONAL/PROFESSIONAL COMMITMENT

Was there any situation when you had a personal commitment and a sudden office commitment at the same time? How did you manage such a situation?

RATIONALE: *We all need to manage our personal and professional activities. It happens when an official task came out, and you have e.g.; finalized a meeting with girlfriend/boyfriend, committed to a wedding, something committed to your parents or family.*

Interviewer wants to understand interviewee experience/view to manage such a type of situation.

SAMPLE ANSWER FROM A PROFESSIONAL POINT OF VIEW

I usually see what should be on priority based on that situation. If I feel office work is more important and without me it's impossible somebody else can do, and then I will surely do.

Example: At some time, my father got some health problem, and I was the only one to manage my father. So I left my work though it was highly important. It all depends on situation to situation, and as an ethical professional, I put my best efforts to manage such a type of situation.

Exercise:	Q:	How you manage the conflicts between the personal and official commitment?

Am I going to answer this question now? And adding the notes on my career note book?

(a).[Yes] (b).[No] (c).[Later] (d).[Its not relevant to my career] (e) [I framed this question on other way]

Date and Time:

PROGRAMMING: CODE DESIGN/REVIEWS

How much experience do you have performing code and design reviews?

RATIONALE: *Based on the business/product/software requirements, professionals get an opportunity to perform code and design review and it all depends on the nature of software product.*

Interviewer wants to know whether interviewee performed code and design reviews.

SAMPLE ANSWER FROM A PROFESSIONAL POINT OF VIEW

I have reasonable experience in terms of performing code and design review and based on the situation I have done thorough review or high level review e.g.

While performing code review, I may inspect (but not limited to) e.g. code's logic

Code is written based on coding guidelines

- Code has been organized appropriately in folders, files, classes, functions, header files,
- Code has been designed based on appropriate design patterns,
- Code is using appropriate language constructs,
- Code is using appropriate algorithmic logic wherever required, Proper function's signature, Optimized Code,
- Coding has considered appropriate implementation of business/product/software requirements,
- Code provides flexibly for possible future changes.

While performing design review, I may inspect (but not limited to) e.g.

- Design's objective,
- Its architecture,
- Appropriate component selection,
- Individual component design and its interaction with another component
- Appropriate selection of technology
- High level design,
- Low level design,

- Consideration of appropriate cases,
- Sequence diagram, data flow diagram, API signatures,
- Flow/logic/sequence of the designed solution,
- Consideration for performance, scalability, appropriate design pattern

Exercise:	Q:	How much experience do you have performing code and design reviews?

Am I going to answer this question now? And adding the notes on my career note book?

(a).[Yes] (b).[No] (c).[Later] (d).[Its not relevant to my career] (e) [I framed this question on other way]

Date and Time:

PROGRAMMING: LARGEST PIECE OF CODE

What is the largest piece of code you've written in terms of lines of code? How many lines was it? What language did you use? What did it do?

RATIONALE: *Writing of source code depends on the type of implementation, and how well code has been written, e.g.*

- *It can use standard template library as an existing library, and it might need to write such a library from scratch.*

- *Coding lines can be very few, but it might solve a big purpose*

Interviewer wants to check your coding ability, that how much source code had interviewee written on any project he or she worked in the past.

SAMPLE ANSWER FROM A PROFESSIONAL POINT OF VIEW

I coded a test tool for voip (voice over ip) based mobile client application from scratch to shipment (C++ /windows platform):

- The voip things used SIP [Session Initiation Protocol] messages for signalling: So I coded the encoding/decoding sip message library, parser to parse the messages, utility functions to test the sequence of SIP signalling protocol by following the rfc-3261/3264 for its must and must not requirements~ 17500 line of codes.

*Coded roughly 300 stubs * 30 ~ 9000 Lines*

- These test stubs validates various SIP signalling scenarios based on must and must not requirements from rfc 3261,3264

Supporting framework: roughly ~ 4000 Lines

- To compose appropriate SIP messages and several SIP encoding and decoding functions

Wrote several other utilities etc–around ~ 4000 Lines

- Test tool related library functions e.g. logging test results

Wrote test shuffling algorithms ~ 500 Lines

- It shuffles certain SIP signalling scenario for stress and interoperability.

Exercise:	Q:	**List out your major coding related work items?**

Am I going to answer this question now? And adding the notes on my career note book?

(a).[Yes] (b).[No] (c).[Later] (d).[Its not relevant to my career] (e) [I framed this question on other way]

Date and Time:

RECOMMENDATION – SUPERVISOR'S COMMENTS ABOUT YOU

If we were to contact your last supervisor what kind of comments would he have about you?

RATIONALE: *A supervisor can evaluate the team member's positive points based on his or her work style, attitude, knowledge, job's accomplishments, communication style, presentation style, and several other professional skill parameters.*

Interviewer wants to understand Interviewee's perception related with his work style, knowledge, work attitude, misc.

SAMPLE ANSWER FROM A PROFESSIONAL POINT OF VIEW

- Disciplined and organized with work
- Always provide timely update
- Try his best to resolve most issues by himself, could be technical or setting up test-bed or anything or working on entirely new topic or any bug or anything related with work
- Take initiatives, organize meetings/discussion on reasonable situations.

SAMPLE ANSWER FROM A PROFESSIONAL POINT OF VIEW

Since last two years I am working on a project, and I developed 'A', 'B' and 'C' from scratch to be a deliverable, and currently I am solving several design issues related with project's next release.

- My manager may say–technical expert in C++/Linux for the VOIP related development, with an organized discipline for deliverables.
- Effective team member, keep friendly attitude and neutral on some situation

| Exercise: | Q: | **What will be your supervisor's comments about you?** |

Am I going to answer this question now? And adding the notes on my career note book?

(a).[Yes] (b).[No] (c).[Later] (d).[Its not relevant to my career] (e) [I framed this question on other way]

Date and Time:

RECOMMENDATION –
TEAM MEMBERS' COMMENTS ABOUT YOU

If we were to contact previous team members, what kind of comments would they have about you?

RATIONALE: *Interviewer wants to understand Interviewee's self-perception related with the recommendations he or she might receive from his team members.*

SAMPLE ANSWER FROM A PROFESSIONAL POINT OF VIEW

I've managed an advanced communication solution team in X Company overseas center as part of a bigger group based in United States. From the US side, Interviewee was responsible for my team's remote activity in terms of S/W involvement and project management.

The plan & integration of our remote efforts wasn't trivial and was impressively conducted by Interviewee, who controlled all technical aspects of our deliveries, mile stone management and general inspection of expectations. All work executed in an outstanding manner of professionalism and extremely good manners.

SAMPLE ANSWER FROM A PROFESSIONAL POINT OF VIEW

I've worked with interviewee on a complex software solution for converged network, interviewee was responsible for integration and has accompanied the project with great mind for details and excellent social skills. He managed to successfully interact with teams across the globe (China, Israel, Korea, USA) managing deliveries and project milestones.

Exercise:	Q:	What type of comments your team members will have about you?

Am I going to answer this question now? And adding the notes on my career note book?

(a).[Yes] (b).[No] (c).[Later] (d).[Its not relevant to my career] (e) [I framed this question on other way]

Date and Time:

SOFTWARE DEVELOPMENT LIFE CYCLE: YOUR INVOLVEMENT

Describe your involvement, if any, and percent of time spent in developing a piece of software during the following life cycle stages:

1) Specification: 2) Design: 3) Development: 4) Testing: 5) Maintenance/ support:

RATIONALE: *A professional might be involved in analysis, e.g. architected the design, decided set of technologies to be used, algorithms to be used for XYZ purpose, how database would be used and its design as well, defined test functionalities and related test tool.*

- *A professional might involve of writing specification e.g. interaction across modules, set of interfaces, user interface requirements.*

- *A professional might involve in development or testing.*

- *A professional might be involved in support, e.g. fixing bugs after releasing the product, applying change-request.*

Interviewer is trying to understand Interviewee's past project experience regarding the software-development life cycle.

SAMPLE ANSWER FROM A PROFESSIONAL POINT OF VIEW

- I joined XYZ project during development phase, when specification, designs were already in place and studied concepts, specification, design, etc. to develop 'A' feature.

- Overall time of this project was 12 months, from which I was involved mostly on development with two months for unit testing and bug fixing, later I was on project support on a per-time basis. My involvement in XYZ project was 70% development, 20% on bug fixing/unit testing and 10% on support.

Exercise:	Q:	Describe your involvement, if any, and percent of time spent in developing a piece of software during the following life cycle stages: 1) Specification, 2) Design, 3) Development, 4) Testing, 5) Maintenance/support?

Am I going to answer this question now? And adding the notes on my career note book?

(a).[Yes] (b).[No] (c).[Later] (d).[Its not relevant to my career] (e) [I framed this question on other way]

Date and Time:

SOFTWARE TESTING:
WHAT EXCITES YOU MOST ABOUT TESTING

What excites you most about testing?

RATIONALE: *Software test professional performs various types of testing activities, e.g. manual and automation testing, development of test tools, designing appropriate test cases.*

Interviewer wanted to understand, which are the main test activities on which interviewee kept a high interest.

SAMPLE ANSWER FROM A PROFESSIONAL POINT OF VIEW

- Excited to consider about functional aspects, afterwards move to non-functional and then work about various advanced techniques for specific use cases and scenarios.

- Excited to have interaction with other internal/cross-cultural /across teams, e.g.; PM, Team Members, Developers, Test Manager, Test Lead, and Technical Program Manager

- Excited to use my experience and current capabilities to write very efficient test cases, automation and do well in all test engineering area, e.g. by clearing requirement, test environment, timeline, project phase, my role, resources, dependency, targeted customer, end user(different age group, or different profession), targeted industry, interoperability, conformance product specification, requirement use cases.

Exercise:	Q:	What excites you most about testing?

Am I going to answer this question now? And adding the notes on my career note book?

(a).[Yes] (b).[No] (c).[Later] (d).[Its not relevant to my career] (e) [I framed this question on other way]

Date and Time:

SOFTWARE TESTING:
HAVE YOU WRITTEN ANY UNIT TESTS

Have you written any unit tests?

RATIONALE: *Interviewer wants to understand how the interviewee tested his or her own written code.*

SAMPLE ANSWER FROM A PROFESSIONAL POINT OF VIEW

While writing unit test I have considered various factors.

- Every test Strategy to do unit testing is entirely different, e.g. it all depends on various parameters, requirement, actual use cases, performance, actual use of this code, platform/environment where it will run, system from which it will interact, given schedule, objectives.

- On some situations unit tests require the use of tools e.g.; Simulators-Code Coverage-Scripts, tests on real environment.

- It also require to consider taken time to tests, dependency on other modules where it is going to be integrate, deadline of delivery, available resources

I have tested the code in exactly the ways this will ultimately going to use it.

E.g. written a library which has set of APIs, so that require to write some unit test cases to test said API e.g. Error/Non-Error cases based on the input accepted by API.

Exercise:	Q:	Have you written any unit tests?

Am I going to answer this question now? And adding the notes on my career note book?

(a).[Yes] (b).[No] (c).[Later] (d).[Its not relevant to my career] (e) [I framed this question on other way]

Date and Time:

STRONG TECHNICAL SKILLS: SCALE FROM 1-TO-10

What are your 3 strongest technical skills? (Please rank your ability on a scale of 1-10 (novice to guru) and years of experience in listed skills.)

RATIONALE: *Over the years professionals gain experience with domain and technical knowledge, which envisage him or her to solve specific problems pertaining to a domain. It could be related to computer networks, banking, health-care industry or any other. Professionals rank their ability on such technical skills based on their level of knowledge, which may or may not be related with the years of experience, e.g. a professional rank his or ability to work on A technology as 5 in three years, another professional may rank his ability to work on same technology as 8 in two years*

SAMPLE ANSWER FROM A PROFESSIONAL POINT OF VIEW

Voip Signalling and Network Protocols Stack (SIP/SDP/TCP/IP) 7

- SIP/SDP/TCP/IP carries core part of the VOIP(Voice Over IP)
  - ▷ Signalling: completely studied rfcs, e.g. 3261, 3264,
  - ▷ Coded appropriate solutions, e.g. Voip Calls signalling scenarios
  - ▷ Sockets Programming, IP routing concepts, TCP handshake, TCP based algorithms
  - ▷ Several network tools e.g. packet capture tools

Programming Languages (C, C++) 6

Designed coding specification, designed code architecture, used appropriate code concepts to implement call signalling API e.g. Design Patterns, Templates, Standard Template's Library, OOPs Concepts. Code optimization tools e.g. Profiler, line count, memory leak.

Platform (Linux) 5

- Understanding of Linux's Kernel Architecture, Memory, Scheduling Algorithms, File system. Several Linux based Tools e.g. GDB debugger, Kdiff3
- Practically used Linux based programming e.g. Multithreading, Signals, Inter-process communication, BSD Socket's API, GTK toolkit

All together, I have technical experience in Network Protocols (Data Communication domain) while using C, C++languages on Linux Platforms (gained during my work with XYZ company/companies in last four years).

Exercise:	Q:	What are your 3 strongest technical skills? (Please rank your ability on a scale of 1-10 (novice to guru) and years of experience in listed skills.)

Am I going to answer this question now? And adding the notes on my career note book?

(a).[Yes] (b).[No] (c).[Later] (d).[Its not relevant to my career] (e) [I framed this question on other way]

Date and Time:

TEAM COLLABORATION: ODD WORK HOURS

Have you worked with others in-different geographical locations, and if so, How did you manage to deal with such situations?

RATIONALE: *Big companies outsource work to many companies located in different geographical locations, e.g.; China, India, Romania, Russia or it has branches in many countries so may be some part of work happening in United States and another part of happening in Ireland.*

Interview more interested to see whether you have experience collaborating with team members who are sitting in different time zones.

SAMPLE ANSWER FROM A PROFESSIONAL POINT OF VIEW

It's a matter of team collaboration, where it involved people from diverse time zone. In my case, I didn't have any strict timeline to be available on an everyday basis. I worked with ISRAEL and China team from United States.

On some case's discussion used to be little unusual than office timings, and that it's again on understanding basis. Now it comes under my work practice and always well known that works happen like this way, especially in MNCs or big companies.

SAMPLE ANSWER FROM A PROFESSIONAL POINT OF VIEW

I truly understand the job's nature, as the world has been globalized. In my past project, I had worked related involvement with Indian team from United States. Initially, it took some time to understand the nature of work, and what can work best to collaborate with the team.

Based on that I defined some of my work practices to overlap my timings with Indian team, e.g.; my morning time and their evening time (vice versa).

SAMPLE ANSWER FROM A PROFESSIONAL POINT OF VIEW

My concept related to the work timings is nine or 10 hours in a day, usually to 8, but at Max nine or 10. Yes I'm flexible with timings, but only on some specific business situations, not everyday, not all the time. I prefer a organized environment where work hours should be organized too.

I totally understand the work culture and the situations where different geographical teams work together, but I might not be the perfect candidate who can work on odd hours. Because I have commitment to my family, commitment to my health, and commitment to many other things which require myself to be organized and disciplined.

Exercise:	Q:	**Are you comfortable with working with different time zones or have some past experience on that?**

Am I going to answer this question now? And adding the notes on my career note book?

(a).[Yes] (b).[No] (c).[Later] (d).[Its not relevant to my career] (e) [I framed this question on other way]

Date and Time:

TEAM MATCHING – TEAM WORK

Please explain a situation when you had a bad time with a co-worker?

RATIONALE: *Employees need to maintain a positive relationship with other team members. It might be possible that on some odd/even situation, a team member might require to support other team members. Interviewer wants to understand your relational skills.*

Interviewer also wants to see what is bad in terms of your view? It may not be exactly bad, but he wanted to understand your feeling towards those situations when something went wrong, and you had a bad time with a co-worker, because working in a team brings great productivity.

SAMPLE ANSWER FROM A PROFESSIONAL POINT OF VIEW

I never had a bad time with co-workers such as something which cannot be bear. We had situations when we got conflict in ideas related with work items, e.g. why X approach is right, Y's product design should be modified, deadline of the X work item. On those situations, I listened to my team members and gave my ideas, and we discussed in an appropriate manner. That always worked out to win-win situations.

Co-workers or team members, e.g. supervisor, manager, mentor, director, leader, juniors.

SAMPLE ANSWER FROM A PROFESSIONAL POINT OF VIEW

In my past projects, I have seen introvert attitude of some people, it is something like they don't talk much, and they don't want to talk much. It is okay, because that is their personality type, but on some work situation such attitude doesn't work well.

And usually when you approach to such type of people for some reasons, especially for some important work reasons e.g. you request a particular thing where the input is very valuable, and that require a good communication. But the reply you might receive that, "sorry I have no idea".

Because of such response from that team member, you might loose the confidence to talk with him again and that surely affect the work productivity.

Exercise:	Q:	**What do you say about your relational skills?**

Am I going to answer this question now? And adding the notes on my career note book?

(a).[Yes] (b).[No] (c).[Later] (d).[Its not relevant to my career] (e) [I framed this question on other way]

Date and Time:

TEAM MATCHING – HARD TIME WORKING WITH CO-WORKERS

Please explain a situation–when you feel that your co-worker is not giving you actual output for what he supposed to be, how you handle such a situation?

RATIONALE: *Teams are organized based on the work type, and team members are assigned for individual responsibilities. It might be possible that a specific team member not handling his or her task very well, and that affect to team.*

Interviewer wants to understand interviewee experience on such scenarios; if you haven't then how effectively you deal with this.

SAMPLE ANSWER FROM A PROFESSIONAL POINT OF VIEW

Actually, I didn't face such a type of situation literally. It happened when my co-worker was unable to provide something on time, but behind that, there was a practical and logical reason. I worked with my co-worker for those situations, and tried on some level to get out from that situation, e.g.; a co-worker got health issue or some personal problem in home, or he was very new on that technology or there was a communication barrier, etc.

SAMPLE ANSWER FROM A PROFESSIONAL POINT OF VIEW

I met with a situation when my co-worker didn't provide me expected output in terms of work, I had a discussion with him and found, initially he didn't understand work correctly because of his less experience on XYZ area, and he was a introvert guy who didn't approach much to people for help or understanding. I took the initiative and stabilized the situation by having a discussion with him and later made myself available for him most of the time.

Such types of situation really exist, but it also requires careful finding of its reason and how to handle it.

Am I going to answer this question now? And adding the notes on my career note book?

(a).[Yes] (b).[No] (c).[Later] (d).[Its not relevant to my career] (e) [I framed this question on other way]

Date and Time:

TEAM MATCHING – OWNERSHIP OF THE WORK

Explain a situation when you took ownership of the work?

RATIONALE: *Companies hires a candidate and includes him in an existing work system, and that system comprises with many parameters e.g. work environment, team type, project type, company's policies, team member's attitude, competitive environment, motivation, value of that team/work to the company, attitude of leader and many more.*

To understand the new environment, it require to take some initiative based on the type of situation e.g. acquire a discipline, follow people to get things done, providing status of the work to intended people, trying to get complete understanding of work by initiatives.

Interviewer would like to understand the interviewee's ownership skills, does he keeps wait and watch attitude or stand-up to speedup the activity?

SAMPLE ANSWER FROM A PROFESSIONAL POINT OF VIEW

It depends on particular individual, how he or she relates the meaning of ownership. In first priority, my job responsibilities are my ownerships. If I am writing a user interface for X application, It's my responsibility or ownership:

- To understand its actual requirements,
- To develop it based on the requirement,
- Analysis those requirements and introduce own creativity, skills to make it formal and professional.
- Develop it based on the given/planned schedule and resources.
- Release it a production ready user interface.
- Discuss items as and when required with related people.
- Work on every single item whichever related with my work.

| Exercise: | Q: | **What is your definition of ownership?** |

Am I going to answer this question now? And adding the notes on my career note book?

(a).[Yes] (b).[No] (c).[Later] (d).[Its not relevant to my career] (e) [I framed this question on other way]

Date and Time:

TECHNICAL SKILLS:
ENCOUNTERED TECHNICALLY COMPLEX PROBLEMS

Can you name any difficult technical problems you have been able to overcome that you are most proud of? Please provide specific information, outlining the problem and how you resolved it.

RATIONALE: *It's obvious that professionals face problems during work, e.g. technical Issues while doing software development or testing. Such problems show how the tough situation can be, and professional didn't have any clue while it seemed as if all roads are blocked. However, he or she stood up and face the problem head-on and analyzed various ways to find solution.*

SAMPLE ANSWER FROM A PROFESSIONAL **POINT OF VIEW**

Technical Problem

- When I made a customized software build for one of my project by making various changes across build flags, modules and dependencies. However, after making that build it was running fine but in some specific scenario, it was showing "XYZ file couldn't be found."

How I approached to solution?

- First, I did trivial ways to solve this problem like checking the path to the file location which was already correct. Later, I also checked if that specific files runs on kernel mode, which requires a flag to be set on build and presence of certain dynamic link libraries. Even doing all these trivial debugging didn't solve the issue.

- All together, I found that I have done everything and everything is on a place, even checked if there are any known bugs, or somebody else experienced this on past, but only for this specific issue; it doesn't work.

- After doing more analysis, I found that for this operation, it picks a file from the directory path, which need to be generated on run time but for this issues this has not happened. Because it was a custom build, and these scenarios were not understood while designing steps to make this custom build, and then system defined path.

Why did you make that decision?

- Because I tried most of the trivial ways first, and then tracked to build steps from beginning.

- On studying build files, I found some scripts, which generate files on run time and path as well.

- Because it was a custom build, and these scenarios were not understood while designing steps to make this custom build, and then system defined path.

What was the outcome?

- Problem was solved

In retrospect, how would you handle this type of situation differently?

- Solving of such complex issues provides more ways to think out of the box.

- Every day when I perform testing, I find varied issues, e.g. issues with regard to set up test environment, issue related to creating customized builds, issues related to diverse non-frequent scenarios, issues to write automation for certain complex issues.

- In every situation, my strategy was different I could not make same strategy for all scenarios, because everything was dynamic, and just from system behavior, I needed to find out what could be the possible cause.

- When I need to understand different types of such behavior, I start from basic analysis and slowly advance towards a logical end, check the existing bugs or any open issue, if required, then escalate to developers or some other concerned people, to find out the root cause.

Exercise:	Q:	**Can you name any difficult technical problem you have been able to overcome that you are most proud of? Please provide specific information, outlining the problem and how you resolved it.**

Am I going to answer this question now? And adding the notes on my career note book?

(a).[Yes] (b).[No] (c).[Later] (d).[Its not relevant to my career] (e) [I framed this question on other way]

Date and Time:

TECHNICAL SKILLS: TECHICAL TERMS

Please explain XYZ term on this technology?

RATIONALE: *Project uses various types of technologies, tools, methodology, process and professionals' shows expertise by defining projects and technologies. Interviewer went through from interviewee's resume, and he or she wanted to understand the meaning of a XYZ term mentioned in CV.*

Example – Term: What kind of Security defined with Session Initiation Protocol: (you are talking here about Authentication in your project, May you please explain about the Understanding of SIP authentication and XMPP Authentication)

SAMPLE ANSWER FROM A PROFESSIONAL POINT OF VIEW

Example – Term: *What kind of Security defined with Session Initiation Protocol: (you are talking here about Authentication in your project, May you please explain about the Understanding of SIP authentication and XMPP Authentication)*

SIP allows usage of various algorithms for client authentication. The most commonly used is the SIP-Digest algorithm which is identical to the HTTP digest algorithm defined in RFC2617. It is based on a shared secret (password) known to the client and server.

The server sends the client a one-time challenge, and the client replies with a response that is the result of applying the MD5 cryptographic hashing algorithm to the challenge using the password.

XMPP uses the SASL method for client authentication, which, in essence, uses the same algorithm as the SIP digests.

SAMPLE ANSWER FROM A PROFESSIONAL POINT OF VIEW

Example – Term: *Why J2EE/MySQL was used in X project, Why didn't .NET/SQL Server or ORACLE*

There was a debate in between .Net and J2EE platforms. I am a novice to comment on scalability of .Net but am pretty confident that few J2EE architectures are highly scalable (e.g. EJBs, Hibernate, springs with some well established web frameworks like Struts, Faces etc).

As far as database is concerned, based on the project situation Oracle/SQL-Server support was too expensive, and getting oracle/SQLServer skill set was also expensive, So based on that situation we used MySQL Server .

Exercise:	Q:	**Please explain XYZ term on this technology?**

Am I going to answer this question now? And adding the notes on my career note book?

(a).[Yes] (b).[No] (c).[Later] (d).[Its not relevant to my career] (e) [I framed this question on other way]

Date and Time:

TECHNICAL SKILLS: TECHNOLOGIES DOMAIN

Why did you change your technology domain?

RATIONALE: *On many situations, it happens that professionals do change their technology domain, e.g. people who ever worked on banking domain they make a shift to data communication domain, or people who are working in data communication domain; they may make a shift to banking domain Or health-care domain or advertising domain. Each domain uses a set of applications to solve types of industrial problems (varies from case by case), so a professional might be interested to explore another domain, which is unlike to his or her present domain*

May be because of his or her interest Or May be he or she wanted to relocate to another place, but the best employer exists on another domain Or May be the current domain is fast getting outdated and few opportunities are coming by his or her way, Hence, shifting to another domain, which has a good pay-check and worthwhile in the long-term.

SAMPLE ANSWER FROM A PROFESSIONAL POINT OF VIEW

Service based companies execute projects based on their customer's need, and companies deploy people based on the business requirements. While working in service based companies, I worked on Microsoft's/Linux/Unix platform based technologies. After working many years I understood, how that technologies are fitted to a professional e.g. engineers, and for a business that is its requirements.

Recently, I changed my job role, which requires doing in-depth analysis e.g. architecture, product's requirements, understand the cost, targeted customers and many other projects related parameters.

Though I had more work experience in Microsoft platforms than Linux. But based on the analysis, this project requires working on Linux Area, e.g. implementing server side technologies for Mobile Enterprise Apps. This is the reason my current project reflecting Linux platform related technologies than Microsoft.

SAMPLE ANSWER FROM A PROFESSIONAL POINT OF VIEW

I joined a start-up company and worked on XYZ Technologies, but that company shuttled down his business in less than one year, and that was using propriety technologies. So I changed my technology domain to enter in Banking Domain because of evergreen Industry and stable career.

SAMPLE ANSWER FROM A PROFESSIONAL POINT OF VIEW

Since last few years I generated more interest in Finance Domain, and that gave me ideas to shift my existing technology's domain to Internet Security Domain.

Exercise:	Q:	Why did you change your technology domain?

Am I going to answer this question now? And adding the notes on my career note book?

(a).[Yes] (b).[No] (c).[Later] (d).[Its not relevant to my career] (e) [I framed this question on other way]

Date and Time:

TECHNICAL SKILLS: TECHNOLOGY DIFFERENCES

Why you are using XYZ technologies on your project when other XYZ technologies are available?

RATIONALE: *Professionals analyze various parameters while selecting an appropriate technology for a technical implementation, e.g. budget parameters, performance parameters, ease of use, available expertise, support, maturity, stability, functionality, features and many more.*

Interviewer wants to know interviewee's understanding related with the difference between two similar technologies and could be used for the same purpose.

SAMPLE ANSWER FROM A PROFESSIONAL POINT OF VIEW

While we decided to use GWT (Google Window Toolkit) in our project, we analyzed YUI (Yahoo User Interface Library) as well; here are some of the pros and cons related with GWT.

Pros:

Very good perceived UI responsiveness. In a perfect case response times will be even better than on desktop (local Google Gears caching is great).

- GWT uses component model for UI, so code reuse is easy. And there are many open-source libraries of GWT components too.
- GWT server-side is stateless. So it is highly scalable "by design". In our case we achieved very good performance per single front-end server instance.
- It's possible to make UI similar to desktop GUI with associated sweeties (DND, visual effects & etc)

Cons:

- GWT is built around Java -> JavaScript compilation. So if you get a big Java codebase, the result js files will be big. So some old browsers will not be able to load and run them
- GWT app loading time may be quite significant for big codebase. Of course, browser caching helps here
- GWT renders page content with JavaScript, so indexing of data represented by the app is problematic
- While there is browser history control inside the library, there are restrictions introduced by HTTP/HTML stack. In general case, It will not

be able to reference pages inside GWT app if use HTTP redirect (for example during authentication)

- HTML Browsers are not too good in visualization of dynamic HTML (IE is the worst, Safari 3 is the best). So It may need some tricks to show big number of items)

- GWT components are not easy to debug/implement. They should be cross-browser. And HTML browsers have their own bugs too. So it may need a JS/DHTML guru in Java team.

SAMPLE ANSWER FROM A PROFESSIONAL POINT OF VIEW

Why I used XMPP Signalling in my project, why I didn't use SIP with respect to messenger type application:

Both XMPP and SIP provide the functionality required my project. Each protocol has its leading client side and server-side implementations that claim to offer high performance and scalability.

- Although SIP is a general-purpose session protocol and XMPP, a more IM/Collaboration oriented one; there is no clear winner in this match. In the basic protocol functionality required by my project, both SIP and XMPP may offer a scalable solution.

- One advantage of XMPP over SIP is its ability to run over an HTTP transport. Currently, many firewalls apply a very strict policy on traffic that blocks anything that looks different than plain Web browsing. In addition, many ISPs use traffic shaping that prioritizes

Exercise:	Q:	**Why you are using XYZ technologies on your project when other XYZ technologies are available?**

Am I going to answer this question now? And adding the notes on my career note book?

(a).[Yes] (b).[No] (c).[Later] (d).[Its not relevant to my career] (e) [I framed this question on other way]

Date and Time:

TECHNICAL SKILLS:
VARIOUS TECHNOLOGIES YOU USED

Please describe your past experience and various technologies you have worked with.

RATIONALE: *Usually technology areas refer to a practical application of science in industry. That would also mean what a professional has worked on and learnt from his or her past work experience in the various technologies.*

Individual's experience varies. It could be any, from banking domain to web domain, from java area to adobe dreamweaver.

SAMPLE ANSWER FROM A PROFESSIONAL **POINT OF VIEW**

During my past project experience (5+ Years), I got involved in Telecommunication/Data Communication Software domain, I am experienced in Technology standards, e.g. IETF (Internet engineering Task Force), W3C (World Wide Web Consortium), ITU (International Telecommunication Union) e.g. SIP, TCP/IP, Protocol Stack, Base Station Controller (GSM), Base Transceiver Station (GSM). Often I used programming languages such as C, C++ and JAVA.I have had worked with various known IDE for programming like Eclipse, Visual Studio, Code Blocks. I have also used various debugging and test tools.

SAMPLE ANSWER FROM A PROFESSIONAL **POINT OF VIEW**

I am working in banking domain and got experience in Microsoft Technologies e.g. .NET, C#, Silver Light, Active Server Pages, IIS.

SAMPLE ANSWER FROM A PROFESSIONAL **POINT OF VIEW**

I'm a professional developer specialized in Microsoft Technologies (.NET) with 9 years of experience in development and leadership. I have thorough understanding of current and emerging Microsoft technologies and Development Lifecycle.

I am familiar with the challenges involved in Internet entrepreneurship profile with proven records of successful 4.8 years entrepreneurship with past and current clients and ways to deal with them through vast experiences.

I am ready to be deployed in a senior capacity as a developer or team leader. My broad range of experience in both team management and senior level development makes me a strong candidate for a diverse set of positions.

Exercise:	Q:	**Please describe your past experience and various technologies you have worked with.**

Am I going to answer this question now? And adding the notes on my career note book?

(a).[Yes] (b).[No] (c).[Later] (d).[Its not relevant to my career] (e) [I framed this question on other way]

Date and Time:

TIME MANAGEMENT – SUGGESTION/OWNERSHIP

Provide me an example of how you managed to organize your task schedule?

RATIONALE: *Professionals used to be involved on many tasks from office, and then occupied with personal works as well, e.g.; buy groceries, winter clothing. In office: meeting with Mr.X to discuss A Issue, then write an e-mail to team for some status, work on a draft for Y.*

Interviewer wants to understand Interviewee's way to organize such type of tasks.

SAMPLE ANSWER FROM A PROFESSIONAL POINT OF VIEW

I used Google Calendar, iPhone Calendar to organize my task, I also maintain high level activities on excel sheet. It's all depends how many different types of tasks I have and their priorities. Some time just have one task daily e.g.; come to office and support for X or work on Y.

SAMPLE ANSWER FROM A PROFESSIONAL POINT OF VIEW

It's my natural habit, as soon a task comes to my plate; I add that task in my calendar with comments and timeline. Every morning I used to spend 30 minutes to have a self-check on my tasks, because if something is getting delay, then I might need to take appropriate action.

Exercise:	Q:	How you manage your task schedule?

Am I going to answer this question now? And adding the notes on my career note book?

(a).[Yes] (b).[No] (c).[Later] (d).[Its not relevant to my career] (e) [I framed this question on other way]

Date and Time:

TOP PROGRAMMING LANGUAGES: SCALE FROM 1-TO-10

What are your three top programming languages (rate yourself on a scale from 1-10, 10 being an expert).

RATIONALE: *Interviewer expects to know interviewee involvement in programming related activities. Hence trying to find out the interviewee's competencies, by first looking from his self-evaluation, how interviewee feels about his competency in programming.*

SAMPLE ANSWER FROM A PROFESSIONAL **POINT OF VIEW**

C: 9, C++: 5, Java: 5

I would like to define reasoning behind this rating:

If a professional heavily involved in using C++, e.g. developed a Library or Framework, designed Class diagrams based on the customized design patterns, used OOPS concepts and followed best programming practices, understand real ingredient of a programming language, and worked on at least 2-3 projects. He or she may give rating as 9 and keep 1 point for unknown areas.

If a professional has studied a specific language (c, c++ etc.) in university, but didn't work on any project other than just basic programming. He or she may say: 3 as more than a beginner.

If a professional has used C++ language on any existing project, e.g. done some bug fixes rather made any implementation. He or she may say 5, actually it all depends on professional's confidence and self-evaluation.

After this self-evaluation, Interviewer may ask a set of questions based on rating given to specific language.

- **Interviewee is an expert**, with rating: 9: conceptual question may be from Serializing and Desterilizing using C/C++ (How to serialize objects, which contain pointers to other objects?)

- **Interviewee is average**, with rating: 5: What are some advantages and disadvantages of using friend functions?

- **Interviewee is a beginner**, with rating: 3: May you please describe OOPS concepts and explain how inheritance could be used in C++?

Exercise:	Q:	**What are your three top programming languages (rate yourself on a scale from 1-10, 10 being an expert).?**

Am I going to answer this question now? And adding the notes on my career note book?

(a).[Yes] (b).[No] (c).[Later] (d).[Its not relevant to my career] (e) [I framed this question on other way]

Date and Time:

WORK ATTITUDE: HARD DEADLINE ENVIRONMENT

Have you ever worked in hard deadline environment?

RATIONALE: *Because of urgency or nature of work, some projects are associated with hard deadlines, means no alternatives are possible if a task is not finished on a planned date.*

The Interviewer wants to understand, how the interviewee managed such a situation in the past or does he or she truly understand the nature of business and priorities.?

SAMPLE ANSWER FROM A PROFESSIONAL **POINT OF VIEW**

I worked for a telecom operator's software development project; the objective of this project was to release the next version of a software component in certain deadline, because it was kind of live work. Several telecom operators were already in the use of that software component, and there were some additional requirements from telecom operators (customers) to the software product manufacturer (our company).

We got a deadline, and based on that we planned set of activities to be done. In high level, yes it was hard deadlines type of activity, but we understood the situation very clearly. We made the clear plan, did organized team work, followed a discipline and met with the deadline.

Actually in business, people very well understand what exactly is urgent and what is not, and usually the system makes them automatically ready to handle such situation as a normal situation.

Exercise:	Q:	What is your experience dealing with hard deadline project?

Am I going to answer this question now? And adding the notes on my career note book?

(a).[Yes] (b).[No] (c).[Later] (d).[Its not relevant to my career] (e) [I framed this question on other way]

Date and Time:

WORK ENVIRONMENT – DO OFFICE POLITICS EXIST?

Did you hear a word called official politics? What do you understand from that? Please explain any situation when something was affected to you because of official politics?

RATIONALE: *We hear office-politics word on many occasions e.g. that happened because of office politics.*

Interviewer wants to understand Interviewee's view related with this work office-politics.

SAMPLE ANSWER FROM A PROFESSIONAL POINT OF VIEW

I don't care about this office politics, and not participate much on such a type of talks. I usually follow my work ethics.

On many occasions, I heard the word office-politics. I think; something happens because of some reason. Many times we are unaware of the reason, and imagine reasons by ourselves. Everyone thinks in a different way, and that didn't conclude anything than individual's perception. I am far-far away from such a type of word.

Exercise:	Q:	Did you hear a word called official politics?

Am I going to answer this question now? And adding the notes on my career note book?

(a).[Yes] (b).[No] (c).[Later] (d).[Its not relevant to my career] (e) [I framed this question on other way]

Date and Time:

WORK ENVIRONMENT – SURROUNDING WORK ITEMS

Are you really curious about your colleagues' work items?

RATIONALE: *A professional can learn many things by interacting with his or her colleagues, e.g. knowledge and work related information, understand other's work styles, other's work type, casual feedback, a suggestion on a specific thing and some other work related productivity-parameters.*

Interviewer wants to know whether the interviewee really understands the power of learning from his or her colleagues.

SAMPLE ANSWER FROM A PROFESSIONAL POINT OF VIEW

I always keep a very close association with my colleagues, e.g. maintaining pleasant attitude, listen to them, help them wherever appropriate, having lunch, dinner, tea-breaks together, involvement in ongoing work items, discuss scenarios to have an extra opinion, discuss meaning of XYZ, clear my doubts on certain items if required.

It might happen that few colleagues might not revert back in an expected way, but all together this attitude provides me various opportunities to talk with them for work-related items, and that accelerate my productivity and awareness.

Exercise:	Q:	**Do you really curious related with your colleagues work?**

Am I going to answer this question now? And adding the notes on my career note book?

(a).[Yes] (b).[No] (c).[Later] (d).[Its not relevant to my career] (e) [I framed this question on other way]

Date and Time:

WORK INTEREST:
DEVELOPMENT, TESTING OR ENHANCEMENT OR XYZ

What did you do on this XYZ Project? Was it development, testing, enhancement, maintenance or support?

RATIONALE: *Professional not straight away performs merely development or simply testing.*

Projects start from scratch and over a period of time, it expands. When a project expands, it also incorporates more people, and after that people join projects with different types of job roles, e.g. A software developer for the enhancement of an existing feature on a maintenance project, A software test engineer to test certain functional test cases to provide for project support.

Based on the type of expansion more people get involved,

Explain here your main activities which you have done your project, explain clearly your project was a maintenance project or started the development from scratch etc, and then based on that provide your answers.

SAMPLE ANSWER FROM A PROFESSIONAL POINT OF VIEW

I was purely involved in the test related activities for a project title: "Computer Telephony Integration"

Testing (100%) e.g. worked for a year to write test plans, execution of test cases, test automation, scripts, everything related to test work based on as and when required.

I was involved in development activities for a project title: "Development of Remote monitoring Agent (RMON) agent" and actually I have done following activities:

1. Specifications (10%): Wrote high level use cases e.g. how a end user will use the RMON Agent
2. Design (10%): Major designed item developed by someone else, I did a review and provided few of my comments.
3. Development (50%): Coded in prescribed coding language.
4. Testing (30%): Tested thoroughly via several types of unit test cases and operating environment.

Exercise:	Q:	**What you did on this XYZ Project? Was it development, testing, or enhancement or maintenance or support?**

Am I going to answer this question now? And adding the notes on my career note book?

(a).[Yes] (b).[No] (c).[Later] (d).[Its not relevant to my career] (e) [I framed this question on other way]

Date and Time:

WORK INTEREST: LEARNING FROM WORK

What did you learn from your XYZ project?

RATIONALE: *Interviewer wanted to know interviewee learning attitude towards the project, e.g. other then technical skills what extra did he or she learn on this project.*

SAMPLE ANSWER FROM A PROFESSIONAL POINT OF VIEW

JOB ACTIVITIES

This year, I have done following activities, which gave me learning towards managing a high end project, with technologies, dividing work on teams e.g.

*Implemented/Integrated Netty (Asynchronous JAVA Socket I/O) on a relay server

*Managed actively by working on all end-to-end activities as a Individual contributor with development team (reporting me for project work) for Designing/Documenting/Implementation/Testing overall XMPP Client

Used technical things: libjingle library (libjingle is a collection of open-source C++ code and sample applications that enables you to build a peer-to-peer application), Android Application, XMPP, ICE-UDP (NAT Traversal), Connection Multiplexing feature by working with different teams

LEARNING

*Learnt how to work with a very large codebase, which is using entirely different convergent thoughts/logics/technology and how it could be ported into new technology/innovation.

*Learnt how to work to work in diverse cross –cultural and very big teams, spread different geographical zones, for which I travelled to X and Y locations for couple of weeks.

*The technology was different (A, B technology), and there was not much ready for use expertise available; various brainstorming events were planned to understand the project.

*Learnt how to work with many technologies at once

| Exercise: | Q: | **What did you learn from your XYZ project?** |

Am I going to answer this question now? And adding the notes on my career note book?

(a).[Yes] (b).[No] (c).[Later] (d).[Its not relevant to my career] (e) [I framed this question on other way]

Date and Time:

WORK STYLE: MEETING WITH TEAM MEMBERS

Based on your past experience – when do you prefer to have a formal meeting with team members?

RATIONALE: *The professionals work in a team and team members work together for some objective, and each individual team member is a part of that objective. It happens that on many work-related situations, the team member might require to arrange a meeting so that the joint discussion can be made for work-related reasons. But it is also necessary that a professional need to understand that whether this meeting is really required or If yes, then whether all team members are required or some of them. Overall idea is to make the work hours productive for every one.*

Interviewer wants to understand interviewee attitude to avoid meeting and experience related with team collaboration tools or some other best practices he might suggest.

SAMPLE ANSWER FROM A PROFESSIONAL POINT OF VIEW

I organize meeting where I feel e-mail is a totally inappropriate and joint discussion will work better e.g. discussion requires involvement of multiple people (e.g., more than two), discussion requires deep understanding on a specific topic, discussion requires extended communication with team members. In some scenario, I use team collaboration tools e.g. Microsoft Communicator, WebEx, Live Meeting, because that reduce the cost and effort to organize a meeting.

If above are not helpful, then I might prefer meeting, Some of the best practices I would like to suggest:

- Prepare the clear agenda for the meeting, and notify to attendees before meeting.
- Following should be very as much clear to attendees e.g. Why the attendees are invited, the attendee's role(including the organizer) in meeting, clear agenda of this meeting, expected duration.

Exercise:	Q:	**What is your attitude towards the meeting?**

Am I going to answer this question now? And adding the notes on my career note book?

(a).[Yes] (b).[No] (c).[Later] (d).[Its not relevant to my career] (e) [I framed this question on other way]

Date and Time:

Programming Skills

Most of the core companies, e.g. highly technical product based companies like Microsoft, Google, Apple, Facebook, NetApp, Cisco, QUALCOMM, Intel, Adobe, Oracle and many more, concentrate on producing products and solutions. For providing effective products and solutions, they need capable engineers who can deliver such solutions. A good overall knowledge and skill in this area also provide key inputs for the candidate's problem-solving and programming ability.

APACHE SOLR, GOOGLE'S LIBJINGLE, OPENVPN, LIBUPNP, LINUX KERNEL, NETTY, NODE.JS, MONGODB, BOOST LIBRARY, MYSQL, APACHE – DRUPAL – MEDIAWIKI – MOODLE WORDPRESS JOOMLA TYPO3 COUCHBASE SERVER, MARIADB, HADOOP, QT, ANDROID

TEST

ALGORITHIMS

Asymptotic notation, Recurrences, Dynamic Programming, **Greedy Algorithims**, Graph Algorithims, **Minimum Spanning Trees**, Single source Shortest Paths, **Number-Theoretic Algorithims**, String Matching, NP-completeness, Approximation Algorithms, **Logn, Sqrt(N), N, nLogn, N^2, N^3, 2^n, n!, O-Notation**, acyclic graph, adjacency-list representation, **adjacency-matrix representation,** associative array, AVL Trees, **BackTracking**, Best First Search, Binary Search Tree, Binary Tree, **Brute Force**, Bucket, Bucket Sort, Bubble Sort, Circular List, Circular Queue, Critical Path Problems, Directed acyclic graph directed acyclic graph–**shortest paths**, Decision problem, Depth first search, Dequqe, **Dictionary,** Directed graph, Distribution sort, Divide and conquer, **Double hashing**, Double linked list, Dynamic array, Dynamic hashing, Dynamic programming, Euclid's algorithim, **external memory algorithim,** Factorial, Fat Fourier Transform, Fibonacci number, first in first out, **Floyd-Warshall algorithim**, Garbage Collection, Graph, Graph Coloring, …

DATA STRUCTURES

Container, Deque, Associative array(Map, Dictionary, Multimap), Multiset, Priority queue, Queue, Set, Stack, String, Tree, Graph, Hash, AA Tree, Abstract syntax tree, Adaptive k-d tree, Additional Game Math, Adjacency list, Adjacency matrix, Alternating decision tree, And-inverter graph, Array, AVL tree, B Sharp Tree, B-Tree, B+ tree, B*-tree, B-trie, Beap, Binary tree, Binary search tree, Bit Array, Bitboard, Bitset Class, Bit Field Bitmaps, Bin, Binary decision diagram, Binary heap, Binary Space Partitioning Trees, Binomial heap, Bloom filter, Boolean, Bounding interval hierarchy, Bounding Volumes, BSP tree, Bx-tree, Cartesian tree, Character, Circular buffer, Cover tree, Container, Control table, Custom Array.

CODING

AJAX, Assembly Language, Action Script, AWK, C, **C++**, C#, **Cobol**, ECMAScript, HTML, **IBM** Informix-4GL, Java Language, **JavaScript**, Mac OS X Programming, **MySQL**, Perl, Python, **PHP**, PostScript, **PL/SQL**, Unix Shell, **VBScript**, Visual Basic .NET, Visual **C++**, Visual C++, Net, X, **XML**

The main concept for the interview is to keep the interview active and this requires some action from your side, such as the following:

- You need to talk
- You need to explain
- You need to discuss
- You need to express your views
- You need to understand clearly the questions given to you
- You need to understand the interviewer's expression and mindset to understand those questions
- You might need to ask appropriate questions to understand the question or any other discussion item.

Let's take a scenario where an interviewer will discuss about the coding problem. Usually the duration of such type of interview varies from 45 to 60 minutes. On that 45 to 60 minutes the interviewer will explain the coding problem and you will also clarified to properly understand the coding problem. So it means you will spend 5 to 10 minutes to understand the problem, and another five minutes for other talks.

So it means you have 20 minutes to actually solve the problems, or other ways It may be 20 to 30 minutes. You might need to prepare something more towards the presence of mind and the way of solving the coding problems while in person.

It might be possible, that certain companies will give you the computer machine, and you are required to use a specific tool to actually solve the problem. But whatever be the case an organize practice will yield the desired results.

Here is a example steps to solve the coding problem:

Step 1: First you need to understand the problem. Don't take the problem as is, because the given problem to you is just a statement or a line. Until unless you don't understand it, don't go for solution.

It's a good practice, that if interviewer has explained a coding problem, then it would be great if you can re-explain it to the interviewer e.g. to clarify whether you understood properly or he/she explained the same what you understood.

Step 2: On this particular step you need to do some analysis, you need to define a way to write the solution of the problem. You cannot jump straight forward for a regular solution. You need to clear to your self in front of the interviewer e.g. that this would be the solution that you are expecting, and that way you are going to write the code for that solution.

It is very important and be careful, that you are required to talk with the interviewer or think loudly, better to make environment active.

And it's better that write the design, discuss the approach with the limitations/assumptions and anything else which appeared to be appropriate before giving the solution. Because it shows the completeness, organized behavior and a right attitude towards solving the problem.

Step 3: On this step, you are required to write the solution. It might be that you have to write a function which takes the arguments, perform the logic and return the result based on the asked question.

On this situation, you are required to explain to the interviewer, why this solution is the ideal solution. There might be many other ways exist to write the solution, but it was a situation where he thought it's best.

If you feel that you got some idea while explaining the answer or writing the solution, then you can improve it if applicable or keep a point-list on a side e.g. review list.

Once the solution is written or explained to the interviewer, you might need to review the following:

- Did you consider all the logical cases
- Did you consider the return values
- Did you consider the appropriate error cases
- Have you given the appropriate variable names
- Is the code readable
- Did you use the proper coding concepts
- Are you confident with the code you wrote

Step 4: on this step use some sample values for the test cases to show the output of the function.

You may create a table on which you can keep the column name as the name of the arguments. Trace the code and write values as the code does e.g. code might perform 6 logical steps and on those steps the value changes then mention the values like that.

So it does not mean that you need to only concentrate on coding. You need to concentrate the proper way of doing coding if you follow the proper way then that definitely will lead to the solution.

The concepts of algorithms, and a way to write the logical statements will definitely help on **step-1.**

The concepts of arrays, strings, linked lists, queues, rooted trees, graphs, hash, set, multiset, containers, associative arrays and the other important data structure will help on **step-2.**

You can have a choice of programming language, which can reduce certain operations or functions based on what already exist. Example the Java and C++ they are there for different business solutions. However everything is possible in Java and C++ but still C++ has his own specific case than Java. Such programming concepts will help on **step-3.**

Writing the appropriate test cases, possibly so called unit test cases to verify the code functioning will help on **step-4.**

Above is one of the sample approach to solve coding problems during interviews. It might be differ based on the situation, problem type, candidate's background, the way discussion would be carried and many others dynamic parameters.

ALGORITHMS WALK THROUGH: WHAT IS AN ALGORITHM?

An algorithm is a method of solving a problem using a computer. The implementation of an algorithm consists of a finite set of steps, each of which can consist of one or more operations. We hear about algorithms increasingly often in different contexts nowadays.

Back in the medieval era, mathematicians regarded algorithms as a rule for making arithmetic calculations. With the development of computers, however, the term has acquired a special meaning, turning from a specific instrument used in mathematics into a fundamental way to address problems in various fields.

In computer science, an algorithm is a method of solving problems of a certain type. Solving a problem means producing the right output for any given input data. The algorithm itself consists of a sequence of operations that describe, step by step, how to compute the output data (the result) based on the input. For example, an algorithm for computing the greatest common factor of two numbers would produce '5' as output for the input consisting of '10' and '15'.

As mentioned above, each step of an algorithm requires one or more operations. These operations must be clearly defined before we can implement them on a computer. Secondly, any operation must be effective. This means, in principle, that any person can perform it in a finite amount of time using just pencils and paper. For example, integer arithmetic is effective. Real number arithmetic, on the other hand, is not, because some numbers can be expressed by infinite sequences of digits. Generally, we consider that any algorithm must end after a finite number of operations in a reasonable, finite time period.

A good algorithm for finding the solution to a problem is one whose correctness can be proved. In addition, the use of appropriate data structures and choosing a programming language that can adapt the algorithm well are also important steps. For example, let's consider we have to compute the greatest common factor of two given positive integers. Given the inputs 35 and 14, we could perform the following steps:

- Subtract the smaller number from the bigger one and replace the bigger with the result of the subtraction (in our example 35 – 14 = 21, so we end up with 21 and 14);

- Repeat until the two numbers become equal (21 – 14 = 7, so now we have the pair 14 and 7, and finally 14 – 7 = 7, so we end up with 7 and 7).

- The greatest common factor is the value we have obtained at the end of the previous step (7 in this case).

The steps just mentioned represent an algorithm. In order to prove its correctness, we must show that it terminates after a finite amount of steps and it produces the right result. The algorithm just described always terminates because regardless of the two positive integers we give as an input, they will always end up with an equal value after repeated subtractions. Finally, we know that the greatest common factor of any two numbers divides both their sum and their difference, which means our algorithm produces the right result as well. One could write algorithms to solve problems in any domain. For example, any recipe can be considered an algorithm because it starts with raw materials (input) and leads to a finished product (output), obtained after a finite sequence of operations.

ALGORITHMS WALK THROUGH: TIME/SPACE COMPLEXITY

Time complexity, space complexity, and the big O notation

There are two important performance criteria established for an algorithm: the time and resources needed to output the solution of a problem.

First, the memory space used by an algorithm in a programming language consists of all the variables and data structures allocated statically (before the execution of the program begins). The following example illustrates the difference between an efficient and a non-efficient algorithm in terms of the amount of space used.

Suppose we want to write an algorithm that, given n as an input, $0 < n < 100$, computes the sum of the first n natural numbers. A first approach can be as follows:

```
1.   int sum(int n)
2.   {
3.       int a[100], s = 0;
4.       for (int i = 0; i < n; i++)
5.             a[i] = n;
6.       for (int i = 0; i < n; i++)
7.             s = s + a[i];
8.       return s;
9.   }
```

This program is not efficient in terms of the amount of memory, as it uses an array of 100 integer elements and an extra integer for holding the sum. On the other hand, here is an efficient approach to the same problem:

```
1.    int sum(int n)
2.    {
3.        int s = n*(n + 1) / 2;
4.        return s;
5.    }
```

This algorithm uses just a single integer value to produce the same output. This approach is based on the formula $1 + 2 + ... + n = n * (n + 1) / 2$;

Next, analysis of the execution time complexity of an algorithm involves determining the number of elementary operations performed by the algorithm, since the number of operations is proportional to the execution time. The first program of the two we have just analyzed performs 2 * n operation (n operations for each for loop) to produce an output, while the second one only performs one operation. We say the first program is linear (depends on n), while the second one is constant (performs one operation, regardless of the value of n).

Finally, the big O notation is used to classify algorithms based on their efficiency. The categories of algorithms based on the big O notation are as follows:

- O (1) – constant number of operations (just as the second program of the two discussed above);
- O (log n) – logarithmic number of operations (for example, if the program above took 8 as an input and needed 3 steps to produce the output its complexity would have been logarithmic);
- O (n) – a program performing n operations is said to have linear time complexity;
- O (n2) – a program performing n2 operations is said to have quadratic time complexity;
- O (n3) – cubic time complexity;
- O (nk) – polynomial time complexity;
- O (2n) – exponential time complexity;
- O (n!) – factorial time complexity.

For the purpose of the big O notation, we are not interested in the coefficients of functions. For example, if a program performed 3n + 2 operations, it would still be linear (O(n)).

ALGORITHMS WALK THROUGH: BEST/WORST/AVERAGE CASE

The best-case, worst case and average-case performance of an algorithm

- The best-case performance of an algorithm refers to its behavior when the input is optimal. For example, in the case of an algorithm that sorts an array of integers, the optimal input is an array that is already sorted;

- The worst-case performance of an algorithm, on the other hand, occurs when the input is the most challenging. It is often impossible to determine the worst-case input exactly, but in theory this input should maximize the steps performed by the algorithm to reach the right result;

- The average-case performance of an algorithm is the average numbers of steps it would perform to terminate. For example, if given an algorithm that searches for an element in an array of N entries by a single iteration over the array we would expect N/2 steps on average.

ALGORITHMS WALK THROUGH: ALGORITHMS COMPLEXITIES EXAMPLES

Examples of algorithms and their complexity

- A program that returns the first element of a given array has constant complexity – $O(1)$ – as it only performs one step.

- An algorithm that searches for an element in an array of integers by iterating over the array has linear complexity – $O(N)$.

- An algorithm that searches for an element in an array of integers using binary search has logarithmic complexity – $O(\log N)$.

- An algorithm that searches for an element in a binary tree has logarithmic complexity – $O(\log N)$.

- A sorting algorithm with two for loops has quadratic complexity – $O(N2)$.

- More advanced sorting algorithms, such as quick sort and heap sort have complexity – $O(N \log N)$.

- A recursive function for computing the Fibonacci numbers has exponential complexity – $O(2N)$.

- An algorithm that computes the Cartesian product of three sets has cubic complexity – $O(N3)$ – as it needs three nested loops to achieve this.

ALGORITHMS WALK THROUGH: SORTING APPROACHES

Sorting is one of the most used programming methods. It has various applications in fields such as mathematics (mathematical statistics) and even in languages (implementation of dictionaries). Therefore, it is ideal to find the most convenient sorting algorithm for the task we are given. We can do that by knowing the advantages and disadvantages of different sorting methods.

Sorting methods are classified into direct methods and advanced methods. Direct methods are based on algorithms of a lower difficulty, easy to find and understand. Some examples of direct methods are selection sort and bubble sort. Advanced methods, on the other hand, are based on more complicated algorithms, but do not require advanced algorithmic knowledge. Some of the most common are quick sort, merge sort and heap sort.

SORTING APPROACHES: BUBBLE SORT

This method is based on comparing pairs of two elements and interchanging them if they are not in the right order in the given array. These comparisons are made until all the elements are sorted. The code for bubble sort is as follows:

```
1.   void bubble_sort(type a[], int size)
2.   {
3.   bool sorted;
4.      do
5.      {
6.            sorted = true;
7.            for(int i=0; i<size-1; i++)
8.                    if (a[i]>a[i+1])
9.                    {
10.                           interchange(a[i],a[i+1]);
11.                           sorted=false;
12.                    }
13.      }
14.      while (!sorted);
15.   }
```

The following table shows a step-by-step example of bubble sort:

Step no.	a[0]	a[1]	a[2]	a[3]	a[4]
1	6	2	10	1	12
2	2	6	1	10	12
3	2	1	6	10	12
4	1	2	6	10	12

The best case time complexity for bubble sort is O(n), when the list is already sorted, while the worst case complexity is O(n2). Hence the average is O(n2 / 2), which is still O(n2). The advantage of this algorithm lies in its simplicity, so if the execution time is not an issue you can choose bubble sort as the simplest method for solving a task.

SORTING APPROACHES: SELECTION SORT

Suppose you have an array of integers a with n elements. At step "i" a selection sort algorithm would compute the minimum between a[i+1], a[i+2], ... a[n] and interchange it with a[i], as follows:

```
1.   selection_sort(int a[], int n)
2.   {
3.      for (int i = 0; i < n; i++)
4.      {
5.            min = a[i];
6.      for (int j = i + 1; j < n; j ++)
7.        if (a[j] < min) min = a[j];
8.            interchange(a[i], min)
9.      }
10.  }
```

The following table should make this clearer. The red element is the minimum at each step, while the elements in bold are those that are already sorted.

Step no	a[0]	a[1]	a[2]	a[3]
1	5	3	7	2
2	2	3	7	5
3	2	3	7	5
4	2	3	5	7
5	2	3	5	7

The time complexity of this algorithm is also O(n2), in both worst case and best case, because selection sort performs n2 operations regardless of the input.

SORTING APPROACHES: QUICK SORT

Quick sort is one of the fastest sorting algorithms, with a time complexity in the best case of O(n log n). The basic idea is as follows:

- Pick an element from the array to be sorted. This is the pivot of the array;
- Iterate through the array and re-arrange the entries, making sure the pivot is in the right place, the entries smaller than the pivot are on its left and the entries larger than the pivot are on its right;
- Repeat for the sub-array on the left of the pivot and on the right of the pivot.

For example, suppose we need to sort the array 3, 10, 5, 7, 4 and we choose 5 as our pivot. We start from both ends (3 and 4) and look for the first element bigger than 5 to its left and the first smaller than 5 to its right. In this case, these numbers are 10 and 4, which we swap, obtaining 3, 4, 5, 7 and 10. As opposed to bubble sort, quick sort is able to sort this array by iterating over it only once. Finally, the average and worst-case complexities for quick sort are also O(n2).

SORTING APPROACHES: HEAP SORT

A heap is a binary tree structure with special properties, as follows:

- All the levels, except for the last one, need to be complete;
- All the children of a parent need to be bigger (min heap) or smaller (max hip) than it.

For example, the following is the min-heap for the array (4, 7, 2, 13, 5):

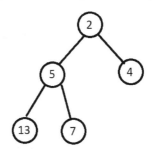

The heap sort algorithm is as follows:

- Build a heap with the elements of the array to be sorted;
- Create an empty array;
- While the heap is not empty
  - ▷ Get the root of the heap (the minimum) and add it to the array created in the second step;
  - ▷ Update the heap so that its properties are still respected.

The time complexity of the heap sort algorithm is also O(n log n) in the best, average and worst cases.

SORTING APPROACHES: RADIX SORT

Radix sort is generally more efficient for large arrays than all the other sorting algorithms. The steps of execution for radix sort are as follows:

1. Sort the elements in the array based on their least significant digit – for example the array [109, 34, 25, 19, 91] would be sorted as [91, 34, 25, 109, 19]. Notice that if two elements have the same least significant digit the one encountered first has priority.

2. Take the sorted array and repeat for the second least significant digit, third significant digit, etc. until the numbers are sorted. For the example above, we would obtain [109, 19, 25, 34, 91] after the second step and [19, 25, 34, 91, 109] after the third, when the algorithm stops.

The time complexity of radix sort is O(n * k) for the worst and average cases, where n is the number of items and k is their size. The best case is O(n), if the elements are all one digit numbers.

SORTING APPROACHES: BUCKET SORT

Bucket sort is based on splitting the elements in the given array in 'buckets', usually based on their value. For example, if we were given the task to sort the array [10, 96, 35, 70, 46, 57, 36, 91, 80] it would be reasonable to create the following 'buckets': (0-9), (10 – 19), (20 – 29), ..., (90 – 99). The steps for performing the algorithm are as follows:

1. Set up an array of empty "buckets" (categories).
2. Assign each element in the initial array to its corresponding bucket.
3. Use any sorting algorithm to sort the buckets internally.

4. Iterate over every bucket and place the elements back in the original array.

In the example above, we would obtain the following distribution of elements in buckets:

0-9	10-19	20-29	30-39	40-49	50-59	60-69	70-79	80-89	90-99
	10		35	46	57		70	80	96
			36						91

After sorting the buckets internally and iterating over all buckets we would obtain the sorted array. The worst case time complexity of bucket sort is $O(n2)$, the average-case complexity is $O(n + k)$, while the worst case performance of the algorithm is $O(n * k)$, where k is the size of the largest number in the data set.

SORTING APPROACHES: POINTS TO REMEMBER

- When you have to sort small arrays it would be best to use one of the direct methods, while an advanced sorting method is recommended for sorting big arrays;
- If time efficiency is important then you should choose either quick sort or heap sort;
- Quick sort is implemented in the stdlib.h library of C++ under the name qsort.
- Choosing the appropriate sorting problem depends on the type of problem we are trying to solve, as well as the programming language used. For example, in Python the most efficient way of sorting an array is by using list.sort, which makes use of the technique called timsort.
- There is a concept called a sorting network, which is a model that performs compare-exchange operations and can be used for sorting a sequence of numbers. An example of a sorting networks is as follows:

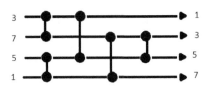

You can see that every pair of numbers from the given array are compared along the way and interchanged if necessary.

ALGORITHMS WALK THROUGH: SEARCHING APPROACHES

When presented with the task of searching for an element in a given data structure, you should know there are various techniques to do this. In the following lines we will analyze searching approaches for arrays, hash tables, linked lists and binary search trees.

SEARCHING APPROACHES: SEARCHING IN ARRAYS AND LINKED LISTS

There are two main searching approaches when it comes to arrays, linear search and binary search.

First, linear search is the most straightforward method of searching for an element. All we need to do is iterate through the array and stop when the element we are looking for was found. Suppose a is an array of N integers. Then the algorithm would be as follows:

```
1.   int find(int value)
2.   {
3.       for (int i = 0; i < N; i++)
4.               if (a[i] == value)
5.                       return i;
6.       return -1; // not found
7.   }
```

As you can see, linear search performs N steps, where N is the size of the array, which often makes it inefficient. On the other hand, if the array is sorted we can perform a binary search on it, which would only take log N steps, as follows:

```
1.   int find(left, right, value)
2.   {
3.       if (right < left)    // value not found
4.               return -1;
5.       int middle = (left  + right) / 2;
6.       if (a[middle] == value) return middle;   // value found at
         index middle
7.       else if (a[middle] < value)  // if value is greater than
         the middle index we need to look to the right
8.               return find(middle + 1, right, value);
9.       else // if the value is smaller need to look for it to the
         left
10.              return find(left, middle - 1, value);
11.  }
```

For example, a=(1, 5, 7, 9, 10) and value = 9, after the first step the method would split a into (1, 5) and (9, 10) and search for the value in (9, 10).

Linear search also works for linked lists. Because of the way linked lists are represented, we cannot use binary search for them.

SEARCHING APPROACHES: HASH TABLES AND BINARY SEARCH TREES

In hash tables, every single element has a unique key associated with it, which is computed in advance. The element is then stored at a location corresponding to this key. Therefore, when searching for a value in a hash table all we need to do is re-compute its key in advance and retrieve the element at the corresponding index. This can be done in constant time, so it can be said that hash table searching has complexity $O(1)$.

As their name suggests, binary search trees are binary trees optimized for searching, as follows:

- The left sub-tree of any node contains only elements that are smaller than the node;
- The right sub-tree of any node contains only elements that are larger than the node.

For example, the following is the binary search tree for (5, 2, 10, 6, 9, 1) is as follows:

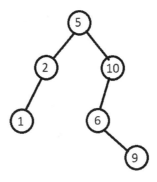

When searching for 9, for example, we start from the top, and compare 9 with every element found along the way, moving left or right accordingly. Because 9 is greater than the root of the tree (5), we move right, then left (9 < 10) and so on. The complexity of searching in a binary tree is $O(\log N)$, where N is the number of elements stored in the tree.

SEARCHING APPROACHES: STRING SEARCH

String search is defined as the problem of searching for a sequence of characters (a string) in a larger string. For example, we could be given the task to find "aba" in "ababacdeababa". There are four occurrences, at positions 0, 2, 8 and 10, respectively.

The naïve algorithm is to iterate through the larger string and check whether the string "aba" can be found there. Generally this approach has complexity O(n*k), where n is the length of the larger string and k the length of the smaller one. A more efficient way to tackle this kind of problem is to use the KMP algorithm, which is based around the idea that if we have failed to find the small string at a certain position, we can tell exactly at which position in the big string we could continue looking for it. The complexity of this algorithm is reduced to O(n + k).

ALGORITHMS WALK THROUGH: BRUTE-FORCE APPROACH

Every programmer should know that the brute-force approach (also known as the backtracking method) is one of the most popular programming techniques. The idea behind this kind of approach is to generate all possible solutions and discard those that do not correspond to the requirements of the task. Intuitively, the generation of all solutions leads to a very large time complexity of a backtracking algorithm, but the advantage is that we do not miss out any solution and almost always produce a correct result. Backtracking can always be used to solve any kind of problem in case a reasonably more efficient algorithm cannot be found.

The structure of a backtracking function generally, the template that can be used to write any backtracking function is as follows:

```
1.    function back(int step)
2.    {
3.        if (solution_is_complete)
4.                check if solution is valid
5.                return
6.        build solution at current step
7.        back (step + 1);
8.    }
```

BRUTE-FORCE APPROACH: EXAMPLE – GENERATE ALL PERMUTATIONS

Problem: generate all permutations of the set {1, 2, ... N} in lexicographic order. Solution: Since the problem asks for the generation of all solutions, a brute-force approach can be used.

The code is as follows:

```
1.   int perm[4] = {0};  int element_used[4] = {0};
2.   void backtracking (int step)
3.   {
4.      static int k = 1;
5.      if (step == N) // if a complete solution was built print it
6.      {
7.              printf("%d:", k);
8.              for (int pIndex = 0; pIndex < N; pIndex++)
                printf("%d", perm[i]); // pIndex = permutation
                index
9.              printf("\n");
10.             ++k;
11.             return;
12.  }
13.  // build the solution at current step
14.  for (int sIndex = 0; sIndex < N; sIndex++)  // iterate
     through all possible values in the given set ({1, 2, 3, …,
     N}) sIndex = set index
15.             if(!element_used[i])  // check if we have used an
                element in one of the previous steps
16.             {
17.                     element_used[i] = 1;
18.                     perm[step] = i;           // add the element
                        to the array containing the permutation
19.                     backtracking(step + 1);
20.                     element_used[i] = 0;
21.             }
22.  }
```

The output for n = 3 is as follows:

1: 123

2: 132

3: 213

4: 231

5: 312

6: 321

As you have seen, the program produces N! lines of output for any given N.

Note that we need to check whether the element we are trying to add to the permutation has already been added in a previous step. We do this using the element_used array. This invalidates permutations such as (1 1 1 1 1), because once we add the first '1' we know we cannot use it anymore. Another aspect to mention is that the function needs to be called with back(0) initially.

If N = 5, for example, the method would behave as follows:

- First iterate from 1 to 5, mark each of them as 'used' and form the valid permutation (1 2 3 4 5)
- Mark 5 as unused and go back to step 4
- Mark 4 as unused and form the valid permutation (1 2 3 5 4)
- Mark 4 and 5 as unused and go back to step 3, where the valid permutation (1 2 4 3 5) is formed

And so on…

BRUTE-FORCE APPROACH: COMMON APPLICATIONS OF BACKTRACKING

You can usually use backtracking to perform tasks such as:

1. Generating permutations or combinations
2. The Eight queens puzzle (given a 8x8 chess board find all ways of placing 8 queens on the board such that they do not attack each other).
3. Generating Cartesian products of sets
4. Longest prefix problems

BRUTE-FORCE APPROACH: CONCLUSION

The brute-force approach is a highly prevalent technique in programming, being very useful for the generation of all solutions of a problem. For most tasks there are more efficient algorithms, but a backtracking technique can always be used to find the right result, even though the execution time would be larger.

ALGORITHMS WALK THROUGH: DIVIDE AND CONQUER ALGORITHMS

The Applicability of Divide and Conquer algorithms: Divide and Conquer methods of solving can be applied to problems that can be decomposed into sub-problems of the same nature as the main problem, but smaller.

On some problems this possibility of decomposition into sub-problems of the same type is obvious. However, there are cases when decomposition is not straightforward at all.

DIVIDE AND CONQUER: HOW DO DIVIDE AND CONQUER ALGORITHMS WORK?

The main question is "how can we solve the sub-problems?" The answer is: "In the same way that we solved the main problem." The Divide and Conquer method relies mainly on recursive implementations. Since we know how to divide the main problem into sub-problems, we can also divide the sub-problems into sub-sub-problems, and so on. But when do we stop this process? The answer is simple. When we reach a problem that is so small that its solution is trivial.

DIVIDE AND CONQUER: IMPLEMENTATION OF DIVIDE AND CONQUER ALGORITHMS

The overall implementation of the Divide and Conquer method is by recursive functions. Usually we have one function that receives the information needed as parameters. A template would look as follows:

```
1.   function divide (parameters that define the current sub-problem)
2.   {
3.       if (sub-problem is trivial)
4.       {
5.           Solve sub-problem directly
6.           Returns result
7.       }
8.       else
9.       {
10.          split sub-problem into sub-sub problems
11.          for each sub-sub-problem
12.              call divide (sub-sub-problem)
13.          Combine the results of the sub-sub-problems
14.          return result of sub-problem
```

```
15.      }
16.  }
```

To solve the main problem, all you have to do is to call this recursive function with the parameters that define the main problem.

DIVIDE AND CONQUER: EXAMPLE-1 – FIBONACCI NUMBERS

As you already know, the formula for computing the Fibonacci numbers is a[i] = a[i-1] + a[i -2], with a[0] = a[1] = 1. In other words, any number is equal to the sum of the two previous numbers in the array. With respect to the code above, each call to the recursive function represents a sub-problem. Any sub-problem is considered trivial if we have reached one of the base cases, index = 0 or index = 1, because we then know our function needs to return 1. The code would be as follows:

```
1.    function fibo(int index)
2.    {
3.       if(index == 0 || index == 1) return 1;
4.       else return fibo (index - 1) + fibo(index - 2);
5.    }
```

DIVIDE AND CONQUER: EXAMPLE-2 – FACTORIAL

A similar example is writing a function to compute the factorial of a given integer. The base case in this example is factorial (0) = 1. The function would look as follows:

```
1.    function factorial(int n)
2.    {
3.       if (n == 0) return 1;
4.       else return n * factorial(n-1);
5.    }
```

ALGORITHMS WALK THROUGH – GREEDY APPROACHES

Greedy algorithms are generally simple and are used in optimization problems such as: finding the best order for executing tasks, finding the shortest path in a graph, etc. Generally, greedy problems are characterized by the following:

- A set of candidates (tasks to be executed, the nodes of a graph etc.);
- A function that checks if a certain set of candidates represents a solution, not necessarily optimal, to the problem;
- A function that checks if a set of candidates can be part of a feasible solution, i.e. if it is possible to add more candidates to the current set and reach a solution;
- A selection function that indicates at any time what the most promising candidate is, out of those still unused;
- An objective function that gives the value of a solution - this is the function that we want to optimize (minimize / maximize).

To solve an optimization problem with a greedy technique, our main goal is to optimize the value of the objective function. A greedy algorithm builds the solution step by step. Initially, the set of selected candidates is empty. At each step, we try to add the most promising candidate to the set according to the selection function. If, after the addition, the set of selected candidates is not feasible, we eliminate the last added candidate. If, on the other hand, the set is feasible, we continue adding candidates to its current configuration.

Every time we expand the set of selected candidates we also check if the current set is a possible solution to our problem. If the greedy algorithm works correctly, the first solution found is also the optimal solution to the problem. Also note that the optimal solution is not necessarily unique. A description of a general greedy algorithm is as follows:

```
1.  greedy function (C)   // C - set of candidates
2.  {
3.      S = {};   // the set we use to construct the solution
4.      while not S is not a solution to the problem and C is not
        empty
5.      {
6.          select(x)   // x - a candidate that maximizes /
            minimizes our objective function
7.          C = C - {x}
8.          if feasible (S + {x}) then S = S + {x}   // if the
            addition of x would lead to a feasible solution
            add x to S
9.      }
10.     if solution (S) then return S
11.     else return «no solution»
12. }
```

It is now understandable why such an algorithm is called "greedy". At each step, the procedure chooses the best candidate at the time, without worrying about the future additions and without 'changing its mind'. If a candidate is included in the solution, it stays there, but if a candidate is excluded from the solution, it will never be reconsidered.

GREEDY APPROACHES:
EXAMPLE 1 – TASK SCHEDULING ALGORITHM

The task scheduling algorithm can be expressed as follows:

You have to complete a series of tasks. Each task has a deadline by which it should be completed, and also a penalty if the deadline is missed. The problem is finding a schedule of all tasks such that the penalty obtained is minimal. Using the greedy approach, we need the following data:

- The set of candidates – this is the list of the tasks that need to be completed;
- A selection function – at each step this function should select the task with the largest penalty (because this needs to be implemented first).
- An objective function that gives the value of a solution – trivial to implement; just compute the total penalty of the elements in the set describing the solution.

The steps for computing the smallest penalty are as follows:

1. First, sort the elements in the set of candidates (the tasks) in descending order with respect to the penalties they incur.

2. Iterate through the set of candidates and accept those tasks that can be performed at the current step without incurring any penalty and reject those whose deadline has already passed.

3. Finally, iterate through the array again and also select the tasks that have not been performed in the previous iteration.

Let's have a look at an example. Here is a list of tasks, along with their deadlines and the penalties, already sorted in descending order:

task$_i$	1	2	3	4	5
deadline$_i$	2	2	1	3	5
penalty$_i$	90	80	70	50	40

In this case, the algorithm would firstly select task 1 for step 1 and task 2 for step 2. Task 3 is rejected, as the deadline for it was the first step. Next, task 4 is selected, because we have not selected task 3 for step 3, so it would still be executed before the deadline. Finally, task 5 is also selected for completion in step 4. The algorithm will then iterate through the array of tasks again to find those rejected in the first place and will also add 3 to the final configuration, which will look as follows: (1, 2, 4, 5, 3).

The total penalty is hence 70.

GREEDY APPROACHES:
EXAMPLE 2 – HUFFMAN CODES

Huffman codes are used to find a minimal encoding for a text. This is done by assigning the code with the shortest length to the characters that appear most often in the text and vice-versa.

For example, if we want to encode the string "aabacad", the first thing to notice is that 'a' is the character that appears most frequently. It would then be best if we assigned the shortest code to it (let's use '0'). Then, b, c and d, respectively, only appear once, so we can assign them codes of equal lengths. Because we have not used '1' yet, we will assign it to b, and then c will be encoded by '00' and d by '01'. The encoded string would then be 0 0 1 0 00 0 01 (spaces are there just for liability). This encoded version uses only 9 bits, while the initial string required 7 * 8 = 56 bits in the memory of the computer.

In the following lines we will present how Huffman coding is actually performed algorithmically. Consider we have a text containing the following characters (the number in brackets represent the frequency of the characters): T(10), A(29), O(9), P(4), S(5). The first step we would perform is sort the elements in ascending order, obtaining P(4), S(5), O(9), T(10) and A(29). At each step we group the two elements with the least frequency and build a binary tree. For the first group, we would obtain the following tree, marking the branches with 0 (right) and 1 (left):

At this point, our set of candidates is {P, S}(9), O(9), T(10) and A(29). After the second step we would obtain the following tree and the set of candidates {P, S, O} (18), T(10) and A(29).

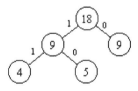

After the last step, the tree will be the following:

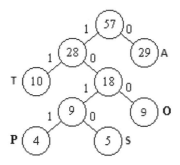

The characters would then be encoded as follows, following the shape of the tree:

A – 0

T – 11

O - 100

P – 1011

S – 1010

We notice that the characters that appear more often have the shortest encoding, as required by the task. In the example above, the initial string occupied 57 * 8 = 456 bits, while after the encoding the total number of bits used can be computed as follows, for each individual character:

T: 10 * 2 = 20;

A: 29 * 1 = 29;

O: 9 * 3 = 27;

P: 4 * 4 = 16;

S: 5 * 4 = 20;

The total is hence 20 + 29 + 27 + 16 + 20 = 112. We have therefore saved no less than 344 bits!

The algorithm is a **greedy** one because at each step it chooses the best solution, by merging the two nodes that appear less often in the array. Huffman coding is particularly useful for file compression. One of the most famous algorithms that uses this technique is PKZIP, but Huffman coding also appears in multimedia codecs like MP3 and JPEG. The technique has some other important applications, such as fax transmission.

ALGORITHMS WALK THROUGH: DYNAMIC PROGRAMMING APPROACHES

Dynamic programming is a programming method that applies to problems whose solution can be build dynamically, in time. The decisions that lead to finding the result of a given task may be taken step by step, based on decisions from preceding steps. Usually, dynamic programming is suitable for problems requiring the computation of an optimal value (minimum or maximum), following a decision making process that takes place in stages. This starts from an initial state and at each step a decision that results in a new state is made, until the final optional solution is reached.

Generally, the steps of solving a task using dynamic programming are as follows:

1. Identifying sub-problems

2. Choosing a structure to hold the solutions to the sub-problems

3. Determining the recurrence relations that characterize the optimal solution to the sub-problems.

4. Solving the recurrence using a bottom-up approach (from the smallest sub-problem to the initial problem).

DYNAMIC PROGRAMMING: EXAMPLE – LONGEST COMMON SUBSEQUENCE

The longest common subsequence problem is defined as follows:

Let $X = (x1, x2, ..., xn)$ and $Y = (y1, y2, ..., ym)$, i.e. two arrays of integers. Determine the subsequence of the biggest length that appears in both arrays. For example, for the arrays $(1, 2, 7, 3, 4, 8, 5)$ and $(1, 2, 3, 4, 5)$, the longest subsequence is $(1, 2, 3, 4, 5)$.

The dynamic programming approach for solving this problem is as follows:

1. The sub-problems are defined as follows: Determine the longest common subsequence starting from position i in X and j in Y.

2. Choose an appropriate data structure for storing partial solutions to the sub-problems. In this case, a bi-dimensional array (a matrix) is what we need. We construct $L(n+1, m+1)$ and define it as follows:
   ▷ $L[i][j]$ = longest common subsequence beginning at position i in X and j in Y.

3. Find the recurrence relation. For the purpose of this task this can be defined like:
   a) $L[i][0] = 0$ for all values of i

b) L[0][j] = 0 for all values of j

c) L[i][j] = L[i-1][j-1] + 1, if X[i]=Y[j]
= max(L[i-1][j], L[i][j-1]), otherwise

Notice that points a and b represent the two base cases of the recurrent formula established in point c. What point c really tells us is that if we have reached two values that are equal in the two given arrays then the length of the longest subsequence at the current position can be obtained by adding 1 to the length of the longest substring at the previous position. Otherwise (if the elements at the current position are not equal) then we keep the maximum value obtained so far in one of the previous steps (either i-1 or j-1). The solution to the initial problem will be stored in l[n - 1][m - 1] (-1 because we index the arrays from 0).

The algorithm that uses these three points works in $O(n * m)$, as only one iteration over the two-dimensional array is required. Here is how the code looks like in C++:

```
1.    int longest (int x[], int y[])
2.    {
3.        for (int i = 0; i < n; i++)   // base case 1
4.                L[i][0] = 0;
5.        for (int j = 0; j < m; j++) // base case 2
6.                L[0][j] = 0;
7.
8.        // apply the formula
9.        for (int i = 1; i < n; i++)
10.               for (int j = 1; j < m; j++)
11.                   if (x[i] == y[j])
12.                       L[i][j] = L[i-1][j-1] + 1;
13.                   else
14.                       L[i][j] = max(L[i-1][j], L[i][j-1]);
15.
16.       return L[n - 1][m - 1];
17.   }
```

Consider x = (2 2 3 9 8 7 6 8 6 5 5 7 8 9 7 6 5 3) and y = (1 2 3 9 1 4 5 5 7)

The function described above will return 6, which is the length of the longest common subsequence of the two arrays (bolded above). The idea of a subsequence is that if we eliminate all the elements that are not bolded we would obtain two equivalent arrays. (2, 3, 9, 5, 5, 7) is the longest subsequence with this property.

The algorithm for finding the longest common subsequence is commonly used in various biology applications, out of which perhaps the most famous is matching the DNA of multiple organisms.

DYNAMIC PROGRAMMING:
EXAMPLE – MATRIX MULTIPLICATION

Let A[m][n] and B[n][p] be two matrices. We already know that for multiplying them we need to perform m * n * p multiplications. What if we actually need to multiply 3 or more matrices? Dynamic programming offers an approach to reduce the number of operations required in this situation.

Take, for example, a[10][100], b[100][5] and c[5][50].

(AB)C would require 10 * 100 * 5 + 10 * 5 * 50 = 7500 multiplications. On the other hand,

A(BC) would require 100 * 5 * 50 + 10 * 100 * 50 = 75000 multiplications, i.e. 10 times more operations to be executed.

However, we already know that matrix multiplication is associative ((AB)C = A(BC)). This means that we could actually save on execution time by finding an optimal order of execution for the multiplications. We will describe the dynamic programming approach for this task step by step, on the following example:

Suppose we have to multiply the following matrices: M1[2][4], M2[4][5], M3[5][1], M4[1][10], M5[10][3].

The steps for the algorithm are as follows:

1. Define the array m[n][n], where n is the number of matrices that we want to multiply (5 in our example), and m[i][j] represents the minimum number of multiplications required for computing the Mi*Mi+1, ..., * Mj. For example, m[2][3] is the number of multiplications required to multiply M2 * M3.

2. Furthermore, suppose d[n] is the array storing the dimensions of the matrices, such that Mi has d[i-1] rows and d[i] columns. In order to be able to multiply two matrices, they must share a common dimension, which is why we only need a 1D array to store their sizes. For our example, d[] = {2, 4, 5, 1, 10, 3}.

3. Start with two base cases are as follows:

    a) m[i][i] = 0, for all values of i – there is no multiplication required between position i and itself, i.e. m[1][1] = the number of multiplications required to compute M1, which is 0.

    b) m[i][i+1] = d[i-1] * d[i] * d[i+1], for all values of i – the number of multiplication of any two consecutive matrices; for example (m[2][3] = the number of multiplications required for M2 * M3 = d[1] * d[2] * d[3] = 4 * 5 * 1 = 20.

4. Apply the following formula for the rest of the matrix:

a) m[i][i+d] = min(m[i][k] + m[k+1][i+d] + d[i-1] * d[k] * d[i+d]), i < k < i + d.

b) For example, suppose we have to compute m[2][5] (the number of multiplications required for M2 * M3 * M4 * M5. Applying the formula above gives m[2][5] = min(m[2][3] + m[4][5] + d[1] * d[3] * d[5], m[2][4] + m[5][5] + d[1] * d[4] * d[5]).

c) Let's analyze m[2][3] + m[4][5] + d[1] * d[3] * d[5].

d) m[2][3] is the number of multiplications required to compute M2 * M3

e) m[4][5] is the number of multiplications required to compute M4 * M5

f) d[1] * d[3] * d[5] is the number of multiplications required to compute (M2 * M3) * (M4 * M5).

g) Hence this first term corresponds to (M2 * M3) * (M4 * M5).

h) If we do a similar analysis for the second term we would see that it corresponds to M2 * (M3 * M4) * M5.

i) Therefore, according to this formula, the minimum number of multiplications required to compute M2 * M3 * M4 * M5 is the minimum out of the number of the multiplications required to compute (M2 * M3) * (M4 * M5) and the one required for M2 * (M3 * M4) * M5.

After the algorithm is complete, the required value will be stored in m[1][n], i.e. the minimum number of operations required to multiply M1*M2*...*Mn.

Suppose we have are given 4 matrices, with the dimensions defined by the following array:

(13 5 89 3 34) (A[13][5], B[5][89], C[89][3], D[3][34]).

The program built by following the steps above will return 2856, which is the lowest number of operations required to perform the multiplication of the four matrices, which corresponds to *(A(BC))D. The complexity of this algorithm is O(n3).

DYNAMIC PROGRAMMING: EXAMPLE – THE TRAVELLING SALESMAN PROBLEM

The travelling salesman problem (often abbreviated to TSP) can be defined as follows:

Given: a list of locations and the distance between each two

Find: the shortest path that starts from one location, visits every other location exactly once and returns to the initial location.

For the purpose of the dynamic programming example, suppose we always start from location 0 and the distance between every two locations i and j, given by the matrix d[i][j]. Here are the steps the dynamic programming algorithm would perform for this task:

1. Define the string visited, of length n (the number of locations), composed of only 0s and 1s, showing whether a certain location has been visited or not. For example, if 4 destinations were given visited="1111" means all destinations have been visited at the current step.

2. Define the array best[visited][end], which stores the shortest path from the start to end for the configuration defined by 'visited'. For example, best["1101"][2] means "the shortest path from the start location to location 2, by visiting only locations 1, 2 and 4".

3. We use the following formula to populate the array for every value of 'visited':

   a) best[visited][end] = min(best[subset − "end"][i] + dist[i][end]), $1 <= i <= n$, i != end.

   b) For example, let's see how we would compute best ["1110"][3], which is the shortest path from start to location 3, by visiting only locations 1,2 and 3.

      i. According to the formula, we would obtain the following: best["1110"][3] = min(best["1100"][1] + dist[1][3], best["1100"][2] + dist[2][3], best["1100"][4] + dist[4][3]).

      ii. In English, this would be expressed as the minimum out of:

         • The shortest path so far to location 1 + the distance from 1 to 3;

         • The shortest path so far to location 2 + the distance from 2 to 3;

         • The shortest path so far to location 4 + the distance from 4 to 3;

Basically, what this formula tells us is that the shortest path to the current node is the one obtained by summing the distance to an intermediate node i and the distance from i to the node we are trying to reach.

The final result would then be given by best["111..1" (n times)][end] (the shortest path from the starting location to the final location when all the nodes have been visited) + distance[end][0] (because we also need to return to the origin).

In order to make the implementation simple, instead of using a string as an index to the matrix we can use an integer with the same properties. In our example "0000" would correspond to 0, "0001" would correspond to 1, "0010" would correspond to 2, ..., "1111" would correspond to 15. This algorithm has complexity O(2n).

ALGORITHMS WALK THROUGH: STRING ALGORITHMS

In the following lines we will revise some of the most common algorithms involving strings, which you may encounter in your career as a programmer. We will go through some examples and we will also discuss when it is best to use every such algorithm.

STRING ALGORITHMS: TRIE

A trie tree (from "retrieve") is a tree used for storing strings of different lengths that share some common prefixes. The nodes of such a data structure do not contain data and a string is a path from the root to a leaf node or some internal nodes. A trie is not a binary tree. The number of successors of a node is equal to the number of distinct character in the strings stored.

The following picture shows a trie storing the strings (words): cup, sing, curve, singer, small, ball.

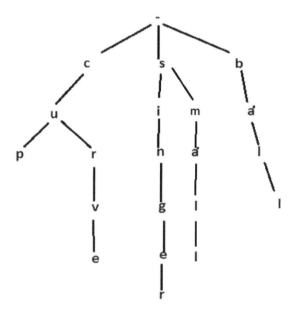

The advantages of a trie tree are as follows:

- They enable fast retrieval of a given string or checking whether a given string is part of a dictionary; the number of comparisons is determined only by the length of the string searched for, regardless of the number of strings stored in the dictionary. This can be important when building a spellchecker-like program, which requires checking whether each word belongs to a dictionary;

- Determining the longest prefix of a given string is also fast when using a trie;
- Trie structures offer a significant reduction of storage space if arrays are used instead of pointers.

The trie data structure has lead to the formation of suffix trees, which are a particular case of this data structure. The property that makes suffix trees different is that they hold each of the suffixes of a word. For example, the tree for the word "carpet" would hold "carpet", "arpet", "rpet", "pet", "et", and "t". Suffix trees are particularly useful when trying to search for substrings of a given string.

STRING ALGORITHMS: NAÏVE STRING MATCHING

The problem of searching for the occurrence of a string inside another can be solved using a naïve approach. This involves checking whether the string we are looking for can appear at each of the positions in the bigger string. Searching for an instance of "aab" in a string such as "aabaaaabbaabba" would take 15 * 3 steps (the size of the big string x the size of the smaller one). The complexity of this approach is therefore O(n*m).

STRING ALGORITHMS: THE KNUTH-MORRIS-PRATT ALGORITHM

The Knuth-Morris-Pratt algorithm (commonly referred to as KMP) is an improvement for the naïve string matching approach and is based on the following idea: when a mismatch is detected, we have already iterated through some positions in the big string. We can use this information to set the new index to a position where we know the small string can be found, rather than going back to characters we have already discovered as part of the search, like in the naïve approach.

Let's consider the example presented above again. When we look for "aab" in "aabaaaabbaabba"and we check the position in bold, we already know that the following two letters cannot represent the start of "aab" because we have already iterated through them once. We then set resume searching at the position in red (the next 'a' character). The complexity of KMP is reduced to O(n + m).

The steps of the KMP algorithm are as follows:

1. Compute the function array prefix[m] for the string we are looking for (the smaller string). prefix[i] has the following meaning: the length of the longest prefix matching a suffix of the substring that starts at 0 and ends at i.

   a) For example, let's compute this array for "ababab":

i. prefix[0] = 0 (the substring is "a", so the length of the longest prefix matching a suffix is 0).

ii. prefix[1] = 0 (the substring is "ab", there is still no prefix that matches a suffix)

iii. prefix[2] = 1 (the substring is "aba", the longest prefix matching a suffix is "a", which has the length 1).

iv. prefix[3] = 2 (the substring is "abab", the longest prefix matching a suffix is "ab", which has the length 2).

v. prefix[4] = 3 (the substring is "ababa", the prefix matching a suffix is "aba").

vi. prefix[5] = 4 (the substring is "ababab", the prefix matching a suffix is "abab").

2. Place the smaller string (the one we are looking for) under the bigger one (we will call it this one a template). Start matching until a mismatch occurs. In case of a mismatch there are two situations:

   a) If the mismatch occurs at the first position in the smaller string then just shift it one position to the right;

   b) Otherwise, if the mismatch occurs at position j (j > 0), shift it j – prefix[j - 1] positions to the right.

3. If there is a match, just shift the smaller string one position to the right and continue matching.

Suppose we want to find "ababab" in "abaabababa".

a	b	a	a	b	a	b	a	b	a
a	b	a	b	a	b				

The first mismatch occurs in the column marked with red, at position 3 (remember, we are indexing from 0). prefix[2] = 1, so we shift "ababab" to the right 3 -1 = 2 positions, as follows:

a	b	a	a	b	a	b	a	b	a
		a	b	a	b	a	b		

This time a mismatch occurs at character 1 in the smaller string, so we shift it 1 – prefix[0] = 1 position.

a	b	a	a	b	a	b	a	b	a
			a	b	a	b	a	b	

A match occurs. We note this and then shift the smaller string one position to the right.

a	b	a	a	b	a	b	a	b	a
			a	b	a	b	a	b	

There is a mismatch at the first character, but the algorithm ends because the length of the template has now been reached.

STRING ALGORITHMS: RABIN-KARP ALGORITHM

The Rabin-Karp algorithm is a string matching algorithm that uses hashing techniques. When searching for a string of length m in a string of length n the best case complexity of this algorithm is O(n). On the other hand, the worst case complexity is still O(n*m), just as the naïve approach, which is the main reason why the algorithm is not widely used.

The first thing you need to know about the Rabin-Karp technique is that uses a hash function to convert any string into a numerical value, exploiting the property according to which any two equal strings have the same hash value. One of the most common hash functions used by Rabin-Karp is the one that uses the ASCII value of the characters in a string to convert the string into a number in base q.

For example, if the string to be converted is "abc" and q = 101, then "abc" = 97 * 101^2 + 98 * 101 + 99 (97 is the ASCII value for 'a', while 98 corresponds to 'b' and 99 corresponds to 'c' in the same system).

Suppose we are looking for "abc" in "ababcdab". The steps are as follows:

1. Choose a reasonable value for base q, as described above. This value is usually a prime number and for the purpose of this example we will use 13. A prime number is used for the same reason it is used in most hashing functions, mainly because it provides an even distribution across the hash space.

2. Compute the value of the smaller string, as described above. In our example, abc = 97 * 13^2 + 98* 13 + 99.

3. Take each substring of length m in the bigger string and compute its value. Try to match only at the positions that produce the same value as our template. For example we want to skip the first position in the larger string because "aba" = 97 * 13^2 + 98 * 13 + 97, which is different from what we obtained for "abc".

Note that, as the values can get quite large when converting from strings to integers, it is a common practice to choose a number m and perform a %m operation on all the values computed using the algorithm.

STRING ALGORITHMS: THE BOYER-MOORE ALGORITHM

One last algorithm we will be discussing for string search is the Boyer-Moore algorithm. The idea behind this approach is that it iterates through the bigger string from right to left. Consider the following example:

Find "ababac" in "abbdbeababacad". We firstly align the strings as follows:

abbdbeababacad

ababac

We compare 'c' with 'e'. Since 'e' does not appear in the string we are searching for, so we know the match cannot occur for any of the positions 0, ..., 5. Therefore we can move the smaller string 6 positions to the right, as follows:

abbdbeababacadc

      ababac

Again, we compare 'c' with 'c', 'a' with 'a', and so on, until we notice that a matching has occurred. Next, we move one position to the right.

abbdbeababacadc

      ababac

We compare 'c' with 'a' and, since a match does not occur, this means in theory we could move 5 positions to the right again. The algorithm stops here because this means we would exceed the capacity of the bigger string.

ALGORITHMS WALK THROUGH: NP-COMPLETENESS ALGORITHMS

The algorithms we use to solve programming tasks are deterministic. This means that at any given time the evolution of the algorithm is uniquely determined, and is specified by the instruction to be executed in a particular moment. There is another category of algorithms, however, which bring a great theoretical value. Non-deterministic algorithms are not directly applicable, but their study raises some important concepts.

The definition for the correctness of non-deterministic algorithms is the first surprising aspect about these. Such an algorithm is correct if there is a possibility that it finds the right answer after its execution. Take a look at the following example of a non-deterministic algorithm that searches for the exit in a maze:

```
1.  exit (current_position) ->
2.      if (there is no wall to the north)
3.              current_position = north of current_position;
4.      or if (there is no wall to the south)
5.              current_position = south of current_position;
6.      or if (there is no wall to the east)
7.              current_position = east of current_position;
8.      or if (there is no wall to the west)
9.              current_position = west of current_position;
10.  end
```

Briefly, the algorithm behaves like this: if there is no wall to the north go north, or maybe if there is no wall to the south move south and the same for east, or west. What makes it non-deterministic is that the direction of movement is not specified. It is clear that if there's an exit and it can be reached, there is a suite of applications of these rules that leads to the exit.

The practical utility of such an algorithm is not immediately apparent and it is clear that such algorithms cannot be directly implemented on a programmable machine. In reality, however, the existence of non-deterministic algorithms shows us that a problem can be solved algorithmically.

Secondly, one can show that any deterministic algorithm can be transformed into a deterministic one automatically. Once we know how to solve a problem in a deterministic way, we can solve it deterministically too! The transformation is relatively simple. For the example above, this would mean trying every direction step by step. This is often known as "flood fill".

The class of all problems that can be solved by non-deterministic algorithms in polynomial time is denoted by NP (non-deterministic polynomial). It is clear that any problem that is in P is also in NP, because non-deterministic algorithms are only an extreme case of the deterministic ones. On the other hand, it is thought NP problems are not solvable in polynomial time. This is one of the most important debates in modern computer science, as it is still unclear whether the P complexity class is different from NP. What we do know for sure that for every NP problem we can write a program that runs in polynomial time that can check whether the solution produced by a non-deterministic algorithm is actually correct.

NP-COMPLETENESS ALGORITHMS: NP-COMPLETENESS

Before explaining what NP-Completeness actually means, let's explain the concept of NP-hardness first. NP-hard is the class of problems that are "at least as hard as all the problems in NP". The NP-complete class, on the other hand, contains the NP-hard problems that are in NP. The following diagram will help you get the picture:

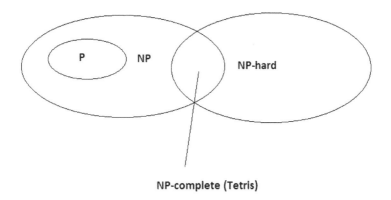

NP-complete (Tetris)

Another aspect worth mentioning is that the NP-Complete complexity class is a class of decision problems. Decision problems are those problems that, given an input, output "yes" or "no". Take, for example, Tetris. Determining whether a player can survive on a Tetris board given a configuration of pieces is a decision problem. There is no efficient way to compute the order of moves the player can make in order to survive, so the task is NP-hard.

However, we could certainly write a program that runs in polynomial time to simulate the way the player has arranged the given pieces and check whether they survived or not. This means Tetris is also in NP because, as mentioned above, for any problem in NP we can write a program in polynomial time to check whether a solution holds or not. But since it is also NP-hard, we can say Tetris is NP-complete.

Finally, it has been observed that some instances of known problems that are normally not in NP are part of this complexity class. For example, the classic knapsack problem can be solved in polynomial time with various methods, including a greedy approach or dynamic programming. However, the decision problem form of knapsack (i.e. Can a value V be achieved without going over a given weight W?) appears to be part of the NP-complete class, as there is no algorithm that can solve this problem in polynomial time. The same can be said about graph coloring, for example.

DATA STRUCTURE WALK THROUGH: ARRAY

There are various problems that can be solved using arrays as data structures. The first thing to know about arrays is that generally the memory used by arrays is static and is allocated at compile time. Arrays can be regarded as a contiguous block, split into sections. The size of the block determines the number of elements that can be stored inside it. For example, a block of 80 bytes can hold up to 20 integers, since each 32-bit integer occupies 4 bytes in the memory.

In addition to this property of contiguity, there are a couple of key points that would be useful to remember when it comes to arrays, as follows:

1. Arrays can be declared on compile time both as an empty block and with pre-defined elements. In the first case, we just need to specify the maximum number of elements the array will hold (e.g. int array[10]), while in the second case we would write int array[]={0, 1, 2, 3, 4, 5, 6, 7, 8, 9}.

2. Alternatively, we can define arrays using a combination of the methods we have described. The declaration a[10] = {0, 1, 2, 3, 4, 5, 6, 7, 8, 9, 10} is also considered valid.

3. There is a way to declare arrays dynamically, but the exact size of the block also needs to be known. In C, for example, such a declaration would be *array = (int *) malloc (10 * sizeof(int)). Sizeof is the function that returns the exact size of the type given as a parameter.

4. We can always use the name of the array to refer to the base address of the memory we have allocated. For the declaration array[10] = {0, 1, 2, 3, 4, 5, 6, 7, 8, 9} a[0] points to 0, a[1] points to 1 and so on. Furthermore, *(arr) will also give 0, while *(arr + 1) will give 1. * is used to retrieve the value at the given address.

5. In C/C++, array indexing starts from 0, so for example, if we declare an array of 10 elements, the indexes corresponding to these will be 0, 1, 2, ..., 9.

6. As opposed to linked lists, we can retrieve an element at a given index in O(1) (e.g. array[4]). In the case of linked lists the index is usually not hold in the memory, so there is no way to refer to it.

7. If needed, resizing the array can be done as follows:

    a) Define a new array, larger than the initial one;

    b) Copy the contents from the initial array to the array just defined;

    c) Free up the memory occupied by the initial array.

   It is also worth mentioning that certain programming languages provide methods to do this automatically (in C, for example, we can always use realloc).

8. When deleting an element from the array we usually have to shift every element after the one deleted to the left to fill the gap. The size of the memory needed by the array is not shrunk automatically.

9. Inserting and modifying an element in the array can simply be done using the "=" attribute (for example, array[4] = 10).

10. Inserting an element into an array can easily be done at the end of the array, but if the task requires the insertion at a certain index, then we need to shift the elements after this index to the right.

11. Arrays can be of multiple dimensions, which may be useful if the task we are given requires this. For example, a two-dimensional array (a matrix) can be defined as int matrix[10][10] and used in a similar manner as a regular array.

ARRAY: EXAMPLE –
FINDING THE MAXIMUM VALUE IN AN ARRAY

A classic example of a task requiring the use of an array is finding the maximum / minimum value of the elements it holds. In this example we will consider finding the maximum value. The steps for doing this are as follows:

1. Consider the first value in the array is the maximum value.
2. Iterate through all the remaining values and update the maximum as soon as we find an element that is larger than it.

In C++, the code would be as follows:

```
1.   int maximum(int array[], int N) // N is the number of items
     in the array
2.   {
3.      int max = array[0];
4.      for (int i = 1; i < N; i++)
5.             if (array[i] > max)
6.                     max = array[i];
7.      return max;
8.   }
```

ARRAY: THE "VECTOR" TYPE

In addition to the standard representation of an array, which was discussed above, there is another way of declaring and working with arrays. This is by using the data structure known as vector. The main differences between an array and a data structure of type vector are as follows:

- The memory necessary for storing a vector is allocated dynamically, so there is no need to know the maximum number of elements that need to be stored in the vector in advance.

- When iterating through a vector we can either use an integer for each position or a special object, of type iterator; an iterator is basically a pointer which, if set to the first element in a vector, can iterate through the other elements.

- The vector data type is directly available in the Standard Template Library (STL) of C++.

- Declaring an element of such a type can be done by vector <type> name (e.g. vector <int> v).

- Insertion into a vector is performed by using pre-defined functions (e.g. in C++ this is done with push_back(element), which adds an element at the end of the data structure).

- Deleting all the elements in the vector can also be done with pre-defined functions (e.g. in C++ this is usually through v.clear()).

- Operators such as "=" or "==" can be used directly on variables of type vector, without the need to iterate through all the elements, which is one of the benefits of using vector instead of regular arrays.

- Here are some other functions that you may find useful:

  ▷ The empty() function returns true if the vector is empty, false otherwise;

  ▷ The size() function returns the size of the vector;

  ▷ An element can be accessed either as in a usual array or by using v.at(index);

Here is an example program in C++ that makes use of the vector type:

```
1.    #include <cstdio>
2.    #include <vector>
3.
4.    using namespace std;
5.
6.    int main()
7.    {
8.        vector <int> v1, v2;
9.
10.       v1.push_back(1);  v1.push_back(2);  v1.push_back(3);
11.       v2.push_back(1);  v2.push_back(2);  v2.push_back(4);
12.
13.       // print the contents of v1
14.       for (int i = 0; i < v1.size(); i++)
15.               printf("%d ", v1[i]);
16.       // compare the two vectors
17.       if (v1 == v2)
18.               printf("The two vectors are equal!");
19.       else
20.               v1 = v2;
21.       return 0;
22.   }
```

DATA STRUCTURE WALK THROUGH: STRINGS

Strings are a particular case of arrays, holding only data of type char. They are therefore often referred to as arrays of characters. Most of the properties we have discussed in the previous chapter apply to strings as well (for example, we can declare strings as char string[20]), but there are also some special properties that you will need to take into account. Some of these properties are as follows:

• PROGRAMMING SKILLS •

1. Since strings are generally variable in length, a convention was established, which tells us that the last character of a string is always '\ 0', which is known as the terminator sequence; thus, a string declared as char string [10] would actually hold a maximum of only 9 characters, as the last one is reserved for this special sequence.

2. In C and C++, there are a number of features that assist the programmer when it comes to working with strings. These functions require the inclusion of the string.h header file. All these features assume that the strings they are used with have '\0' in the end.

3. Generally, strings are composed of single-byte characters. However, if we need to hold characters that require more than one byte of memory (multi-byte characters), we can either encode the special characters by mapping each of them to a number (many such mappings already exist), or use one of the libraries that facilitate working with such characters. One of these libraries is known as ICU(International Components for Unicode) and can be accessed at http://site.icu-project.org/.

We may wish to use multi-byte characters in a string when we want to work with characters from a language such as Chinese or Japanese. These characters are not part of the standard 8-biy encoding system, which only allows 255 characters. For example, the character '\u0B95' (க) requires no less than 3 bytes of memory. Perhaps the simplest way to work with multi-byte characters in C++ would be to use the chart16_t data type, as follows:

```
1.   char16_t testing[40];
2.   testing[0] = u'\u0B95';
3.   testing[1] = u'\u0BA3';
4.   testing[2] = u'\u0B82';
5.   testing[3] = u'\0';
```

STRINGS: MAJOR STRING FUNCTIONS

In the C/C++ string.h library, there are a couple of very useful string functions every programmer needs to be aware of when writing code in this language. These are as follows:

- strlen(char s[]) – takes a string as a parameter and returns its length; this is not equal to the size of the memory allocated at compile time, but to the number of characters preceding the '\0' at the end of the string;

- strcpy(char s1[], char s2[]) – takes two strings as parameters and copies the contents of the second one (in this case s2) to the first one (s2 in this case).

- strcat(char s1[], char s2[]) – similar to strcpy, but instead of copying the contents of the second string in the first one, this function appends it. For example, strcat("program", "ming") would change the first string to "programming".

- strcmp(char s1[], char s2[]) – takes two strings as parameters and compares them, returning one of the following results:

  ▷ if the first string is larger or lexicographically bigger than the second one, a value bigger than 0 is returned;

  ▷ if the two strings are equal the function returns 0;

  ▷ if the first string is smaller in size or lexicographically smaller than the second one, a value smaller than 0 is returned.

- strstr(char s1[], char s2[]) – searches for the occurrence of s2 in s1 and returns a pointer to the first position where s2 is found or NULL if s2 does not appear in s1.

- strchr(char s1[], char c) – searches for character c in the string s1 and returns a pointer to the first position where c is found or NULL if c does not appear in s1 at all.

- strrev(char s[]) – reverses the contents of the string given as a parameter.

STRINGS: EXAMPLE –
CHARACTER FREQUENCY IN A STRING

Suppose that we are given a sentence represented by a string and we want to compute how many times each letter in the alphabet appears in the sentence. The following code performs this:

```
1.   void frequency(char s[])
2.   {
3.       int frequency[26]; // there are 26 letters in the alphabet
4.       for (int i = 0; i < strlen(s); i++)
5.               if (s[i] >= 'a' && s[i] <='z') // if s[i] is a
                 lowercase letter
6.                       frequency[s[i] - 'a']++;
7.               else if (s[i] >='A' && s[i] <= 'Z') // if s[i] is
                 an upper-case letter
8.                       frequency[s[i]-'A']++;
9.   }
```

An additional thing to mention for this example would be that by subtracting two characters we will always obtain an integer. For example, if s[i] == 'b', s[i] – 'a' would return 1. The explanation behind this is that the program subtracts the ASCII codes of the two characters.

DATA STRUCTURE WALK THROUGH: STACKS

A stack, is a structure of type LIFO (Last In First Out) and is a particular case of linear list in which all insertions and deletions are made at one end of the list, called the top of the stack. This node can be accessed, modified or delete. In the case of insertion, the newly inserted node becomes the head of the stack.

In order to understand the mechanics of a stack, it would be useful to picture this data structure as a pile of books. Once you form such a structure you only have direct access to the element at the top of the pile. This is the only element that can be removed or replaced. Here are some points to remember about stacks:

- A stack can be implemented as a linear list for which the access operations (insertion, deletion, access element) are restricted as follows:
    ▷ Insertion is only performed at the top of the stack, with the inserted element becoming the top of the stack.
    ▷ Accessing an element and deletion can only be performed on the last element added to the list;
- A stack can be implemented using a static (array) or dynamic (linked list) data structure; in the static approach, great attention need to be paid to the storage space allocated to the stack. A **stack overflow** occurs when we are trying to add an element to a stack that is already full. In this case we need to perform a deletion before the insertion.
- When it comes to stacks, the insertion is commonly referred to as a "push" operation, while "pop" describes a deletion operation.

Here is an example that will help you visualize this data structure better:

push(9)	push(8)	pop()	push(10)	pop()
	8		10	
9	9	9	9	9

STACKS: EXAMPLE –
EVALUATING MATHEMATICAL EXPRESSIONS

Normally, computers cannot tell the difference between expressions such as (4 * 2) + 3 and 4 * (2 + 3), which are written in the so-called infix form. In order to make this possible, we need to translate such mathematical expressions into a computer-understandable representation. There are two forms that have this property: the prefix and the infix form. Here is how to obtain these two forms from an expression written in infix:

- The main idea behind the **prefix form** is that each operator must be placed right before the two terms it is applied to. For example, the translation for the infix expression a + b in prefix is + a b. Let's look at a more complicated example. Consider the expression mentioned above, (4 * 2) + 3. The steps for its conversion into prefix are as follows:

  ▷ First, the operation in brackets is converted to * 4 2, by applying the rule mentioned above.

  ▷ Next, the final operation to be performed is a + applied to the term in brackets and the term '3', so we write it as + (* 4 2) 3. In prefix and postfix there is no need to use brackets, so the final form is + * 4 2 3. The computer will automatically know the multiplication needs to be performed before the addition, because '*' directly precedes two numbers.

- The process is similar for the **postfix** form of an expression. Consider 4 * (2 + 3):

  ▷ The first operation to be performed is the addition, which we write at 2 3 +.

  ▷ Next, the multiplication operator is applied to '4' and the term in the previous step, so the final postfix form is 4 2 3 + *.

We have so far looked at the conversion from infix to prefix and postfix, respectively. But what if we want to convert from prefix to postfix, for example? One of the simplest algorithms of converting a mathematical expression from its prefix notation into postfix uses a stack. The steps of this algorithm are as follows:

- Iterate through the expression in prefix and add any operator encountered along the way to the stack; if the value encountered is a term, on the other hand, output it.

- For every two terms outputted perform a pop() operation on the stack and output its head.

Take, for example, + * 4 2 3. The algorithm starts with the empty stack s={} and then behaves as follows:

- Add '+' and '*' to the stack, as they are operators;

- Output 4 and 2. Now that we have outputted two terms, also output the head of the stack, which is '*'. The output at this step is 4 2 *. This is now regarded as a single term.

- Output 3. This term and the one in the previous step count as two terms, so we perform another pop() operation on the stack. The final output is 4 2 * 3 +, which is the postfix notation corresponding to the given expression in prefix.

- The algorithm is now over, as there are no other elements to iterate over.

DATA STRUCTURE WALK THROUGH: QUEUES

A queue is a structure of type FIFO (First In First Out), in which all insertions are made at one end (called the head of the queue) and all deletions are performed at the other end (commonly referred to as the tail of the queue). The following properties apply to queues in general and it is best for any programmer to be aware of them:

- In order to represent a queue we need two pointers, one for the head and the other for the tail of this data structure; the two addresses these pointers point to are usually apart, but in the case of a **circular queue** they are located next to each other (the element immediately following the tail of the queue is its head).

- In a static approach, a queue can be implemented using an array. In this case, we need to integers, one for indicating the beginning of the queue and one showing its end; hence when we perform an insertion we add the element to the end of the array and increment the corresponding index, while a deletion only requires increasing the index pointing to the start of the queue.

- In a dynamic approach, a queue can be implemented using a simple linked list; again, in this case, we need to have two separate pointers, for each end of the data structure;

- As opposed to stacks, the insertion operation is commonly referred to as enqueue() and the deletion as dequeue().

The following picture will hopefully help you have a clearer idea about how a queue works:

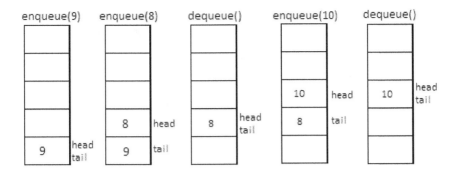

QUEUES:
PRIORITY QUEUES AND DOUBLE-ENDED QUEUES

A priority queue is a special case of queue, in which every element has a priority associated with it. Thus the elements with a highest priority are served first. Otherwise, if two elements have the same priority the properties of the regular queue hold. A priority queue is usually implemented with a heap.

Double-ended queues, on the other hand, are often referred to as dequeues (pronounced "decks") and enable the insertion or deletion at both ends. Such a data structure may be useful for solving problems such as task scheduling.

QUEUES: EXAMPLE – SIMULATING CHECK-OUT LINES

Suppose customers queue up for the self check-out machines of a supermarket. A program that simulates this uses a queue and performs the following steps:

- Once a new customer joins the check-out queue, he / she is added to the tail of the data structure.
- Once a check-out machine becomes available the customer at the head of the queue has priority and can use the machine.

DATA STRUCTURE WALK THROUGH: LINKED LISTS

Arrays are simple and efficient data structures to store objects in a certain order, but they also have disadvantages, being often not very adaptable. For example, inserting and deleting items is difficult because the elements in the array need to be moved to accommodate the insertion or to fill the gaps that result after deleting an element. Therefore we often need an alternative data structure.

A single linked list is a collection of nodes arranged in a linear order (but not in successive locations in memory - as in the case of vectors). Each node has at least a pointer to the next node, which we often call "next" by convention. The first node is called the head of the list and the last node is called the tail, but of course there is no strict rule on these names.

A single linked list is called as such because each node only stores one pointer to the next node. Unlike vectors, the list does not have a fixed size, being easily scalable by adding or deleting nodes. Think of a node as an object (item) that contains some information and a link to the next object. To signal the end of the list we mark the "next" pointer of the last object by NULL. Here is a picture that will help you picture a single linked list better:

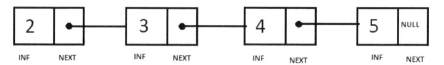

Here is how to perform an insertion or deletion operation on the list:

- To insert an element into a single linked we perform the following steps:

    ▷ if we want to perform the insertion at the end of the list we simply link the last element in the list with the newly created element; the image below shows the addition of '6' at the end of the list above:

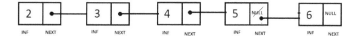

    ▷ if we want to perform the insertion between any two nodes all we need to do is alter the "next" field of the node after we are inserting to point to the new element and make the new element point to the next one in the list.

- Deletion is even simpler than insertion, as we only need to modify the "next" field of the element before the one deleted.

    ▷ If we want to delete the first element in a list all we need to do is move the head of the list to the address specified by the 'next' pointer of the first element. The first element will therefore be omitted.

    ▷ If we want to delete the last element of the list we simply assign 'NULL' to the "next" pointer of the next to last element in the list. This will make it the last element in the list.

    ▷ Finally, if the element we want to delete is not the first or last element of the list we need to make the element before it to point to the element after it. The following picture illustrates the deletion of 4 from the initial list:

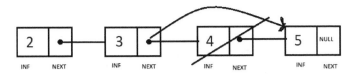

In C/C++, a list is normally represented with a 'struct', as follows:

```
1.   struct node
2.   {
3.       type inf;  // the information
4.       node *next; // the pointer to the next object
5.   } *list;
```

Note that we only hold a pointer to the first location of the list. One of the disadvantages that arise from this is that we cannot access an element at a given index directly as in the case of arrays. We have to start from the head of the list and iterate in order to access it.

LINKED LISTS: EXAMPLE – DELETING AN GIVEN ELEMENT FROM A SINGLE LINKED LIST

The following function searches for a given value in a single linked list and deletes it once found. The list is defined in the manner described above.

```
1.   void delete (node *list, int value)
2.   {
3.       // if the list is empty do nothing
4.       if (list == NULL) return;
5.
6.       // if the value is contained by the first element move the
         head of the list
7.       if (list -> inf == value)
8.       {
9.           list = list -> next;
10.          return;
11.      }
12.
13.      // all the other cases
14.      for (node *current = list; current -> next != NULL;
         current = current -> next)
15.      {
16.          if (listIndex -> next -> inf == value)  // if
             the value of the next element is the one we are
             looking for skip it
17.          {
18.              if(listIndex -> next -> next != NULL) // if
                 element is not the last one
```

```
19.                         listIndex -> next = listIndex ->
                            next -> next;
20.                 else    // at this step the element is the
                    last one
21.                         listIndex -> next = NULL;
22.             }
23.     }
24.
25. }
```

LINKED LISTS: DOUBLE LINKED LISTS

The concept of a double linked list is similar to the one of the single linked list. The only difference is that each node has a connection to two other nodes, the one preceding it and the one after it. This time we have to assign null to the "prev" field of the first element and the "next" field of the last one, as in the following picture:

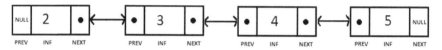

The operations of insertion, deletion or searching for an element are performed in a similar way to single linked lists, but we need to take into account that there are two pointers associated with each element.

LINKED LISTS: EXAMPLE – REVERSING A DOUBLE LINKED LIST

Suppose a double linked list is defined as follows:

```
1.  struct node
2.  {
3.      int inf;
4.      node *prev, *next;
5.  } *list;
```

Here is a C++ function that returns the reversed list:

```
1.  node * reverse_list(node *list)
2.  {
3.      node *reversed_list;
4.
5.      node *last = list;
6.      while (last -> next) last = last -> next; // after the loop
        'last' will point to the last element of the given list
```

```
7.
8.      reversed_list = last; // first element in the reversed list
        is the last one in the initial list
9.      reversed_list -> prev = NULL; // there is no element
        before the first one
10.
11.     while(last -> prev != NULL)
12.     {
13.             last = last -> prev;
14.             reversed_list -> next = last;  // keep adding to
                the back of the reversed list
15.             reversed_list = reversed_list -> next;
16.     }
17.     return reversed_list;
18. }
```

LINKED LISTS: THE USEFULNESS OF SINGLE AND DOUBLE LINKED LISTS

Lists are generally used when we need to cut on the amount of space the programs we write use. One of the most common applications is representing graph in the memory of a computer. Because the number of nodes any node in the graph is connected to varies from node to node, it is more advantageous to use a linked list instead of a 2D array.

Consider the following graph:

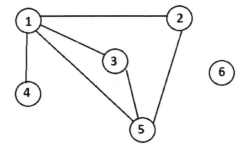

If we were to represent it using a 2D array, it would look as follows:

```
0 1 1 1 1 0
1 0 0 0 1 0
1 0 0 0 1 0
1 0 0 0 0 0
1 1 1 0 0 0
0 0 0 0 0 0
```

Notice that, regardless of the number of edges in the graph, we always need 36 memory entries to store the information about the graph, because in the case of a regular array we need to allocate the memory statically, at compile time.

On the other hand, linked lists for the same graph would only require as many elements as the number of edges in the graph. A linked list is created for each node, as follows:

list[1]: 2, 3,4, 5
list[2]: 1, 5
list[3]: 1, 5
list[4]: 1
list[5]: 1, 2, 3
list[6]: -

DATA STRUCTURE WALK THROUGH: ROOTED TREES

Trees are a recursive data structure. They are a finite set of nodes, with the following properties:

- There is a single node called the **root**;
- All the nodes, except for the root, have a single parent;
- There are no cycles. This means that if we start from a certain node and try to find a path within the tree there is no way to get back to the original node.
- The nodes that have no descendants are called **leaves**;
- The descendants of every node are called the **children** of that node.

Here is a visual representation of a tree:

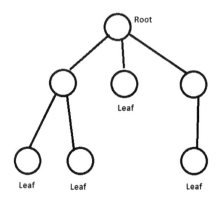

Like in the case of linked lists, any node can contain any type of information, along with a pointer to the next node. The trees in which any node has at most two children are called **binary trees**. The tree represented above is not binary, because the root has three children.

ROOTED TREES: BINARY SEARCH TREES

A tree is called a binary search tree if all the nodes contain some information (key) and have the following properties:

- The key of a node is greater than or equal to the key of all children on its left;
- The key of a node is smaller than all the key of all its right children.

A **balanced binary search tree** is a tree in which every node has the same number of descendants to its left and right.

The following is a (non-balanced) binary search tree:

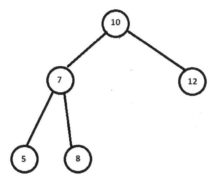

As their name suggest, binary search trees are particularly useful for searching for an element in a data collection. The complexity of this operation is log(N) because of the way the nodes are arranged in a binary search tree. Let's now look at some of the basic operations that can be performed using this data structure.

1. Insertion can be performed with the following steps:

    a) Start with the root. Consider the root is the current node.

    b) Compare the key of the current node with the key of the node to be inserted.

        i. If the key of the node to be inserted is smaller than or equal to the key of the current node go left.

        ii. If the key of the node to be inserted is greater than the key of the current node go right.

c) Repeat step b for all the nodes until a free space is found.

d) Place the element in the free space.

For example, if we were inserting '11' in the binary search tree above, after the insertion the tree would look as follows:

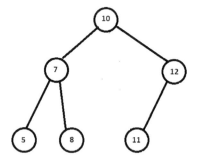

We start with the root and compare 10 to 11. 11 > 10, so we move right. Then 11 < 12, so we move left, where a free space is found. The element is then inserted at the free space.

1. Searching for an element in the tree is done in a similar fashion. We start at the root and at each step we compare the key of the current node with the value we are looking for, moving left and right according to the result of this comparison. For example, searching for '8' in the tree above would only take 2 steps, as we move left and right from the root. The value we are looking for is not in the tree if there is nowhere to go. For example, if we were looking for '13' we would go from 10 to 12 and then stop because there is nothing on the right.

2. The deletion operation needs to take into account the following cases:

    a) if the node we are trying to delete is a leaf, then just mark it as 'NULL' (delete it).

    b) if the node has only one direct child then delete it and bring the child to its original location. For example, deleting '12' in the tree above only requires replacing the node with '11'.

    c) if the node has two children things become a little more complicated:

        i. We firstly delete the information in the node, but keep the node.

        ii. Place the largest value in the left sub-tree in the node whose information we have just deleted.

        iii. Delete the node containing the largest value in the left sub-tree.

Let's see what happens if we are trying to delete '10' from the tree given as an example. We firstly delete '10', but keep the node, as follows:

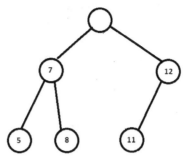

Then we notice the largest value in the left sub-tree is 8. Generally, this can easily be determined, because we only need to go right in the left sub-tree to find the largest value. We then place 8 in the empty space and delete the node that contained it initially. The final tree is as follows:

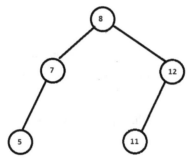

There are three ways of **traversing a binary search tree**. We will list them and give an example based on our initial tree from above (before deletion):

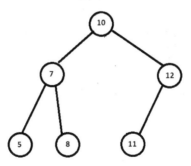

- Inorder traversal – recursively list the key of the node in the order left – root – right. For example, in the tree above we start from the root, move left and repeat the process for the left sub-tree (write down the left part of the root first – 5, then the root itself – 7 and then the right key – 8). The result is 5 7 8 10 11 12. Not that the inorder traversal of a binary search tree always results in the **sorted keys**, in ascending order.

- Pre-order traversal: similar to inorder, but the order is now root – left – right. For the tree above we would obtain 10 7 5 8 12 11.

- Post-order traversal: also similar to inorder, with the order left – right – root. For the tree above, this type of traversal gives 7 8 7 11 12 10. The root is always the last element.

ROOTED TREES: RED-BLACK TREES

A red-black tree is a binary search tree that has an extra bit of information for each node: its color, which can be red or black. Each node of the tree contains the fields color, key, left, right and parent. If the parent or any of the left or right children does not exist, the respective field is set to null. A binary search tree is red-black tree if it meets the following properties:

1. Each node is either red or black.
2. The root is always black.
3. If a node is red then both is children must be black.
4. Every path from a node to a leaf contains the same number of black nodes.

We will refer to the number of these properties later in our examples, so it is good to know them.

Here is an example of a red-black tree:

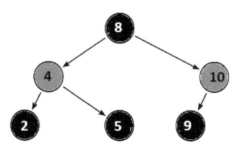

The number of black nodes on any path from a node down to a leaf node will be called the black height of the node. The notion of black height is well defined on the basis of property 4, according to which all paths from a node to a leaf have the same number of black nodes. We define the black height of a red-black tree as the black height of its root.

Theorem A red-black tree with n nodes has height $h < 2\log(n + 1)$.

This means that whenever a new node is inserted into the tree it will not become significantly unbalanced, because the properties need to be maintained, which is the major advantage of using this type of data structure. Let's now look at some operations that can be performed on red-black trees:

1. When we execute insertions and deletions on a red-black tree with n nodes, it could happen that some of the properties of this data structure are not respected. In order to restore these properties, the colors of some of the nodes in the tree and the pointer structure need to be changed.

   The structure of the pointers is changed by rotation. There are two types of rotation: left and right rotation. In order to be able to perform a right rotation on a node x, the left child of the node must not be null. The tree is then rotated to the right, so in our example 8 becomes the right child of 4. If the left child of the initial root already had a right child (in our case it did – 5), we make its right child the left child of the initial root (the left child of 8 in our example). Finally, all the nodes that are located on a different level in the rotated tree change their color (in our example, all of them, except 5). The process of left rotation is symmetrical to the left rotation. The following image describes these two techniques:

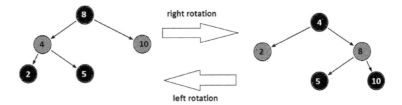

2. Inserting a node in a red-black tree with n nodes can be done in time O (lg n). We will firstly used the procedure of inserting into a binary search tree to insert a node x in the tree. Next, we will color x with red. To guarantee the preservation of the red-black properties, we recover the resulting tree by node re-coloring and by performing rotations. After insertion only the third property can be broken, which states that a red colored node cannot have a child colored in red. Specifically, property 3 is violated if the parent of x is red. There are a couple of cases to consider:

   a) If the parent of the newly inserted node is red, then this must mean that its parent is black, because the tree was a red-black tree before. In this case we color both the inserted node and its parent with black, then color the grandparent of the newly inserted node with red, in order to preserve the fourth property. For example, if we were to insert '1' in the tree shown in the picture above in the right, we would firstly insert it to the left of '2'. We would then color both 1 and 1 in black and 4 in red.

   b) If the parent of the newly inserted node is black, then we can keep the red color of the node, because it does not break the fourth property.

For example, if we were to insert 9 in the red-black tree above, we would firstly follow the insertion procedure that applies to regular binary search trees and obtain the following tree, which violates properties 3 and 4:

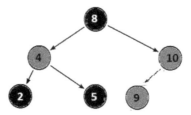

All we need to do now is change the color of 9, which will restore all the properties of a red-black tree:

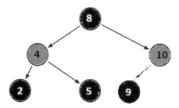

3. Deletion in red-black trees is not much more complicated than insertion.

    a) If the node we want to remove is red then we would still end up with a red-black tree after its deletion. This means we can use exactly the same algorithm as with regular binary search trees.

    b) If the node we want to remove is black its descendants must be given another black ancestor in order not to break the fourth property. If both descendants are red then we can color the one that will replace the black node removed in black. If not, we will need to restructure the tree.

For example, suppose we want to delete the root of our red-black tree above. Following the steps described in the section corresponding to regular binary search trees, we delete the root's key and replace it with the largest value in the left subtree (in this case 5), as follows:

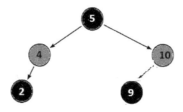

This tree does not violate any of the four properties, so this time we do not need to change colors.

The key thing to remember about red-black trees is that they enable the implementation of all dictionary operations in O(log n). The four properties discussed make this data structure more balanced than regular binary search trees.

ROOTED TREES: B-TREES

- B-Trees are a special category of trees, defined by the property according to which each node can hold **multiple keys**;
- The nodes of a B-tree are called pages;
- There is an internal sorting mechanism for the pages of the B-tree, which makes a page very easy to find;
- The keys are usually sorted within a page, which makes finding a certain key possible with a binary search.
- The number of children of a page is always equal to the maximum number of pages + 1.

Here is how a B-tree looks like:

In this particular tree, the maximum number of keys in a page is, so the maximum number of children for a key is 5 (4 + 1). We observe the following property:

- The left children of 8 (2, 3, 5) contains only keys that are smaller than 8. Similarly, the right children of 8 (which is also the left children of 19, the element (10, 12, 14, 17)) contains only keys that are larger than 8. This is valid for all keys in a B-tree.

Suppose we want to look for '12' in the tree above. The steps are as follows:

- We use binary tree to search for the key in the root of the tree;
- 12 is not there, so we then look for the interval in which 12 fits. In this case this interval is [8, 19], so we then move to the page that is common to these 2 keys, which in our case is the second page of the second level (10, 12, 14, 17).
- We perform a binary search again and this time we find the key.

Next, inserting a key in a B-tree is done by firstly finding the page in which the key fits and then checking whether we can add it or not. If the page is already full, then we have to make some changes, as follows:

For example, if we wanted to add the key 18 in the B-tree above, then normally it would go in the second page of the first level, which is already full. Remember that a page cannot contain more than 4 keys in this case. The solution in this case would be to insert the new value in the place of the parent node (19 in this case), and then re-insert the value just replaced. The final tree would look as follows:

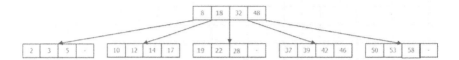

Finally, deleting a key from a B-Tree is always done from a leaf. We firstly look for the key to be deleted by using the searching algorithm described above, and then update the page accordingly. For example, deleting '3' from the tree above would result in the page (2,5) on the first level.

DATA STRUCTURE WALK THROUGH: GRAPHS

A graph (undirected or directed) is an ordered pair of sets G = (V, E), where set V is a nonempty and finite set of elements known as **vertices** and E is the set of **edges.** The following properties define a graph:

- Each edge connects exactly two vertices;
- In the case of an undirected graph, the edge connects the vertices both ways.
- In the case of directed graphs, the edge has a direction and is commonly referred to as an arc.
- Here is a visual representation of an undirected graph:

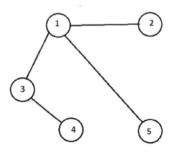

- There are 5 vertices (1, 2, 3, 4, 5) and 4 edges ([1 2], [1 3], [1 5], [3 4]).
- The degree of a vertex is given by the total number of edges incident to that vertex. For example, 1 has degree 3.

- A path in a graph is a sequence of vertices connected by edges. For example, (2, 1, 3, 4) is a path in the given graph.

- A cycle is a path that starts and ends in the same vertex. For example, if 1 and 4 were connected in the graph above, the sequence (1, 3, 4, 1) would be a cycle.

- A complete graph is a graph if any two vertices are directly connected by an edge.

- A connected graph is a graph in which there is a path between every 2 vertices. The graph drawn above is connected.

GRAPHS: GRAPH TRAVERSALS

Traversing a graph requires systematic examination of the graph's vertices in order to process the information associated with them. There are two basic methods of traversing a graph, as follows:

1. Depth – first search (DFS)
2. Breadth - first Search (BFS)

Depth first search is performed as follows:

3. Browsing begins with an initial vertex, called the starting vertex.
4. Then the first unvisited neighbor of the starting vertex is visited. Vertex y is considered a neighbor of vertex x if there exists a direct edge (x, y) in the graph.
5. Next the first unvisited neighbor of the first unvisited neighbor of the starting vertex is visited, and we repeat the process until there are no unvisited neighbors for a vertex. When we reach such a vertex, we go back to the vertex we visited previously and continue looking through the rest of the unvisited neighbors.
6. The algorithm can be easily implemented with the use of a stack. We will look at an example so you can have a better understanding of the concept.

Suppose we want to perform a DFS traversal on the following graph:

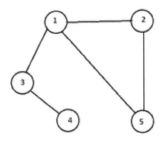

We start with an empty stack. If 1 is our starting vertex, then we firstly added it to the stack. Then we add its first unvisited neighbor, which is 2. We repeat the same for 2 and add 5 to the stack. At this point our stack is (1, 2, 5). Since there are no unvisited neighbors of 5 (2 and 1 have already been visited), we perform a pop() operation on the stack and go back to 2 and then to 1. At this point we add the next unvisited neighbor of 1 (3), and finally 4. The DFS traversal is 1 2 5 3 4.

Next, breath first search is done with the following steps:

1. We choose a starting vertex and visit it first.
2. We visit all unvisited neighbors of the starting vertex one by one.
3. The simplest algorithm for BFS uses a queue. Let's look at an example.

Suppose we want to perform a BFS on the same graph and we choose 1 as a starting node again. We firstly add all unvisited neighbors of 1 to an initially empty queue, which would look like (1, 2, 3, 5). We then perform a dequeue operation, obtaining (2, 3, 5). We then expand 2, which has no more unvisited neighbor, so we perform another dequeue operation, removing it from the queue. At this point the queue is (3, 5). We finally expand 3, which has 4 as an unvisited neighbor. The final BFS traversal is therefore 1 2 3 5 4.

GRAPHS: TOPOLOGICAL SORT

Given a directed graph with no cycles, topological sorting performs a linear arrangement of nodes based on the edges between them. The edge orientation corresponds to a sequence relationship from the source node to the destination. Thus, if (u, v) is one of the edges of the graph, u must appear ahead of v in the listing. Topological sorting can be seen as placing nodes along a horizontal line so that all edges are directed from left to right.

The most common algorithm for topological sort uses DFS. Consider the following directed graph:

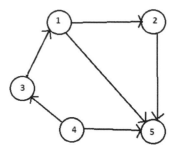

The steps the algorithm would perform are as follows:

- Perform a DFS traversal from any vertex (let's suppose we start with 4).

- As opposed to a regular traversal, we are now interested in all the nodes we run into during the search, even they have been marked as visited or not. For example, when we start from 4 we would output 4 3 1 2 5 5 5 (the last two 5s were outputted when visiting from 1 and 4, respectively).

- We consider the output in the step above and we iterate through it from right to left, removing any duplicates. In the example above we would remove the first and second 5.

- The topological sort in this case is 4 3 1 2 5.

GRAPHS: EXAMPLE – TASK MANAGEMENT

Suppose you are assigned a list of tasks, dependent on each other. For example, suppose you have 5 tasks, numbered 1, 2, 3, 4 and 5, respectively, and you know you must start with either task 3 or 5. Furthermore, you know that task 2 cannot be performed until task 3 is finished, while task 4 cannot be performed until task 2 and 5 are finished and task 5 depends on the result of task 1, so it must be performed after it. This is a classic example of a problem that can be solved using topological sort. The steps are as follows:

1. We build a graph, with the following properties:

   a) Every task is assigned a vertex of the graph;

   b) There is an edge between vertex x and vertex y if x must be completed before y.

The graph for the problem above would look as follows:

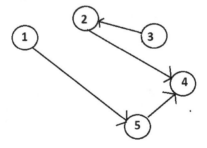

2. We apply the topological sort algorithm from any of the starting nodes, which in this case are 3 or 5. Any solution obtained at this step is a valid one. For example, the solution 3 1 2 5 4 is valid.

Finally, it is also worth mentioning that topological sort is also often used in real-world contexts. For example, when installing packages under Linux, there are dependencies between them and we often need to install one package before another. A good order for installing these files is based on finding a topological sort with the algorithm we have just described.

DATA STRUCTURE WALK THROUGH: HASH TABLES

In many applications we work with large data structures that we need to use to search, insert, modify or delete an element. These structures can be vectors, matrices, lists etc. In the best case, these can be sorted in O(log n). However, there are some data structures for which we do not need sorting in order to find an element, which would definitely save us some precious time. Hash tables are data structures that have this property. Imagine we have four string elements, as follows:

B = ("abc", "painter", "abacus", "fuss")

We build a vector Index to indicate the order in which we should place the words in a sorted vector. The alphabetical order for these words is "abacus", "abc", "fuss", "painter", so the Index vector would look like:

Index = (2, 4, 1, 3)

signifying that the first word in the array should be placed on the second position in the sorted array and so on. The way in which we can obtain the sorted vector is as follows:

B '= (B [Index (1)], B [Index (2)], B [Index (3)], B [Index (4)]).

This procedure is called indexing. The construction of the Index vector cannot be constructed in less than O(N log N), but this only needs to be done once. After this, searches can be made really quickly. If along the way are adding or deleting items, we will lose some time to maintain the index, but in practice this time is much less than the time that would be lost if searching took longer.

In some situations, unfortunately, you cannot do any indexing on a data structure. Consider the case of a program that plays chess. The number of possible positions for the pieces on the chessboard is too high. In such cases we use the data structures known as a **hash table.**

Suppose we want to build a hash table H with 1000 Boolean elements. Initially, all elements of H are set to False (or 0). If the number 400, for example, was found in the list, we would only have to set the value of H (400) to True (or 1). Next time we search for this element we would only need to examine the element H (400) and because it is True, it means that this number was found. If we delete an item in the hash table, all we need to do is set the corresponding index to False.

Now suppose that instead of 1000 numbers we have to represent up to 2 billion elements. We surely cannot use a regular array in this situation. The solution is to use a mod operation to establish a common property of some elements. If we can store up to 100,000 elements in our array, we choose M = 100,000 and insert each element at position f(value) % M, where f is called a hashing function. Our hash table will end up like an array of lists.

HASH TABLES: THE DIVISION METHOD

One of the most common approaches when working with a hash table is to insert elements at a position given by x % M, where M is the number of table entries. The challenging aspect about this method is to choose the right value for M, such that the number of collisions for any input will be small. In addition, if M is maximized then the number of keys assigned to the same index will be smaller. Suppose, for example, that we are only allowed to store 5 variables in our array and we need to store the keys 0, 10, 7, 9, 3, 4.

- At index 0 we would store 0, 10: 0 % 5 = 0, 10 % 5
- At index 1 we would not store anything
- At index 2 we would store 7: 7 % 5 = 2
- At index 3 we would store 4: 3 % 5 = 3
- At index 4 we would store 9, 4: 9 % 5 = 4, 4 % 5 = 4.

A good choice for M is represented by prime numbers that are not close to any power of 2. For example, instead of a table with M = 10,000 entries we can use one with 9973 entries. This would decrease the number of items stored at the same index and, as a consequence, searching in the hash table would be faster.

HASH TABLES: THE MULTIPLICATION METHOD

The multiplication stores the items at an index given by the hash function h(x) = M * A * x

For this method hash function is h (x) = [M * {A * x}]. A is a positive number, 0 < A < 1, and {x * A} means the fractional part of x * A, i.e. x * A - [x * A]. For example, if we choose M = 1234 and A = 0.3, for x = 1997, we would obtain h (x) = [1234 * {599.1}] = [1234 * 0.1] = 123. Note that the function h produces numbers between 0 and M-1, just as the mod function used in the division method.

In this case, the value of M has no importance, as opposed to the division method. We can therefore choose it according to our needs in terms of the number of elements that we need to store.

HASH TABLES: HASHING – POINTS TO REMEMBER

- The value of M (the size of the table) is important and greatly influences the efficiency of the hashing algorithm we choose to implement. It has been proven that the best performance is given by prime numbers that are not close to a power of 2. For example, if we choose M = 100, we would just take the last two digits of the elements and insert them at the same position (e.g. 123, 23 and 223 would all go to the same position), which would result in an increased number of collisions and hence and inefficient implementation of our hashing algorithm.

- A good real-world example that would require the use of a hash table is the implementation of a router table for an ISP. Just imagine that there can be up to millions of routers handled by such a company. When a package of information needs to be routed to a certain IP address, searching for the optimal route can be done efficiently if a hash table is used to store all these addresses.

HASH TABLES:
DEALING WITH COLLISIONS – OPEN ADDRESSING

In the examples we have seen so far our hash table was basically an array of lists. But what happens if we really do not want to store multiple elements at the same index? If this is the case we could use the technique known as open addressing. In case we want to add an element and a collision with another item already stored in the hash table occurs, this technique uses **probing**, which means scanning for alternate locations to place the current element at.

There are multiple types of probing:

1. Linear probing – simply search for the next position available in the array linearly, usually in steps of 1. If, for example, our hash function indicates an element should be stored at position 3, which already holds some values, we start looking for the next available location, examining 4, 5, 6 and so on, until the first free position has been found.

2. Quadratic probing: The difference from linear probing is in the interval between probes. Take the same example as above. Instead of examining every single position from 4 onwards, we could examine every $x^2 + 2$ positions. For example, we start with 4, then $4 + 1^2 + 2 = 7$, then $4 + 2^2 + 2 = 10$, then $4 + 3^2 + 2 = 15$, and so on.

3. Double hashing: The interval between probes is computed by an additional hash function, usually different from the one we used initially.

HASH TABLES:
UNIVERSAL HASHING AND BUCKET HASHING

For a better performance for our hashing algorithm and for minimizing the number of collisions, we can use more than one hash function and pick a random function every time we are computing the index at which an element will be stored. This technique is known as **universal hashing** and such a collection of hashing functions is called a family of functions. For example, we can pick the functions (x + 1, 2x + 3, 3x + 4 and 4x + 2). Choosing a random function every time we want to compute the index of an element in the hash table will ensure a more uniform distribution across the table and hence a smaller number of collisions.

In order to improve the performance of the hash table even more, we could also make use of the concept known as **bucket hashing**. The main idea is to divide the M slots available in the hash table into B buckets. Thus every bucket would consist of M / B slots. The hash function would then assign values only to the first slot of every bucket. If this is unavailable, then we linearly search for the next free slot within the bucket. If, however, the bucket is full, we insert the element into an **overflow bucket** at the end of the hash table. This bucket has infinite capacity and is shared by all the other buckets. It is ideal to have as few elements as possible deposited in the overflow bucket.

DATA STRUCTURE WALK THROUGH: SETS AND MULTI-SETS

Sets are a special case of arrays, having the following properties:

- They store only unique element, which follow a specific order, in ascending order by default;
- In the set each element is uniquely identified by its value, as opposed to arrays, where there is an index associated with each element, this makes iteration by index impossible with sets;
- Iterating through the set is done by an iterator object which firstly points to the start of the set;
- Once an element is inserted into the set it cannot be modified, but it can be deleted; another value can then be re-inserted;
- An internal **comparison object** gives the order of the elements in the set; this is defined as a function applied to two elements of the set, which returns true if the first element needs to be placed before the second one in the set and false otherwise; by default, this comparison object is '<' (<(a,b) returns true if a<b, false otherwise), so the elements are stored in ascending order, but this function can be overridden.
- Because the sets
- Sets are typically implemented by using binary search trees.

The operations that can be performed on sets are the same as the ones that use vectors. In the C++ STL library, a set can be declared as set<int> s; Some functions that can be used in the context of sets are as follows:

- s.insert() – adds an element to the set s;

- s.begin() and s.end() – return a pointer to the beginning of set s and to its end, respectively;
- s.find(value) – find the value in the given set;
- s.empty() – empty the set s;
- s.size() – returns the capacity of set s;
- s.insert(iterator, value) – inserts a value into set s; in case of duplicates nothing is done;
- s.erase(iterator, value) – deletes a value from set s.

We can normally use sets to perform any operation that can be done with arrays containing unique values.

SETS AND MULTI-SETS: MULTI-SETS

The difference between sets and multi-sets is that in multi-sets multiple elements can have the same value. All the properties mentioned above are applicable to multi-sets and the only different aspect is with the insert() function, which inserts any value, without checking for duplicates. Here is an example program showing the functionality of sets and multi-sets, making use of the STL library of C++:

```
1.   #include <cstdio>
2.   #include <set>
3.
4.   using namespace std;
5.
6.   int main()
7.   {
8.       set<int>s;
9.       multiset<int>m;
10.
11.      set<int>::iterator i1;
12.          multiset<int>::iterator i2;
13.
14.      s.insert(10);
15.      s.insert(10);
16.      s.insert(5);
17.
18.      for (i1 = s.begin(); i1 != s.end(); i1++)
19.              printf("%d ", *i1);
20.      printf("\n");
21.
22.      m.insert(10);
23.      m.insert(10);
24.      m.insert(5);
25.
26.      for (i2 = m.begin(); i2 != m.end(); i2++)
```

```
26.              printf("%d ", *i2);
27.    printf("\n");
28.
29.    return 0;
30. }
```

The output of the program is:

5 10

5 10 10

SETS AND MULTI-SETS:
WHEN TO USE SETS AND MULTI-SETS?

- Generally, it is best to use sets when we want to keep the elements we are storing in a specific order. For example, if we want to keep track of a list of friends we might wish to store their names in alphabetical order. If we use a set, regardless of the number of insertions or deletions, the list will be kept in order. With a vector this is not the case and we often have to re-arrange the elements manually.

- If, on the other hand, we have multiple friends with the same name, we may wish to use a multi-set instead, in order to allow duplicate entries. Multi sets behave in the same way as sets and allowing multiple entries with the same value is the only difference.

DATA STRUCTURE WALK THROUGH: CONTAINERS

We use the concept of containers in real life more often than you probably imagined. Most of the things we buy come in a box, while the books of every page we read are kept in the same cover. We can call these boxes or covers holders of objects. The concept is similar in programming. Containers are the holders, while the objects are variables or functions.

Containers can hold multiple objects of different types. The set of these objects is known as the **collection** of the container. Here are some properties of containers, worth mentioning:

- Containers are implemented as class templates, which makes them flexible to use and adaptable to fit any kind of data; templates are a parameterization of code fragment, generally denoted with angle brackets. Hence, a container would be written as Container<type>, where type is the type of the objects held in the container;

- Containers are responsible for the management of the space required in the memory to store all its objects;

- The elements of a container can be accessed directly using a member function and iterating through the elements can be done using an object of type iterator;

- Member functions can be common to multiple containers, as well as bits of functionality;

- Choosing an appropriate type of container for a certain task is usually done by taking into account the efficiency of its member functions;

In the C++ STL library, some of the most common types of data structures are in fact implementations of the type container and are also known as container classes. This gives rise to the following classification of containers:

1. Sequence containers – list, vector, deque (double ended queue);
2. Associative containers – set, multi-set, bitset, map, multi-map;
3. Container adaptors: - stack, queue, priority_queue

The key thing to remember is that whenever you see a class declared as name_of_class<data_type> then this is most certainly a container class (e.g. vector<int> v).

Generally, container classes are particularly useful because of their built-in functionality. For example, in the case of arrays, using the container class vector is more advantageous because it provides dynamic resizing of the data structure, as opposed to the traditional implementation (type v[number_of_elements]), when we would have to manually resize the array in case of an overflow.

In addition to this, containers are standardized and intuitive to use (functions such as pop(), push() or empty() are common for most data collections implemented with containers).

DATA STRUCTURE WALK THROUGH: ASSOCIATIVE ARRAYS

Maps and multi-maps : As the name of this data structure suggests, its main property is that it performs a mapping between a set of keys and a set of values. In this sense maps are similar to hash tables, but the keys are not generated randomly with a hash function. The main idea is that every value to be inserted in this data structure has a key associated with it. Suppose we want to store titles of web pages. A good key for this would be the URL at which they are stored. For example, we would store the string "The Career Tools" at the key given by "http://thecareer-tools.com/".

You can think of maps as look-up tables, in order to get a clearer idea of how they really work. For example, if we wanted to fetch the title of the web page hosted at the http://thecareertools.com, we would just need to access the memory address corresponding to this key. Here are some interesting properties of maps:

- Any key in the map must be unique, but this property does not have to hold for values;

- Keys do not have to be integers, they can have any data type, as you have seen in the example with the web pages, given above;

- Similar to sets, iteration through the elements of a map is performed by using an object of type iterator.

- A map is usually implemented as a balanced binary search tree (sometimes as a red-black tree), as opposed to hash tables, which are in most cases regular arrays.

ASSOCIATIVE ARRAYS: EXAMPLE – ANAGRAMS

Suppose we want to write a program that identifies all the anagrams of a given word that are in the English dictionary. A good choice would be to use the sorted letters of the word as a key and use a map to store it. For example, the key for the word "car" would be "acr". We notice, however, that the word "arc", for example, has the same key. In this case we could use a **multi-map**. A multi-map is the same as a map, but it allows multiple elements to have the same key.

As a consequence, in our example we could, for every given word, sort its letters to obtain the key and look in the multi-map to see which other words share the same key. The words with this property are all anagrams of the initial word.

Here is how to use a multi-map in C++'s STL library:

```
1.   #include <cstdio>
2.   #include <map>
3.
4.   using namespace std;
5.
6.   int main ()
7.   {
8.      multimap<char*, char*> m;
9.      multimap<char*, char*>::iterator i;
10.
11.     m.insert(pair<char*, char*>("acr", "car"));
12.     m.insert(pair<char*, char*>("acr", "arc"));
13.
14.     for (i = m.begin(); i != m.end(); i++)
15.             printf("key: %s  element: %s\n", i->first,
                i->second);
```

```
16.     return 0;
17. }
```

The program outputs the following:

key: acr element: car

key: acr element: arc

Sometimes associative arrays are also referred to as **dictionaries**. This term is common for programming languages such as Python and .Net.

ALGORITHM/CODING WARM UP: ALGORITHMS DURING INTERVIEWS

Why algorithms question during interviews?

RATIONALE: *Most of the professional work on varied projects which are associated with varied business cases and technologies. But all the work uses the concepts of algorithms, data structures and coding, so these things are common in between the interviewer and interviewee. It is also a interesting way to judge the interviewee's problem solving capabilities and way of solving the problem.*

SAMPLE ANSWER FROM A PROFESSIONAL POINT OF VIEW

Nearly all algorithms books talk about following key areas viz, Divide and Conquer, Sorting, Searching, Hash Tables,; Trees (Binary Search Trees, Red-Black Trees), Dynamic Programming, Greedy Algorithms, Graphs, Data Structures like (Stack, Queue, Linked list, Array, etc.), Minimum Spanning Trees, NP-Complete problems, Linear programming, etc.

Most of the core companies, e.g. highly technical product based companies like Microsoft, Google, Apple, Facebook, NetApp, Cisco, QUALCOMM, Intel, Adobe, Oracle and many more. All these companies concentrate on producing products and solutions. For providing effective products and solutions, they need able engineers who can deliver such solutions. A good overall knowledge and skill in this area also provide key inputs from the candidate's problem-solving and algorithmic programming ability.

Even though if you join a company on an entry level or mid level or more in research areas of software engineering division, you are expected to solve complicated problems related to the field of computer science in your day to day life in work and solving such problems will require some amount of algorithmic knowledge.

Below is an example of the usage of Stack and Queue. You are given a deck containing n cards, while holding the deck:

1. Take the top card off the deck and set it on the table
2. Take the next card off the top and put it on the bottom of the deck in your hand.
3. Continue steps 1 and 2 until all cards are on the table. This is a round.
4. Pick up the deck from the table and repeat steps 1-3 until the deck is in the original order.

HERE IS APPROACH TO SOLVE THIS KIND OF PROBLEM

SIMULATING STACK'S PUSH OPERATION: STEP-1

1. Take the top card off the deck
2. Set it on the table

SIMULATING QUEUE'S ENQUEUE OPERATION: STEP-2

- Take the next card off the top
- Put it on the bottom of the deck in your hand

STEP -3

- Continue steps 1 and 2 until all cards are on the table. This is a round.

STEP-4

- Compare original order with current order
- If equal - success
- Else - continue
- Pick up the deck from the table
- Repeat steps 1-3 until the deck is in the original order

Table side simulating a stack's push operation, and putting the card from top to bottom on hand simulating a queue's enqueue operation.

If the problem observed carefully, it might look like a game, but if you think algorithmically and if your concepts related with stacks and queue are clear, then this problem could be solved in 1-2 hours.

[COMPLETE SOLUTION OF THIS PROBLEM IS PROVIDED IN CODING SECTION]

ALGORITHIM/CODING WARM UP: WHAT ABOUT ALGORITHIMS

What about Algorithms?

RATIONALE: *Algorithms carries several mathematical, optimal and logical concepts. It also talks about the well known problems and the design/ analysis of the relevant solutions.*

Interviewer would like to know, how as a professional think about algorithms?

SAMPLE ANSWER FROM A PROFESSIONAL **POINT OF VIEW**

In terms of practical algorithm's definition, it's something like precise solution of a XYZ programmatic problem. So the core area of the solution must be using a very interesting and right logic to lead the problem into a solution domain.

Example: There is a situation on which software receives input of consecutive numbers in every hour, means in every hour it receives 1 to 999 numbers or on next hour it may receive 1 to 7775 numbers, and it requires calculating the sum of these numbers.

The core area of this problem is to calculate the sum of consecutive number. Because you can use existing time functions to compute start time and end time, but how efficiently to calculate the sum of these numbers?

- Naive approach is to use a loop from 1 to N and calculate the sum.
- Algorithmic approach: $N/2(N+1)$

See following behaviour (It shows calculations of the sum from 1 to 10):

Pair-1: 1,10

Pair-2: 2,9

Pair-3: 3,8

Pair-4: 4,7

Pair-5: 5,6

- Sum of each Pair = 11 = $(N+1)$
- Total Pair =5 = $(N/2)|$
- Actual result = 5X11 = $N/2(N+1)$

Because while working on practical projects during our job assignment, we encounter many situations where we cannot write the code just via using for/while, etc., we need to design an algorithm to get the optimal solution.

ALGORITHIM/CODING WARM UP: EXPERIENCE WITH ALGORITHMS

May you please tell me based on your experience if you have solved any problem on which you have used algorithmic skills?

RATIONALE: *Algorithmic skills truly help to write an optimized solution, it may be directly related with the problem where algorithmic skills are required to design the solution.*

Interviewer would like to know that how algorithmic skills helped you to solve the complex logical problems.

SAMPLE ANSWER FROM A PROFESSIONAL POINT OF VIEW

We occasionally design any algorithms, means out of 100 or 1000 software engineers may be **one** work directly with any known algorithm, e.g.; you might be working for a particular product company, and designing an algorithm for XYZ problem, i.e.; image compression or cryptography or parsing a specific type of document or anything else. In general how a professional use algorithmic skills.

Algorithmic skills talks about precise and optimized solutions. Nearly all situations require an optimized solution and that may simulate an algorithmic approach.

EXAMPLE

To provide a network client/server software (e.g. ftp client/server)– largely consist of BSD kind of customized sockets API(socket, read, write, listen, accept, close etc) designed for file transfer.

USE CASE

File Transfer: Each single file transfer from one computer to another (running client on one machine and server on another machine): It requires to set up the connection, perform data transfer and disconnect once data transfer is over

PROBLEM WHICH MIGHT REQUIRE OPTIMIZED APPROACH

For Multiple File Transfer e.g. if it requires to transfer 10 files, then for every file transfer it will open a connection and once file transfer will be over it will close the connection.

OPTIMIZATION-TECHNIQUE

For this situation if multiplexing could be done, means if logic could be changed, which says if connection going to same destination than rather every time creating a new connection, it can use existing connection.

PERFORMANCE

Performance could be deduced by several types of comparison, e.g. data›s transfer rate based on single connection vs. multiple connections to same destination, single connection and single thread vs. multiple connections and multiple threads vs multiple connections and single thread.

ALGORITHM/CODING WARM UP: DATA STRUCTURES

Which are the main data structures used while writing programming based solutions?

RATIONALE: *Using the appropriate data structures are depends on the type of problem, but still there are a standard set of data structures.*

SAMPLE ANSWER FROM A PROFESSIONAL POINT OF VIEW

It depends on the situation to situation, but most of the times following data structures used to write the programmatically solution:

EXAMPLE

Major data structures which are self-explainable, e.g. Container, Deque, Associative array(Map, Dictionary, Multimap), Multiset, Priority queue, Queue, Set, Stack, String, Tree, Graph, Hash.

Vectors are something like dynamic array, Its contiguous as Array,

Set/Multi-Set like a collection of unique unordered element, e.g.; set of integers or strings. Its internal implementation uses balanced binary tree for lookup, insertion and deletion. However, multiset may have duplicated elements.

Map/Multi-Map usually stores data in key value pair, map keeps unique keys association though multimap allow duplicates keys.

Hash is kind of a hash function, which map values to algorithmically generated keys.

Tree is a data structure like a tree in real life, many branches with data hanging on several keep going left-right nodes.

Graphs are data structures as a set of cities in some area (e.g.; in a country) interconnected to each other.

Strings to store set of characters, several algorithms exist to perform various manipulations on strings, e.g.; compare, replace.

Stacks data structure defines its top and bottom, and keeps adding an element via PUSH operation and gets the element from POP operation, works on Last In First Out Fashion.

Queue works as queue works in real life as First in First Out.

Priority Queue as priority defined over the elements means similar priorities elements follow the same queue orders, but high priority will come first.

It's really required to understand the concept of above data structures, means what exactly they meant more. On actual situation, it doesn't mean to use as is data structures, but yes these data structures are used very frequently.

ALGORITHM/CODING WARM UP: DATA STRUCTURES AND ALGORITHMS

How data structures are related with algorithms?

RATIONALE: *Algorithms carries the optimized logical steps to deduce the solution, and while deducing the solution it receives the input in the form of data e.g. to provide the shortest path from destination A to destination B, it require the requisite set of data to deduce the solution.*

SAMPLE ANSWER FROM A PROFESSIONAL **POINT OF VIEW**

Programmatically or algorithmically writing a solution means all over manipulation of data.

Data is flowing in a form of parameters; functions performed diverse logic on it, and on some situation, it's deduced to intermediate or final output.

A programmer uses data structures to keep the storage and significances of these data, e.g. array, linked list, etc. based on the situation.

ALGORITHM/CODING WARM UP: ARRAY OR LINKED LIST

Provide your observation related with the use of array or linked List?

RATIONALE: *Array and linked lists are important data structures. These data structures are used based on the situation for what they meant for.*

Interviewer would like to understand some of the use cases where array can work and linked list not or vice versa.

SAMPLE ANSWER FROM A PROFESSIONAL POINT OF VIEW

One of the major difference to point in between array and linked list is: Array is one complete block, and Linked List include several blocks of memory.

Array – contiguous blocks of memory, e.g. 4-Bytes *1024 = 1024 blocks of four bytes. O (1) to reach to a particular index. If one has to include any element in between the array, then it might require shifting elements.

Linked List – various blocks of linked memory, e.g.; 4-bytes->10-bytes->4-bytes .So to reach to a particular node, it requires to traverse to that node from the beginning (If we talk about single linked list), though insertion or deletion doesn't require to shift element on either side.

One of the use case would be:

If the situation require to use a contiguous block of memory, exact data set (e.g. set of n integers or n records)and its memory size known in advance, then array can be use.

If the situation require to use to handle the requirements where the exact data set and its memory size would be known on run time (e.g. relevant data set : first received x size of data and then receive y size of data and then may receive z type of data).

ALGORITHM/CODING WARM UP:
ALGORITHMIC SOLUTION

Given an array like this {13, 14, 35, 1, 2, 10, 25} print all the increasing sequences in the array. The sequences may not necessarily be contiguous. So for this example (a). 13, 14, 25, 35 (b).14,25,35, (c).35 (d). 1, 2,10,13,14, 25, 35... Provide all of your thinking while writing its solution.

SOLUTION: A solution of a programming problem can be direct solution, here interviewer would like to understand the interviewee's thought process while designing the solution.

SAMPLE ANSWER FROM A PROFESSIONAL **POINT OF VIEW**

Assumptions and thoughts while writing the solution of this problem:

THOUGHTS

- Solution requires a sorting algorithm: To print increasing sequence of integers
- Solution requires a search algorithm: To find the new location of original array's element in sorted array

ASSUMPTIONS

- This problem doesn't provide any specific target to solve this problem, e.g. what is the real use case to solve this issue, from where these inputs coming.
- This problem just provides one example of series, e.g. It's not known the behavior of the received input stream; it's received by once or keep coming.
- It doesn't talk about the number of elements in array.

It doesn't provide much other information, if provided, then those would be taken into consideration. So at this point, this problem just wants basic prototypical solution. In this core part - We need to select sorting and search algorithm.

- Merge Sort: average/worst case O(NlogN)
- Binary Search: worst case O (log N)

LOGIC

- Get Input of array elements as original array
- Have an auxiliary array, copy of all existing values of original array into this array
- Input auxiliary array as input and get sorted auxiliary array
  - ▷ Sort the elements on this auxiliary array [use merge sort] return sorted array
- Get one by one element from the original array and write all of Its increasing sequence.
- Get the index location of original array elements into sorted array.
- Print all increasing sequence from the found index to the end index.

NOTES

- This algorithmic problem could be made open ended, by considering various factors, e.g. its performance, memory allocation, why an auxiliary array, printing values on standard output. However, it would be better to choose based on necessity.
- This problem just considers some assumptions and based on that derived the solution.
- This solution may not be perfect and require much-2 optimization, the only intention to explain here - how to conclude to a solution by using an approach.
- Solution of this problem is based on thoughts; one can treat it as a guideline, it's nowhere mentioning that this is the perfect solution and could be used anywhere.

ARRAY: CREATING A SERIES 123456789001234567890...

Write a program which, given input n, creates and prints an array containing the first n elements of the series 0123456789012345678901234567890...

SOLUTION: For example, if given input 11 - It should create the series 01234567890 and if given input is 5 it should create 01234.

The algorithm we will be using generates the elements in the series one by one and stores them into an array. When the n-th element is reached, the algorithm stops, so exactly n steps are performed.

Suppose we have n=25. We build the series as follows:

- Series[0] = 0, series[1] = series[0] + 1 = 1, ..., series[10] = series[9] + 1 = 9 + 1 = 10.

- At this point, because 10 is not in our initial sequence, we make series[10] = 0 and continue.

- When we reach series[25] = series[24] + 1 = 3 + 1 = 4 we stop.

There are a couple of useful clarification points you may wish to establish before implementing the problem, based on which we can draw assumptions / limitations, as follows:

PSEUDO CODE:

```
1.   CreateSeries(lengthOfSeries, series[]):
2.   series[0] = 0
3.     for seriesIndex from 1 to lengthOfSeries
4.           series[seriesIndex] = previous element + 1
5.           if series[seriesIndex] = 10
6.                 series[seriesIndex] = 0
```

CLARIFICATION POINT-1:

What is the maximum value for N?

This is very useful in case of a static array, since we need to know the number of elements the array stores at compile time.

CLARIFICATION POINT-2:

Is the array indexed from 0?

This is always a good question to ask when given a task that makes use of arrays, so you can do the indexing according to the problem.

ASSUMPTION/LIMITATION:

Elements from 0 to 9 ->

Array of integers

* We will assume array will be static.)

--If Dynamic Array then?

(See discussion points)

DEVELOPMENT ENVIRONMENT:

Eclipse IDE for C/C++ Developers

Version: Juno Service Release 1

Build id: 20120920-0800

MAJOR DATA STRUCTURES:

Array of integers

UNIT TESTS:

POSTIVE FUNCTIONAL TEST CASES

INPUT	EXPECTED OUTPUT
n = 1	{0}
n = 2	{0,1}
n = 4	{0,1,2,3}
n = 10	{0,1,2,3,4,5,6,7,8,9}
n = 20	{0,1,2,3,4,5,6,7,8,9,0,1,2,3
n = 25	,4,5,
	6,7,8,9}
	{0,1,2,3,4,5,6,7,8,9,0,1,2,3,
	4,5,6,7,8,9,0,1,2,3,4}

NEGATIVE FUNCTIONAL TEST CASES

n = 0	Invalid input
n < 0	Invalid input

Here is a sample answer, running in O(N):

```
1.    #include <cstdio>
2.    #define maxLengthOfSeries 10001
3.    using namespace std;
4.    void create_series(int lengthOfSeries, int series[])
5.    {
6.       if (series < 0)
7.       {
```

```
8.                  printf("Input Invalid!");
9.                  return;
10.     }
11.
12.     if (lengthOfSeries <= 0) return;
13.
14.     series[0] = 0;
15.     for (int seriesIndex = 1; seriesIndex < lengthOfSeries;
        seriesIndex++)
16.     {
17.             series[seriesIndex] = series[seriesIndex - 1] + 1;
18.             if (series[seriesIndex] == 10)
19.                     series[seriesIndex] = 0;
20.     }
21. }
22.
23. int main()
24. {
25.     int series[maxLengthOfSeries];
26.     create_series(25, series);
27.
28.     // print the result
29.     printf("Here is the series for 25:\n");
30.     for (int seriesIndex = 0; seriesIndex < 25; seriesIndex++)
31.             printf("%d ", series[seriesIndex]);
32.
33. }
```

OUTPUT:	FURTHER EXERCISE:
For n=25: Here is the series for 25: 0 1 2 3 4 5 6 7 8 9 0 1 2 3 4 5 6 7 8 9 0 1 2 3 4	Q: What if the array was dynamic? A: We would not need to know the maximum value for N in advance. However, if N is really big we can expect a stack overflow (i.e. our program is using too much memory). Q: What happens if N is so large that we cannot store the series in an array? A: If N is large we can just print the elements of the sequence as we compute them, one by one, taking advantage of the fact that we only need to store the previous value to compute the next one.

ARRAY: THE INCREASING SEQUENCES IN THE ARRAY

Given an array of N integers, print all the sequences of ordered elements in the array. The sequences may not necessarily be contiguous. So for this example, if given the array {13, 14, 35, 1, 2, 10, 25}, the following will be valid sequences:
13,
13,14,
13,14,35,
13,14,25,
14,35,
14,25

SOLUTION: The algorithm we will use is based on a backtracking approach, trying all possible valid sequences and performs the following steps:

- Start with an empty 'sequence' array;
- Iterate through the initially array and append to the sequence array all numbers that are bigger than or equal to the previous value in this array, one by one. The key is to remember the previous index of the array, which is needed for the subsequent calls to the recursive function.

For example, suppose we have {1, 3, 2}. We start with sequence {1}, print it and call the function again, knowing that we have already used the first element. We then add 3, obtaining {1, 3} and print the sequence. When we call the function again, we cannot add '2', because this is smaller than 3, so we go back to {1}, adding the {2} this time, obtaining the sequence {1,2}. Finally, we go back to where we started, at the empty sequence {} and add {3} and then {2}, which are our final sequences.

PSEUDO CODE:

```
print_sequences(array, sequence, lengthOfSequence, sequenceIndex,
prevArrayIndex):

1.   print current sequence
2.   for arrayIndex from prevArrayIndex to lengthOfSeq
3.      if array[arrayIndex] >= sequence[sequenceIndex]
4.             sequence[sequenceIndex] = array[arrayIndex]
5.             print_sequences(array, sequenceIndex + 1,
               arrayIndex)
```

CLARIFICATION POINT-1:

What is the maximum size for the array?

This is very useful in case of a static array, since we need to know the number of elements the array stores at compile time.

CLARIFICATION POINT-2:

What is the maximum value for an element in an array?

For example, if the array can have an element whose value is more than $2^{32} - 1$ then we may need to use the type long instead of int.

CLARIFICATION POINT-3:

What is the minimum length of a sequence? Does a single element count as a sequence?

CLARIFICATION POINT-4:

Are there any duplicates in the array? If yes, is the sequence 13 13, for example, a valid one?

ASSUMPTION/LIMITATION:

All elements in the array fit in the type int -> Array of integers

- We will assume array will be static and the maximum number of elements it can store is 10,000

- We will also assume the length of a valid sequence is at least 1.

- We will also assume that the array is not sorted.

- Finally, we will assume the array can contain duplicates.

MAJOR DATA STRUCTURES:

Array of integers

POSTIVE FUNCTIONAL TEST CASES	
INPUT	EXPECTED OUTPUT
N = 2 {0, 1}	{0}, {1}, {0, 1}
N = 2 {1, 0}	{1}, {0}
N = 3 {0, 0, 1}	{0}, {0,0}, {0,0,1}, {0,1},
N = 5 {10, 7, 6, 4, 3}	{0}, {0,1}, {1}
N = 4 {10, 12, 5, 6}	{10}, {7}, {6}, {4}, {3}
n = 5 {10, 12, 5, 6, 13}	{10}, {10,12}, {12}, {5}, {5,6}, {6}
	{10}, {10,12}, {10,12,13}, {10,13}, {12}, {12,13}, {5}, {5,6}, {5,6,13}, {5,13}, {6}, {6,13}, {13}

NEGATIVE FUNCTIONAL TEST CASES	
N = 0	Invalid input
N < 0	Invalid input

Here is a sample answer, which uses a recursive function, based on the backtracking approach.

```
1.    #include <cstdio>
2.    #define maxSequenceLength 10001 // maximum number of elements
3.
4.    using namespace std;
5.
6.    void print_sequences(int array[], int sequence[],  int
      lengthOfSequence, int sequenceIndex, int prevArrayIndex)
7.    {
8.        if (lengthOfSequence <= 0)
9.        {
10.               printf("Invalid input!");
11.               return;
12.       }
13.
14.       // print current sequence
15.       for (int i = 0; i < sequenceIndex; i++)
16.               printf("%d ", sequence[i]);
17.       printf("\n");
18.
19.       for (int arrayIndex = prevArrayIndex + 1; arrayIndex <
          lengthOfSequence; arrayIndex++)
20.       {
21.               // condition for the valid sequence
22.               if (sequenceIndex == 0 || array[arrayIndex] >=
                  sequence[sequenceIndex-1])
23.               {
```

```
24.                          sequence[sequenceIndex] =
                             array[arrayIndex];
25.                          print_sequences(array, sequence,
                             lengthOfSequence, sequenceIndex + 1,
                             arrayIndex);
26.              }
27.      }
28. }
29.
30. int main()
31. {
32.     int sequenceLength = 4; // number of elements
33.     int sequence[maxSequenceLength];
34.
35.     int array[maxSequenceLength] = {10, 12, 3, 5};
36.
37.     // print the sequences
38.     printf("Here are the sequences:\n");
39.
40.     // initialize prev index with -1 because we start from
        preIndex + 1 initially
41.     print_sequences(array, sequence, sequenceLength, 0, -1);
42.
43.     return 0;
44. }
```

OUTPUT:	FURTHER EXERCISE:
For N = 4, {10, 12, 3, 5}:	Q: Is there a more efficient approach?
Here are the sequences:	A: No, we need to generate all sequences
10	
10 12	Q: Can this program be done iteratively?
12	
3	A: Yes, but the program would get tedious, with too many lines of code. The recursive solution is always more elegant in such cases.
3 5	
5	

ARRAY: PARTITION THE ARRAY OF BALLS

Given an array of balls, which can be one of two colors (RED or BLUE), write a function that partitions the array in place such that on exit from the function all the balls of the same color are contiguous.

It does not matter whether the red or blue balls come first. The return value from the function is the index of the first ball of the second color. If there is only one color of balls in the array then the return value should be 0. It is not legal to change the color of a ball. They must be moved. Consider performance, memory utilization and code clarity and elegance of the solution when implementing the function.

C++ Prototype

```
class Ball
{
public:
        enum BallColor { RED, BLUE };
        BallColor Color() const { return _color; }
private:
        BallColor _color;
        // Other data in class (unrelated to assignment)
};

unsigned Partition( Ball aBalls[], unsigned
numberOfBalls )
{
// Your code goes here
}
```

SOLUTION: The first thing we need to do is build a constructor method, which is necessary for testing our partitioning function. In C++, every constructor comes with a destructor, so we also have to build this one. In terms of the actual function, the idea is to store the color of the first ball in a variable and then start the partitioning from both ends. When we find two balls whose colors do not correspond to what we want to achieve in the end, we swap them.

For example, consider we have the array RRBBRBR, where each R represents a red ball and each B represents a blue ball. The color of the first ball is red, so on the left we stop at the first blue ball, which is the third one. Simultaneously, we also consider the right side of the array and stop at the very last ball, which should be a blue one. We then swap the elements at index (2,6), obtaining RRRBRBB. We continue the process and we do one more stop, obtaining the final distribution of the balls, RRRRBBB. In this case the index required by the problem is 4.

PSEUDO CODE:

```
1.   Partition(aBalls[], numberofBalls):
2.      frontIndex = 0; backIndex = numberOfBalls - 1;
3.      while (frontIndex < backIndex)
4.             while color of ball at frontIndex=color of ball1
5.             frontIndex++
6.      while color of ball at backIndex!=color of ball1
7.             backIndex--
8.      swap aBalls[frontIndex] and aBalls[backIndex]
```

CLARIFICATION POINT-1:

What is the maximum size for the array?

This is very useful in case of a static array, since we need to know the number of elements the array stores at compile time.

CLARIFICATION POINT-2:

What input is given from the user? Solely the colors of the balls is sufficient to create instances of the class and store them in an array

CLARIFICATION POINT-3:

Do we need to create a constructor / destructor function for the given class?

ASSUMPTION/LIMITATION:

- We will assume a maximum of 10,000 balls, so the memory can be statically allocated.

- We will also assume the user gives the input as a sequence of 'R's or 'B's, representing red balls and blue balls, respectively. For example, 'BRRBB' is a sequence of 5 balls, 3 blue and 2 red.

- We will also create a constructor for the class, so we can initialize the elements.

- Finally, we will always place the red balls first in the array

MAJOR DATA STRUCTURES:

Array of elements of type Ball[]

UNIT TESTS:

POSTIVE FUNCTIONAL TEST CASES

INPUT	EXPECTED OUTPUT
N = 1 "B"	0
N = 1 "R"	0
N = 5 "RRBRR"	4
N = 5 "RBBBR"	3
N = 10 "RRRRRRRRRR"	0

NEGATIVE FUNCTIONAL TEST CASES

| N = 0 "" | Invalid input |
| N < 0 | Invalid input |

Here is a sample answer. Note the efficiency in terms of memory, as we only use two index variables to do the partitioning.

```
1.   #include <cstdio>
2.   #define maxN 10001
3.
4.   using namespace std;
5.
6.   class Ball
7.   {
8.      public:
9.              enum BallColor { RED, BLUE };
10.             Ball(Ball::BallColor);
11.             Ball();
12.             ~Ball();
13.             BallColor Color() const { return _color; }
14.      private:
15.             BallColor _color;
16.      // Other data in class (unrelated to assignment)
17.   };
18.
19.  // constructor method
20.  Ball::Ball(Ball::BallColor color)
21.  {
22.     _color = color;
23.  }
24.
25.  // we also need this to declare arrays initially
26.  Ball::Ball()
27.  {
28.  }
```

```
29.
30.  // destructor method
31.  Ball::~Ball()
32.  {
33.
34.  }
35.
36.  unsigned Partition(Ball aBalls[], unsigned numberOfBalls)
37.  {
38.     if (numberOfBalls <= 0)
39.     {
40.             printf("Invalid input!\n");
41.             return 0;
42.     }
43.
44.     // the color that goes first in the partition
45.     Ball::BallColor colorOfFirstBall = aBalls[0].Color();
46.
47.     int frontIndex = 0, backIndex = numberOfBalls - 1;
48.
49.     while (frontIndex < backIndex)
50.     {
51.             while (aBalls[frontIndex].Color() ==
                 colorOfFirstBall && frontIndex < numberOfBalls)
52.                     frontIndex++;
53.             while (aBalls[backIndex].Color() !=
                 colorOfFirstBall && backIndex > 0)
54.                     backIndex--;
55.
56.             if (frontIndex >= backIndex) break; // need to
                 check again
57.
58.             // swap the two balls
59.             Ball tempBall = aBalls[frontIndex];
60.             aBalls[frontIndex] = aBalls[backIndex];
61.             aBalls[backIndex] = tempBall;
62.     }
63.
64.     printf("Here is the partition of the balls:\n");
65.     for (int i = 0; i < numberOfBalls; i++)
66.             if(aBalls[i].Color() == aBalls[i].RED)
67.                     printf("R");
68.             else
69.                     printf("B");
70.     printf("\n");
71.
72.     for (int i = 1; i < numberOfBalls; i++)
73.
74.             if (aBalls[i].Color() != colorOfFirstBall)
75.                     return i;
76.
```

```
77.        return 0;
78.    }
79.
80.    int main()
81.    {
82.        int numberOfBalls; //number of balls
83.        char colors[6]="BBRRB";
84.
85.        Ball *balls = new Ball[maxN];
86.
87.        numberOfBalls = 5;
88.
89.        for (int i = 0; i < numberOfBalls; i++)
90.        {
91.                Ball newBall;
92.                if (colors[i] == 'B')
93.                        newBall = Ball(newBall.BLUE);
94.                else if(colors[i] =='R')
95.                        newBall = Ball(newBall.RED);
96.                balls[i] = newBall;
97.        }
98.
99.        unsigned result = Partition(balls, numberOfBalls);
100.       printf("The result is: %d", result);
101.       return 0;
102.   }
```

OUTPUT:	FURTHER EXERCISE:
For N = 5, "BBRRB":	Q: What if more colors were given?
Here are the sequences:	A: We could use bucket sort.
Here is the partition of the balls:	Q: Is there a naïve approach?
BBBRR	A: The naïve approach uses a temporary array to store the balls in the initial array and is inefficient in terms of memory use.
The result is: 3	

ARRAY: ADDING TWO N-BIT BINARY INTEGERS

Consider the problem of adding two n-bit binary integers, stored in two N-element arrays A and B. The sum of the two integers should be stored in binary form in an (N+1) element array C. Write a function which accepts an array of M N-bit binary integers and returns their sum.

SOLUTION: The idea we will be using in this example is similar to the addition we were taught in primary school. For example, if we have the numbers 1010 and 1011 we firstly align them and start from their end, adding the digits one by one, and propagating the carry further one if there is one.

1010 +

1011

10101

$1 + 1 = 10$, so we place 0 and remember that carry is '1'. At the next step, $0 + 0 = 0$, but since the carry is 1, we output 0. The final result is 10101.

PSEUDO CODE:

```
1.   Sum(n1[], n2[]):
2.      carry = 0;
3.      for i = max(n1.length, n2.length) to 1 step -1
4.            sum[i] = n1[i] + n2[i]
5.            if n1[i] = 1 and n2[i] = 1
6.                  if carry = 1 sum[i] = 1 else sum[i] = 0
7.            carry = 1
8.      else if n1[i] = 0 and n2[i] = 1 or vice-versa
9.            if carry = 1 sum[i] = 0 else sum[i] = 1
10.     else
11.           sum[i]+= carry
12.           carry = 0
```

CLARIFICATION POINT-1:

What is the maximum size for N?

This is very useful in case of a static array, since we need to know the number of elements the array stores at compile time.

CLARIFICATION POINT-2:

What is the maximum value for M?

This is useful to consider, because when adding two numbers we have to increase the capacity of the array storing the sum by 1.

CLARIFICATION POINT-3:

Does the sum need to be returned as an array or as an integer?

Assumption/Limitation:

- We will assume N is at most 500 and M is at most 100. Hence we will need an array of length 600 to store the sum.

- We will also return the sum in the form of an array.

- We will also store the length of each array at position 0 of the array, while the actual digits will be stored between positions 1 and N.

MAJOR DATA STRUCTURES:

2D array of integers

UNIT TESTS:	
POSTIVE FUNCTIONAL TEST CASES	
INPUT	EXPECTED OUTPUT
M = 1 N = 1 {0}	{0}
M = 1 N = 1 {1, 0}	{1, 0}
M = 2 N = 1 {0, 0}	{0}
M = 2 N = 2 {1, 0}, {1, 1}	{1, 0, 1}
M = 3 N = 2 {1,1}, {1,1},	{1,0,0,1}
{1,1}	{1,0,1,0}
M = 5 N = 3 {0,0,0}, {0,0,1},	
{0,1,0}, {0,1,1}, {1,0,0}	
NEGATIVE FUNCTIONAL TEST CASES	
N = 0 {}	Invalid input
N < 0	Invalid input

Here is a sample answer, which runs in O(N*M), where M is the number of numbers and N is their length:

```
1.    #include <cstdio>
2.    #include <cstring>
3.    #define maxNumberOfNumbers 601
4.    #define maxNumberLength 101
5.
6.    using namespace std;
7.
```

```
8.   // method to compute the sum of two numbers and store it in
     sum
9.   void sum_of_two(int number1[maxNumberLength], int
     number2[maxNumberLength], int sum[maxNumberLength])
10.  {
11.    int carry = 0;
12.
13.    // do the addition
14.    // iterate from the least significant digit (Backwards)
15.    for (int i = number2[0]>number1[0]?number2[0]:number1[0];
       i >= 1; i--)
16.    {
17.        sum[i] = number2[i] + number1[i];
18.
19.        // case 1 + 1
20.        if (sum[i] == 2)
21.        {
22.            if (carry == 1)
23.                sum[i] = 1;
24.            else
25.                sum[i] = 0;
26.            carry = 1;
27.        }
28.
29.        // case 0 + 1 or 1 + 0
30.        else if (sum[i] == 1)
31.        {
32.            if (carry == 1)
33.                sum[i] = 0;
34.            else
35.                sum[i] = 1;
36.        }
37.
38.        // case 0 + 0
39.        else
40.        {
41.            sum[i] += carry;
42.            carry = 0;
43.        }
44.
45.    }
46.
47.    // if carry is 1 at this point we need to shift and add an
       extra digit
48.    if (carry == 1)
49.    {
50.        // shift the result to the right
51.        for (int i = number2[0]>number1[0]?number2[0]:numb
           er1[0] + 1; i>1; i--)
52.            sum[i] = sum[i-1];
53.        sum[1] = 1;
```

```
54.                sum[0]++;
55.        }
56.
57. }
58.
59. void compute_sum(int numbers[maxNumberOfNumbers]
    [maxNumberLength], int sum[maxNumberLength], int
    numberOfNumbers)
60. {
61.     if (numberOfNumbers <= 0)
62.     {
63.             printf("Invalid input!\n");
64.             return;
65.     }
66.
67.     // initialize sum with the the first number
68.     for (int index = 0; index <= numberOfNumbers; index++)
69.             sum[index] = numbers[0][index];
70.
71.     for (int numberIndex = 1; numberIndex <
        maxNumberOfNumbers; numberIndex++)
72.             sum_of_two(sum, numbers[numberIndex], sum);
73. }
74. int main()
75. {
76.     int numberOfNumbers, lengthOfNumbers;
77.
78.     // index 0 will store the number of bits for each number
79.     int numbers[maxNumberOfNumbers][maxNumberLength] = {{3,0,
        0, 0}, {3, 0, 0, 1}, {3, 0, 1, 0}, {3, 0, 1, 1}};
80.     int sum[maxNumberLength];
81.
82.     numberOfNumbers = 4; lengthOfNumbers = 3;
83.
84.     compute_sum(numbers, sum, numberOfNumbers);
85.
86.     printf("The binary sum is:\n");
87.     for (int sumIndex = 1; sumIndex <= sum[0]; sumIndex++)
88.             printf("%d ", sum[sumIndex]);
89.             printf("\n");
90.
91.     return 0;
92. }
```

For M = 4, N = 3
4 3
0 0 0
0 0 1
0 1 0
0 1 1

The binary sum is:

1 1 0

Q: What if we had to perform subtraction / multiplication instead of addition?

A: The principle is the same, we align the numbers and then perform the operation as we do with a pen and some paper. In fact, the last step of the multiplication operation is the one we have implemented (addition of multiple numbers).

ARRAY: TWO ELEMENTS IN SET WHOSE SUM IS EXACTLY X.

Given a set S of N real numbers and another real number x, determine whether or not there exist. two elements in S whose sum is exactly x.

S = { 1,3,5,2,15,14,10,9,6 }

X = 8

Sum Pairs = { 5,3}, {2,6}

SOLUTION: We store whether an element is present in the set or not by using a hash table of Boolean values, such that hash[x] = true if and only if x is an element of the set. All we need to do after building this hash table is check whether there is an i between 0 and x/2 - 1 such that hash[i] and hash[x − i] are both true. For example, take the following input:

N = 4, X = 10

{1, 6, 4, 10}

In this case we would just iterate through the array and mark hash[1], hash[6], hash[4] and hash[10] with true. Finally, since x is 10 we iterate from 1 to 4 (10 / 2 − 1) and check whether the pairs (1, 9), (2,8), (3,7) and (4,6) are present in our hash table. We find 6,4, since hash[4] = true and hash[6] = true, so in this example there is a pair of elements that add up to 10.

PSEUDO CODE:

```
1.   Check_for_pairs(table, x):
2.       for iterator from 0 to x/2
3.               iterator and x - iterator are in table
4.                   return true
5.       return false
```

CLARIFICATION POINT-1:

What is the maximum value for an element in the set?

In our approach we could use the numbers as indexes, so this question is important.

CLARIFICATION POINT-2:

Are the elements positive? If not, we would not be able to use the
method described in the previous clarification point.

ASSUMPTION/LIMITATION:

- We will firstly assume all the elements in the data set are integers, between 0 and 10000

- We will assume we stop when the first pair has been detected, considering how the problem is formulated.

MAJOR DATA STRUCTURES:

Array of Boolean values

UNIT TESTS:

POSTIVE FUNCTIONAL TEST CASES

INPUT	EXPECTED OUTPUT
N=1 X=2 {0}	No pair
N=2 X=2 {1, 1}	No pair (all elements in a set are unique)
N=3 X=3 {1, 2, 3}	
N=4 X=10 {10, 11, 12, 13}	There is a pair that adds up to 3 (<1,2>)
N=10 X=11	
{1,2,3,4,5,6,7,8,9,10}	No pair
N=2 X=10 {4,6}	There is a pair that adds up to 11 (<5,6>)
	There is a pair that adds up to 10 (<4,6>)

NEGATIVE FUNCTIONAL TEST CASES

N = 0	Invalid input
N < 0	Invalid input

Here sample answer uses a look-up table / hash table of type Boolean and uses the value of the elements in the initial set as keys. This is done in O(N). The algorithm then performs x/2 steps to determine whether the pair (y, x − y) is present in the set. The total complexity is hence O(N + X/2).

```
1.    #include <cstdio>
2.    #define maxNumberOfElements 10001
3.    using namespace std;
4.
5.    bool check_for_pairs(int array[], int numberOfElements, int x)
6.    {
7.        if (numberOfElements <= 0)
8.        {
9.            printf("Input Invalid!\n");
10.           return false;
11.       }
12.
13.       // the hash table
14.       bool hashTable[maxNumberOfElements];
```

```
15.
16.     for (int i = 0; i < numberOfElements; i++)
17.             hashTable[array[i]] = true;
18.
19.     for (int i = 0; i <= x / 2; i++)
20.             if(hashTable[i] && hashTable[x-i])
21.                     return true;
22.     return false;
23. }
24.
25. int main()
26. {
27.     int numberOfElements;
28.     int x;
29.
30.     numberOfElements = 4;
31.
32.     int array[maxNumberOfElements] = {1, 6, 4, 10};
33.
34.     x = 10;
35.
36.     if (check_for_pairs(array, numberOfElements, x))
37.             printf("There is a pair of elements with sum
                %d!\n", x);
38.     else
39.             printf("There is no pair of elements with sum
                %d!\n", x);
40.
41.
42.     return 0;
43. }
```

OUTPUT:

N = 4, X = 10

{1, 6, 4, 10}

There is a pair of elements
with sum 10!

FURTHER EXERCISE:

Q: What if the set contained
duplicates?

A: If the set contained duplicates, we would use an
array that counts how many
times an item is present in
the set, rather than just
marking whether they are
there or not.

Q: What if the set contained
real numbers? A: In this
case a viable solution
would be the naïve ap-
proach, which uses two for
loops to iterate over the
array and runs in O(n2).

ARRAY: MEDIAN/MEAN/MODE/RANGE OF TWO ARRAYS

Let X[1..n] and Y[1..n] be two arrays, each containing n numbers already in sorted order. Give an O(logn)-time algorithm to find the median/mean/mode/range of all 2n elements in arrays X and Y.

SOLUTION: Take the following sorted array: {1, 6, 7, 9, 10}. The median of the array is the element in the middle (in this case 7). If the array had an even number of elements (e.g. {1, 2, 3, 4}) the median would be obtained by averaging the two elements in the middle (in our example 2 + 3 / 2 = 2.5).

The mean of an array is simply the average of the elements (sum of all elements / number of elements). In the example above, the mean is (1 + 6 + 7 + 9 + 10) / 5 = 33 / 5. Next, the mode is the value that appears most often in the data. In the example above, all the five elements are modes of the array because they all appear once, but in the array {1, 3, 3, 5}, for example, 3 is the mode element.

Finally the range is simply the difference between the largest and smallest element in the array. Our initial array given as an example has range 10 − 1 = 9.

The algorithm for computing the median will takes the following steps:

- Compute the median of both arrays
- If the median of the first array is smaller than the median of the second array
    - ▷ Discard the first half of the first array
    - ▷ Discard the second half of the second array
- Else
    - ▷ Discard the second half of the first array
    - ▷ Discard the first half of the second array
- Repeat until both arrays have only one element left; their average is the median required.

In order to find the mean of two arrays of n elements each, we simply iterate through both at the same time and add up the value of their elements. In the end we divide this value by 2n, which is the total number of elements. Furthermore, the range of two arrays is even simpler to detect and only requires two comparisons. Suppose we have the sorted arrays A = {a, b, c} and B = {d, e, f}. The steps are as follows:

- If a < d then a is surely the smallest element in the two arrays, as they are already sorted; otherwise this element is d.

- If c > f then c is surely the largest element in the two arrays, because they are already sorted, otherwise, this element is f.

- The range of the two arrays is obtained by subtracting the smallest element from the larger one.

Finally, suppose we have arrays a={1, 2, 2, 3, 4} and b={1, 3, 3, 3, 5} and we want to compute the mode of the two arrays. We can do this in the following way:

- Have two iterators, one for each array, and set them at position 0 initially. Let's call them position1 and position2.

- If (a[position1] == b[position2]) increment position 1 and position 2 until a different element is found and count the increments.

- If (a[position1] < b[position2]) increment position1 until a different element is found; count the increments.

- If (a[position1] > b[position2]) increment position2 until a different element is found; count the increments.

- The mode of the two arrays is the element that corresponds to the largest number of increments.

In our initial example we start at position 0 in both arrays (elements 1 and 1) and, because these are equal, increment position1 once and position2 once (so 2 increments in total), reaching the pair (2,3). 2 < 3, so we increment position1 two times, finding (3,3). This time we increment position 1 once and position 2 three times (so 4 increments in total, i.e. 3 appears 4 times in our arrays). 3 is therefore the mode of our arrays.

We will now see the algorithm required to compute the median in practice, as this is the most challenging of the four.

PSEUDO CODE:

```
1.   Find_median(x[], y[])
2.       startx=0; endx=N; starty=0; endy=N;
3.       repeat
4.               medianx=median of sub-array (startx,endx) of x
5.               mediany=median of sub-array (starty,endy) of y
6.               if (median < mediany)
7.                       discard left-half of x
8.                       discard right-half of y
9.               else
10.                      discard right-half of x
11.                      discard left-half of y
12.      until (endx-startx=1 and endy-starty=1)
```

CLARIFICATION POINT-1:

What is the maximum value for N?

This is useful to know, so we can ensure we can store the arrays statically.

CLARIFICATION POINT-2:

 Can the same number appear in both arrays? In this problem we will assume the answer to this clarification is positive.

CLARIFICATION POINT-3:

What is the maximum value of an element in any of the arrays? For the purpose of this example we will assume they all fit in the type int.

ASSUMPTION/LIMITATION:

- We will firstly assume all the elements in the data set are integers.

- We will assume a maximum of 10000 for N.

MAJOR DATA STRUCTURES:

Array of Integers

UNIT TESTS:	
POSTIVE FUNCTIONAL TEST CASES	
INPUT	EXPECTED OUTPUT
N=3 X={1,2,3} Y={1,2,3}	2
N=2 X={1,1},Y={1,1}	1
N=3 X={1,2,3},Y={4,5,6}	3.5
N=4 X={1,2,3,4},Y={6,7,8,9}	5
NEGATIVE FUNCTIONAL TEST CASES	
N = 0	Invalid input
N < 0	Invalid input

The sample answer provided below works in O(logN) and does the following:

- Start with both arrays at the same time;
- Compute their mean;
- If the mean in x < mean in y discard the left half of x and right half of y, because the mean must be smaller/ greater than N/2 elements

- Repeat until there is only one element left in each array
- The mean is the average of the two elements left.

```
1.   #include <cstdio>
2.   #define maxLengthOfArrays 10001
3.
4.   using namespace std;
5.
6.   // returns the mean in sub-array of array[], defined by
     positions start to end
7.   int median_of_array(int array[], int start, int end)
8.   {
9.       int lengthOfArray = end - start;
10.
11.      // if length is odd median is at position (length-1)/2
12.      if (lengthOfArray %2 == 1)
13.              return array[start + (lengthOfArray - 1)/2];
14.
15.      // if length is even return the average of the two
         elements in the middle
16.      return (array[start + lengthOfArray/2] + array[start +
         lengthOfArray/2-1]) / 2;
17.  }
18.
19.  float find_median(int x[], int y[], int lengthOfArrays)
20.  {
21.      if (lengthOfArrays <= 0)
22.      {
23.              printf("Invaild input!\n");
24.              return 0;
25.      }
26.
27.      // the two iterators for x and y
28.      int startX = 0, endX = lengthOfArrays;
29.      int startY = 0, endY = lengthOfArrays;
30.
31.      // the meadian of each array
32.      int medianX, medianY;
33.
34.      while (1)
35.      {
36.              // compute the medians individually
37.              medianX = median_of_array(x, startX, endX);
38.              medianY = median_of_array(y, startY, endY);
39.
40.              // if there is only one element left in each array
                 stop
41.              if (endX - startX == 1 && endY - startY == 1)
42.              break;
43.
```

```
44.              // if the median of x is smaller
45.              // discard left half of x and right half of y
46.              if (medianX < medianY)
47.              {
48.                      startX = startX + (endX - startX)/2;
49.                      endY = endY - (endY - startY) / 2;
50.              }
51.
52.              // if the median of y is smaller
53.              // discard left half of y and right half of x
54.              else
55.              {
56.                      startY = startY + (endY - startY)/2;
57.                      endX = endX - (endX - startX) / 2;
58.              }
59.      }
60.
61.      // return the average of the two elements left
62.      return float(medianX + medianY) / 2;
63. }
64. int main()
65. {
66.      int lengthOfArrays = 3;
67.      int x[maxLengthOfArrays] = {1, 2, 3};
68.      int y[maxLengthOfArrays] = {4, 5, 6};
69.
70.      float median = find_median(x, y, lengthOfArrays);
71.
72.      printf("The median of the two arrays is %g\n", median);
73.
74.      return 0;
75. }
```

OUTPUT:	FURTHER EXERCISE:
N = 3, X={1,2,3}, Y={4,5,6}	Q: Is there a naïve approach?
3	A: There is also a naïve approach, inefficient in terms of memory, which stores the elements of both arrays into a single array and computes the median. The complexity of this method is O(N).
1 2 3	
4 5 6	
The median of the two arrays is 3.5	
	Q: Write a program to compute the mean, the range and the mode of two arrays.
	A: Use the algorithms described.

ARRAY: TWO STACKS IN ONE ARRAY A[1..N]

Write a function to implement two stacks in one array A[1..n] in such a way that neither stack overflows unless the total number of elements in both stacks together is n. The Push and Pop operations run in O(1) time.

SOLUTION: The best way to do this is to place the base of the two stacks at an end of the given array and let the first stack 'grow' from the left and the right one 'grow' from the right. For example, if we had an array of 10 elements available and two stacks, s1={0,1,2} and s2={4,5,6}, the array would look as follows:

A = 0, 1, 2, x, x, x, x, 6, 5, 4

x denotes an unused space. Notice that if s1.length + s2.length > n an overflow will occur. If we store the stacks in this way it will be easy to implement push and pop operations in O(1) for both of them.

PSEUDO CODE:

```
1.    Stacks_to_array(s1,s2):
2.        Place elements of s1 from 0 to s1.length in array
3.        Place elements of s2 from N-s2.length to N in array
```

CLARIFICATION POINT-1:

Can any stack be empty?

CLARIFICATION POINT-2:

Can we implement separate push / pop operations for the stack?

ASSUMPTION/LIMITATION:

- We will implement separate push / pop operations for the two stacks, in O(1)

- The first stack will start from index 0 in the array and 'grow' to the right, while the second one will start at index N-1 in the same array and 'grow' to the left. In this way an overflow would only occur if the sum of the number of elements of the two stacks exceeds the capacity of the array.

MAJOR DATA STRUCTURES:

Array of integers

POSTIVE FUNCTIONAL TEST CASES	
INPUT	EXPECTED OUTPUT
S1={0,1,2} S2={3,4,5}, N=10	Array={0, 1, 2, 0, 0, 0, 0, 5, 4, 3}
S1={1}, S2={3}, N=3	Array={1, 0, 3}
S1={1}, S2={3}, N=2	Array={1, 3}
S1={1,2,3}, S2={1,2,3}, N=6	Array={1,2,3,3,2,1}
NEGATIVE FUNCTIONAL TEST CASES	
N1 + N2 > N	Invalid input
N <= 0	Invalid input

Here sample answer, which implements the idea defined above. We implement separate push and pop functions for the two array, which both run in O(1). We also test these methods by performing a pop and a push for each stack.

```cpp
1.    #include <cstdio>
2.    #define maxLengthOfArray 10001
3.
4.    using namespace std;
5.
6.    void pop1(int &head)
7.    {
8.        head--;
9.    }
10.
11.   void pop2(int &head)
12.   {
13.       head++;
14.   }
15.
16.   void push1(int array[], int &head, int value)
17.   {
18.       array[++head] = value;
19.   }
20.
21.   void push2(int array[], int &head, int value)
22.   {
23.       array[--head] = value;
24.   }
25.
26.   void stacks_to_array(int array[], int lengthOfArray, int
      s1[], int lengthOfs1, int s2[], int lengthOfs2)
27.   {
28.       if (lengthOfArray <= 0 || lengthOfs1 + lengthOfs2 >
          lengthOfArray)
29.       {
```

```
30.              printf("Invalid input!\n");
31.              return;
32.        }
33.
34.     // stack 1 'grows' from 0
35.     for (int index1 = 0; index1 < lengthOfs1; index1++)
36.              array[index1] = s1[index1];
37.     int head1 = lengthOfs1 - 1; // head of stack 1
38.
39.     // stack 2 starts at N-1 (the other end of the array)
40.     // and grows to the left
41.     for (int index2 = 0; index2 < lengthOfs2; index2++)
42.              array[lengthOfArray - index2 - 1] = s2[index2];
43.     int head2 = lengthOfArray - lengthOfs2; // head of stack 2
44.
45.     // we now define the push and pop operations for each stack
46.     // all these are O(1)
47.     pop1(head1); pop2(head2);
48.     push1(array, head1, 10); push2(array, head2, 10);
49.
50.     // print contents of stack 1
51.     printf("Stack 1: ");
52.     for (int index1 = 0; index1 <= head1; index1++)
53.              printf("%d ", array[index1]);
54.     printf("\n");
55.
56.     // print contents of stack 2
57.     printf("Stack 2: ");
58.     for (int index2 = lengthOfArray - 1; index2 >= head2;
        index2--)
59.              printf("%d ", array[index2]);
60.     printf("\n");
61. }
62.
63. int main()
64. {
65.     int lengthOfArray = 10;
66.     int lengthOfs1 = 2, lengthOfs2 = 3;
67.     int array[maxLengthOfArray];
68.     int s1[maxLengthOfArray] = {1, 2}, s2[maxLengthOfArray] =
        {4, 5, 6};
69.
70.     stacks_to_array(array, lengthOfArray, s1, lengthOfs1, s2,
        lengthOfs2);
71.
72.     return 0;
73. }
```

OUTPUT:

```
N = 10, N1=2, N2=3
S1={1,2} S2={4,5,6}
10
2
1 2
3
4 5 6
Stack 1: 1 10
Stack 2: 4 5 10

(After a pop() and a push(10))
```

FURTHER EXERCISE:

Q: Is it possible to store multiple stacks in a single array? How?

A: We could divide the array into more chunks, but chances for an overflow would then increase considerably. Suppose we had an array of 10 and three stacks of 3 elements each.

A = {s11,s12,s13,x,s21,s22,s23,s31,s32,s33}

If we perform a push on stack 2, it would clash with the third stack, even though there is one space available, where the element inserted could fit.

ARRAY: S1 UNION/INTERSECTION S2

Set S1 and Set S2 consist of n and m elements each, write a function to compute the union/intersection of these sets S1 U S2, S1 Intersection S2.

SOLUTION: The algorithm we will use takes advantage of the fact that sets are sorted data structures. The union can be performed as follows:

- Iterate through bots sets at the same time, remembering the current position for each;
- If s1[position1] < s2[position2] output s1[position1] and increase position1
- Else output s2[position2] and increase position2

The intersection uses the same principle, but we only output elements when they are equal, because we are interested in finding values that appear in both sets.

Suppose we had the sets {1, 3, 5} and {2, 4, 5, 6}. We would then perform the following steps for the union:

- Start from the beginning of both sets.
- 1 < 2, so output 1 and increase index of first set.
- 3 > 2, so output 2 and increase index of second set,
- And so on..

The intersection is performed as follows:

- 1 < 2, so increase the index of the first set.
- 3 > 2, so increase index of the second set.
- 3 < 4, so increase index of the first set.
- Repeat until we reach 5 = 5, when we output 5.

PSEUDO CODE:

```
1.    Union(s1[], s2[]):
2.        position1=position2=0
3.        while position1<N || position2 <M
4.            if s1[position1] < s2[position2]
5.                print s1[position1]
6.                increase position1
7.            else
8.                print s1[position2]
9.                increase position2
```

```
10.
11.  intersection(s1[], s2[]):
12.      position1=position2=0
13.      while position1<N && position2<M
14.              if s1[position1] = s2[position2]
15.                      print s1[position1]
16.                      increase position1 and position2
17.              else if s1[position1] < s2[position2]
18.                      increase position1
19.              else
20.                      increase position2
```

CLARIFICATION POINT-1:

Can the sets be stored statically? How many values do they contain at most?

ASSUMPTION/LIMITATION:

- We will firstly assume the sets can hold at most 10000 elements

- We will build two separate functions, one for computing the intersection and the other for computing the reunion

MAJOR DATA STRUCTURES:

Array of Boolean values

UNIT TESTS:	
POSTIVE FUNCTIONAL TEST CASES	
INPUT	EXPECTED OUTPUT
S1={0,1,2} S2={1,2,3}	U={0,1,2,3} I={1,2}
S1={0} S2={0} S1={1,2,3} S2={1,2,3,4} S1={1,3,5,7} S2={2,4,6,8}	U={0} I={0} U={1,2,3,4} I={1,2,3} U={1,2,3,4,5,6,7,8} I={}
NEGATIVE FUNCTIONAL TEST CASES	
N < 0 or M < 0	Undefined

Here sample answer, which works in O(N), where N is the length of the biggest set.

```
1.    #include <cstdio>
2.    #define maxLengthOfs1 10001
3.    #define maxLengthOfs2 10001
4.
5.    using namespace std;
6.
7.    void compute_union(int s1[], int s2[], int lengthOfs1, int
      lengthOfs2)
8.    {
```

```
9.      if (lengthOfs1 <= 0 || lengthOfs1 <= 0)
10.     {
11.             printf("Invalid input!");
12.             return;
13.     }
14.
15.     int currentPos1 = 0, currentPos2 = 0;
16.
17.     while (currentPos1 < lengthOfs1 || currentPos2 <
        lengthOfs2)
18.     {
19.             // if there are no more elements in the first set
                but there are more in the second one
20.             if (currentPos1 == lengthOfs1 && currentPos2 <
                lengthOfs2)
21.             {
22.                     printf("%d ", s2[currentPos2]);
23.                     currentPos2++;
24.                     continue;
25.             }
26.
27.             // if no more elements in the second set but more
                in the first one
28.             if (currentPos1 < lengthOfs1 && currentPos2 ==
                lengthOfs2)
29.             {
30.                     printf("%d ", s1[currentPos1]);
31.                     currentPos1++;
32.                     continue;
33.             }
34.
35.             if (s1[currentPos1] < s2[currentPos2])
36.             {
37.                     printf("%d ", s1[currentPos1]);
38.                     currentPos1++;
39.             }
40.
41.             else
42.             {
43.                     printf("%d ", s2[currentPos2]);
44.                     currentPos2++;
45.             }
46.     }
47.     printf("\n");
48. }
49.
50. void compute_intersection(int s1[], int s2[], int lengthOfs1,
    int lengthOfs2)
51. {
52.     if (lengthOfs1 <= 0 || lengthOfs1 <= 0)
53.     {
```

```
54.                 printf("Invalid input!");
55.                 return;
56.         }
57.
58.     int currentPos1 = 0, currentPos2 = 0;
59.
60.     // while we have not reach the end of any of the two sets
61.     while (currentPos1 < lengthOfs1 && currentPos2 <
        lengthOfs2)
62.     {
63.             if (s1[currentPos1] == s2[currentPos2])
64.             {
65.                     printf("%d ", s1[currentPos1]);
66.                     currentPos1++;
67.                     currentPos2++;
68.             }
69.             else if (s1[currentPos1] < s2[currentPos2])
70.                     currentPos1++;
71.             else
72.                     currentPos2++;
73.     }
74.     printf("\n");
75. }
76.
77. int main()
78. {
79.     int lengthOfs1 = 3, lengthOfs2 = 4;
80.
81.     int s1[maxLengthOfs1] = {1, 3, 5};
82.     int s2[maxLengthOfs2] = {2, 4, 5, 6};
83.
84.     printf("The union of the two sets:\n");
85.     compute_union(s1, s2, lengthOfs1, lengthOfs2);
86.
87.     printf("The intersection of the two sets:\n");
88.     compute_intersection(s1, s2, lengthOfs1, lengthOfs2);
89.     return 0;
90. }
```

OUTPUT:	FURTHER EXERCISE:
N=3	Q: Is there a naïve approach?
s1=1 3 5	
M=4	A: The naïve approach merges
s2=2 4 5 6	the two sets in the same
The union of the two sets:	array to perform the union.
1 2 3 4 5 5 6	
	Q: How do you perform the union
The intersection of the two	/ intersection of three or
sets:	more sets?
5	A: We use the same principle,
	with an index for each set.
	However, because of the ex-
	tra number of comparisons,
	the complexity of the al-
	gorithm increases consid-
	erably.

ARRAY: LARGEST SUB ARRAY(RECTANGLE)

Given a 2D binary array (2D array of 0's and 1's) with 'm' rows and 'n' columns, give an efficient algo to find area of the largest sub array(rectangle) consisting entirely of 1's.

SOLUTION: Before we look at the pseudo-code, clarification points and all the other aspects, let's start by explaining how an efficient algorithm works. The naïve approach would consider all the rectangles and compute their area individually, leading to a very large complexity. A more efficient approach is as follows:

- We firstly compute an auxiliary matrix derived from the initial one, such that aux[i][j] = the number of '1's above the position (i,j) in the initial matrix; in order to save space, we will use the initial 2D array to store this auxiliary matrix; at this point our matrix is similar to a histogram;

- We then iterate through each row i in the auxiliary matrix and compute the maximum area for the row, as follows:

  ▷ We compute height(j) for each column j, which is the maximum 'height' that can be obtained for column j at row i

  ▷ We compute l(j) and r(j), which define the number of larger or equal values to the left and to the right of column j of row i

  ▷ The maximum area for row i is therefore max(h(j) * (l(j) + r(j) + 1)), i.e. the column at which the biggest height * width can be obtained.

- The global maximum is the maximal area obtained at any of the rows.

For example, given the matrix:

```
0 0 0 1 1 1
0 0 0 1 1 1
0 0 0 1 1 1
1 1 1 1 0 0
1 1 1 1 0 0
1 1 1 1 0 0
```

We compute the following auxiliary matrix:

```
0 0 0 1 1 1
0 0 0 2 2 2
0 0 0 3 3 3
1 1 1 4 0 0
2 2 2 5 0 0
3 3 3 6 0 0
```

This can simply be done by iterating through the initial matrix and every time we reach a '1' make the element at the current position equal to the one above it, increased by 1. For example, after traversing the second row of the initial matrix we would have:

```
0 0 0 1 1 1
0 0 0 2 2 2 (= 1 + 1)
```

After the third and fourth rows are traversed we would obtain

```
0 0 0 1 1 1
0 0 0 2 2 2
0 0 0 3 3 3 (= 2 + 1)
1 1 1 4(= 3 + 1) 0 0
```

Next, the naïve approach for computing l(j) and r(j) for each column j in the current row runs in $O(N^2)$ and iterates from 0 to j (N to j for r(j)), computing the number of larger or equal values encountered along the way. A more clever solution uses a stack and performs the following steps:

- As we iterate through each column j we push j into the stack and, when we want to find out how many larger values are on its left (or right) we just pop the elements already pushed in the stack until a smaller one is found or the stack is empty.

- For example, suppose we have row 1 1 1 4 0 0 and we want to compute l(j) for every column j. By the time we get to 4, the third 1 will have already been pushed to the stack, so we know there is no adjacent value larger than or equal to 4 to the left. When we get to 0, the stack will have 4 elements, so we need to do 4 pop operations, so l(4) = 4.

We then iterate through each row in the auxiliary matrix and perform the steps described above. The maximum is obtained at the element marked with red in the auxiliary matrix above (3 * (2 + 1 +1) = 3 * 4 = 12).

This algorithm has complexity $O(M * N)$, where M is the number of rows in the matrix and N is the number of columns.

PSEUDO CODE:

```
1.   Largest_area (int a[][]):
2.       maxarea = 0
3.       for rowIndex from 0 to M - 1
4.              if area(rowIndex) > maxarea
5.                     maxarea = area(rowIndex)
6.       return maxarea
```

CLARIFICATION POINT-1:

What is the maximum value for m and n? Can the array be stored statically?

ASSUMPTION/LIMITATION:

- We will assume a maximum of 10000 rows and 10000 columns for the initial matrix;

- We will use the same data structure to hold the auxiliary matrix

MAJOR DATA STRUCTURES:

2D array of integers

UNIT TESTS:

POSTIVE FUNCTIONAL TEST CASES

INPUT	EXPECTED OUTPUT
M=6 N=6, A= 0 0 0 1 1 1 0 0 0 1 1 1 0 0 0 1 1 1 1 1 1 1 0 0 1 1 1 1 0 0 1 1 1 1 0 0	12

NEGATIVE FUNCTIONAL TEST CASES

N<0 or M<0	Input invalid
Array with elements other than 0/1	Input invalid

Here is the sample answer described in the first paragraph:

```
1.    #include <cstdio>
2.    #define maxN 10001
3.    #define maxM 10001
4.
5.    int array[maxM][maxN];
6.
7.    using namespace std;
8.
9.    int area_for_row(int row[], int numberOfColumns)
10.   {
11.       int area[numberOfColumns]; // area at each column position
                                     // in the row
12.
13.       int top;
14.       int stack[maxN], stackHead = -1;
15.
16.       // find Li
17.       for (int colIndex = 0; colIndex < numberOfColumns;
          colIndex++)
18.       {
19.               while (stackHead != -1)
```

```
20.                         if(row[colIndex] <= row[stack[stackHead]])
21.                                 stackHead--;
22.                         else
23.                                 break;
24.
25.                 if(stackHead == -1)
26.                         top = -1;
27.                 else
28.                         top = stack[stackHead];
29.
30.                 area[colIndex] = colIndex - top - 1;
31.                 stack[++stackHead] = colIndex;
32.         }
33.
34.     // empty the stack to find Ri
35.     while (stackHead != -1)
36.             stackHead --;
37.
38.     for (int colIndex = numberOfColumns - 1; colIndex >= 0;
        colIndex--)
39.     {
40.             while (stackHead != -1)
41.                     if(row[colIndex] <= row[stack[stackHead]])
42.                             stackHead--;
43.                     else break;
44.
45.             if(stackHead == -1)
46.                     top = numberOfColumns;
47.             else
48.                     top = stack[stackHead];
49.
50.             // area[i] = Li + Ri after this point
51.             area[colIndex] += top - colIndex -1;
52.             stack[++stackHead] = colIndex;
53.     }
54.
55.     int maxArea = 0;
56.
57.     //calculating Area[i] with the following formula in order
        to find max
58.     for (int colIndex = 0; colIndex < numberOfColumns;
        colIndex++)
59.     {
60.             area[colIndex] = row[colIndex] * (area[colIndex] +
                1);
61.             if (area[colIndex] > maxArea)
62.                     maxArea = area[colIndex];
63.     }
64.
65.     return maxArea;
66. }
```

```
67.
68.  int compute_area(int array[maxM][maxN], int numberOfRows,
     int numberOfColumns)
69.  {
70.     for (int rowIndex = 1; rowIndex < numberOfRows;
        rowIndex++)
71.             for (int colIndex = 0; colIndex < numberOfColumns;
                colIndex++)
72.                     if (array[rowIndex][colIndex] != 0 &&
                        array[rowIndex][colIndex] != 1)
73.                     {
74.                     printf("Input invalid!");
75.                     return 0;
76.                     }
77.
78.     if (numberOfRows < 0 || numberOfColumns < 0)
79.     {
80.             printf("Input invalid!\n");
81.             return 0;
82.     }
83.
84.     // store the auxiliary matrix in the initial array
85.     for (int rowIndex = 1; rowIndex < numberOfRows;
        rowIndex++)
86.             for (int colIndex = 0; colIndex < numberOfColumns;
                colIndex++)
87.                     if (array[rowIndex][colIndex] == 1)
88.                             array[rowIndex][colIndex] =
                                array[rowIndex - 1][colIndex] + 1;
89.
90.     int maxArea = 0;
91.
92.     for (int rowIndex = 0; rowIndex < numberOfRows;
        rowIndex++)
93.     {
94.             int tempArea = area_for_row(array[rowIndex],
                numberOfColumns);
95.             if (tempArea > maxArea)
96.                     maxArea = tempArea;
97.     }
98.
99.     return maxArea;
100. }
101.
102. int main()
103. {
104.    int numberOfRows = 6, numberOfColumns = 6;
105.    array[0] = {0, 0, 0, 1, 1, 1};
106.    array[1] = {0, 0, 0, 1, 1, 1};
107.    array[2] = {0, 0, 0, 1, 1, 1};
108.    array[3] = {1, 1, 1, 1, 0, 0};
```

```
109.    array[4] = {1, 1, 1, 1, 0, 0};
110.    array[5] = {1, 1, 1, 1, 0, 0};
111.
112.    int area = compute_area(array, numberOfRows,
        numberOfColumns);
113.
114.    printf ("The area of the largest rectangle is %d\n",
        area);
115.
116.    return 0;
117. }
```

OUTPUT:

```
6 6
0 0 0 1 1 1
0 0 0 1 1 1
0 0 0 1 1 1
1 1 1 1 0 0
1 1 1 1 0 0
1 1 1 1 0 0
```

The area of the largest rectangle is 12

FURTHER EXERCISE:

Q: Is there a naïve approach for this problem? What is its complexity:

A: The naïve approach for this problem has complexity O(N2 * M2) and computes the area of every single square, being very inefficient.

Q: What if the array contained more values rather than just 0s and 1s?

A: This problem is known as the maximum sub-array problem and there are plenty of algorithms for solving it, including a divide-and-conquer approach.

ARRAY: SEQUENCE OF THE FORM
0123456789101112131415.

Imagine you have a sequence of the form 0123456789101112131415... where each digit is in a position, for example the digit in the position 5 is 5, the digit at position 13 is 1, the digit at position 19 is 4, etc. Write a function that given a position returns the digit in that position.

SOLUTION: Again, let's start with a description of the algorithm we will be using. First, it would be tedious to generate the entire sequence, because we would waste too much memory. The idea of the algorithm is based on the fact that there are 10 1-digit numbers, followed by 90 2-digit numbers, 900 3-digit numbers, 9000 4-digit numbers, etc. Because of this, given the position, we can firstly deduce which number it points to. Once we have this information, computing the digit at the given position becomes trivial. We consider the following steps:

- Consider the case position < 10 separately and return the position itself in this case.

- We subtract 10, 90 * 2, 900 * 3, 9000 * 4 (remember, there are 10 1 digit numbers, 90 2-digit numbers, etc.) from the position until we would obtain a negative number when subtracting;

- For example, if we had position = 1001 we would perform 1001 – 10 – 90 * 2 = 811; at this point position points to the 811th digit of the sequence formed by the 3-digit numbers (i.e. the sequence 100101102103...; we have eliminated the 1-digit and 2-digit numbers with the subtraction);

- Following the logic of the example above, in order to be able to tell which number the digit we are looking for belongs to we need to know that the number has 3 digits (let's call this variable howManyDigits) and also that there are 900 such numbers (let's call this variable base).

- We reconstruct the number at the given position using number = position / howManyDigits + base / 9.

- In order to know which digit of the number reconstructed is required we can use:

  ▷ positionOfDigit = howManyDigits - position % howManyDigits -1;

- If we had position 5, for example, of the sequence formed by 3-digit numbers. 4 % 3 = 1. This is the second digit from the start of the number we have reconstructed. However, we can only extract a digit one by one form the end of the number, rather than the start, which is why we have to use

howManyDigits – position % howManyDigits – 1, to tell us the position of the digit starting from the back of the number.

For example, for input 1001, we perform the following:

- 1001 – 10 – 90 * 2 = 811; we stop at this point, because 811 – 3 * 900 would give a negative number;

- We reconstruct the number: number = 811 / 3 + 900 / 9 = 370.

- positionOfDigit = 3 – 811 % 3 – 1 = 3 – 1 – 1 = 1; in this example this digit is 7.

PSEUDO CODE:

```
1.   digitAtPosition(position):
2.       count=2, base=90
3.       if position < 10 return position
4.       position -= 10
5.       while position > base-count
6.               position -= base * count
7.               count++
8.               base = base * 10
9.       number=position/count + base/9
10.      position_in_number=count-position%count-1
11.      return number/10^position_in_number % 10
```

CLARIFICATION POINT-1:

What is the maximum position? This will help us determine if we can generate the sequence and store it in an array.

CLARIFICATION POINT-2:

How much memory are we allowed to use? For the purpose of this example we will not use any array

CLARIFICATION POINT-3:

Are we allowed to use non-standard libraries to simplify our calculations? (e.g. math.h in C/C++)

ASSUMPTION/LIMITATION:

- We will assume the given position fits in the type int

- We will also use the external library math.h to help with the calculations

MAJOR DATA STRUCTURES:

Integers

POSTIVE FUNCTIONAL TEST CASES	
INPUT	EXPECTED OUTPUT
N=1	1
N=2	2
N=10	1
N=11	0
N=1000	3
NEGATIVE FUNCTIONAL TEST CASES	
N < 0	Undefined

Here is the sample answer that implements the solution described above:

```
1.    #include <cstdio>
2.    #include <math.h>
3.
4.    using namespace std;
5.
6.    int digitAtPosition(int position)
7.    {
8.       if (position <= 0) {printf("Invalid input!"); return 0;}
9.
10.      int howManyDigits = 2, base = 90;
11.
12.      if (position < 10) return position;
13.
14.      position -= 10;
15.      while (position > base * howManyDigits)
16.      {
17.              position -= base * howManyDigits;
18.              howManyDigits++;
19.              base *= 10;
20.      }
21.
22.      int number = position/howManyDigits+ base/9;
23.
24.      int positionOfDigit = howManyDigits - position %
         howManyDigits -1;
25.      int whichDigitInNumber = int(number/pow(10,
         positionOfDigit)) % 10;
26.
27.      return whichDigitInNumber;
28.   }
29.
30.   int main()
31.   {
32.      int position = 1001;
33.
```

```
34.    printf("The digit at position %d is %d\n", position,
       digitAtPosition(position));
35.
36.    return 0;
37. }
```

OUTPUT:	FURTHER EXERCISE:
N = 1001 1001 The digit at position 1001 is 7	Q: Is there a naïve approach? A: The naïve approach stores the entire sequence in an array and is very inefficient in terms of space.

ARRAY: PRINTS OUT A 2-D ARRAY IN SPIRAL ORDER

Write a routine that prints out a 2-D array in spiral order!

A spiral traversal of a 2D array is shown in the following picture:

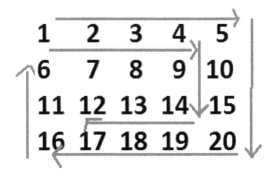

The order of the elements is 1, 2, 3, 4, 5, 10, 15, 20, 19, 18, 17, 16, 11, 6, 7, 8, 9, 14, 13, 12.

The easiest and most intuitive way to tackle this problem is by a recursive algorithm, with four separate for-loops to print the elements in the array from left to right, from top to bottom, from right to left and from bottom to top, respectively. The parameter 'level' of the recursive function we will use is how 'deep' we have gone in to the matrix. It starts with 0 and as we enter each sub-layer (with another call to the same method) it increases.

PSEUDO CODE:

```
1.    Print_array_in_spiral(N, M, level)
2.        If N = 1 print first row of sub-matrix
3.        If M = 1 print first column of sub-matrix
4.
5.        Print row[level] from left to right
6.        Print column[level + N] from top to bottom
7.        Print row [level + M] from right to left
8.        Print column[level] from bottom to top
9.
10.       Print_array_in_spiral(N-2,M-2,level+1)
```

CLARIFICATION POINT-1:

What is the maximum size of the array? Can it be stored statically?

ASSUMPTION/LIMITATION:

- We will assume the given array can be stored statically and can hold up to 10000 x 10000 elements.

MAJOR DATA STRUCTURES:

2D array of integers

UNIT TESTS:

POSTIVE FUNCTIONAL TEST CASES	
INPUT	EXPECTED OUTPUT
M=1 N=1 1	1
M=1 N=5 1 2 3 4 5 M=2 N=2 1 2 3 4	1 2 3 4 5 1 2 4 3
M=2 N=3 1 2 3 4 5 6	1 2 3 6 5 4

M=4 N=4 1   2   3   4
       5   6   7   8
       9 10 11 12
     13 14 15 16
	1 2 3 4 8 12 16 15 14 13 9 5
	6 7 11 10

NEGATIVE FUNCTIONAL TEST CASES	
N < 0 or M < 0	Invalid input

Here is the sample answer that implements the solution described above:

```
1.   #include <cstdio>
2.   #define maxNumberOfRows 10001
3.   #define maxNumberOfColumns 10001
4.
5.   using namespace std;
6.
7.   int array[maxNumberOfRows][maxNumberOfColumns];
8.
9.   void print_array_in_spiral(int array[maxNumberOfRows]
     [maxNumberOfColumns],
10.                             int numberOfRows, int
                               numberOfColumns, int level)
11.  {
12.     if (numberOfRows <= 0 || numberOfColumns <= 0)
13.            return;
14.     if (numberOfRows == 1)
15.     {
16.            for (int colIndex = 0; colIndex < numberOfColumns;
               colIndex++)
17.                    printf("%d ", array[level][level +
                       colIndex]);
18.            return;
19.     }
20.     if (numberOfColumns == 1)
21.     {
```

```
22.            for (int rowIndex = 0; rowIndex < numberOfRows;
               rowIndex++)
23.                    printf("%d ", array[level + rowIndex]
                       [level]);
24.            return;
25.    }
26.    //print from left to right
27.    for (int colIndex = 0; colIndex < numberOfColumns-1;
       colIndex++)
28.            printf("%d ", array[level][level + colIndex]);
29.    //print from top to bottom
30.    for (int rowIndex = 0; rowIndex < numberOfRows - 1;
       rowIndex++)
31.            printf("%d ", array[level + rowIndex][level +
               numberOfColumns - 1]);
32.    //print from right to left
33.    for (int colIndex = 0; colIndex < numberOfColumns-1;
       colIndex++)
34.            printf("%d ", array[level + numberOfRows - 1]
               [level + numberOfColumns - 1 - colIndex]);
35.    //print from bottom to top
36.    for (int rowIndex = 0; rowIndex < numberOfRows - 1;
       rowIndex++)
37.            printf("%d ", array[level + numberOfRows - 1 -
               rowIndex][level]);
38.    print_array_in_spiral(array, numberOfRows - 2,
       numberOfColumns - 2, level + 1);
39. }
40.
41. int main()
42. {
43.    int numberOfRows = 6, numberOfColumns = 3;
44.
45.    array[0] = {1, 2, 3};
46.    array[1] = {4, 5, 6};
47.    array[2] = {7, 8, 9};
48.    array[3] = {10, 11, 12};
49.    array[4] = {13, 14, 15};
50.    array[5] = {16, 17, 18};
51.
52.    printf("The array printed in spiral order:\n");
53.    print_array_in_spiral(array, numberOfRows,
       numberOfColumns, 0);
54.
55.    return 0;
56. }
```

OUTPUT:	FURTHER EXERCISE:
6 3	Q: Is there an iterative approach?
1 2 3	
4 5 6	A: Yes, but the code would be tedious because of the large number of lines of code.
7 8 9	
10 11 12	
13 14 15	
16 17 18	

OUTPUT:

6 3
1 2 3
4 5 6
7 8 9
10 11 12
13 14 15
16 17 18

The array printed in spiral order:

1 2 3 6 9 12 15 18 17 16 13 10
7 4 5 8 11 14

FURTHER EXERCISE:

Q: Is there an iterative approach?

A: Yes, but the code would be tedious because of the large number of lines of code.

Q: How do you print the same matrix in zig-zag?

A: We just need to take into account whether the current row is odd or even and print it normally or in reverse.

ARRAY: SPLIT THE ARRAY IN ODD AND EVEN

Write a function which takes an integer array as input and split this array as all existing Odd Integers come first and then Even Integers into this Array SplitOddAndEvenFromAPostiveIntegersArray()

SOLUTION: The idea behind the algorithm we will be using performs the following steps:

- Start from both ends of the array;
- We will use the index at the left of the array to find an even number and the index to the right to find an odd number;
- When we find two such numbers we swap them, as the odd number needs to appear before the even one in the modified array.
- Stop when the index on the left has exceeded the value of the index on the right.

Consider the example {2,3,2,5,4,7,8,8}. We would perform the following steps in this case:

- Start from 2 and 8 at the same time. The first odd number starting from the right is 7 and the first even number from the left is 2, so we swap them. Our array is now {7,3,2,5,4,2,8,8}.
- The next even element from the left is 2 (the third element), while the next odd element from the right is 5, so we swap them. Our array is {7,3,5,2,4,2,8,8}. We now stop as the two indexes will overlap.

PSEUDO CODE:

```
1.   SplitOddAndEvenFromAnIntegersArray :
2.       Keep two Index :
3.       StartIndex -> Starting from the (Index - 0)
4.       EndIndex   -> Starting from the (Index - (N -1))
5.   ( * N-> N length of the Array)
6.           Scan the array : from start to end until StartIndex
                 Less than EndIndex
7.           If Array[StartIndex] == Odd number then
8.                   Increment the Start Index,
9.           Scan another Item, go back to Scan the array;
10.  If Array[EndIndex] == Even number then
11.          Decrement the EndIndex,
12.                  Scan another Item, go back to Scan the
                     array;;
13.          If (Array[StartIndex] != Odd (OR) Array[EndIndex]
             != Even)
```

14.		Swap the Array's odd values from the end with
15.		the even values from the start

CLARIFICATION POINT-1:

What is the maximum value for N?

This is very useful in case of a static array, since we need to know the number of elements the array stores at compile time.

CLARIFICATION POINT-2:

Does the order of the elements need to be preserved?

ASSUMPTION/LIMITATION:

- For the purpose of this example we will use an array with only 8 elements.

- We will also assume the order of elements in the initial array does not need to be preserved.

MAJOR DATA STRUCTURES:

Array of integers

UNIT TESTS:

POSTIVE FUNCTIONAL TEST CASES

INPUT	EXPECTED OUTPUT
{0]	{0}
{2,5} {2,2,2} {5,5,5} {2,3,2,3}	{5,2} {2,2,2} {5,5,5} {3,3,2,2}

NEGATIVE FUNCTIONAL TEST CASES

Input size = 0	Invalid input
Input size = random size N	Invalid input

Here is a sample answer, running in O(N):

```
1.   #include <iostream>
2.
3.   using namespace std;
4.
5.   enum ReturnValue
6.   {
7.     INVALID_PARAMETER_VALUE=-1,
8.     TRUE
```

```
9.    };
10.
11.   ReturnValue SplitOddAndEvenFromAnIntegersArray
12.      (int *Array , unsigned short ArrayLen);
13.
14.   int main()
15.   {
16.      int array[] = {2,3,2,5,4,7,8,8};
17.      int retVal;
18.
19.      retVal = SplitOddAndEvenFromAnIntegersArray(array,8);
20.
21.      for (int index = 0; index< 8;index++)
22.      {
23.            cout<<" "<<array[index];
24.      }
25.
26.      return 0;
27.   }
28.
29.   ReturnValue SplitOddAndEvenFromAnIntegersArray
30.      (int *Array , unsigned short ArrayLen)
31.   {
32.   unsigned int StartIndex = 0;
33.   unsigned int EndIndex = ArrayLen -1;
34.   unsigned int TempValue = 0;
35.
36.   /* Validation of Input Parameter */
37.
38.   if(NULL == Array)
39.    return INVALID_PARAMETER_VALUE;
40.
41.   if(0 == ArrayLen)
42.    return INVALID_PARAMETER_VALUE;
43.
44.   /*
45.      Split the values in this received array,
46.      odd numbers will come on front and even
47.      numbers will be on end
48.   */
49.      while(StartIndex < EndIndex)
50.      {
51.      /* 0 is a even value, if result is 0
52.       treat is as even, put odd values in front
53.       and even values on last    */
54.      if(Array[StartIndex] % 2 !=0)
55.      {StartIndex++;
56.            continue;
57.      }
58.
59.      if(Array[EndIndex]%2 == 0)
```

```
60.    {
61.         EndIndex--;
62.         continue;
63.    }
64.
65.    if((Array[StartIndex] % 2 == 0) || Array[EndIndex]%2 != 0)
66.    {
67.                 TempValue = Array[StartIndex];
68.                 Array[StartIndex] = Array[EndIndex];
69.                 Array[EndIndex] = TempValue;
70.                 StartIndex++;
71.                 EndIndex--;
72.    }
73.    //return TRUE;
74.    }
75.    return TRUE;
76. }
```

OUTPUT:	FURTHER EXERCISE:
7 3 5 2 4 2 8 8	Q: How does the function receive the input? Will the function modify the input array, or just create a new copy?
	The function receives a pointer to the initial array as an input, so it also changes the initial array. In fact, you can see that our code outputs the final configuration for the array from the initial variable. We have done this to make this process more visible.

ARRAY: KTH LARGEST VALUE IN THE ARRAY

Find the kth largest value in the array efficiently. You may assume that k is much smaller than n, the number of elements in the array.

SOLUTION: The approach we will be using is straightforward and performs the following simple steps:

- We find the maximum value in the array;
- We eliminate this maximum value (e.g. mark it as 0);
- We decrease k and stop when k reaches the value 1.

Suppose we are given the array {220,14,73,19,1,3,100,55,12,7,100,44,99} and we want to find the third largest value. The steps we would perform are as follows:

- We notice 220 is the largest value in the array, so we mark it as 0 and decrease k, which is now 2.
- We notice 100 is the next largest value in the array, so we mark it as 0 and decrease k, which is now 1.
- The next biggest value is also 100 (notice that our algorithm also works if the array contains duplicate elements) and, this time, because k has already reached 1 we return 100 and stop.

PSEUDO CODE:

```
1.   kThLargest(n,array,k):
2.       while (k >= 1)
3.               temp = maximum value in array
4.               remove maximum value from array
5.               k--;
6.       return temp
```

CLARIFICATION POINT-1:

What is the maximum value for N?

This is very useful in case of a static array, since we need to know the number of elements the array stores at compile time.

ASSUMPTION/LIMITATION:

For the purpose of this example we will use an array with only 13 elements.

MAJOR DATA STRUCTURES:

Array of integers

POSTIVE FUNCTIONAL TEST CASES

INPUT	EXPECTED OUTPUT
Array={0} k=1	0
Array={1,2} k=1	1
Array={1,2} k=2	2

NEGATIVE FUNCTIONAL TEST CASES

Input size = 0	Invalid input
Input size = random size N	Invalid input

Here is a sample answer:

```
1.   #import <stdio.h>
2.
3.   /* FUNCTION INFORMATION: kthLargest(int n, int *array, int
     k)*/
4.   int kthLargest(int n, int *array, int k)
5.   {
6.       int *tempArray;
7.       int count,valIndex;
8.       int MaxVal = 0;
9.       // Validate Input Parameters
10.      if ( (0 == n) || (array == NULL) || (*array == NULL) || (k
         == 0))
11.      {
12.              printf(" INALID PARAMETER ");
13.              return 0;
14.      }
15.
16.      tempArray = (int *)malloc(sizeof(int)*n);
17.
18.      // Validate Memory Allocation
19.      if(tempArray == NULL)
20.      {
21.              printf(" MALLOC ERROR ; Could not allocate
                 memory");
22.              return 0;
23.      }
24.
25.      // Copy Original Array to Temporary Buffer
26.      for (count =0 ;count< n;count++)
27.              tempArray[count] = array[count];
28.
```

```
29.    // Compute Kth Largest element from Array
30.    while(k >= 1)
31.    {
32.            MaxVal = 0;
33.            // Compute Largest element
34.            for (count =0 ; count < n ;count++)
35.            {
36.                    if(MaxVal < tempArray[count])
37.                    {
38.                            MaxVal = tempArray[count];
39.                            valIndex = count;
40.                    }
41.            }
42.
43.            // Compute Largest Value Element to Zero
44.            tempArray[valIndex] = 0;
45.            // Compute Duplicate Largest Value Element to Zero
46.            for (count =0 ; count < n ;count++)
47.            {
48.                    if(MaxVal == tempArray[count])
49.                    {
50.                            tempArray[count]= 0;
51.                    }
52.            }
53.
54.            //Iterate untill kth largest element
55.            k--;
56.    }
57.    // Free Allocated Memory
58.    free (tempArray);
59.    return MaxVal;
60. }
61.
62. int main()
63. {
64.    int retVal =0 ;
65.    int kthLargestVal = 0;
66.    int array[] = {220,14,73,19,1,3,100,55,12,7,100,44,99};
67.    int n = sizeof(array)/sizeof(int);
68.    //int *p = array;
69.    for (kthLargestVal = 1;kthLargestVal <=n;kthLargestVal++)
70.    {
71.            retVal = kthLargest(n, array,kthLargestVal); //
                returns 220
72.            printf("\n\n %d th Largest is : %d in sizeof %d
                Array",kthLargestVal,retVal,n);
73.    }
74.    return 0;
75. }
```

```
OUTPUT:
1 th Largest is : 220 in sizeof 13 Array

2 th Largest is : 100 in sizeof 13 Array

3 th Largest is : 99 in sizeof 13 Array
```

ARRAY: REMOVING DUPLICATES

Suppose you have an integer array a of size n that is ordered but has duplicates. For example a = [0, 0, 0, 2, 3, 3, 5, 5, 5, 7, 9, 9] (n = 12). Write a function that "reduces" a by removing duplicates, and returning the new size. For the example above, a becomes [0, 2, 3, 5, 7, 9] and returns 6. (Answer this question in the language you are most comfortable with).

SOLUTION: The idea behind our algorithm is straightforward and performs the following steps:

- Initiate a new array, which will store the original array without duplicates;
- Iterate through the initial array, and if the current element has not been added to the duplicate array add it.

For the input {0,0,0,2,3,3,5,5} we will perform the following steps:

- Initiate the new empty array, new={}
- Add 0 to the new array, so new ={0}
- The following 2 elements have already been added to the temp array, so we skip over them.
- Add the 2 to the new array, new ={0, 2},
- Add the 3 to the new array, new ={0,2,3}, and so on.

PSEUDO CODE:

```
1.  RemovingDuplicates :
2.      reScan the array from start to end
3.      If Array[arrIndex] == Array[arrIndex+1];
4.          Skip the Value Array[arrIndex + 1];
5.      else
6.      Keep the Value[arrIndex + 1];
7.      increment the arrIndex
```

CLARIFICATION POINT-1:

Array will be Static or Dynamic

If Static - then Its shrinking is not possible

(after the reduction it will keep the same size, one possible solution is to mark remaining element as zero e.g. Array with duplicates: Size: 14

2,2,2,2,2,2,2,2,2,2,2,2,2,2,

Array without duplicates: Size: 1

2,0,0,0,0,0,0,0,0,0,0,0,0,0,)

If Dynamic Array - then

- receive the dynamic array - dArray

- remove the duplicates - dArray - duplicates

- reCompute the array size - <u>sizeof</u> (dArray - duplicates)

- create a new contiguous memory block - <u>sizeof</u>(reducedArray) = <u>sizeof</u>(dArray - duplicates)

- copy the element into this array - reducedArray = elementsOf (dArray -duplicates)

- free the last array - free(dArray)

- the new array is the array - return this array - reducedArray

CLARIFICATION POINT-2:

Given value e.g. [0, 0, 0, 2, 3, 3, 5, 5, 5, 7, 9, 9]

2.1 Will it be given in ascending order?

2.2 Does this RemovingDuplicates function require to make a ascend-
    ing order check ?

CLARIFICATION POINT-3:

Will this function be able to remove only those duplicates which
will be consecutive?

ASSUMPTION/LIMITATION:

Duplicate Array -> Array of integers

- Array will be Static or Dynamic

--If Static then what would be the limit ?

- (static array may not shrink its size)

--If Dynamic Array then?

(See discussion points)

MAJOR DATA STRUCTURES:

Array of integers

Sample Answer from a professional point of view:

```
1.   #include <iostream>
2.   using namespace std;
3.
4.   #define ARRAY_VALUE_ERROR -1
5.   #define ARRAY_SIZE_ERROR  -2
6.   #define FAIL              -3
7.   #define SUCCESS            0
8.
9.   int RemovingDuplicatesFromAStaticArray(int *dupArray, int
     arrSize);
10.  int RemovingDuplicatesFromADynamicArray(int **dupArray, int
     arrSize);
11.  int test_RemovingDuplicatesFromAStaticArray();
12.  int test_RemovingDuplicatesFromADynamicArray();
13.
14.  int main() { // Call Main
15.     test_RemovingDuplicatesFromAStaticArray();/* If input is
        static array */
16.     test_RemovingDuplicatesFromADynamicArray();/* if input is
        dynamic array */
17.     return 0;
18.  }
19.
```

```
20.  int RemovingDuplicatesFromAStaticArray(int *dupArray, int
     arrSize)
21.  { /* If input is static array */
22.  int countSize, reducedSize = 0;
23.  if (NULL == dupArray)
24.          return ARRAY_VALUE_ERROR ;
25.    if(arrSize <= 0)
26.          return ARRAY_SIZE_ERROR;
27.
28.  /* Starting from the first element, compare subsequent element
     in array for same value,
29.  if its same skip it, else keep it */
30.  for (countSize = 1; countSize < arrSize; countSize++) {
31.                     if (dupArray[reducedSize] !=
                        dupArray[countSize]) {
32.                             dupArray[reducedSize+1] =
                                dupArray[countSize];
33.                 reducedSize++;
34.          }
35.     }
36.
37.  /* set the remaining element as zero */
38.  for (countSize = reducedSize + 1; countSize < arrSize;
     countSize++) {
39.                     dupArray[countSize] = 0
40.  }
41.
42.  /* return the size of this new reduced array */
43.  return (reducedSize + 1);
44.  }
45.
46.
47.  int RemovingDuplicatesFromADynamicArray(int **dupArray, int
     arrSize)
48.  {/* if input is dynamic array */
49.  int countSize, reducedSize = 0;
50.  if (NULL == *dupArray)
51.                  return ARRAY_VALUE_ERROR ;
52.  if(arrSize <= 0)
53.          return ARRAY_SIZE_ERROR;
54.
55.  /* Starting from the first element, compare subsequent element
     in array for same value,if its same skip it, else keep it */
56.  for (countSize = 1; countSize < arrSize; countSize++) {
57.  if (*(*dupArray + reducedSize) != *(*dupArray + countSize)) {
58.  *(*dupArray + reducedSize + 1) = *(*dupArray + countSize);
59.      reducedSize++;
60.  }
61.  }
62.
63.  int *reducedArray = new int[reducedSize + 1];
```

```cpp
64.  int *tempArray;
65.
66.  /* copy the non-duplicate array elements to reduced Array */
67.  for (countSize = 0; countSize <= reducedSize; countSize++) {
68.     *(reducedArray + countSize) = *(*dupArray + countSize);
69.  }
70.
71.  tempArray = *dupArray;
72.  *dupArray = reducedArray;
73.  delete tempArray;
74.
75.  /* return the size of this new reduced array */
76.  return (reducedSize + 1);
77.  }
78.
79.  /* Test Remove duplicate function if input array is a static
     array */
80.  int test_RemovingDuplicatesFromAStaticArray()
81.  {
82.  int dupArray[] ={0, 0, 0, 2, 3, 3, 5, 5, 5, 7, 9, 9};
83.  int returnVal;
84.  int *ptrdupArray = dupArray;
85.  int arrIndexSize = sizeof(dupArray)/sizeof(int);
86.
87.  cout <<"Array with duplicates: Size: "<<arrIndexSize << endl;
88.  for (int arrIndex =0 ; arrIndex< arrIndexSize;arrIndex++)
89.  {
90.     cout<<dupArray[arrIndex]<<",";
91.  }
92.  cout <<endl;
93.
94.  returnVal = RemovingDuplicatesFromAStaticArray(ptrdupArray,a
     rrIndexSize);
95.
96.  if (returnVal < 0)
97.  {
98.     cout<<"An Error occured :-("<<endl;
99.     return FAIL;
100. }
101.
102. cout <<"Array without duplicates: Size: "<<returnVal << endl;
103. for (arrIndex =0 ; arrIndex< returnVal;arrIndex++)
104. {
105.    cout<<dupArray[arrIndex]<<",";
106. }
107. cout <<endl;
108.
109. return SUCCESS;
110. }
111.
```

```
112. /* Test Remove duplicate function if input array is a dynamic
     array */
113. int test_RemovingDuplicatesFromADynamicArray()
114. {
115. int returnVal;
116. int *ptrdupArray ;
117. int arrIndexSize ;
118.
119. cout<<"enter the size of the array"<<endl;
120. cin>>arrIndexSize;
121.
122. ptrdupArray = new int [arrIndexSize];
123.
124. std::cout <<"(With duplicates )Memory Address of ptrdupArray:
     "<< static_cast<void*>
125. (ptrdupArray)<< " :Size:"<<arrIndexSize<< std::endl;
126.
127. for (int arrIndex =0 ; arrIndex< arrIndexSize;arrIndex++)
128. {
129.    cout<<"enter the array Index : "<<arrIndex<<endl;
130.    cin>>ptrdupArray[arrIndex];
131.    cout <<endl;
132. }
133.
134. cout <<"Array with duplicates: Size: "<<arrIndexSize << endl;
135.
136. for (arrIndex =0 ; arrIndex< arrIndexSize;arrIndex++)
137. {
138.    cout<<ptrdupArray[arrIndex]<<",";
139. }
140. cout <<endl;
141.
142. returnVal = RemovingDuplicatesFromADynamicArray(&ptrdupArray
     ,arrIndexSize);
143.
144. std::cout <<"(Without duplicates )Memory Address of
     ptrdupArray: "<< static_cast<void*> (ptrdupArray)<< "
     :Size:"<<returnVal<< std::endl;
145.
146. cout <<"Array without duplicates: Size: "<<returnVal << endl;
147.
148. for (arrIndex =0 ; arrIndex< returnVal;arrIndex++)
149. {
150. cout<<ptrdupArray[arrIndex]<<",";
151. }
152. cout <<endl;
153.
154. return SUCCESS;
155. }
```

OUTPUT:	FURTHER EXERCISE:
Array with duplicates: Size: 12	If the interviewer will "validate the received input array for its ascending order check" ?
0,0,0,2,3,3,5,5,5,7,9,9,	
Array without duplicates: Size: 6	What would be the maximum size of an array?
0,2,3,5,7,9,	

ARRAY: SORTED ARRAY ROTATION

Implement the following function, FindSortedArrayRotation, which takes as its input an array of unique integers that has been sorted in ascending order, then rotated by an unknown amount X where 0 <= X <= (arrayLength - 1). An array rotation by amount X moves every element array[i] to array[(i + X) % arrayLength]. FindSortedArrayRotation discovers and returns X by examining the array. Consider performance, memory utilization and code clarity and elegance of the solution when implementing the function.

SOLUTION: First, let's see what happens when we rotate an array. Suppose the initial array is [1 3 5 6 7 8 10] and this array was rotated by 2, obtaining [8 10 1 3 5 6 7]. What this task asks for is to find that part of the array where two consecutive elements are not sorted. In this example this occurs at the second position in the array, as 10 > 1, which means the array was rotated by 2.

A first naïve approach arises from this idea. Instinctively, we could iterate through the array and check every two consecutive elements. The worst case complexity of such an algorithm is O(N). Even though this may seem efficient at first, there is an even more efficient approach to this task, which is based on binary search.

An interesting property is that if we split the rotated array into two halves then one half will always be sorted. The only exception to this rule is when the 'disruption' occurs exactly in the middle of the array (for example, the array [8, 10, 11, 1, 2, 3] has two sorted halves). Based on this idea, we will build the following algorithm:

- Split the array into two halves;
- Check which of the halves is the sorted one;
- Descend into the half that is unsorted, by making a recursive call to the main search function, just as the usual binary search.
- Stop when both halves are sorted. The index of the element we have landed on is the value of the rotation.

Let's consider the example, below, with the array [8 10 1 3 5 6 7]. The steps our algorithm will perform on this example are as follows:

- Split the array into [8 10 1] and [3 5 6 7]. We notice that the right half is the sorted one, so we descend into the first half.

- We split this into [8 10] and [1]. We notice that both halves are sorted, so the element in the index of the element in the middle (10, with the index 2) is the value of the rotation.

The algorithms runs in O(log N), as opposed to the previous solution, and is much more efficient.

PSEUDO CODE:

```
1.    FindSortedArrayRotation(array,left,right):
2.        middle = (left + right) / 2
3.        if array[left] > array[middle]
4.                FindSortedArrayRotation(array,left,middle)
5.        Else if array[middle] > array[right]
6.        FindSortedArrayRotation(array,middle+1, right)
7.        Else return middle;
```

CLARIFICATION POINT-1:

What is the maximum value for N?

This is very useful in case of a static array, since we need to know the number of elements the array stores at compile time.

ASSUMPTION/LIMITATION:

- We will assume an array of 7 elements for the purpose of this example, in order to illustrate the concept better.

MAJOR DATA STRUCTURES:

Array of integers

UNIT TESTS:	
POSTIVE FUNCTIONAL TEST CASES	
INPUT	EXPECTED OUTPUT
{0,1,2}	0
{1,0}	1
{8,1,3,6}	1
NEGATIVE FUNCTIONAL TEST CASES	
Array size < 0	Invalid input

Here is a sample answer:

```
1.    #include <cstdio>
2.
3.    using namespace std;
4.
5.    int FindSortedArrayRotation(int array[], int left, int right)
```

```
6.   {
7.       int middle = (left + right) / 2;
8.
9.       // if left half is unsorted
10.      if (array[left] > array[middle])
11.              return FindSortedArrayRotation(array, left,
                 middle);
12.
13.      // else if right half unsorted
14.      // descend into it
15.      else if (array[middle] > array[right])
16.              return FindSortedArrayRotation(array, middle + 1,
                 right);
17.
18.      // at this point both halves are sorted, so
19.      // the value of the rotation is the middle
20.      else
21.              return middle;
22.  }
23.
24.  int main()
25.  {
26.      int array[] = {8, 10, 1, 3, 5, 6, 7};
27.      int numberOfElements = 7;
28.
29.      printf("The value of the rotation is %d\n",
         FindSortedArrayRotation(array, 0, numberOfElements));
30.
31.      return 0;
32.  }
```

OUTPUT:

The value of the rotation is 2

STRINGS: BACKSPACE FUNCTION TO ONE OR TWO BYTES

A stream of characters is given to you. It has a mixture of two kinds of characters. ASCII –which is a byte long with the most significant bit 0. JAPANESE – which is three bytes and has the MSB in the higher byte set. Given a stream, Implement a backspace function which will erase the last character of the given stream, depending on whether it is represented on one or three bytes.

SOLUTION: The first thing to mention about the algorithm we will be using is that the input file needs to be saved as UTF-8 format, which ensures the stream is read correctly. Also make sure the editor you are using knows how to open UTF-8 files correctly, in order to test the correctness of the program. The library we will use is wchar.h, which stands for wide character. This was included into C/C++ in order to adapt the language to the use of multi-byte characters. Functions such as puts, have or strlen, have been adapted to getws, putws and wcslen.

In the backspace function we will be building, it is sufficient to check if the last character in the stream is in standard ASCII (its ASCII code is between 0 and 127) or not (in which case, it means it is a Japanese character) and delete the appropriate number of bytes.

PSEUDO CODE:

```
1.   Backspace(stream)
2.      If last character of the stream has ASCII code between 0
        and 127
3.              Delete the last byte in the stream
4.      Else
5.              Delete the last three bytes in the stream
6.   return stream
```

CLARIFICATION POINT-1:

What is the maximum size of the given message?

ASSUMPTION/LIMITATION:

• We will assume the given message has at most 200 bytes.

MAJOR DATA STRUCTURES:

Array of multi-byte characters (wchar_t).

UNIT TESTS:	
POSTIVE FUNCTIONAL TEST CASES	
INPUT	EXPECTED OUTPUT
"hi" MEANS は	"hi" MEANS
は means hi	は means h
NEGATIVE FUNCTIONAL TEST CASES	
No stream	No output

Here is the sample answer that implements the solution described above:

```
1.    #include <cstdio>
2.    #include <wchar.h>
3.
4.    using namespace std;
5.
6.    void backspace(wchar_t stream[])
7.    {
8.       // if the last character is ASCII
9.       if (stream[wcslen(stream) -  1] >=0 &&
          stream[wcslen(stream) - 1] <= 127)
10.              stream[wcslen(stream) - 1] = '\0';
11.
12.      // if not then it must be Japanese (3 bytes)
13.      else stream[wcslen(stream) - 3] = '\0';
14.   }
15.
16.
17.   int main()
18.   {
19.      wchar_t stream[200];
20.
21.      FILE *input = fopen("test.in", "r");
22.      FILE *output = fopen("test.out", "w");
23.
24.      // read stream from input file
25.      fgetws(stream, 200, input);
26.
27.      // perform backspace
28.      backspace(stream);
29.
30.      //output the stream
31.      fputws(stream, output);
32.
33.      return 0;
34.   }
```

OUTPUT:	FURTHER EXERCISE:
Stream = I am learning 日本人 I am learning 日本	Q: How can we allocate the array dynamically without knowing anything about the size of the stream in advance? A: We can use wscanf, which does not require specifying the limit in terms of the length of the string.

STRINGS: STRING REPRESENTATION OF THE INTEGER

Write a function that takes an int and returns a chararray containing the string representation of the integer.

SOLUTION: Assume that the chararray has enough space to contain the int. Use the following function header:

```
void convert(int x, char * buf) {};
```

Perhaps the trickiest part of this problem is to handle negative numbers. All we need to do in this case, however, is to multiply the number by -1 and remember that its initial value was negative. The algorithm we will be using performs the following steps:

- Start with an empty string;
- Take every digit of the integer one by one, starting with the least significant one, and append it to the string;
- If the number was initially negative append a '-' character to the string
- Reverse the string.

For example, given the input -318513513, we would add 3,1,5,3,1,5,8,1,3 and – in the string and then reverse it, producing the initial number.

PSEUDO CODE:

```
1.   Convert(x, buf)
2.       If x is negative
3.              x = x * -1
4.                 remember x was negative
5.       while there are digits in x
6.              digit = last digit of x
7.              buf = buf + digit;
8.              x = x / 10
9.       if x was initially negative
10.             buf = buf + '-'
11.      reverse buf
```

CLARIFICATION POINT-1:

What is the maximum size of the number? If it's more than 10, we may need to use the type long instead of integers.

CLARIFICATION POINT-2:

Can the number be negative? Does the sign need to be stored in the string?

ASSUMPTION/LIMITATION:

- We will assume the given number is an integer.

- Our program will also handle negative integers.

MAJOR DATA STRUCTURES:

Array of characters (string).

UNIT TESTS:	
POSTIVE FUNCTIONAL TEST CASES	
INPUT	EXPECTED OUTPUT
X = 1	"1"
X = 0	"0"
X = 1234	"1234"
X = -12345	"-12345"
NEGATIVE FUNCTIONAL TEST CASES	
313158205942551	Overflow

Here is the sample answer that implements the solution described above:

```
1.   #include <cstdio>
2.   #include <string.h>
3.
4.   using namespace std;
5.
6.   char array[100];
7.
8.   void convert(int x, char *buf)
9.   {
10.      // remember if the number is negative, so we can add '-'
         at the end
11.      bool negative = false;
12.      if (x < 0)
13.      {
14.             negative = true;
15.             x *= -1;
16.      }
17.
18.      // append digits to array of chars one by one, in reverse
         order
19.      int digit;
20.      while(x)
21.      {
22.             digit = x % 10;
23.             buf[strlen(buf)] = digit + '0';
24.             x = x / 10;
```

```
25.    }
26.
27.    // add the '-' if necessary
28.    if (negative)
29.            buf[strlen(buf)] = '-';
30.
31.    // reverse the string
32.    strrev(buf);
33. }
34.
35. int main()
36. {
37.    int number = -318513513;
38.
39.    convert(number, array);
40.    printf("Here is the converted number: %s\n", array);
41.    return 0;
42. }
```

OUTPUT:	FURTHER EXERCISE:
-318513513 Here is the converted number: -318513513	Q: How to we convert the number back to its integer representation? A: We iterate through the string, and add them to an integer, initially set to 0. For example, given "1443" we would do the following steps: Assign 1 to the integer, multiply it by 10, add 4, multiply by 10, add 4, and so on. We also need to keep track of the sign and multiply the integer in the end.

STRINGS: TO SEE IF IT CONTAINS PALINDROMES

Check a given string to see if it contains palindromes.

SOLUTION: We will assume the given string is in fact a sentence of words, separated by a single or multiple space characters. In this case, we can use a standard function such as strtok() in order to split the given sentence into words, using the delimiter " ". A word is a palindrome if it is equal to its reversed form.

For example, given "this is aba a sample string", we split it into words and check whether the word is a palindrome. For example, "this" and "siht" are not equal, but "aba" and "aba" are, which means "aba" is a palindrome.

PSEUDO CODE:

```
1.   Contains_palindromes(s)
2.      Split s into words, separated by " "
3.      For each word
4.             Reverse word
5.             If initial word = reversed word
6.                    Return true
7.      Return false;
```

CLARIFICATION POINT-1:

Is the given string a word or a sentence containing multiple words?

CLARIFICATION POINT-1:

How will the words be separated? What kind of characters does the string contain?

CLARIFICATION POINT-3:

What is the maximum size of the given string?

ASSUMPTION/LIMITATION-2:

- We will assume our string contains at most 200 characters.

- We will also assume it only contains letters of the English alphabets and spaces, while spaces separate the words

MAJOR DATA STRUCTURES:

Array of characters (string)

POSTIVE FUNCTIONAL TEST CASES	
INPUT	EXPECTED OUTPUT
S = "I am here"	No palindromes
S = "test string"	No palindromes
S = "test aba"	The string contains palindromes
S = " "	No palindromes
S = "abcabc abccba ab"	The string contains palindromes
NEGATIVE FUNCTIONAL TEST CASES	
String contains other charac- ters than " " and letters	Invalid input!

Here is the sample answer that implements the solution described above:

```
1.    #include <cstdio>
2.    #include <string.h>
3.
4.    using namespace std;
5.
6.    bool contains_palindromes(char s[])
7.    {
8.        for (int stringIndex = 0; stringIndex < strlen(s);
          stringIndex++)
9.                if (s[stringIndex] != ' ' && !(s[stringIndex] >=
                  'a' && s[stringIndex] <= 'z')
10.                        && !(s[stringIndex] >= 'A' &&
                           s[stringIndex] <= 'Z'))
11.                {
12.                        printf("Invalid input!\n");
13.                        return false;
14.                }
15.
16.        // split the string into words using strtok
17.        char *word = strtok(s, " ");
18.        char word_reversed[200];
19.
20.        while(word)
21.        {
22.                // reverse current word and store it
23.                strrev(word);
24.                strcpy(word_reversed, word);
25.                // bring initial word back to its initial form
26.                strrev(word);
27.
```

```
28.                // if current word == its reversed form then it's
                   a palindrome
29.                if (!strcmp(word, word_reversed))
30.                        return true;
31.                word = strtok(NULL, " ");
32.        }
33.
34.     return false;
35. }
36.
37. int main()
38. {
39.     char s[200];
40.     strcpy(s, "this is aba a sample string");
41.
42.     if (contains_palindromes(s))
43.             printf("The string contains palindromes!");
44.     else
45.             printf("The string does not contain palindromes!");
46.     return 0;
47. }
```

OUTPUT:	FURTHER EXERCISE:
this is aba a sample string	Q: Can you extend the problems to handle more than just words?
The string contains palindromes!	A: Yes, string reversal works for any character.
	Q: What if the sentences contained punctuation marks?
	A: We would need to use multiple separators for the strtok function.

STRINGS: TRIE DATA STRUCTURE TO STORE WORDS.

Use a trie data structure to store words. Every node contains a list of all letters (pointers to the same node structure) and flags for each letter to indicate the length of the word. Write a method to insert into this kind of data structure. What would you use to store each node?

SOLUTION: Unlike other data structures, in a trie keys are not identified by information from a single node, but by the path from the root of the tree to a particular node. Thus, each node has a number of children equal to the letters in the alphabet being used, and each edge is labeled with the corresponding letter of the alphabet. The following picture shows a trie storing the strings (words): cup, sing, curve, singer, small, ball:

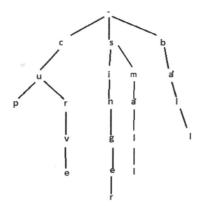

Before we get to the insertion algorithm, let's start by analyzing how a representation of this type of data structure would look like:

```
1.   struct trie
2.   {
3.       int noOfWordsThatEndHere, noOfChildren;
4.       trie *letters[26];
5.       trie()
6.       {
7.           noOfWordsThatEndHere = noOfChildren = 0;
8.           memset(letters,0,sizeof(letters));
9.       }
10.  };
```

As you can see, a trie is a recursive data structure that stores 26 other tries within its internal representation (one for each letter in the alphabet). Some other information we are storing here is the number of words that end at the current trie and the number of non-NULL children. Insertion can be easily performed recursively. Given a string, we just increase noOfWordsThatEndHere if we reach the end of a word or, otherwise, create a new trie at the position corresponding to the next letter in the word. Insertion in a trie can be done in O(n), where n is the length of the string inserted.

PSEUDO CODE:

```
1.   Insert(t, s):
2.       If (current position in s is end of word)
3.               t.number_of_words++
4.               return
5.       if (sub-trie for current letter is NULL)
6.               create sub-trie
7.               increase t.number of children
8.       insert (t.sub-trie, s+1)
```

CLARIFICATION POINT-1:

What is the maximum size of the string given as input?

CLARIFICATION POINT-2:

What kind of characters can the given string contain?

ASSUMPTION/LIMITATION:

- We will assume the given string to be inserted into the trie data structure is no longer than 200 characters.

- We will also assume the given string contains only lower case and upper case letters and the words are separated by ' ' or a newline.

MAJOR DATA STRUCTURES:

Array of characters (string), trie

UNIT TESTS:	
POSTIVE FUNCTIONAL TEST CASES	
INPUT	EXPECTED OUTPUT
S = any string with lower case / upper case letters and spaces	Program terminates
NEGATIVE FUNCTIONAL TEST CASES	
S = any other string	Undefined

Here is the sample answer that implements the solution described above:

```
1.    #include <cstdio>
2.    #include <string.h>
3.
4.    using namespace std;
5.
6.    char s[200];
7.
8.    struct trie
9.    {
10.       int noOfWordsThatEndHere, noOfChildren;
11.       trie *letters[26];
12.       trie()
13.       {
14.               noOfWordsThatEndHere = noOfChildren = 0;
15.               memset(letters,0,sizeof(letters));
16.       }
17.    };
18.
19.    void insert(trie *t,char *s)
20.    {
21.       for (int stringIndex = 0; stringIndex < strlen(s);
          stringIndex++)
22.               if (s[stringIndex] != ' ' && !(s[stringIndex] >=
               'a' && s[stringIndex] <= 'z')
23.                          && !(s[stringIndex] >= 'A' &&
                           s[stringIndex] <= 'Z'))
24.               {
25.                       printf("Invalid input!\n");
26.                       return;
27.               }
28.
29.       if(*s == '\n' || *s == ' ' || strlen(s) == 1)
30.       {
31.               t->noOfWordsThatEndHere++;
32.               return;
33.       }
34.
35.       int position = *s-'a';
36.
37.       if(t -> letters[position]==0)
38.       {
39.               t -> letters[position]=new trie;
40.               t -> noOfChildren ++;
41.       }
42.       insert(t -> letters[position],s+1);
43.    }
44.
45.    int main()
46.    {
```

```
47.    trie *t=new trie;
48.
49.    strcpy(s, "test sentence for trie");
50.
51.    insert(t, s);
52.
53.    return 0;
54. }
```

FURTHER EXERCISE:

Q: Write a function that searches for a word in a trie. What is its complexity?

A: We would just need to start at the root and search for each subsequent letter, going along the path corresponding to the word. The complexity is O(N), where N is the length of the word we are searching for.

STRINGS: STRTOK FUNCTION

Write your own implementation of the strtok function.

SOLUTION: The algorithm we will be using performs the following steps:

- Store the contents of the initial string in a static variable, call it initial.
- At each recursive call of the function work with the value of this static variable.
- Find the first character that matches a delimiter and end the string at that position.
- Return the modified string.

Suppose we are given the string "test for strtok" and a " " as a delimiter. When the function is called for the first time, we return 'test' and keep 'for strtok' in the static variable. Then, for every subsequent call we return the next word ('for' and 'strtok', respectively).

PSEUDO CODE:

```
1.   Mystrtok(s, delimiter)
2.       If first call
3.             Initial = s
4.
5.       Word = initial
6.       For i = 0 to word.length
7.             If word[i] is a character of delimiter
8.                   Word[i] = 0
9.             While word[i] is still a character of delimiter
10.                   I++
11.             Initial = initial + I;
12.       Return word;
```

CLARIFICATION POINT-1:

What is the maximum size of the given input string? What kind of characters can it contain?

ASSUMPTION/LIMITATION:

- We will assume our given string is a sentence of words separated by a single space character.

- We will also assume the given string can store up to 200 characters.

MAJOR DATA STRUCTURES:

Arrays of characters (strings)

Here is the sample answer that implements the solution described above:

```
1.    #include <cstdio>
2.    #include <string.h>
3.
4.    using namespace std;
5.
6.    char s[201];
7.
8.    char *mystrtok(char *s, char *delimiter)
9.    {
10.      // we need a static variable to save current state
11.      static char *initial;
12.
13.      char * word = new char[201];
14.
15.      // if first call (a call with an actual string, not with
         NULL)
16.      if (s != NULL)
17.      {
18.             initial = s;
19.
20.             // check input for validity
21.             for (int stringIndex = 0; stringIndex < strlen(s);
                stringIndex++)
22.                     if (s[stringIndex] != ' ' &&
                        !(s[stringIndex] >= 'a' &&s[stringIndex] <=
                        'z')
23.                                     &&!(s[stringIndex] >= 'A' &&
                                        s[stringIndex] <= 'Z'))
24.                     {
25.                             printf("Invalid input!\n");
26.                             return "";
27.                     }
28.      }
29.
30.      if (initial == NULL) return NULL;
```

```
31.
32.     strcpy(word, initial);
33.
34.     // in the last step, initial will have no more delimiter
        characters
35.     // so the program will not enter the if condition
36.     // we need to take this into account
37.     bool enteredloop = false;
38.
39.     for (int i = 0; i < strlen(word); i++)
40.             if(strchr(delimiter, word[i]))
41.             {
42.                     word[i] = 0;
43.                     while(strchr(delimiter, initial[i])) i++;
44.                     initial = initial + i;
45.                     enteredloop = true;
46.             }
47.
48.     if (!enteredloop) initial = NULL;
49.
50.     return word;
51. }
52.
53. int main()
54. {
55.     strcpy(s, "test   string for   mystrtok");
56.
57.     char *word = mystrtok(s, "! ");
58.
59.     printf("The string delimited by space:\n");
60.     while(word)
61.     {
62.             printf("%s ", word);
63.             word = mystrtok(NULL, "! ");
64.     }
65.
66.     return 0;
67. }
```

OUTPUT:	FURTHER EXERCISE:
test string for mystrtok	Q: How do you implement strchr?
The string delimited by space:	A: The idea is similar, but we need to return the position at which the first character is found in the given string. Furthermore, at each subsequent call, we return the next position. We can use the same method (a static char array) to 'remember' the current state of the string.
test string for mystrtok	

STRINGS: PARSE REGULAR EXPRESSIONS

How do you parse regular expressions?

SOLUTION: First, what is a regular expression? A regular expression, in short RegEx or RegExp, is a string describing a search pattern for another string, or even a whole file. With regular expressions you can find or replace specific parts of a text easily. They are also a powerful way of checking the validity of e-mail addresses, Internet domains or postal codes.

RegEx expressions define models (or templates). For example, a regular expression for an email address would tell us that it needs to contain an @ symbol and a domain. All we need to do at this point is parse the expression and check whether a given string matches the template it defines.

Let's see how we write patterns using regex. The following characters are allowed:

^ [A-Z] {2}[0-9] +*% $

That and nothing more. Seems puzzling, but this is actually very simple. First, the character ^ marks the beginning of the string, and $ marks its end. Between these two characters we write the actual expression. % denotes any punctuation character.

Square brackets [] are used to denote a sequence of characters. We can define them some selectors, or by writing directly the characters we can think of. If, for example, we want our expression to only accept digits, we would use the selector: [0-9]. If we want a lower case letter we use [a-z] and [A-Z] for upper case letters. These selectors can be combined to make a sequence such as [a-zA-Z0-9_]. This tells us that the only strings accepted are those that start with a lowercase letter, continue with an uppercase one and with a digit, followed by a white space.

Braces {} are used to define lengths. For example, [AZ] {2} means a sequence of exactly two upper case letters. If you want to set limits on both sides, we can do this using, for example, {2,5}, which tells us that a sequence must have 2 to 5 characters. The operators + and * are also used for lengths. For example [a-z]+ means at least one (but could be more than one) lower-case letter and [a-z]*denotes any number of lower case letters.

Knowing this, we can write a regular expression that would serve for the validation of an email address, as follows:

^[A-Z0-9._%-]+@[A-Z0-9.-]+.[A-Z]{2,4}$

This means we are allowing at least one lower-case, upper-case, digit or punctuation character, followed by '@', followed by at least one letter/digit/punctuation character, name, a '.', and a domain made of letters, between 2 and 4 characters.

Every programming language comes with support for regular expressions. In C++, for example, we can use the <regex> library. This standard C++ library provides support for various regular expressions, with useful functions such as regex_match and regex_search. In C++ the difference to the general regular expression form we presented so far is that instead of right brackets ([,]) we use round brackets. For example, the expression a+, which we will use in our simple example, accepts a sequence of 'a' characters.

PSEUDO CODE:

```
1.    Regex_match:
2.        regex expression(expression value)
3.        s = string we are checking
4.        if (string matches regular expression)
5.                return true
6.        else
7.                return false
```

CLARIFICATION POINT-1:

What kind of characters does the regular expression contain? What is the maximum length of the strings it can accept?

ASSUMPTION/LIMITATION:

• We will assume our regular expression is a standard one, of type regex in C++

• The strings we are checking against this regular expression will have at most 100 characters.

MAJOR DATA STRUCTURES:

Strings, regular expressions

UNIT TESTS:	
POSTIVE FUNCTIONAL TEST CASES	
INPUT	EXPECTED OUTPUT
Expression = "aa" string = "a"	false
Expression = "a+" string = "aa" Expression = "(0-9)" string = "0"	true true
NEGATIVE FUNCTIONAL TEST CASES	
Expression="#%!#^#!" string=any	Undefined (Regex error)

Here is the sample answer that implements the solution described above:

```cpp
1.    // regex_match example
2.    #include <cstdio>
3.    #include <string>
4.    #include <regex>
5.
6.    using namespace std;
7.
8.    int main ()
9.    {
10.      char string1[100] = "aaa9";
11.      char string2[100] = "aaa";
12.
13.      regex expression("a+");
14.
15.      if (regex_match(string1, expression))
16.              printf("String %s matches expression!\n", string1);
17.      else
18.              printf("String %s does not match expression!\n",
                 string1);
19.
20.      if (regex_match(string2, expression))
21.                      printf("String %s matches expression!\n",
                         string2);
22.              else
23.                      printf("String %s does not match
                         expression!\n", string2);
24.      return 0;
25.   }
```

String
aaa9
does not
match
expres-
sion!

String
aaa
matches
expres-
sion!

Q: How would you implement the regex_match function manually?

A: This process requires turning the regular expression into a graph, where each node is a vertex in the graph and each character is used to label an edge. For example, the expression "a*b" would have 2 states, one of which can be reached with character 'a', while the other can be reached with character 'b':

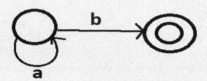

We have marked the vertex on the right with a double line because it is a final state. Given a string, we would then have to determine whether there is a path to the final state, in which case the string is accepted by the regular expression. For example, 'aa' would not be accepted by the regular expression represented in the graph, because there is no path to the final state just by using a sequence of 'a's.

Because of the complexity of regular expressions, and the various operators it can contain, writing a manual parser is a complex task that requires plenty of lines of code. This is why every programming language comes with a pre-defined library, to facilitate working with such expressions.

A very basic parser, on the other hand, can be implemented without building a graph, simply by iterating through the regular expression and splitting it. There are three basic operations to take into account, concatenation (e.g. ab), union (e.g. a|b) and frequency (e.g. a{2} or a*). Suppose we have [a-z]{2}[0-9]. Given a string to match against this expression, this basic parser would firstly iterate through the regular expression and check the values between the sets of straight brackets. If a '-' is detected, it would just check its two extremities (a and z in this case) and check whether the first character of the given string has an ASCII character between these two values. Finally, it would also check the frequency when iteration through the regular expression continues, and so on..

STRINGS: GENERATE COMBINATIONS OF A STRING

Write a program to generate combinations of a string.

SOLUTION: Consider a set A = {a, b, c, d, e}. A combination of this set is a sub-set that contains one or more different elements. The order of the elements is not important in combinations, just the value of the elements. For example, {a, b, c} and {c, b, a} are considered the same sub-set, because they contain the same elements.

Some valid combinations for the set given above are as follows: {a}, {b}, {c}, {d}, {e}, {a, b}, {a, b, c}, {b, d}, etc.

The principle is the same for strings. The set of all combinations of a string is the set of substrings that contain different values. This algorithm can be implemented recursively, with only a few lines of code, as described in the pseudo-code section below.

Let's explain how the pseudo-code works. First of all, we notice that at every call of the function we start iterating through the string from the index given as a parameter. This is because we do not want to repeat the same elements twice. For example, if we have "abcd", by the time we get to index 2 (character 'c'), all the combinations containing 'a' and 'b' will have already been created, so considering them again would lead to duplicates. For abcd, the algorithm performs the following steps:

- Start with a and append it to the combination;
- Output the combination and make a recursive call with index 1
- Append b to the combination and output "ab". Notice that this is equivalent to "ba", so at this point we make a call with index 2.
- Append c to the combination and output "abc". Make a call with index 3 (index of c + 1).
- Append d to the combination and output "abcd". Make a call with index 4 (index of d + 1).
- At this point, the program does not enter the for loop anymore, so it returns; it then goes back to the previous call (index 3). Again, there is nothing more to add (d was already added), so we go back to index 2, where we had "ab".
- Append d to "ab" and output "abd". Make a call with index 4 (index of d + 1), etc.

PSEUDO CODE:

```
1.   generate_combinations(string s,int currentPosition):
2.       for index = currentPosition to s.length
3.               append string[index] to combination
```

```
4.                output combination
5.                generate_combinations(s, index + 1)
6.                delete string[index] from combination
7.        return
```

CLARIFICATION POINT-1:

Can the string contain duplicates? Do these count as separate elements?

CLARIFICATION POINT-1:

Do we need to print the combinations in lexicographic order?

ASSUMPTION/LIMITATION:

• We will assume the initial string holds no more than 100 characters.

• We will also print the combinations in lexicographic order.

• Finally, we will consider that duplicate characters count as separate elements, i.e., for the string 'aa', the first 'a' and second 'a' count as separate combinations.

MAJOR DATA STRUCTURES:

Arrays of characters (strings)

UNIT TESTS:	
POSTIVE FUNCTIONAL TEST CASES	
INPUT	EXPECTED OUTPUT
String = "a"	a
String = "ab"	a, ab, b
String = "abc"	a, ab, abc, b, bc, c
String = "test"	t,te,tes,test,tet,ts,tst,tt, e,es,est,et,s,st,t
NEGATIVE FUNCTIONAL TEST CASES	
String length > 100	Overflow

Here is the sample answer that implements the solution described above:

```
1.    #include <cstdio>
2.    #include <string.h>
3.
4.    using namespace std;
5.
6.    char combination[100];
7.
```

```
8.   void generate_combinations(char s[], int positionInString)
9.   {
10.      for (int stringIndex = positionInString; stringIndex <
         strlen(s); stringIndex++)
11.      {
12.             combination[strlen(combination)] = s[stringIndex];
13.             printf("%s\n", combination);
14.             generate_combinations(s, stringIndex + 1);
15.             combination[strlen(combination) - 1] = '\0';
16.      }
17.  }
18.
19.  int main()
20.  {
21.      char s[100] = "abcd";
22.      printf("Combinations for %s:\n", s);
23.      generate_combinations(s, 0);
24.      return 0;
25.  }
```

OUTPUT:	FURTHER EXERCISE:
Combinations for abcd:	Q: How would you print the permutations of a string?
a	
ab	A: With permutations the order of the elements is important, so the change would be to always start at the same index and remember which character was previously used. This can be done by implementing a look-up table of Boolean values.
abc	
abcd	
abd	
ac	
acd	
ad	
b	
bc	
bcd	
bd	
c	
cd	
d	

STRINGS: FIND ALL PALINDROMES FROM AN INPUT STRING

Write a prog. to find all palindromes (of length > 2) from an input string. e.g. Input aabbabb. Ans: abba, bbabb, bab

SOLUTION: The naïve (trivial) approach for this problem has complexity O(N^3) and is as follows:

```
1.    For index1 from 0 to length of string
2.        For index2 from index1 + 2 to length of string
3.                If the sub-string between positions index1 and
                  index2 is a palindrome output it
```

This is not efficient because, for example, when given string "aabbabb" we call it with (0,6) and (1,5), which checks if sub-strings such as (2, 4) are palindromes twice. This tells us that we can use this information to obtain a more efficient algorithm. Next we will describe a more efficient O(N^2) implementation of this task. This takes advantage of the fact that a palindrome remains a palindrome if we remove its first and last characters and uses a dynamic programming approach as follows:

- Build an array palindrome[i][j] which tells us whether the sub-string that starts and index i and ends at index i + j is a palindrome or not. We only need to store Boolean values for this purpose;

- First, we will populate palindrome[i][0] with true for all 'i's, as every character taken on its own is a palindrome.

- The other base case is to make palindrome[i][1] true when this is the case. In our example input, "aabbabb", we would have palindrome[0][1] = true, as the sub-string that starts at 0 and ends at 0+1, 'aa' is a palindrome.

- For all other elements palindrome[i][j] = true if and only if palindrome [i+1][j-2] is true. This uses the property according to which a palindrome remains a palindrome if we remove its first and last characters. For example, palindrome [1][3] ('abba') will be true because palindrome [2][1] ('bb') is also true.

```
PSEUDO CODE:

1.    Find_palindromes(string s)
2.        Palindromes[i][0] = true for all 'i's
3.        Palindromes[i][1] = true for all applicable 'i's
4.
5.        For offset = 2 to s.length
6.                For startIndex = 0 to s.length
7.                        If s[startIndex] = s[startIndex + offset]
                          and
```

```
8.                              Palindrome[startIndex + 1]
                                [offset-2] = true
9.                                      Palindrome[startIndex]
                                        [offset] = true
10.
11.     Print all palindromes using the palindrome matrix
```

CLARIFICATION POINT-1:

What is the maximum length of the given string?

ASSUMPTION/LIMITATION:

- We will assume the given string holds no more than 100 characters.

MAJOR DATA STRUCTURES:

Array of characters (string), 2D array of Boolean values

UNIT TESTS:	
POSTIVE FUNCTIONAL TEST CASES	
INPUT	EXPECTED OUTPUT
String = "aabb"	No palindromes
String = "aaa"	aaa
String = "abbbabbba"	abbba, abbbabbba, bbb,
String = "testtset"	bbbabbb, bbabb, bab, abbba,
	bbb
	stts, esttse, testtset
NEGATIVE FUNCTIONAL TEST CASES	
String length > 100	Overflow
String length = 0	Invalid input

Here is the sample answer that implements the solution described above:

```
1.    #include <cstdio>
2.    #include <string.h>
3.
4.    using namespace std;
5.
6.    void find_palindromes(char s[])
7.    {
8.      if (strlen(s) == 0)
9.      {
10.             printf("Invalid input!\n");
11.             return;
12.     }
13.
```

```
14.     bool palindrome[100][100];
15.
16.     // the two base cases
17.     for (int startIndex = 0; startIndex < strlen(s);
        startIndex++)
18.     {
19.             // every single character is a palindrome in
                itself
20.             palindrome[startIndex][0] = true;
21.             // every sequence of two equal characters is a
                palindrome
22.             if (startIndex < strlen(s) - 1 && s[startIndex +
                1] == s[startIndex])
23.                     palindrome[startIndex][1] = true;
24.     }
25.
26.     // for each offset (2, .. ,N) apply the dynamic
        programming algorithm discussed
27.     for (int offset = 2; offset < strlen(s); offset++)
28.     for (int startIndex = 0; startIndex + offset < strlen(s);
        startIndex++)
29.             if(s[startIndex] == s[startIndex + offset] &&
                palindrome[startIndex + 1][offset - 2])
30.                     palindrome[startIndex][offset] = true;
31.
32.     // print the solutions using the matrix we just built
33.     // note that we are only interested in palindromes of
        length > 2,
34.     // so we start with offset = 2
35.     for (int startIndex = 0; startIndex < strlen(s);
        startIndex++)
36.             for (int offset = 2; offset < strlen(s); offset++)
37.                     if (palindrome[startIndex][offset] == true)
38.                     {
39.                             for (int pos = startIndex; pos <=
                                startIndex + offset; pos++)
40.                                     printf("%c", s[pos]);
41.                             printf("\n");
42.                     }
43. }
44.
45. int main()
46. {
47.     char s[100] = "aabbabb";
48.
49.     printf("Here are the palindromes:\n");
50.     find_palindromes(s);
51.
52.     return 0;
53. }
```

OUTPUT:	FURTHER EXERCISE:
S="aabbabb" Here are the palindromes: abba bbabb bab	**Q:** What if we extended the problem to finding just the palindrome of maximum length? **A:** A more efficient approach can be taken for finding the largest palindromic substring of a given string. The algorithm also uses dynamic programming and runs in O(N).

STRINGS: IF S2 IS SUBSTRING OF S1

Given two strings S1 and S2, implement and test a program to find if s2 is substring of s1.

SOLUTION: This problem is essentially a string matching one, as we need to find an occurrence of string s2 in s1. First, a naïve approach has complexity O(N*M), with n and m being the lengths of the two strings, and checks every single position in the bigger string. A more efficient approach, running in O(N+M) uses the KMP algorithm, which was described in detail in the 'String algorithms' chapter. We will see it in action in the following section.

The example given is s1='testtest' and 'esttes'. The first step is to build the prefix function for s2. As explained in the String algorithms section, prefix[i] is the length of the longest suffix that is also a prefix of s + i the string. For 'esttes' this is as follows: prefix[] = {0, 0, 0, 0, 1 ('e'='e'), 2('es'='es')}. This means that if we are trying to search for 'esttes' in 'esttesttes', we find a first match (positions 0-5), we would normally do the first match from position 6, but because prefix[5] = 2, we start at position 6 – 2, where we find another match.

PSEUDO CODE:

```
1.    Match(s1, s2):
2.        Build prefix function for s2
3.        nextPosition = 0
4.        for index = 0 to s1.length
5.              while s2[nextposition] != s1[index]
6.                     nextPosition = prefix[nextPosition]
7.              if s2[nextPosition] = s1[index]
8.                     return true
9.        return false
```

CLARIFICATION POINT-1:

What is the maximum length of the two strings?

ASSUMPTION/LIMITATION:

• We will assume the given strings hold no more than 100 characters.

MAJOR DATA STRUCTURES:

Array of characters (strings), array of integers (for the prefix function)

UNIT TESTS:

POSTIVE FUNCTIONAL TEST CASES	
INPUT	EXPECTED OUTPUT
S1="ababab" s2= "ab"	S2 is a substring of S1
S1="ababab" s2= "ac"	S2 is not a substring of S1
S1="test123"s2 = "12"	S2 is a substring of S1
NEGATIVE FUNCTIONAL TEST CASES	
String length > 100	Overflow
S1.length < S2.length	S2 is not a substring of S1

Here is the sample answer that implements the solution described above:

```
1.   #include <cstdio>
2.   #include <string.h>
3.
4.   using namespace std;
5.
6.   void compute_prefix(int prefix[], int nextPosition, char s[])
7.   {
8.      for(int i = 1; i <strlen(s); i++)
9.      {
10.             while(nextPosition && s[nextPosition]!=s[i])
11.                 nextPosition=prefix[nextPosition];
12.             if(s[nextPosition]==s[i])
13.                 nextPosition++;
14.             prefix[i+1]=nextPosition;
15.      }
16.  }
17.
18.  bool match(char s1[], char s2[])
19.  {
20.      int prefix[100],nextPosition = 0;
21.      compute_prefix(prefix, nextPosition, s2);
22.
23.      if (strlen(s1) < strlen(s2))
24.              {
25.              printf("Invalid input!\n");
26.              return false;
27.              }
28.
29.      nextPosition=0;
30.
31.      for(int index = 0; index < strlen(s1); index++)
32.      {
33.              while(nextPosition && s2[nextPosition]!=s1[index])
34.                  nextPosition=prefix[nextPosition];
35.              if(s2[nextPosition]==s1[index])
36.                  nextPosition++;
```

```
37.                    if(nextPosition==strlen(s2))
38.                        return true;
39.    }
40.    return false;
41. }
42.
43. int main()
44. {
45.    char s1[100]="testtest";
46.    char s2[100] = "esttes";
47.
48.    if (match(s1, s2))
49.            printf("S2 is a substring of S1!\n");
50.    else
51.            printf("S2 is not a substring of S1!\n");
52.
53.    return 0;
54. }
```

OUTPUT:	FURTHER EXERCISE:
S1="testtest" S2="esttes" S2 is a substring of S1!	Q: Is there an alternative algorithm for this task? A: Yes, another commonly used algorithm for string matching is the Rabin-Karp algorithm.

STRINGS: ALGORITHM TO DO WILD CARD STRING MATCHING

Implement an algorithm to do wild card string matching.

SOLUTION: The idea behind wild card string matching is similar to the one behind regular expression, but is a little simplified. We still have to deal with a pattern and match a string against it, but this time there are only three cases that we need to consider and only two special characters in the alphabet that we use to build the pattern, '?' and '*'. The three cases are as follows:

1. 'Any character' match – any character in the given string matches character '?' in the pattern. The '?' is like the joker in a pack of cards. For example, "a?" matches "ab", but also "aa", "a," and all the other combinations.

2. 'Any character repeat' match – any character or sequence composed of multiple instances of the same character in the given string matches character '*' in the pattern. For example, 'a*' matches 'aaaa', but also 'abbbbb', 'a]' and 'a]]'.

3. Exact match – the character in the string needs to match the character in the pattern exactly – this is the case for all characters other than '?' and '*'. For example, the pattern "aba" matches only string "aba", as there are no occurrences of '?' or '*'.

An algorithm in O(N), where N is the length of the given string, can be easily implemented to achieve this task. The steps are as follows:

- Suppose we have the pattern "Th?s ?s a t*st *tring" and we want to check whether the string "This is a test sssstring" matches the pattern.

- We start at the beginning of both strings with two indexes, one for the pattern and one for the string. We iterate through both strings by increasing both indexes at each step. We then consider the three cases as follows:

  ▷ If the current character in the pattern is a '?' we match the current position in the string regardless of its value and continue by increasing both indexes one more time;

  ▷ If the current character in the pattern is a '*' then we match the current position in the string and we increase the index of the string as long as the character is repeated. In our example, when we reach the second *, we firstly compare it with s and then increase the index of the string until we reach the 't'. When we reach the 't' we also increase the index of the pattern.

  ▷ If the current character in the pattern is any other character we only match the current character in the string if it is the same; this is the exact-case match. For example, character 'a' matches only 'a', but does not match any of the other characters (e.g. 'b', 'c', '[', etc).

- These three cases can be included in a switch statement in order to improve the readability of the code; furthermore, their names can be expressed with an enum structure, to make the code even clearer.

CLARIFICATION POINT-1:

What is the maximum length of the two strings?

ASSUMPTION/LIMITATION:

- We will assume the given strings, both the pattern and the string to be matched, hold no more than 100 characters.

MAJOR DATA STRUCTURES:

Array of characters (strings), enum

UNIT TESTS:	
POSTIVE FUNCTIONAL TEST CASES	
INPUT	EXPECTED OUTPUT
Str="abcd"Pattern"ab?*"	String matches pattern
Str="abaaac"Pattern"ab*"	String does not match pattern
Str="abbbb"Pattern"ab*"	String matches pattern
NEGATIVE FUNCTIONAL TEST CASES	
Str.length = 0	Invalid input
Pattern.length = 0	Invalid input

Here is the sample answer that implements the solution described above:

```
1.    #include <cstdio>
2.    #include <string.h>
3.
4.    using namespace std;
5.
6.    bool wildcard_match(const char *str, const char *pattern)
7.    {
8.        if (strlen(str) == 0 || strlen(pattern) == 0)
9.        {
10.            printf("Invalid input!\n");
11.            return false;
12.        }
13.
14.        // an enum can be used for a more readable repreentation
15.        // of the possible states in the pattern
16.        enum State {
17.            Exact,                  // exact match
```

```
18.                Any,                    // ?
19.                AnyRepeat               // *
20.        };
21.
22.        // the part of pattern that comes after '*'
23.        const char *afterStar = 0;
24.        int state = 0;
25.
26.        bool canMatch = true;
27.
28.        // while the string can still match the pattern
29.        // and we have not reached the end of the pattern
30.        while (canMatch && *pattern)
31.        {
32.                // set the corresponding state
33.                if (*pattern == '*')
34.                {
35.                        state = AnyRepeat;
36.                        afterStar = pattern+1;
37.                }
38.                else if (*pattern == '?')
39.                        state = Any;
40.                else state = Exact;
41.
42.                // if the string has ended we are done
43.                if (*str == 0) break;
44.
45.                switch (state)
46.                {
47.                        // character needs to match exactly
48.                        case Exact:
49.                                canMatch = *str == *pattern;
50.                                str++;
51.                                pattern++;
52.                                break;
53.
54.                        // any character matches, go to next one
55.                        case Any:
56.                                canMatch = true;
57.                                str++;
58.                                pattern++;
59.                                break;
60.
61.                        // any character can match + they can
                           repeat
62.                        case AnyRepeat:
63.                                canMatch = true;
64.                                str++;
65.
66.                                // if no repeat then continue
                                   matching after *
```

```
67.                              if (*str == *afterStar) pattern++;
68.                              break;
69.                 }
70.     }
71.
72.     // return the corresponding result based on the final state
73.     if (state == AnyRepeat)
74.                 return (*str == *afterStar);
75.     else if (state == Any)
76.                 return (*str == *pattern);
77.     else
78.                 return canMatch && (*str == *pattern);
79. }
80.
81. int main()
82. {
83.     char str[100] = "This is a test sssstring";
84.     char pattern[100] = "Th?s ?s a t*st *tring";
85.
86.     if (wildcard_match(str, pattern))
87.                 printf("string matches pattern!\n");
88.     else
89.                 printf("string does not match pattern!\n");
90.
91.     return 0;
92. }
```

OUTPUT:	FURTHER EXERCISE:
string This is a test sssstring matches pattern Th?s ?s a t*st *tring	Q: Can you think of a naïve approach?
	A: A naïve approach would take the pattern as an input and generate all strings of length equal to the string we are trying to match. This has exponential complexity, especially if the pattern contains multiple *s.

STRINGS: DISPLAY ALL OF
THE ANAGRAMS WITHIN THE ARRAY

Assume you have an array that contains a number of strings. Each string is a word from the dictionary. Your task, described in high-level terms, is to devise a way to determine and display all of the anagrams within the array (two words are anagrams if they contain the same characters; for example, tales and slate are anagrams).

SOLUTION: Perhaps the first thought when looking at this task would be to count the frequency of each letter in the given words and then compare each word with all the other words given to see whether these frequencies correspond. This approach is inefficient in terms of memory, because we would need an array of 26 integer values (because there are 26 letters in the alphabet) for every single word.

A much more efficient approach is to use a multimap. This data structure was described in detail in the section dedicated to data structures of this book. The steps our algorithm will perform are as follows:

- Iterate through the list of given words;

- Sort the letters in each word and insert the word in the map at the key given by the sorted letters; for example, the word "cba" would be stored at key "abc", and so will the word "cab". This is the reason behind the use of a multimap, because anagrams will be inserted at the same key.

- Insert the keys in a set, as we insert the words into the map. This ensures we save a unique copy of each key, so we can easily iterate through all the keys in the next step.

- Once the map is created, iterate through all keys and print the group of elements at the current key – these are anagrams of each other.

Because it can get quite tedious to implement a multimap manually, we can take advantage of the STL library of C++ and implement a multimap<string, string> object, which comes with pre-defined methods for inserting an element or iterating through the keys, for example. Furthermore, we will use the iostream library instead of stdio this time, because of compatibility issues.

CLARIFICATION POINT-1:

What is the maximum length of each word in the map?

ASSUMPTION/LIMITATION:

- We will assume the given words will be of no more than 100 characters.

PSEUDO CODE:

```
1.    Find_anagrams(words[]):
2.        Multimap={}, set={}
3.        For index = 0 to words.length
4.                Key = sorted letters of words[index]
5.                Insert words[index] into the map at key Key
6.                Insert Key into set
7.        For all keys in set
8.                Print the words at current key in the multimap
```

MAJOR DATA STRUCTURES:

Multimap, set, string

UNIT TESTS:	
POSTIVE FUNCTIONAL TEST CASES	
INPUT	EXPECTED OUTPUT
Words={help,lost,slot,pleh} Words={car,rac,drive,cra, open,poen} Words={abc,bca,cba,aabb,bbba, babb,test}	{help, pleh}, {lost, slot} {car, rac, cra}, {drive}, {open, poen} {aabb, bbba, babb}, {abc, bca, cba}, {test}
NEGATIVE FUNCTIONAL TEST CASES	
Number of words <= 0 Length of any word = 0	Invalid input Invalid input

Here is the sample answer that implements the solution described above:

```
1.    #include <iostream>
2.    #include <string>
3.    #include <algorithm>
4.    #include <map>
5.    #include <set>
6.
7.    using namespace std;
8.
9.    void find_anagrams(int numberOfWords, string words[])
10.   {
11.       if (numberOfWords <= 0)
12.       {
13.               cout<<"Invalid input!"<<endl;
14.               return;
15.       }
16.
17.       multimap<string, string> strCharsMap;
18.
19.       set <string> keys;
20.
```

```
21.     string wordSorted;
22.
23.     // iterate thorugh all words, sort them and build the map
24.     for(int wordIndex = 0; wordIndex < numberOfWords;
        wordIndex++)
25.     {
26.             wordSorted = words[wordIndex];
27.             sort(wordSorted.begin(), wordSorted.end());
28.             strCharsMap.insert(pair<string, string>(wordSorted,
                words[wordIndex]));
29.             keys.insert(wordSorted);
30.     }
31.
32.     // display the results for all keys
33.     for (set<string>::iterator it = keys.begin(); it != keys.
        end(); it++)
34.     {
35.             pair <multimap<string, string>::iterator,
                multimap<string, string>::iterator> keyPair;
36.             keyPair = strCharsMap.equal_range(*it);
37.
38.             // print all elements with key *it
39.             for (multimap<string, string>::iterator it2 =
                keyPair.first; it2 != keyPair.second; ++it2)
40.                     cout << it2 -> second << " ";
41.             cout << endl;
42.     }
43. }
44.
45. int main()
46. {
47.     int numberOfWords = 7;
48.     string words[100]{"abc", "bca", "cba", "abbb", "bbba",
        "babb", "test"};
49.     cout << "Here are the anagrams: " << endl;
50.
51.     find_anagrams(numberOfWords, words);
52.
53.     return 0;
54. }
```

Here are the anagrams:

abbb bbba babb
abc bca cba

test

Q: Suppose you are given another word and you are asked to print all the anagrams of the given word, which were discovered so far. What is the complexity of this operation with the multimap approach? How about the naïve approach?

A: With the multimap approach, the group of anagrams for any word can be retrieved in constant time, because we do not need to iterate through all the keys. On the other hand, the naïve approach requires iterating over all the words and comparing the letter frequency with the given word, which has complexity O(N).

Internally, in the STL library, multimap is implemented with a red-black tree. An alternative approach to the solution given is therefore to implement a red black tree directly. As mentioned in the data structure chapter, red-black trees are balanced binary search trees, which maintain this balancing property by assigning colors to each node and following four important rules.

Suppose we have the strings "abc", "aab", "bdf", "bdg "bcd" and "bcef". A red-black tree built with these items is as follows:

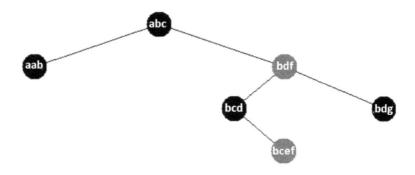

Remember, in a red-black tree, insertion is done in the same way as in binary search trees, but an extra step is taken, which allocates a color to each node. Then, suppose we are given the string "aba" and find whether there are any anagrams stored in our tree. We sort its letters and obtain the key 'aab', which was previously inserted in the tree. This means 'aab' is an anagram of the word.

In order to make our red-black tree work as multimap, we need to store a vector of strings in each node, rather than a single string. For example, after processing 'aba', the node that previously stored 'aab' will store 'aab' and 'aba'. In this way, if we are given string 'baa' at a later point, for example, we would be able to find both anagrams stored in the red-black tree.

All the operations that require fast execution time in a multimap, including insertion, deletion and retrieval of a node, can be done very quickly with a red-black tree, mainly because of its approximately balanced structure.

STRINGS: K-SUBSTRINGS DOES AN N-STRING HAVE

How many k-substrings does an n-string have? (Consider identical k-substrings at different positions as different.) How many substrings does an n-strings have in total?

SOLUTION: This task is actually easier than it may seem at first sight. Let's work on an example that will help us deduce a formula. Suppose our string (let's call it s) is "abcdefg" and k = 3. Then the k-substrings of the initial string are "abc", "bcd", "cde", "def" and "efg". Because k-substrings always start at position 0 and end at position s.length we can see there are always s.length – k – 0 + 1 = s.length – k + 1 k-substrings.

The second task basically requires us to count all the k-substings of a given string, with k from 1 to the length of the string. Let's consider the same example. The number of all substrings of "abcdefg" is equal to the number of 1-substrings + the number of 2-substrings + .. + the number of 7-substrings. This can easily be done with a for loop.

PSEUDO CODE:

```
1.  Count_k_substrings(s[]):
2.      Return s.length – k + 1
3.
4.  Count_substrings(s[]):
5.      Count = 0
6.      For k from 1 to s.length
7.              Count = Count + number of k-substrings of s
8.      Return count
```

CLARIFICATION POINT-1:

What is the maximum length of the given string?

ASSUMPTION/LIMITATION:

• We will assume the given strings hold no more than 100 characters.

MAJOR DATA STRUCTURES:

Array of characters (string)

UNIT TESTS:

POSTIVE FUNCTIONAL TEST CASES

INPUT	EXPECTED OUTPUT
S=abcd k = 1	4 1-substrings, 10 substrings
S=tesssst k = 3	in total
S=abc k = 3	4 3-substrings, 21 substrings
	in total
	1 3-substring, 6 substrings
	in total

NEGATIVE FUNCTIONAL TEST CASES

S=abc k = 4	Invalid input
S.length = 0	Invalid input

Here is the sample answer that implements the solution described above:

```
1.   #include <cstdio>
2.   #include <string.h>
3.
4.   using namespace std;
5.
6.   int count_k_substrings(char s[], int k)
7.   {
8.      if (k <= 0 || k > strlen(s) || strlen(s) == 0)
9.      {
10.             printf("Invalid input!\n");
11.             return 0;
12.     }
13.     return strlen(s) - k + 1;
14.  }
15.
16.  int count_substrings(char s[])
17.  {
18.     if (strlen(s) == 0)
19.     {
20.             printf("Invalid input!\n");
21.             return 0;
22.     }
23.
24.     int numberOfSubstrings = 0;
25.
26.     // add together the number of k-substrings for all 'k's
27.     for (int k = 1; k <= strlen(s); k++)
28.             numberOfSubstrings += strlen(s) - k + 1;
29.
30.     return numberOfSubstrings;
31.  }
32.
33.  int main()
```

```
34.  {
35.      char s[100] = "thisisastring";
36.
37.      int k = 10;
38.
39.      printf("The string %s has %d %d-substrings\n", s, count_k_
         substrings(s, k), k);
40.      printf("The string %s has %d substrings in total\n", s,
         count_substrings(s));
41.
42.      return 0;
43.  }
```

OUTPUT:	FURTHER EXERCISE:
The string thisisastring has 4 10-substrings The string thisisastring has 91 substrings in total	Q: What if we had to count the number of k-substrings different from each other? A: Then we would need to determine how many equal k-substrings exist and simply subtract this number from the total number of k-substrings, which can be computed in the same way. Determining how many of the k-substrings are equal can be done in multiple ways. An efficient algorithm would be to use a hash table and check whether a substring had been previously encountered in constant time.

STRINGS:
LARGEST BLOCK OF REPEATED CHARACTERS

Given a string, find the start position of the largest block of repeated characters.

SOLUTION: A simple algorithm can be implemented in O(N), because we only need to consider blocks of consecutive characters (substrings) in the given string. The algorithm we will implement takes the following steps:

- Suppose our string (call it s) is "aacdefaaaabbccc";

- We start from first position and move to the right as long as the character stays the same, stopping when we encounter another character; for example, the first step would consider the first two 'aa's and stop at 'c';

- Every time we stop count whether the length of the current block is larger than any block we have encountered so far. For example, when we stop at the 'b' after 'aaaa', we would set the global maximum to be 4.

- Finally, we simply return the position corresponding to the start of the longest substring containing the same characters.

PSEUDO CODE:

```
1.    Largest_block_position(s):
2.        CurrentPosition = 0
3.        Max = 0, maxposition = 0
4.        While CurrentPosition < s.length
5.                Increase currentPosition while it holds the
6.                same character and count the number of increases
7.                if number of increases > max
8.                        max = number of increases
9.                        maxposition = currentPosition - max
10.       return maxposition
```

CLARIFICATION POINT-1:

What is the maximum length of the given string?

CLARIFICATION POINT-2:

Which substring we consider if two or more substrings have equal lengths?

ASSUMPTION/LIMITATION:

- We will assume the given string hold no more than 100 characters.

- We will also consider the leftmost substring in case of an equality.

MAJOR DATA STRUCTURES:

Array of characters (strings)

UNIT TESTS:	
POSTIVE FUNCTIONAL TEST CASES	
INPUT	EXPECTED OUTPUT
S = aacdefaaaabbccc	6
S = abc	0
S = aaaabbbbccccc	8
NEGATIVE FUNCTIONAL TEST CASES	
S.length = 0	Invalid input

Here is the sample answer that implements the solution described above:

```
1.   #include <cstdio>
2.   #include <string.h>
3.
4.   using namespace std;
5.
6.   int largest_block_position(char s[])
7.   {
8.      if (strlen(s) == 0)
9.      {
10.             printf("Invalid input!\n");
11.             return 0;
12.      }
13.
14.      // start from beginning of a string and count
15.      // how many subsequent letters we can find
16.      int currentPosition = 0;
17.      int maxLength = 0, maxPosition = 0;
18.
19.      while (currentPosition < strlen(s))
20.      {
21.             int currentLength = 1;
22.
23.             while (s[currentPosition + 1] ==
                   s[currentPosition])
24.             {
25.                    currentPosition++;
26.                    if (currentPosition == strlen(s) - 1)
                       break;
27.                    currentLength++;
28.             }
```

```
29.
30.                          // increase currentPosiiton again, just in
                             case it was not increased
31.                          // in the loop above
32.              currentPosition++;
33.
34.                          // if the current substring is the longest
                             so far store it
35.              if (currentLength > maxLength)
36.              {
37.                      maxLength = currentLength;
38.                      maxPosition = currentPosition - maxLength;
39.              }
40.      }
41.
42.      return maxPosition;
43. }
44.
45. int main()
46. {
47.      char s[100] = "aacdefaaaabbccc";
48.
49.      int result = largest_block_position(s);
50.
51.      printf ("The start position of the largest block of
         repeated characters is %d\n", result);
52.
53.      return 0;
54. }
```

OUTPUT:	FURTHER EXERCISE:

The start position of the largest block of repeated characters is 6

Q: What is a naïve approach to this task and what is its complexity?

A: A naïve approach runs in O(N3) and considers all the substrings of the given string, checking whether all the letters they contain are equal. It then records the maximum length of all substrings with this property.

STRINGS: DELETE FROM S2 ALL THOSE CHARACTERS WHICH OCCUR IN S1

Given two strings S1 and S2. Delete from S2 all those characters which occur in S1 also and finally create a clean S2 with the relevant characters deleted.

SOLUTION: An efficient algorithm for performing this task uses a look-up table of Boolean values to mark the characters in S1 that need to be deleted from S2. We will allocate 256 slots in memory to this look-up table, so it can support the extended ASCII characters as well (With ASCII codes from 0 to 255). We perform the following steps:

- Iterate through S1 and make table[ASCII code of current character in S1] true, meaning this character needs to be deleted from S2;

- In order to save memory, we copy the contents of S2 into S1, because we do not need S1 anymore, and empty S2

- Iterate through the new S1 (holding the value of the initial S2) and append to S2 just those characters for which table[ASCII code of character] = false.

For example, if S1 = "abcde" and S2 = "azhbcdi", then we mark table[a], table[b], .. table[e] with true, and when we iterate through "azhbcdi" we ignore a, b, c and d. The final value in S2 will be "zhi".

PSEUDO CODE:

```
1.   remove(s1, s2):
2.       for s1index from 0 to s1.length
3.             table[s1[s1index]] = true
4.       copy s2 to s1
5.       empty s2
6.       for s1index from 0 to s1.length
7.             if table[s1[s1index]]= false
8.                   append s1[s1index] to s2
9.       return s2
```

CLARIFICATION POINT-1:

What is the maximum length of the two given strings?

ASSUMPTION/LIMITATION:

- We will assume the given string can hold no more than 100 characters.

MAJOR DATA STRUCTURES:

Arrays of characters (strings)

UNIT TESTS:	
POSTIVE FUNCTIONAL TEST CASES	
INPUT	EXPECTED OUTPUT
S1="ab" s2= "ab"	S2=empty string
S1="ab" s2= "ac"	S2=c
S1="abcdef"s2 = "efghia"	S2=ghi
NEGATIVE FUNCTIONAL TEST CASES	
S1.length = 0 or s2.length = 0	Input invalid

```
1.    #include <cstdio>
2.    #include <string.h>
3.
4.    using namespace std;
5.
6.    void remove(char s1[], char s2[])
7.    {
8.       if (strlen(s1) == 0 || strlen(s2) == 0)
9.       {
10.              printf("Invalid input!\n");
11.              return;
12.      }
13.
14.      bool toBeRemoved[256];
15.
16.      int s2Index = 0;
17.
18.      // mark all characters in s1
19.      for(int s1Index = 0; s1Index < strlen(s1); s1Index++)
20.              toBeRemoved[s1[s1Index]] = true;
21.
22.      // we no longer need s1, so we can copy the contents of s2
         in it
23.      strcpy(s1, s2);
24.
25.      // empty s2
26.      strcpy(s2, "");
27.
28.      for(int s1Index = 0; s1Index < strlen(s1); s1Index++)
29.              if(!toBeRemoved[s1[s1Index]])
30.                      s2[s2Index++]=s1[s1Index];
31.
32.      // end of s2
33.      s2[s2Index]='\0';
34. }
```

```
35.
36.  int main()
37.  {
38.      char s1[100] = "abcde";
39.      char s2[100] = "azhbcdi";
40.
41.      remove (s1, s2);
42.      printf("After removal S2 = %s", s2);
43.      return 0;
44.  }
```

OUTPUT:	FURTHER EXERCISE:
After removal S2 = zhi	Q: How can you add support for multi-byte characters?
	A: If any of the two strings contains a multi-byte character then we would firstly need to allocate more than 256 memory slots for the look-up table. In principle, the other steps remain the same.

STRINGS: REVERSE THE ORDER OF WORDS

Given an array of characters which forms a sentence of words, give an efficient algorithm to reverse the order of the words (not characters) in it.

SOLUTION: Given an array of characters which forms a sentence of words, give an efficient algorithm to reverse the order of the words (not characters) in it.

An efficient method for reversing the order of the words in a sentence performs the following steps:

- Reverse the entire string;
- Iterate through each word and reverse it individually.

For example, if we have the string "this is a test string", we would firstly reverse it completely, obtaining "gnirts tset a si siht". By then considering each word and reversing it individually, we obtain the final result, which is "string test a is this".

PSEUDO CODE:

```
1.    Reverse_words(s):
2.        Reverse s
3.        tempString = s
4.        empty s
5.        For each word in tempString
6.                Reverse word
7.                Add reversed word to s
8.        Return s
```

CLARIFICATION POINT-1:

What is the maximum length of the given string?

CLARIFICATION POINT-2:

How are the words in the sentence separated?

ASSUMPTION/LIMITATION:

- We will assume the given string can hold no more than 100 characters.

- We will also assume the words in the given sentence are separated by a single blank space.

MAJOR DATA STRUCTURES:

Arrays of characters (strings)

This is an implementation of the algorithm discussed above:

```
1.    #include <cstdio>
2.    #include <string.h>
3.
4.    using namespace std;
5.
6.    void reverse(char s[])
7.    {
8.        // have a start and end index
9.        int startIndex = 0, endIndex = strlen(s) - 1;
10.
11.       while (startIndex < endIndex)
12.       {
13.               // swap elements at startIndex and endIndex
14.               char temp = s[startIndex];
15.               s[startIndex] = s[endIndex];
16.               s[endIndex] = temp;
17.               startIndex++;
18.               endIndex--;
19.       }
20.   }
21.
22.   void reverse_words(char s[])
23.   {
24.       if (strlen(s) == 0)
25.       {
26.               printf("Invalid input!\n");
27.               return;
28.       }
29.
30.       // reverse the string normally
31.       reverse(s);
32.
33.       // copy the contents of s into temp
34.       char tempString[100];
35.       strcpy(tempString, s);
36.
37.       // empty s
```

```
38.      strcpy(s, "");
39.
40.      // reverse each word individually
41.      char *word = strtok(tempString, " ");
42.      while (word)
43.      {
44.              reverse(word);
45.              strcat(s, word);
46.              // add a space
47.              strcat(s, " ");
48.              word = strtok(NULL, " ");
49.      }
50. }
51.
52. int main()
53. {
54.      char s[100] = "this is a test string";
55.      reverse_words(s);
56.      printf("The string with reversed order of words: %s\n ", s);
57.      return 0;
58. }
```

OUTPUT:	FURTHER EXERCISE:
The string with reversed order of words: string test a is this	Q: Can you describe a naïve approach for this task? A: A naïve approach would iterate through all the words in the given sentence and switch them one by one, until their order is reversed. For example, given the string "this is me", the algorithm would perform the following: "this is me" -> "is this me"-> "is me this"-> "me is this". This algorithm is very inefficient if the number of words in the given sentence is fairly large.

STRINGS: PRINT ALL OF
THE PERMUTATIONS OF A STRING.

Write a function to print all of the permutations of a string.

SOLUTION: As opposed to combinations, permutations are about re-ordering the elements of a given string. For example, the permutations for 'abc' are 'abc', 'acb', 'bac', 'bca', 'cab' and 'cba'. Notice that each character in the string is only used once and that the order of the characters is everything that matters. Because we are asked to print all the permutations of a string, rather than counting them, we will use a backtracking approach. Let's call the recursive function we will be using throughout print_permutations. The steps are as follows:

First, call print_permutations with the following parameters:

> ▷ Initial string

> ▷ Permutation – this is the string that we will use to build a permutation of the initial one

> ▷ Level – this is the position we will use to store an element in the current permutation (the 'level' of our recursive function)

> ▷ usedInCurrentPermutation – an array of Boolean values (true/false) or integers (0/1) that we will use to mark that an element was added to the current permutation (remember, a character cannot appear multiple times in a valid permutation).

• Iterate through the string. Add each character that was not used so far to Permutation and mark it as used in usedInCurrentPermutation.

• Call print_permutations with Initial string, Permutation, level + 1 and usedInCurrentPermutation.

• After a successful call, mark the current character as unused, as we may need it for a future permutation.

Again, suppose we are working with the string 'abc'. We would then perform the following steps, as per the algorithm we have described above:

• Add 'a' to permutation and mark it as used in usedInCurrentPermutation. We will mark it as unused again once the recursive function returns to this step.

• Call the recursive function one more time (with level = 1).

• Add 'b' to the current permutation ('a' was already used). Call the recursive function with level=2.

• The same for 'c'. Call the recursive function with level = 3.

- Because level = length of the initial string (we have constructed a complete permutation), print the current permutation and return to the previous step (level = 2).
- There is nothing else to add (all the elements were used, so mark c as unused and go back).
- Again, nothing more to do, so mark b as unused and go back to level = 0.
- We repeat the same process, building 'acb', and so on, until we have exhausted all the possibilities.

PSEUDO CODE:

```
1.   Print_perm(s,perm,level,usedInCurrentPermutation):
2.       If perm is complete
3.            Print perm
4.            Return
5.       For sIndex from 0 to s.index
6.            If (usedInCurrentPermutation[sIndex] == 0)
7.                 usedInCurrentPermutation[sIndex] = 1
8.                 permutation[level] = s[sIndex]
9.                 print_perm(s,perm,level+1,usedInCurrent)
10.                usedInCurrentPermutation[sIndex] = 0
```

CLARIFICATION POINT-1:

What is the maximum length of the given string?

ASSUMPTION/LIMITATION:

- We will assume the given string can hold no more than 100 characters.

MAJOR DATA STRUCTURES:

Arrays of characters (strings)

UNIT TESTS:

POSTIVE FUNCTIONAL TEST CASES

INPUT	EXPECTED OUTPUT
S=a	{a}
S=ab	{ab},{ba}
S=123	{123},{132},{213},{231}, {312},{321}

NEGATIVE FUNCTIONAL TEST CASES

S.length = 0	Input invalid

Here is an algorithm that implements the idea described above:

```
1.    #include <cstdio>
2.    #include <string.h>>
3.
4.    using namespace std;
5.
6.    void print_permutations(char s[], char permutation[], int
      level, int usedInCurrentPermutation[])
7.    {
8.       if (strlen(s) == 0)
9.       {
10.              printf("Invalid input!\n");
11.              return;
12.      }
13.
14.      // if the current permutation is complete print it
15.      // complete = an element has been added to level strlen(s)
16.      if (level == strlen(s))
17.      {
18.              printf("%s\n", permutation);
19.              return;
20.      }
21.
22.      for (int sIndex = 0; sIndex < strlen(s); sIndex++)
23.              // if the element at sIndex was not used in the
                 current permutation so far
24.              if (!usedInCurrentPermutation[sIndex])
25.              {
26.                      // mark it as used and add it
27.                      usedInCurrentPermutation[sIndex] = 1;
28.                      permutation[level] = s[sIndex];
29.                      print_permutations(s, permutation, level +
                         1, usedInCurrentPermutation);
30.
31.                      // at this point mark it as unused, so it
                         can be used in other permutations
32.                      usedInCurrentPermutation[sIndex] = 0;
33.              }
34.    }
35.
36.    int main()
37.    {
38.       char s[100] = "abcd";
39.       char permutation[100] = "";
40.       int usedInCurrentPermutation[100];
41.
42.       // empty the indexUsed array
43.       memset(usedInCurrentPermutation, 0, sizeof(usedInCurrentPe
          rmutation));
```

```
44.     printf("The permutations of the string are as follows:\
        n\n");
45.     print_permutations(s, permutation, 0,
        usedInCurrentPermutation);
46.     return 0;
47. }
```

OUTPUT:	FURTHER EXERCISE:
The permutations of the string are as follows:	Q: What if we only needed to count the number of permutations?
abcd	
abdc	A: The number of permutations of a given string is equal to N!, where N is the length of the string, so we would only need to use this formula.
acbd	
acdb	
adbc	
adcb	
bacd	
badc	
bcad	
bcda	
bdac	
bdca	
cabd	
cadb	
cbad	
cbda	
cdab	
cdba	
dabc	
dacb	
dbac	
dbca	
dcab	
dcba	

STRINGS: COMPRESS STRING

Write a function which compress string AAACCCBBD to A3C3B2D and another function to generate the initial string from the compressed one (decompression function).

SOLUTION: The solution to this task, both for compression and for decompression, is fairly straightforward, and runs in O(N). For compression, we perform the following steps:

- Iterate through the string from left to right. For every step:
  - ▷ count how many times the current character repeats at the indexes that follow;
  - ▷ add the number of times it repeats to an initially empty string.

For example, given AAACCCBBD, we start with an empty string, let's call it compressed. We firstly noiice that A is repeated 3 times, so add A3 to compressed, then C also repeats 3 times, so add C3 to compressed, etc.

For decompression, we would basically reverse the process described above, as follows:

- Iterate through the characters in the compressed string.
- Append the current character n times to an initially empty string, where n is the number of times dictated by the number that follows it.

PSEUDO CODE:

```
1.    compress(s):
2.        compressed=""
3.        for i = 0 to s.length
4.                count how many times s[i] repeats
5.                append s[i] to compressed
6.                append frequency to compressed
7.        return compressed
8.    decompress(s):
9.        decompressed=""
10.       for i = 0 to s.length step 2
11.               for k = 0 to s[i+1]
12.                       append s[i] to decompressed k times
13.       return decompressed
```

CLARIFICATION POINT-1:

What is the maximum length of the given string?

ASSUMPTION/LIMITATION:

- We will assume the given string can hold no more than 100 characters.

MAJOR DATA STRUCTURES:

Arrays of characters (strings)

UNIT TESTS:

POSTIVE FUNCTIONAL TEST CASES

INPUT	EXPECTED OUTPUT
S=A	S=A1
S=2133A	S=211132A1
S=AAAABBBBCCCCC	S=A4B4C5

NEGATIVE FUNCTIONAL TEST CASES

S.length = 0	Input invalid

Here is a C++ solution for the algorithm described above:

```
1.    #include <cstdio>
2.    #include <string.h>
3.
4.    using namespace std;
5.
6.    void compress(char s[])
7.    {
8.       if (strlen(s) == 0)
9.       {
10.             printf("Invalid input!\n");
11.             return;
12.       }
13.
14.       // variable for holdingthe compressed string, initially
         empty
15.       char compressed[100] = "";
16.
17.       int currentPosition = 0, currentLength;
18.       while (currentPosition < strlen(s))
19.       {
20.             currentLength = 1;
21.             while (s[currentPosition + 1] ==
                s[currentPosition])
22.             {
23.                   currentLength++;
24.                   currentPosition++;
25.             }
26.
```

```c
27.            // append the character and frequency to the
               compressed string
28.            compressed[strlen(compressed)] =
               s[currentPosition];
29.            compressed[strlen(compressed)] = currentLength +
               '0';
30.
31.            currentPosition++;
32.     }
33.
34.     // copy back to the initial string;
35.     strcpy(s, compressed);
36. }
37.
38. void decompress(char s[])
39. {
40.     if (strlen(s) == 0)
41.     {
42.            printf("Invalid input!\n");
43.            return;
44.     }
45.
46.     // variable for holding the uncompressed string, initially
        empty
47.     char decompressed[100]="";
48.
49.     // iterate through each character
50.     // we know the next element is its frequency
51.     for (int sIndex = 0; sIndex < strlen(s); sIndex += 2)
52.            for (int numberOfTimes = 0; numberOfTimes <
               s[sIndex + 1] - '0'; numberOfTimes++)
53.                   decompressed[strlen(decompressed)] =
                      s[sIndex];
54.
55.     // copy back to s
56.     strcpy(s, decompressed);
57. }
58.
59. int main()
60. {
61.     char s[100] = "AAAABBCCCDDAA";
62.
63.     compress(s);
64.     printf("The compressed string: %s\n", s);
65.     decompress(s);
66.     printf("The initial, uncompressed string: %s\n", s);
67.
68.     return 0;
69. }
```

```
OUTPUT:

The compressed string: A4B2C3D2A2

The initial, uncompressed string: AAAABBCCCDDAA
```

STRINGS: RETURNS THE NUMBER OF TIMES ANY CHARACTER IN STRING

Write a function "int count(const char *s, const char *a)" that returns the number of times any character in string a occurs in string s. For example, count("programming", "aemgx") returns 5 (a->1, e->0, m->2, g->2, x->0). Assume standard ASCII characters. If you can think of more than one way to code, emphasize speed over memory. (Answer this question in the language which you are most comfortable with).

SOLUTION: The idea of the algorithm is the following:

1. Build a frequency table for all characters in string s. This can be done as follows:

   a) Assume a='0', b='1', etc.

   b) Start with an empty array of integers, of 26 elements (there are 26 letters in the alphabets).

   c) Iterate through the string s and increase the corresponding position in the frequency table. For example, if the current character is 'd' then we would perform table[4] = table[4] + 1.

2. Iterate through all the characters in string a and add the value that corresponds to the frequency table of the current character along the way. For example, if the current character is 'a', then we would add table[0].

3. The result will be the sum of the values added in the previous step,

PSEUDO CODE:

```
1.   Count(s,a)
2.      For index = 0 to s.length
3.              Table[s[index]]++
4.      S = 0
5.      For index = 0 to a.length
6.              S = S + table[a[index]];
7.      Return S
```

CLARIFICATION POINT-1:

Do the strings contain uppercase / lowercase characters or both?

CLARIFICATION POINT-2:

Are the characters in the two strings unique?

ASSUMPTION/LIMITATION:

- The two strings can contain both upper and lower case characters. We will use the 'tolower' function to handle both. At the
  same time, the strings can also contain duplicates.

MAJOR DATA STRUCTURES:

Array of characters (Strings)

UNIT TESTS:	
POSTIVE FUNCTIONAL TEST CASES	
INPUT	EXPECTED OUTPUT
S="abc" A="d"	0
S="abc" A="b"	1
S="abbc" A="abc"	4
NEGATIVE FUNCTIONAL TEST CASES	
a.size = 0 or s.size = 0	Invalid input

Here is a sample answer:

```
1.   int count(const char *s, const char *a)
2.   {
3.       unsigned int alphabetCount[26] = {0};
4.       unsigned int srcStrLen;
5.       unsigned int charSearchStrLen;
6.       unsigned int charSum;
7.
8.       srcStrLen = strlen(s);
9.       charSearchStrLen = strlen(a);
10.
11.      if(NULL == *s || NULL == *a || (0 == srcStrLen) || (0 ==
         charSearchStrLen))
12.          return PARAMETER_ERROR;
13.
14.      /* alphabetCount array store the repetitive
15.      counts of characters occurs in string s */
16.      while(*s!='\0')
17.      {
18.              alphabetCount[tolower(*s) - 'a'] =
19.              alphabetCount[*s - 'a'] + 1;
20.              *s++;
21.      }
22.
23.      /* Search the string a characters in
24.      alphabetCount array, and sum their occurrence
25.      */
26.      charSum = 0;
```

```
27.    while(*a!='\0')
28.    {
29.            charSum = alphabetCount[tolower(*a) - 'a'] +
               charSum;
30.            *a++;
31.    }
32.    return charSum;
33. }
```

FURTHER DISCUSSIONS:

Q: What if the two strings contained characters other than letters?

A: In this situation we would have had to extend the size of
   the frequency table to support various other characters. For
   example, if standard ASCII was used, then 128 elements would
   have been enough. Otherwise, in the case of Unicode, for
   example, we would have needed to extend the size even more.

STRINGS: CONVERT AN INTEGER N INTO ITS ASCII STRING REPRESENTATION

Write a function to convert an integer n into its ASCII string representation for a given base.

SOLUTION: The idea of the algorithm includes the following steps:

- Start with an empty string, which will eventually contain the representation of the given integer in the given base; let's call this string s, so at this step s="";

- Extract every digit from the given integer, one by one, using the % operator. However, we will not use '%10' as usual, because this operator extracts the digit in base 10. What we will do instead, is perform a '%base' operation, which will return the digit in the given base. The following cases arise:

  ▷ If number % base < 10 we just append the digit to the string in the first step, for example, given n=152 and base = 5, n % 5 = 2, which is smaller than 10, so we just append 2 to the initial string.

  ▷ If the number % base > 10, we need to start using letters. The association is the following:

    - 10 = a, 11 =b, 12= c, and so on..

  ▷ For example, 109%16 = 13 = d. In this case we append 'd' to the initial string.

- Finally, because the % operator extracts the digit from the end of the number, we also need to reverse the initial string. After the string is reversed, it will contain the desired result.

Let's say we are given n=76 and b=11. The conversion is as follows:

- S="".
- 76 % 11 = 10 = a, so we append a to s; s="a".
- 76/11 = 6.
- 6 % 11 = 6 < 10, so we append 6 to s. s = "a6".
- 10 / 11 = 0 and the algorithm stops.
- We reverse s, so s="6a". 76 in base 11 is "6a".

```
CLARIFICATION POINT-1:

What is the maximum value for n?
```

ASSUMPTION/LIMITATION:

- We will assume the integer given as input to our function fits into the int type in C++.

MAJOR DATA STRUCTURES:

Array of integers

UNIT TESTS:	
POSITIVE FUNCTIONAL TEST CASES	
INPUT	EXPECTED OUTPUT
N=10, base=2	1010
N=10, base=5	20
N=10, base=10	10
NEGATIVE FUNCTIONAL TEST CASES	
Base < 0	Invalid input

Here is a sample answer:

```
1.    char* itoa(int n, int base)
2.    {
3.        /* Four Byte Integer - If base 2
4.        then its require 32 bits max */
5.        char tmpStr[33];
6.        char *tp = tmpStr;
7.        char *retStr;
8.        int i;
9.        unsigned v;
10.       int sign;
11.       char *sp;
12.       /* Check Validity for Base Range */
13.       if (base > 16 || base <= 1)
14.       {
15.             printf(" INVALID BASE :Base Range should be between
                  2 to 16");
16.             return 0;
17.       }
18.       /* Check Intger signed or unsigned */
19.       sign = (base == 10 && n < 0);
20.       v = n;
21.
22.       /* Prepare Ascii Value String from given integer Value */
23.       while (v || tp == tmpStr)
24.       {
25.             i = v % base;
26.             v = v / base;
27.             if (i < 10)
28.                   *tp++ = i+'0';
```

```
29.            else
30.                    *tp++ = i + 'a' - 10;
31.     }
32.
33.     retStr = (char *)malloc((tp-tmpStr)+sign+1);
34.     if(retStr == NULL)
35.     {
36.             printf(" MALLOC ERROR ; Could not allocate
                memory");
37.             return 0;
38.     }
39.
40.     sp = retStr;
41.     if (sign)
42.             *sp++ = '-';
43.
44.     /* Reverse Ascii String */
45.     while (tp > tmpStr)
46.             *sp++ = *--tp;
47.     *sp = 0;
48.
49.     /* Return Ascii String representation String */
50.     return retStr;
51. }
52.
53. /* Test Function: test_itoa_function()*/
54. int test_itoa_function()
55. {
56.     char string[33];
57.     int integer;
58.     int base;
59.     integer = 12345;
60.
61.     for (base = 2;base <=16;base++)
62.     {
63.             strcpy(string,itoa(integer,base));
64.             printf("\n\nIntger: %d Base : %d , ASCII
                Representation String :%s \n",integer,base,string);
65.     }
66.     return 0;
67. }
```

```
Integer: 12345 Base : 2 , ASCII Representation String
:11000000111001
Integer: 12345 Base : 3 , ASCII Representation String
:121221020
Integer: 12345 Base : 4 , ASCII Representation String
:3000321
Integer: 12345 Base : 5 , ASCII Representation String
:343340
Integer: 12345 Base : 6 , ASCII Representation String
:133053
Integer: 12345 Base : 7 , ASCII Representation String
:50664
Integer: 12345 Base : 8 , ASCII Representation String
:30071
Integer: 12345 Base : 9 , ASCII Representation String
:17836
Integer: 12345 Base : 10 , ASCII Representation String
:12345
Integer: 12345 Base : 11 , ASCII Representation String
:9303
Integer: 12345 Base : 12 , ASCII Representation String
:7189
Integer: 12345 Base : 13 , ASCII Representation String
:5808
Integer: 12345 Base : 14 , ASCII Representation String
:46db
Integer: 12345 Base : 15 , ASCII Representation String
:39d0
Integer: 12345 Base : 16 , ASCII Representation String
:3039
```

STACKS: QUEUE USING TWO STACKS

How do you implement a queue using two stacks?

SOLUTION: An efficient algorithm for implementing a queue using two stacks performs the following steps:

- We use two stacks, initially empty, let's call them inbox and outbox, for a better understanding of the concept;
- Whenever we need to perform an enqueue(x) operation (add x to the queue) we add the element to the inbox stack;
- Whenever we need to perform a dequeue() operation (delete an element from the queue) we consider the following cases:
  - ▷ If outbox is empty then populate it with all the contents of inbox (by repeatedly popping the inbox stack and adding its top to the outbox stack).
  - ▷ Return the top of outbox and pop() outbox.

Let's consider the following sequence of operations as an example: enqueue(2), enqueue(10), enqueue(11), enqueue(3), dequeue(), dequeue(), enqueue(15), enqueue(16), dequeue(), dequeue(), dequeue(). We perform the following steps:

- Start with inbox={} and outbox={}.
- For each of the 4 enqueue operations add the elements to the inbox stack; we now have: inbox={2, 10, 11, 3} and outbox={}.
- For the first dequeue() operation, outbox is empty so we repeatedly pop inbox and push the elements into outbox; we now have inbox={} and outbox={3, 11, 10, 2}. We now pop outbox and return 2. Now outbox = {3, 11, 10}.
- For the next dequeue() operation we just pop outbox again, and return 10. Outbox={3, 11}.
- The next two enqueue operations produce inbox = {15, 16} and outbox = {3, 11}.
- For the next two dequeue() operations we pop the two elements from outbox, inbox = {15,16}, outbox={}.
- Finally, as outbox is empty again and we need to perform another dequeue() operation, we empty the contents of inbox and place them into outbox, obtaining inbox={} and outbox = {16,15}. We return 15.

```
1.    Enqueue(inbox,outbox,value):
2.        Add value to inbox
3.    Dequeue(inbox,outbox)
4.        If outbox is empty
5.                While inbox is populated
6.                        Pop inbox
7.                        Push the top of inbox to outbox
8.        Return top of outbox
```

CLARIFICATION POINT-1:

What data structure should we use to implement the two stacks?

CLARIFICATION POINT-2:

What types of elements will the two stacks hold?

ASSUMPTION/LIMITATION:

- We will use linked lists to implement the two stacks.

- We will also assume our stacks only hold integers.

MAJOR DATA STRUCTURES:

Stacks (implemented using linked lists).

Here is an implementation based on the solution described above:

```cpp
1.    #include <cstdio>
2.    #include <string.h>
3.
4.    using namespace std;
5.
6.    struct stack
7.    {
8.       int value;
9.       stack *next;
10.   };
11.
12.   void enqueue(stack *&inbox, stack *&outbox, int value)
13.   {
14.      // all we do is push the value in inbox
15.      stack *temp = new stack;
16.      temp->value = value;
17.      temp->next = inbox;
18.      inbox = temp;
19.   }
20.
21.   int dequeue(stack *&inbox, stack *&outbox)
```

```
22.  {
23.     if (outbox == NULL)
24.           while (inbox != NULL)
25.           {
26.                     stack *temp = new stack;
27.                     temp -> value = inbox -> value;
28.                     temp -> next = outbox;
29.                     outbox = temp;
30.                     inbox = inbox -> next;
31.           }
32.
33.     int top = outbox -> value;
34.     outbox = outbox -> next;
35.     return top;
36.  }
37.
38.  void queue_from_stacks(stack *inbox, stack *outbox)
39.  {
40.     // add 4 elements
41.     enqueue(inbox, outbox, 2);
42.     enqueue(inbox, outbox, 10);
43.     enqueue(inbox, outbox, 11);
44.     enqueue(inbox, outbox, 13);
45.
46.     // perform two dequeues
47.     printf("%d\n", dequeue(inbox, outbox));
48.     printf("%d\n", dequeue(inbox, outbox));
49.
50.     // add 2 more elements
51.     enqueue(inbox, outbox, 15);
52.     enqueue(inbox, outbox, 16);
53.
54.     // perform three dequeues
55.     printf("%d\n", dequeue(inbox, outbox));
56.     printf("%d\n", dequeue(inbox, outbox));
57.     printf("%d\n", dequeue(inbox, outbox));
58.  }
59.
60.  int main()
61.  {
62.     stack *inbox, *outbox;
63.
64.     // start with two empty stacks
65.     inbox = NULL;
66.     outbox = NULL;
67.
68.     queue_from_stacks(inbox, outbox);
69.
70.     return 0;
71.  }
```

OUTPUT:	FURTHER EXERCISE:
2	Q: How can we implement the stacks without using linked lists?
10	
11	A: There are various ways to implement the two stacks. For example, we could use an array of integers, or even the stack object in the C++ STL library, which comes with pre-defined functions for push() and pop(), for example.
13	
15	

STACKS: COMPUTE THE POSTFIX EXPRESSION

Write a program to compute the postfix from of an expression in infix and evaluate it

SOLUTION: Suppose we have this infix expression Q:

5 * (6 + 2) - 12 / 4

The equivalent postfix expression P is:

5 6 2 + * 12 4 / -

The result of the evaluation is : 37

The prefix/infix/postfix forms of an expression were detailed in the 'stacks' section of the data structures chapter. We will now firstly look at an algorithm that can be used to convert an expression from infix to postfix, with the use of stacks. The steps are as follows:

- We need a string to hold the postfix expression and an empty stack for holding the operators. Initially, these are empty.
- Iterate through the string corresponding to the infix expression and consider the following cases:
- If the current character is an operand (in our case, a digit), add it to the postfix string.
- If the current character is a '(' push it onto the operator stack.
- If the current character is a ')'
    a) Pop the operator stack and add the characters to the postfix string until a '(' is reached.
    b) Pop the stack again, as we are not interested in the '(' anymore.
- If the current character is an operator (+, -, * or /)
    a) If the operator stack is empty push the current operator into the stack.
    b) Else
        i. If the top of the stack is an operator with a higher precedence than the current operator pop the stack and add its top to the postfix string.
        ii. Push the current operator into the stack.
- In the end, if there are still more operators into the stack pop them and add them to the postfix string.

Let's consider, for example, the expression 5*(6+2)-12/4. We would then perform the following steps:

- Start with an empty string, postfix="" and with an empty operator stack.
- Append the 5 to the string and push the * to the stack (as it is initially empty)
- Now a '(' is reached, so push it to the stack.
- Add 6 to the postfix string and push '+' to the stack, we now have postfix ="5 6" and stack ="* (+".
- Add the 2 to the postfix string.
- We have now reached a ')' so we pop the stack until we reach the '(', adding its top to the string. We now have postfix = "5 6 2 +" and stack = "*".
- We have reached the '-'. Its precedence is lower than the '*' in the stack, so we pop the stack, append the '*' to the postfix string and add '-' to the stack. At this step postfix = "5 6 2 + *" and stack = '-'.
- We append 12 to the string, we push / to the stack (its precedence is bigger than the – already there), and we also append 4 to the string. We now have postfix = "5 6 2 + * 12 4" and stack = "- /".
- Finally, we pop the stack until it is empty, obtaining "5 6 2 + * 12 4 / -", which is the postfix form of the expression.

Once we have the postfix form, evaluating it can be easily done with the following algorithm:

- Iterate through the postfix expression and, for each character perform the following:
  a) If the current character is a number push it to an initially empty stack
  b) Else (if it is an operator) pop the stack 2 times and perform the operation, pushing the result back into the stack.
- The result will now be on the top of the stack.

For our initial example, 5 6 2 + * 12 4 / -, we perform the following:

- Push 5, 6 and 2 to the stack;
- Pop the stack 2 times, perform 6 + 2 and push 8 to the stack, now we have stack ="5 8".
- Repeat until the end of the string.

PSEUDO CODE:

As described above.

CLARIFICATION POINT-1:

What is the maximum length of the infix expression?

CLARIFICATION POINT-2:

What kind of characters can the infix expression contain?

ASSUMPTION/LIMITATION:

- We will assume the infix expression contains no more than 200 characters;

- We will also assume the infix expression only contains digits and one of the addition, multiplication, subtraction or division operators.

MAJOR DATA STRUCTURES:

Stacks, arrays of characters(string)

UNIT TESTS:	
POSTIVE FUNCTIONAL TEST CASES	
INPUT	EXPECTED OUTPUT
Infix = 1+3+5 Infix = 3*(2+15)-4 Infix = 14/7+2/2 Infix = 1+(2+3+4)-5	Postfix = 1 3 + 5 +, result = 9 Postfix = 3 2 15 + * 4 -, result = 47 Postfix = 14 7 / 2 2 / +, result = 3 Postfix = 1 2 3 + 4 + + 5 -, result = 5
NEGATIVE FUNCTIONAL TEST CASES	
Infix = a + b + z Infix.length = 0	Input invalid Input invalid

Here is a sample solution that implements the steps described above:

```
1.    #include <cstdio>
2.    #include <string.h>
3.    #include <stack>
4.
5.    using namespace std;
6.
7.    char* infix_to_postfix(char infix[])
8.    {
9.        if (strlen(infix) == 0)
10.       {
11.            printf("Invalid input!\n");
```

```
12.                 return "";
13.     }
14.
15.     // if infix contains ther than numbers, brackets or
        operators it is invalid
16.     for (int infixIndex = 0; infixIndex < strlen(infix);
        infixIndex++)
17.             if (infix[infixIndex] != '+' && infix[infixIndex] !=
        '-' && infix[infixIndex] != '*'
18.                     && infix[infixIndex] != '/' &&
                infix[infixIndex] != '('
19.                             && infix[infixIndex] != ')' &&
                        !(infix[infixIndex] >= '0' &&
                        infix[infixIndex] <='9'))
20.                     {
21.                             printf("Invalid input!\n");
22.                             return "";
23.                     }
24.
25.     // postfix string, initially empty
26.     char postfixString[200] = "";
27.     stack<char>operatorStack;
28.
29.     for (int infixIndex = 0; infixIndex < strlen(infix);
        infixIndex++)
30.     {
31.             // if we reach an operand (number)
32.             if (infix[infixIndex] >= '0' && infix[infixIndex] <=
                '9')
33.             {
34.                     // add number to postfix string
35.                     postfixString[strlen(postfixString)] =
                        infix[infixIndex];
36.                     while (infix[infixIndex + 1] >= '0' &&
                        infix[infixIndex + 1] <= '9')
37.                     {
38.                             infixIndex++;
39.                             postfixString[strlen(postfixString)] =
                                infix[infixIndex];
40.                     }
41.                     postfixString[strlen(postfixString)] = ' ';
42.             }
43.
44.             else if(infix[infixIndex] == '(')
45.                     operatorStack.push(infix[infixIndex]);
46.
47.             else if (infix[infixIndex] == ')')
48.             {
49.                     char op = operatorStack.top();
50.
51.                     while (op != '(')
```

```
52.                     {
53.                             operatorStack.pop();
54.                             postfixString[strlen(postfixString)] =
                                op;
55.                             postfixString[strlen(postfixString)] =
                                ' ';
56.                             op = operatorStack.top();
57.                     }
58.
59.             // pop the '(' as well
60.             operatorStack.pop();
61.         }
62.
63.         // case operator
64.         else if (infix[infixIndex] == '+' || infix[infixIndex]
            == '-' ||
65.                         infix[infixIndex] == '*' ||
                            infix[infixIndex] == '/')
66.         {
67.                     if (operatorStack.empty())
68.                             operatorStack.
                                push(infix[infixIndex]);
69.                     else
70.                     {
71.                             char topOperator =
                                operatorStack.top();
72.
73.                             // if operator in the stack
                                has higher precedence
74.                             if ((topOperator == '*' ||
                                topOperator == '/') &&
75.                                     (infix[infixIndex]
                                        == '+' ||
                                        infix[infixIndex] ==
                                        '-'))
76.                             {
77.                                     postfixString
                                        [strlen(post
                                        fixString)] =
                                        topOperator;
78.                                     postfixString[s
                                        trlen(postfixSt
                                        ring)] = ' ';
79.                                     operatorStack.
                                        pop();
80.                                     operatorStack.
                                push(infix[infixIndex]);
81.                                     //break;
82.                             }
83.                             else
```

```
84.                                              operatorStack.
                                       push(infix[infixIndex]);
85.                             }
86.             }
87.     }
88.
89.     while (!operatorStack.empty())
90.     {
91.             postfixString[strlen(postfixString)] = operatorStack.
                top();
92.             postfixString[strlen(postfixString)] = ' ';
93.             operatorStack.pop();
94.     }
95.
96.     return postfixString;
97. }
98.
99.  int evaluate(char postfix[])
100. {
101.    if (strlen(postfix) == 0)
102.    {
103.            printf("Invalid input!\n");
104.            return 0;
105.    }
106.
107.    // if expression contains other than numbers and operators
        it is invalid
108.    for (int postfixIndex = 0; postfixIndex < strlen(postfix);
        postfixIndex++)
109.    {
110.            if (postfix[postfixIndex] != '+' &&
                postfix[postfixIndex] != '-' && postfix[postfixIndex]
                != ' ' &&
111.                postfix[postfixIndex] != '*' &&
                    postfix[postfixIndex] != '/' &&
112.                !(postfix[postfixIndex] >= '0' &&
                    postfix[postfixIndex] <= '9' ))
113.                {
114.                        printf("Invalid input!\n");
115.                        return 0;
116.                }
117.    }
118.
119.    stack<int> numberStack;
120.
121.    for (int postfixIndex = 0; postfixIndex < strlen(postfix);
        postfixIndex++)
122.    {
123.            // if opreator perform operation
124.            if (postfix[postfixIndex] == '+' ||
                postfix[postfixIndex] == '-' ||
```

```
125.                    postfix[postfixIndex] == '*' ||
                        postfix[postfixIndex] == '/')
126.                    {
127.                            // get the two terms from the top of
                               number stack
128.                            // and perform the operation
129.                            int term1 = numberStack.top();
130.                            numberStack.pop();
131.                            int term2 = numberStack.top();
132.                            numberStack.pop();
133.
134.                            int result;
135.                            if (postfix[postfixIndex] == '+')
136.                                    result = term2 + term1;
137.                            else if (postfix[postfixIndex] == '-')
138.                                    result = term2 - term1;
139.                            else if (postfix[postfixIndex] == '*')
140.                                    result = term2 * term1;
141.                            else
142.                                    result = term2 / term1;
143.
144.                            // add the result back to
                               numberstack1
145.                            numberStack.push(result);
146.                    }
147.
148.            else if (postfix[postfixIndex] >= '0' &&
                    postfix[postfixIndex] <= '9')
149.            {
150.                    // form the number and add it to the number
                       stack
151.                    int number = postfix[postfixIndex] - '0';
152.                    while (postfix[postfixIndex + 1] >= '0' &&
                        postfix[postfixIndex + 1] <= '9')
153.                    {
154.                            postfixIndex++;
155.                            number = number * 10 +
                               (postfix[postfixIndex] - '0');
156.                    }
157.                    numberStack.push(number);
158.            }
159.    }
160.
161.    // the result of the evaluation is the top of the stack
162.    return numberStack.top();
163. }
164.
165. int main()
166. {
167.    char infix[200] = "5*(6+2)-12/4";
168.    printf("Expression in infix: %s\n", infix);
```

```
169.
170.    char postfix[200];
171.    strcpy(postfix, infix_to_postfix(infix));
172.    printf("Expression in postfix: %s\n", postfix);
173.
174.    int result = evaluate(postfix);
175.    printf("Result of evaluation: %d\n", result);
176.
177.    return 0;
178. }
```

OUTPUT:	FURTHER EXERCISE:
Expression in infix: 1+(2+3+4)-5	Q: How do you convert from infix to prefix?
Expression in postfix: 1 2 3 4 + + 5 - +	A: One famous algorithm for converting an expression from infix to prefix is called the Shunting-yard algorithm and uses a queue rather than a stack, because the order of the operators needs to be reversed.
Result of evaluation: 5	

QUEUES: STACK USING TWO QUEUES

Implement a stack using two queues, with the use of two linked lists for implementing the queues.

SOLUTION: First of all, a queue can be implemented with the use of a linked list only if we store both the head and tail of the list. This is because we need access to both ends, as enqueue() operations are performed at the tail of the list and as part of the dequeue() operation we need to remove the element from the front of the list.

The algorithm we will be using starts with two empty queues and uses a fairly straightforward idea for the implementation of the push() and pop() functions for the stack. First, the steps for the push() operation are as follows:

- If the first queue is empty
    - ▷ Insert the value to be pushed into the first queue;
    - ▷ Transfer the elements from the second queue to the first queue (by successively performing dequeue() on the second queue and enqueue() on the first queue)
- Otherwise we perform the same steps on the second queue.

Next, for the pop operation, we just perform a dequeue() operation on the stack that is not empty at the current step.

For example, suppose we want to perform the following sequence of operations: push(1), push(2), push(3), pop(), pop(), push(5), push(10), pop(), pop(). The steps are as follows:

1. At first both queues are empty, we insert 1 into the first queue. Q1={1}, Q2={}.
2. When we perform push(2), queue 2 is empty so we insert 2 into it and then transfer the contents of Q1 to Q1. Q1 = {} Q2 = {2, 1}
3. After the third push, we would have Q1 = {3, 2, 1}, Q2= {}.
4. For the next two pop() operations, we just dequeue() Q1 two times. Q1 = {1}, Q2 = {}.
5. After the next two push() operations, we will obtain Q1 = {10, 5, 1}, Q2 = {}.
6. We finally perform two more dequeue() operations, also on Q1 (the non-empty queue), outputting 10 and 5.

PSEUDO CODE:

As described above.

CLARIFICATION POINT-1:

What kind of characters can the queues hold?

ASSUMPTION/LIMITATION:

- We will assume the two queues (and implicitly the stack) will hold only integers.

MAJOR DATA STRUCTURES:

Queue implemented as single linked list

Here is a sample solution that implements the steps described above:

```cpp
1.    #include <cstdio>
2.
3.    using namespace std;
4.
5.    struct queue
6.    {
7.       queue *next;
8.       int value;
9.    };
10.
11.   void push(queue *&q1start, queue *&q1end, queue *&q2start,
      queue *&q2end, int value)
12.   {
13.      // if the first queue is empty
14.      if (q1start == NULL)
15.      {
16.             // push value into the first queue
17.             queue *element = new queue;
18.             element -> value = value;
19.             element -> next = q1end;
20.             q1start = element;
21.             q1end = element;
22.
23.             // transfer contents from the second queue
24.             while (q2start != NULL)
25.             {
26.                     queue *element = new queue;
27.                     element -> value = q2start -> value;
28.                     element -> next = NULL;
29.                     q1end -> next = element;
30.                     q1end = element;
31.                     q2start = q2start -> next;
32.             }
33.
34.             // empty the second queue
35.             q2start = q2end = NULL;
```

```
36.     }
37.
38.     // else do the same thing for the second queue
39.     else
40.     {
41.             // push value into the second queue
42.             queue *element = new queue;
43.             element -> value = value;
44.             element -> next = q2end;
45.             q2start = element;
46.             q2end = element;
47.
48.             // transfer contents from the first queue
49.             while (q1start != NULL)
50.             {
51.                     queue *element = new queue;
52.                     element -> value = q1start -> value;
53.                     element -> next = NULL;
54.                     q2end -> next = element;
55.                     q2end = element;
56.                     q1start = q1start -> next;
57.             }
58.
59.             // empty the first queue
60.             q1start = q1end = NULL;
61.     }
62. }
63.
64. void pop(queue *&q1start, queue *&q1end, queue *&q2start,
    queue *&q2end)
65. {
66.     // just pop an elemnet from whichever queue is not empty
67.     if (q1start != NULL)
68.     {
69.             printf("%d\n", q1start -> value);
70.             q1start = q1start -> next;
71.     }
72.     else
73.     {
74.             printf("%d\n", q2start -> value);
75.             q2start = q2start -> next;
76.     }
77. }
78.
79. void queue_to_stack(queue *&q1start, queue *&q1end, queue
    *&q2start, queue *&q2end)
80. {
81.     // perform some push and pop operations to test the stack
        functionality
82.     push(q1start, q1end, q2start, q2end, 1);
83.     push(q1start, q1end, q2start, q2end, 2);
```

```
84.        push(q1start, q1end, q2start, q2end, 3);
85.        pop(q1start, q1end, q2start, q2end);
86.        pop(q1start, q1end, q2start, q2end);
87.        push(q1start, q1end, q2start, q2end, 5);
88.        push(q1start, q1end, q2start, q2end, 10);
89.        pop(q1start, q1end, q2start, q2end);
90.        pop(q1start, q1end, q2start, q2end);
91.  }
92.
93.  int main()
94.  {
95.      queue *q1start, *q1end, *q2start, *q2end;
96.      q1start = q1end = q2start = q2end = NULL;
97.
98.      queue_to_stack(q1start, q1end, q2start, q2end);
99.
100.     return 0;
101. }
```

```
OUTPUT:

3
2
10
5
```

LISTS: DETECTS WHETHER A LINKED LIST HAS CIRCULAR REFERENCE OR NOT

Implement a circular queue of integers of user-specified size using a simple array. Provide routines to initialize(), enqueue() and dequeue() the queue. Make it thread safe.

SOLUTION: In order to store the queue, we will use a struct containing an array of integers (the elements of the queue), the size of the queue and two other integers representing the head and the tail position in the data structure.

Now, for the initialization function we take the queue and the number of elements as parameter, returning true if the initialization was done successfully and false otherwise. The main purpose of this function is to allocate memory so that we can use the queue at a later point.

Because the task requires the program to be thread safe and avoid deadlocks, our enqueue() and dequeue() function will use an object called "mutex" (comes from "mutual exclusive") which will ensure no two threads access the same memory location at the same time. The enqueue() function performs the following steps:

1. If there is no place in the queue, return.
2. If the element is added at the end of the queue, then after adding it set the tail of the queue to be the first index in the array of integers, as the queue is circular.
3. If the element is added somewhere else, then just insert as in a regular queue.

Finally, the dequeue() function behaves as follows:

1. If there are no elements in the queue then return.
2. Otherwise, increase the index corresponding to the head of the queue (remember, in a queue elements are added at the tail and removed from the head).
3. If after step 2 the tail and head indexes are equal, this means the queue only contained one element and is now empty so we set both indexes to -1.
4. If step 3 does not apply, we just return true after advancing the index of the head.

CLARIFICATION POINT-1:

How many elements will the queue store?

ASSUMPTION/LIMITATION:

- We will assume a reasonable value for the size of the queue, so as not to obtain any segmentation fault.

MAJOR DATA STRUCTURES:

Queue

Here is a sample answer:

```
1.    typedef struct strCircularQueue
2.    {
3.        int *ptrCircularQueue;
4.        int iCircularQueueSize;
5.        int iFrontIndex;
6.        int iRearIndex;
7.    }CircularQueueData;
8.
9.    BOOL initialize(CircularQueueData *CQdata, unsigned int
      QueueLength)
10.   {
11.       if (QueueLength == 0)
12.               printf("QueueLength Length Should be greater than
                  zero");
13.
14.       // Allocate the QueueLength(unsigned int) size of memory
15.       CQdata->ptrCircularQueue = (unsigned int *)
          malloc(QueueLength * sizeof(unsigned int));
16.
17.       if(CQdata->ptrCircularQueue == NULL)
18.   {
19.               printf("Error during memory allocation")
20.               return FALSE;
21.       }
22.
23.       CQdata->iCircularQueueSize = QueueLength;
24.       CQdata->iFrontIndex = -1;
25.       CQdata->iRearIndex = -1;
26.       return TRUE;
27.   }
28.
29.   BOOL enqueue(CircularQueueData *CQdata,int data)
30.   {
31.       // Request ownership of mutex
32.       WaitForSingleObject(g_hMutex, INFINITE);
33.       {
34.               // Check whether Queue has room to enqueue the
                  item;
35.               if((CQdata->iFrontIndex == 0 && CQdata->iRearIndex
                  == CQdata->iCircularQueueSize - 1)||
```

```
36.              (CQdata->iRearIndex + CQdata->iFrontIndex + 1 ==
                 CQdata->iCircularQueueSize) ||
37.              (CQdata->iRearIndex + 1 == CQdata->iFrontIndex)
38.              {
39.                      printf("Circular queue is full.");
40.                      return FALSE;
41.              }
42.              else
43.              {
44.                      // Change the queue index
45.                      if(CQdata->iRearIndex == CQdata-
                         >iCircularQueueSize - 1)
46.                              CQdata->iRearIndex = 0;
47.                      else
48.                              CQdata->iRearIndex++;
49.                              CQdata->ptrCircularQueue[CQdata-
                                 >iRearIndex] = value;
50.
51.                      printf("Enqueued Value Position %d and
                         value %d",CQdata->iRearIndex,value);
52.              }
53.              // If this is first enqueued item,
54.              if(CQdata->iFrontIndex == -1)
55.              CQdata->iFrontIndex = 0;
56.      }
57.      // Release the mutex
58.      ReleaseMutex(g_hMutex);
59.      return TRUE;
60. }
61.
62. BOOL dequeue(CircularQueueData *CQdata)
63. {
64.      int val;
65.      // Request ownership of mutex
66.      WaitForSingleObject(g_hMutex, INFINITE);
67.      {
68.              // Whether queue has any item to dequeue
69.              if(CQdata->iFrontIndex == -1)
70.              {
71.                      printf("Circular queue is empty.");
72.                      return FALSE;
73.              }
74.              else
75.              {
76.                      // Set the front/rear index of queue
77.                      val = CQdata->ptrCircularQueue[CQdata-
                         >iFrontIndex];
78.                      CQdata->ptrCircularQueue[CQdata-
                         >iFrontIndex] = 0;
79.                      if(CQdata->iFrontIndex == CQdata-
                         >iRearIndex)
```

```
80.                      {
81.                             CQdata->iFrontIndex = CQdata-
                               >iRearIndex = -1;
82.                      }
83.                      else
84.                      {
85.                             if(CQdata->iFrontIndex == (CQdata-
                               >iCircularQueueSize -1))
86.                             CQdata->iFrontIndex = 0;
87.                      else
88.                             CQdata->iFrontIndex++;
89.                      }
90.              }
91.      }
92.      printf("Dequeued value at Position %d and value
         %d",CQdata->iRearIndex,val);
93.
94.      // Release the mutex
95.      ReleaseMutex(g_hMutex);
96.      return TRUE;
97. }
```

FURTHER EXERCISE:

Q: Would it be more efficient to implement a circular queue with
   the use of singly-linked lists?

A: Yes, because we would not have needed to know the size of the
   queue in advance and allocate memory accordingly.

LISTS: NTH ELEMENT FROM THE END

Write a function that would return the 5th element from the end of a singly linked list, knowing the following:

- **The list contains only integer**
- **The solution must find the element in one pass**
- **The solution cannot use templates.**

Provide a set of test cases against the function.

SOLUTION: We will use single linked lists implemented with two pointers, one for the head and one for the tail of the list. The algorithm for returning the fifth element from the back of the list is fairly simple and relies on the following steps:

- Have a duplicate pointer to the head of the list and advance it four times;

- Advance both pointers at the same time, until the one we have advanced in the previous step reaches the tail of the list). The result we are looking for will now be stored in the leftmost pointer.

Let's consider an example on the list (1, 2, 3, 4, 5, 6, 7). Initially, the head pointer points to 1, while the tail pointer points to the 7 at the end of this list. The steps would then be as follows:

- Duplicate head, let's call this new pointer tempHead;

- Advance tempHead 4 times, so now it points to 5;

- Advance both pointers in steps of 1, until tempHead points to the tail of the list (the element with the value 7).

- After we do this the first time, head will point to 2 and tempHead will point to 6. We only need to do this one more time, with head pointing to 3 and tempHead to 7. We stop because tempHead points to the tail of the list.

- The answer is the value head points to, which in this case is 3.

CLARIFICATION POINT-1:

How many elements can the list store?

ASSUMPTION/LIMITATION:

- For the purpose of this example, we will work on a list with a maximum of 10 elements. However, as singly linked lists are al-located dynamically, we do not need to know the number of ele-ments in advance.

MAJOR DATA STRUCTURES:

Singly linked list

UNIT TESTS:	
POSTIVE FUNCTIONAL TEST CASES	
INPUT	EXPECTED OUTPUT
List={1,2,3,4,5}	1
List={5,7,10,1,2,3,4}	10
List={10,100,5,200,10,15,10}	5
NEGATIVE FUNCTIONAL TEST CASES	
List = {}	Empty list!
List = {1, 2}	Not enough elements in the list!

Here is a sample solution that implements the steps described above:

```
1.    #include <cstdio>
2.
3.    using namespace std;
4.
5.    struct list
6.    {
7.       list *next;
8.       int value;
9.    };
10.
11.   void insert(list *&head, list *&tail, int value)
12.   {
13.      // if first insertion
14.      if (head == NULL)
15.      {
16.              list *element = new list;
17.              element -> value = value;
18.              element -> next = NULL;
19.              head = tail = element;
20.      }
21.      // if not then insert in the end
22.      else
23.      {
24.              list *element = new list;
25.              element -> value = value;
26.              element -> next = NULL;
27.              tail -> next = element;
28.              tail = element;
29.      }
30.
31.   }
```

```
32.
33.  int return_fifth_element(list *head, list *tail)
34.  {
35.      if(head == NULL)
36.      {
37.              printf("Empty list given!\n");
38.              return 0;
39.      }
40.
41.      // the pointer we advance 5 times
42.      list *tempHead = head;
43.
44.      bool enoughElements = true;
45.      for (int k = 1; k < 5; k++)
46.      {
47.              tempHead = tempHead -> next;
48.              if (tempHead == NULL)
49.              {
50.                      enoughElements = false;
51.                      break;
52.              }
53.      }
54.
55.      if (!enoughElements)
56.      {
57.              printf("Not enough elements in the list!\n");
58.              return 0;
59.      }
60.
61.      // advance both the head and tempHead at the same time
         until
62.      // tempHead reaches the end of the list
63.      while (tempHead != tail)
64.      {
65.              head = head -> next;
66.              tempHead = tempHead -> next;
67.      }
68.
69.      // return value in head (5th from end of list)
70.      return head -> value;
71.  }
72.
73.  int main()
74.  {
75.      // our list, initially empty
76.      list *head, *tail;
77.      int result;
78.
79.      // test 1: empty list;
80.      head = NULL; tail = NULL;
81.      printf ("Test 1: ");
```

```
82.     result = return_fifth_element(head,tail);
83.
84.     // test 2: list with only 1 element
85.     printf ("Test 2: ");
86.     insert(head, tail, 2);
87.     result = return_fifth_element(head,tail);
88.
89.     // test 3: list (1, 2, 3, 4, 5)
90.     head = NULL; tail = NULL;
91.     insert(head, tail, 1); insert(head, tail, 2); insert(head,
        tail, 3);
92.     insert(head, tail, 4); insert(head, tail, 5);
93.     result = return_fifth_element(head, tail);
94.     printf("Test 3: The element is %d\n", result);
95.
96.     // test 4: list (1, 2, 3, 4, 5, 6, 7)
97.     head = NULL; tail = NULL;
98.     insert(head, tail, 1); insert(head, tail, 2); insert(head,
        tail, 3); insert(head, tail, 4);
99.     insert(head, tail, 5); insert(head, tail, 6); insert(head,
        tail, 7);
100.    result = return_fifth_element(head, tail);
101.    printf("Test 4: The element is %d\n", result);
102.
103.    // test 5: list (10, 9, 2, 6, 8, 11, 15, 17, 20, 15)
104.    head = NULL; tail = NULL;
105.    insert(head, tail, 10); insert(head, tail, 9);
        insert(head, tail, 2);
106.    insert(head, tail, 6); insert(head, tail, 8); insert(head,
        tail, 11);
107.    insert(head, tail, 15); insert(head, tail, 17);
        insert(head, tail, 20);
108.    insert(head, tail, 15);
109.    result = return_fifth_element(head, tail);
110.    printf("Test 5: The element is %d\n", result);
111.
112.    return 0;
113. }
```

OUTPUT:	FURTHER EXERCISE:
Test 1: Empty list given!	Q: Is there a naïve approach for this task?
Test 2: Not enough elements in the list!	A: A naïve approach would iterate through the list once to determine how many elements it holds and then iterate again to print the required element. This takes twice as many steps as the approach we have described.
Test 3: The element is 1	
Test 4: The element is 3	
Test 5: The element is 11	

LISTS: MERGES SORTED LINKED LISTS

Write a function that merges two already sorted linked lists into a third, sorted linked list. When the same element exists in both lists, the element from list 1 should come first. The function header is: node * merge(node* sl1, node* sl2){}.

SOLUTION: This problem is pretty much identical to merging two sorted arrays, with the single exception being that we are going to use singly linked lists instead. Because of the header of the function, we will not use two pointers for the lists and we will only store a pointer to the beginning of the lists and assume they are already sorted.

The steps we will perform are the same as if we were working with arrays and are as follows:

- In the beginning the two pointers point to the head of the two lists.
- Create a new list, initially empty, which will hold the sorted elements and will be returned in the end.
- If the element in the first list is smaller than or equal to the element in the second list
  - ▷ Append the element in the first list to the new list;
  - ▷ Advance the pointer corresponding to the first list.

- Else
  - ▷ Append the element in the second list to the new list;
  - ▷ Advance the pointer corresponding to the second list.

- Repeat the steps above until one of the pointers points to a NULL element, which means we have reached the end of either of the lists (or both).
- If there are more elements to be appended to the list holding the sorted elements in any of the lists then do this as a final step.

For example, suppose we have the lists sl1={1, 3, 8, 10} and sl2 = {1, 2, 5, 6, 12}. We perform the following steps:

- Start with the head of both lists and create an empty list, let's call it sorted={}.
- 1 = 1, so append the 1 in the first list to sorted. We advance sl1.
- 3 > 1, so we append the 1 in the second list to sorted and advance sl2. Sorted = {1,1}.

- 3 > 2, so we append 2 and advance sl2. Sorted = {1, 1, 2}.

- We repeat until we reach the end of s1. At this point sorted = {1, 1, 2, 3, 5, 8, 10}.

- There is one more element to be added (in sl2), so we add it to sorted. Finally, sorted = {1, 1, 2, 3, 5, 8, 10, 12}.

PSEUDO CODE:

```
1.   Merge(sl1,sl2)
2.       Merged={}
3.       While (sl1!= NULL and sl2 != NULL)
4.               toBeInserted = 0
5.               if (sl1.value <= sl2.value)
6.                       toBeInserted = sl1.value
7.                       sl1++
8.               else
9.                       toBeInserted = sl2.value
10.                      sl2++
11.              insert toBeInserted into Merged
12.      while there are more elements into sl1
13.              insert them into Merged
14.      while there are more elements into sl2
15.              insert them into Merged
16.      return Merged
```

CLARIFICATION POINT-1:

How many items do the lists hold and what kind of values?

ASSUMPTION/LIMITATION:

- We will assume the lists hold only integer values. For the purpose of this example, we will only work with lists that hold a maximum of 5 elements.

- We will also assume the lists are already sorted by the time the merge function is called.

MAJOR DATA STRUCTURES:

Singly linked lists

UNIT TESTS:	
POSTIVE FUNCTIONAL TEST CASES	
INPUT	EXPECTED OUTPUT
Sl1={} sl2={1,2}	{1,2}
Sl1={1} sl2={2}	{1,2}
Sl1={1,3,5}, sl2={2,4}	{1,2,3,4,5}
Sl1={0,1,4,5,10} sl2={2,3}	{0,1,2,3,4,5,10}

| Sl1={}, sl2={} | Input invalid |
| Sl1 or sl2 - non sorted list | Input invalid |

Here is a sample solution that implements the steps described above:

```
1.   #include <cstdio>
2.
3.   using namespace std;
4.
5.   struct node
6.   {
7.      node *next;
8.      int value;
9.   };
10.
11.  void insert(node *&l, int value)
12.  {
13.     // insert value into list l
14.     node *element = new node;
15.     element -> value = value;
16.     element -> next = l;
17.     l = element;
18.  }
19.
20.  node* merge(node* sl1, node* sl2)
21.  {
22.     // check if sl1 is sorted
23.     node * temp = sl1;
24.     while (temp -> next)
25.     {
26.             if (temp -> next -> value < temp -> value)
27.             {
28.                     printf("Invalid input!\n");
29.                     return NULL;
30.             }
31.             temp = temp -> next;
32.     }
33.
34.     // check if sl2 is sorted
35.     temp = sl2;
36.     while (temp -> next)
37.     {
38.             if (temp -> next -> value < temp -> value)
39.             {
40.                     printf("Invalid input!\n");
41.                     return NULL;
42.             }
43.             temp = temp -> next;
44.     }
```

```
45.
46.
47.    if (sl1 == NULL && sl2 == NULL)
48.    {
49.            printf("Invalid input!\n");
50.            return NULL;
51.    }
52.
53.    node *merged_list_head = NULL;
54.    node *merged_list_tail = NULL;
55.
56.    // iterate through both lists at the same time
57.    while (sl1!= NULL && sl2 != NULL)
58.    {
59.            int toBeInserted;
60.
61.            // current elemnet is smaller in first list
62.            // if equal we also insert from sl1, and insertion
63.            // from sl2 will occur at next step
64.            if (sl1 -> value <= sl2 -> value)
65.            {
66.                    toBeInserted = sl1 -> value;
67.                    sl1 = sl1 -> next;
68.            }
69.
70.            // current element is smaller in second list
71.            else if (sl1 -> value > sl2 -> value)
72.            {
73.                    toBeInserted = sl2 -> value;
74.                    sl2 = sl2 -> next;
75.            }
76.
77.            // insert at the end of merged_list
78.
79.            // if list empty make tail and head equal
80.            if (merged_list_head == NULL)
81.            {
82.                    node *element = new node;
83.                    element -> value = toBeInserted;
84.                    element -> next = NULL;
85.                    merged_list_head = merged_list_tail =
                        element;
86.            }
87.
88.            // else insert at the end of the list
89.            else
90.            {
91.                    node *element = new node;
92.                    element -> value = toBeInserted;
93.                    element -> next = NULL;
94.                    merged_list_tail -> next = element;
```

```
95.                        merged_list_tail = element;
96.                }
97.        }
98.
99.     // if there are values left in either sl1 or sl2 add them
100.    while (sl1 != NULL)
101.    {
102.            node *element = new node;
103.            element -> value = sl1 -> value;
104.            element -> next = NULL;
105.            merged_list_tail -> next = element;
106.            merged_list_tail = element;
107.            sl1 = sl1 -> next;
108.    }
109.
110.    while (sl2 != NULL)
111.    {
112.            node *element = new node;
113.            element -> value = sl2 -> value;
114.            element -> next = NULL;
115.            merged_list_tail -> next = element;
116.            merged_list_tail = element;
117.            sl2 = sl2 -> next;
118.    }
119.
120.    return merged_list_head;
121. }
122.
123. int main()
124. {
125.    node *sl1, *sl2;
126.    sl1 = NULL; sl2 = NULL;
127.
128.    // create the sorted lists
129.    insert(sl1, 10); insert(sl1, 8); insert(sl1, 3);
        insert(sl1, 1);
130.    insert(sl2,12); insert(sl2, 6); insert(sl2, 5);
        insert(sl2, 2); insert(sl2, 1);
131.
132.    node *merged_list = merge(sl1, sl2);
133.
134.    // print the result
135.    printf("The merged lists:\n");
136.    for (node *iterator = merged_list; iterator; iterator =
        iterator -> next)
137.            printf("%d ", iterator -> value);
138.
139.    printf("\n");
140.
141.    return 0;
142. }
```

OUTPUT:	FURTHER EXERCISE:
The merged lists: 1 1 2 3 5 6 8 10 12	Q: Can you think of a naïve approach? A: A naïve approach would append all the elements in the two lists in a third list and then sort the third list. There are some algorithms that can be used to sort a singly linked list, but they will not achieve the same efficiency as the merge function we have seen.

LISTS: REVERSE A SINGLY LINKED LIST

How do you revesre a sinlgy linked list in linear time and constant space, without using recursion and without using the stack object in the STL library?

SOLUTION: As hard as this task may seem, there is actually a pretty simple and efficient solution to complete it. For our implementation, we will use a singly linked list represented with the use of two pointer, one for its head and one for the tail.

The big picture of how our algorithm will perform is as follows:

- Iterate through the list and change the direction of the pointers (i.e. instead of having head point to head -> next we set head -> next to point to head).

- Stop when we have reached the end of the list.

For example, given the list (1, 4, 10, 12, 15), we iterate through it and set 1 to point to NULL, 4 to point to 1, and so on. In the end, 15 (which at this point will point to 12) will become the head of the reversed list.

In practice, in order to achieve this effect, we initially duplicate the head of the list and use this duplicate pointer to iterate through it. At each step, we will be adding elements to the front of the initial head. For example, with (1,4,10,12,15), we will add, 4, 10, 12 and 15, consequently, to the front of '1', in order to obtain 15, 12, 10, 4, 1, which is the reversed list.

PSEUDO CODE:

```
1.    Reverse(head, tail):
2.        Initial_head = head
3.        While (initial_head != tail)
4.            Add initial_head -> next to the front of head
5.        Add tail to the front of head
```

CLARIFICATION POINT-1:

How many elements can the list contain and what type of elements?

ASSUMPTION/LIMITATION:

- For the purpose of this example, our list will contain no more than 5 integers, but lists are dynamically allocated, so we do not need to know the number of elements in advance.

MAJOR DATA STRUCTURES:

Linked lists

UNIT TESTS:	
POSTIVE FUNCTIONAL TEST CASES	
INPUT	EXPECTED OUTPUT
List={2} List={1,2} List={1,5,1,5,2}	{2} {2,1} {2,5,1,5,1}
NEGATIVE FUNCTIONAL TEST CASES	
List={}	Invalid input

Here is a sample solution that implements the steps described above:

```
1.    #include <cstdio>
2.
3.    using namespace std;
4.
5.    struct node
6.    {
7.        node *next;
8.        int value;
9.    };
10.
11.   void insert(node *&head, node *&tail, int value)
12.   {
13.       // if first insertion make head and tail equal
14.       if (head == NULL)
15.       {
16.               node *element = new node;
17.               element -> value = value;
18.               element -> next = NULL;
19.               head = tail = element;
20.       }
21.
22.       // else insert at end
23.       else
24.       {
25.               node *element = new node;
26.               element -> value = value;
27.               tail -> next = element;
28.               tail = element;
29.       }
30.   }
31.
32.   void reverse(node *&head, node *&tail)
33.   {
34.       if (head == NULL)
35.       {
36.               printf ("Invalid input!\n");
37.               return;
```

```
38.     }
39.
40.     // remember what the head was initially
41.     node *initial_head = head;
42.
43.     // set the new head to null
44.     head = NULL;
45.
46.     while (initial_head != tail)
47.     {
48.             // remember what the next node was
49.             node *temp = initial_head -> next;
50.
51.             // change direction of pointer
52.             initial_head -> next = head;
53.             head = initial_head;
54.
55.             // restore the next node
56.             initial_head = temp;
57.     }
58.
59.     // add the last element to the end of the new list
60.     initial_head -> next = head;
61.     head = initial_head;
62. }
63.
64.
65. int main()
66. {
67.     node *head = NULL, *tail = NULL;
68.     insert(head, tail, 1);
69.     insert(head, tail, 4);
70.     insert(head, tail, 10);
71.     insert(head, tail, 12);
72.     insert(head, tail, 15);
73.
74.     // reverse the list
75.     reverse(head, tail);
76.
77.     // print the reversed list
78.     printf("The reversed list: ");
79.     for (node *iterator = head; iterator; iterator = iterator
         -> next)
80.             printf("%d ", iterator -> value);
81.     printf("\n");
82.
83.     return 0;
84. }
```

Output:	Further exercise:
The reversed list: 15 12 10 4 1	**Q:** How efficient is the approach that uses recursion?
	A: The approach that uses recursion uses N memory slots in the program stack, as it needs to make N calls to the function, where N is the number of elements in the list. This does not correspond to the requirements of the task, which says we need to perform this using constant space. The approach we used, on the other hand, only uses one extra pointer to achieve the reversed list, so the space is constant.

LISTS: CONVERT A BST INTO A LINKED LIST

Convert a binary search tree into a linked list

SOLUTION: A binary search tree, as discussed in the data structures section of this book, is a binary tree with the following properties:

- For any node, all the keys stored in the left sub-tree are smaller than or equal to the node's key.
- For any node, all the keys stored in the right sub-tree are larger than the node's key.

The tree we will be working with for this example is as follows:

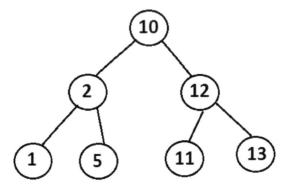

Now we only need to decide on an order for storing the elements in the tree in a singly linked list. Perhaps the most interesting approach would be to perform an in-order traversal of the tree, as this would result in the items being sorted in the list. An in-order traversal of a binary search tree considers every node and recursively processes its left sub-tree, followed by the node itself and the right sub-tree.

For example, in the tree above:

- We start at the root and process the left sub-tree first, so we move left;
- We move left one more time (landing at 1) and we output '1'.
- We have now processed the left sub-tree of '2', so we can output '2'.
- We process the right sub-tree of '2', so we output '5'.
- We have now processed the left sub-tree of the root, so we output '10'.
- We repeat until we have visited all the nodes. The final output will be 1 2 5 10 11 12 13.

In our example we will store the elements in this order in a singly linked list represented with the use of a single pointer (to the head). Instead of outputting an element, we will be adding it to the beginning of the list and update the head correspondingly. Because of this, in the end we will obtain the keys in the binary tree sorted in descending order.

PSEUDO CODE:

```
1.    Build tree
2.    Bst_to_list(node):
3.        If node is NULL
4.                Return
5.        Process left subtree(call bst_to_list(node.left))
6.        Add node.value to list
7.        Process right subtree(call bst_to_list(node.right))
8.    Return list
```

CLARIFICATION POINT-1:

What kind of list should we use?

CLARIFICATION POINT-2:

How many nodes can the tree have?

ASSUMPTION/LIMITATION:

- As mentioned above, we will use a singly linked list represented by a single pointer to the head of the list.

- Our binary tree will store 7 items, but because trees and lists are allocated dynamically there is no need to know the number of elements in advance.

MAJOR DATA STRUCTURES:

Binary search tree, singly-linked list

Here is a sample solution that implements the steps described above:

```
1.    #include <cstdio>
2.
3.    using namespace std;
4.
5.    struct node
6.    {
7.        node *left, *right;
8.        int value;
9.    };
10.
11.   struct list
12.   {
13.       list *next;
14.       int value;
```

```
15.  };
16.
17.  void insert(node* &bst, int value)
18.  {
19.      // if current position is empty insert value
20.      if (bst == NULL)
21.      {
22.              bst = new node;
23.              bst -> value = value;
24.              bst -> left = bst -> right = NULL;
25.              return;
26.      }
27.
28.      // if given value is smaller than or equal to the one
29.      // at current position go left
30.      if (value <= bst -> value)
31.              insert(bst -> left, value);
32.
33.      // else (given value is larger) go right
34.      else
35.              insert(bst -> right, value);
36.  }
37.
38.  void bst_to_list(node * bst, list *&head)
39.  {
40.      if (bst == NULL)
41.              return;
42.
43.      // remember, we are traversing the tree in-order
44.      // i.e. go left -> process current -> go right
45.
46.      // go left
47.      bst_to_list (bst -> left, head);
48.
49.      // process current element (add to list)
50.      list *element = new list;
51.      element -> value = bst -> value;
52.      element -> next = head;
53.      head = element;
54.
55.      // go right
56.      bst_to_list (bst -> right, head);
57.
58.  }
59.
60.  int main()
61.  {
62.      // our bst - initially empty
63.      node *bst = NULL;
64.
65.      // insert some values into the bst
```

```
66.    insert(bst, 10); insert(bst, 2); insert(bst, 12);
       insert(bst, 13);
67.    insert(bst, 1); insert(bst, 5); insert(bst, 11);
68.
69.    // our list, initially empty
70.    list *head = NULL;
71.    bst_to_list(bst, head);
72.
73.    // print list
74.    printf("The list containing an inorder traversal of the
       tree:\n");
75.
76.    for (list *iterator = head; iterator; iterator = iterator
       -> next)
77.            printf ("%d ", iterator -> value);
78.
79.    printf("\n");
80.
81.    return 0;
82. }
```

OUTPUT:	FURTHER EXERCISE:
The list containing an inorder traversal of the tree: 13 12 11 10 5 2 1	Q: How do you store the elements of the tree to the list after a level-based traversal of the tree? (for example, for the tree above the order would be 10 2 12 1 5 11 13). A: In this case we would need to store an extra integer for each node in the tree, for storing the level. We then find the depth of the tree and at each step call the traversal function with an extra parameter, level, from 0 to the depth of the tree, and add the corresponding keys to the list.

Q: Sometimes excessive calls to the recursive functions can cause memory problems. How can you perform an in-order traversal of the tree without using recursion?

A: We can do this using a stack in which we store the node we have visited at each step, along with a flag variable that tells us whether the node has been visited or not. We push the left child of each node to the stack and when we visit the node for the second time we add its key to our list and push its right child to the stack. The pseudo-code is as follows:

```
1.   Traverse(bst, list):
2.       Stack s = {}
3.       Push bst.root to s
4.       While (s is not empty)
5.       {
6.               Top = s.top
7.               If top is not NULL
8.                       If top not previously visited
9.                               s.push(top.left)
10.                      else
11.                              add top.value to list
12.                              s.pop()
13.                              s.push(top.right)
14.              else
15.                      s.pop
16.                      if (s not empty)
17.                              s.top.visited = true
18.      }
```

LISTS: COMPUTE THE MODE OF A LINKED A LIST

Write a program to compute the mode of a singly linked list in which every node has an integer value. In your implementation you should consider the following cases:

- **The list is sorted**
- **The list has only one node**
- **The list is unsorted**

SOLUTION: Write a program to compute the mode of a singly linked list in which every node has an integer value. In your implementation you should consider the following cases:

1. The list is sorted;
2. The list has only one node;
3. The list is unsorted;

Just in the case of arrays, the mode of a singly linked list is the predominant element in the list. Let's consider the three cases individually:

1. First, if the list is sorted then we do not need to have a frequency table to count how many times each number appears. It is enough to just count the longest sequence of repeated characters and store a global maximum.

2. If the list has only one node, then the answer is straightforward. The mode of the list is the only element contained in the list;

3. Finally, if the list is unsorted then we need to use a frequency table, to count how many times each value appears. For example, if 2 appears 3 times in the list, then frequency[2] will be set to 3. After iterating through the list and building the frequency table accordingly, all we need to do is find the maximum value in this table.

Let's consider a couple of examples:

1. If given the list {10}, then our function will return 10, as this is the only element in the list, and hence its mode.

2. If given the sorted list {1, 2, 7, 7, 9} we would count the lengths all of sequences of repeated characters. These lengths are, in order, 1, 1, 2, and 1. The maximum of these is 2, which corresponds to the element 7, so 7 is the mode of the list.

3. If given an unsorted list, for example (23, 7, 23, 2, 42) we build a frequency tables. Its values will be frequency[23] = 2, frequency[7] = 1, fre-

quency[2] = 1 and frequency[42] = 1. The maximum value is 2, which corresponds to the index 23, which is the mode of the list.

4. Finally, another case is when the list has multiple modes. In particular, if all the elements in the list are unique, then they are all modes of the list. Therefore, any element can be considered a mode of the list and our program will print the first one encountered along the way. If we wanted to print all the modes, then we would add an extra condition to our program (i.e. if the length of the current sequence is equal to the maximum length we have encountered so far, then append the current element to the list of modes).

PSEUDO CODE:

```
1.   Mode_of_list(list):
2.       If list has one node
3.               Return value of node
4.       If list is sorted
5.               maxLength = 0, mode = 0
6.               while list
7.                       count = number of times list.value is
                         repeated
8.                       if count > maxLength
9.                               maxLength = count
10.                              mode = list.value
11.              return mode
12.      else
13.              frequency={0}
14.              for each element in list
15.                      frequency[element]++
16.              max = 0, mode = 0
17.              for index = 0 to frequency.length
18.                      if (frequency[index] > max)
19.                              max = frequency[index]
20.                              mode = index
21.              return mode
```

CLARIFICATION POINT-1:

How big are the elements in the list? (This is necessary to establish the length of the frequency table)

CLARIFICATION POINT-2:

How many elements will our list hold?

ASSUMPTION/LIMITATION:

• We will assume the lists given as arguments to our function will not contain elements that are bigger than 10,000.

• For this example, we will only use lists of maximum 5 elements.

MAJOR DATA STRUCTURES:

Singly-linked list

UNIT TESTS:	
POSTIVE FUNCTIONAL TEST CASES	
INPUT	EXPECTED OUTPUT
List={2} List={1,2,2,3,3,3,4} List={1,5,1,5,2}	2 3 5
NEGATIVE FUNCTIONAL TEST CASES	
List={}	Invalid input

Here is a sample solution that implements the steps described above:

```
1.    #include <cstdio>
2.
3.    using namespace std;
4.
5.    struct list
6.    {
7.        list *next;
8.        int value;
9.    };
10.
11.   int mode_of_list(list *head)
12.   {
13.       // empty list => invalid input
14.       if (head == NULL)
15.       {
16.               printf("List is empty -> Invalid input!\n");
17.               return 0;
18.       }
19.
20.       // list with one element => return element
21.       if (head -> next == NULL)
22.               return head -> value;
23.
24.       // sorted list - different algorithm (saves memory space)
25.       bool listSorted = true;
26.       list *tempHead = head;
27.       while(tempHead -> next)
28.       {
29.               if (tempHead -> next -> value < tempHead -> value)
30.                   listSorted = false;
31.               tempHead = tempHead -> next;
32.       }
33.
```

```
34.     // if list is sorted
35.     if (listSorted)
36.     {
37.             // just count how many times the current value is
                repeeated
38.             // and store a global maximum
39.             int maximumLength = 0;
40.             int modeElement = 0;
41.
42.             while (head)
43.             {
44.                     int currentCount = 1;
45.                     int element = head -> value;
46.                     while (head -> next && head -> next ->
                        value == head -> value)
47.                     {
48.                             currentCount++;
49.                             head = head -> next;
50.                     }
51.                     if (currentCount > maximumLength)
52.                     {
53.                             maximumLength = currentCount;
54.                             modeElement = element;
55.                     }
56.                     head = head -> next;
57.             }
58.
59.             return modeElement;
60.     }
61.
62.     // at this point the list is unsorted, so we need to have
        a frequency table
63.     // empty it at first
64.     int frequency[10000] = {0};
65.
66.     // run through the list and increase the corresponding
        value in frequency
67.     for (list *iterator = head; iterator; iterator = iterator
        -> next)
68.             frequency[iterator -> value]++;
69.
70.     // now return the value corresponding to the maximum entry
        in frequency
71.     int maximum = 0;
72.     int modeElement = 0;
73.     for (int fIndex = 0; fIndex < 10000; fIndex++)
74.             if (frequency[fIndex] > maximum)
75.             {
76.                     maximum = frequency[fIndex];
77.                     modeElement = fIndex;
78.             }
```

```
79.
80.     return modeElement;
81.  }
82.
83.  void insert(list* &head, int value)
84.  {
85.      list *element = new list;
86.      element -> value = value;
87.      element -> next = head;
88.      head = element;
89.  }
90.
91.  int main()
92.  {
93.      // our list - initially empty
94.      list *head = NULL;
95.      int result;
96.
97.      // test 1 - empty list
98.      printf("Test 1: ");
99.      result = mode_of_list(head);
100.
101.     // test 2 - list with one element
102.     insert(head, 10);
103.     printf("Test 2: ");
104.     result = mode_of_list(head);
105.     printf("The mode element is %d\n", result);
106.
107.     // test 3 - sorted list
108.     head = NULL;
109.     insert(head, 9); insert(head, 7); insert(head, 7); insert
         (head, 2); insert (head, 1);
110.     result = mode_of_list(head);
111.     printf("Test 3: ");
112.     printf("The mode element is %d\n", result);
113.
114.     // test 4 - unsorted list
115.     head = NULL;
116.     insert(head, 42); insert(head, 2); insert(head, 23);
         insert(head, 7); insert(head, 23);
117.     result = mode_of_list(head);
118.     printf("Test 4: ");
119.     printf("The mode element is %d", result);
120.
121.     return 0;
122. }
```

OUTPUT:	FURTHER EXERCISE:
Test 1: List is empty -> Invalid input!	Q: Can you think of a naïve approach to this task?
Test 2: The mode element is 10	A: A more inefficient approach would firstly sort the list if an unsorted list is given and then perform the steps we performed for the sorted list. This is more inefficient because of the complexity of sorting algorithms for singly linked lists.
Test 3: The mode element is 7	
Test 4: The mode element is 23	

LISTS: ELEMENTS IN LINKED LISTS

Given a list of numbers (a fixed list) and another list, write a function which determines whether any element in the second list appears in the fixed list.

SOLUTION: Given a list of numbers (a fixed list) and another list, write a function which determines whether any element in the second list appears in the fixed list.

In the previous task we have use a frequency table to determine the mode of a singly linked list. For the purpose of this task, it is enough to keep a look-up table of Boolean values, which could tell us whether an element appears in the fixed list or not. Based on this idea, the steps we will perform are as follows:

- Build the look-up table for the fixed list, marking table[value] = true if a value appears in the fixed list.

- Iterate through the second list

  ▷ If the current value is set to true in the look up table then we stop, because we now know an element from the fixed list appears in the second list;

  ▷ If none of the values are marked as true in the table then none of the elements in the fixed list appears in the second list.

For example, suppose we have the fixed list (23, 7, 5, 2, 42) and the second list (11, 44, 7, 10). We firstly build the look-up table for the fixed list, setting table[23] = true, table[7] = true, and so on. Finally, we iterate through the second list and we stop when we reach 7, because table[7] had been previously set to true. An element from the fixed list has now been found in the second list.

PSEUDO CODE:

```
1.    Build tree
2.    Element_in_fixed(list, fixed)
3.        For each element in fixed
4.                Table[element] = true
5.        For each element in list
6.                If Table[element] = true
7.                        Return true
8.        Return false
```

CLARIFICATION POINT-1:

What is the value of the maximum / minimum element the list can contain?

CLARIFICATION POINT-2:

How many elements will the lists hold?

ASSUMPTION/LIMITATION:

- We will assume the lists given as arguments to our function will only contain positive elements that are no bigger than 10,000.

- For this example, we will only use lists of maximum 5 elements.

MAJOR DATA STRUCTURES:

Singly linked list

UNIT TESTS:	
POSTIVE FUNCTIONAL TEST CASES	
INPUT	EXPECTED OUTPUT
List={2}, fixed={}	false
List={2}, fixed={1, 2}	true
List={1,2}, fixed={4,5}	false
List={1,5,1,5,2} fixed={1, 10}	true
NEGATIVE FUNCTIONAL TEST CASES	
List={}	Invalid input

Here is a sample solution that implements the steps described above:

```
1.   #include <cstdio>
2.
3.   using namespace std;
4.
5.   struct list
6.   {
7.       list *next;
8.       int value;
9.   };
10.
11.  void element_in_fixed(list *head, list *fixed)
12.  {
13.      if (head == NULL)
14.      {
15.              printf("Invalid input!\n");
16.      }
17.
18.      // build table for fixed - initially all values are set to
         false
19.      bool table[1000] = {false};
20.      while(fixed)
21.      {
```

```
22.                 table[fixed -> value] = true;
23.                 fixed = fixed -> next;
24.         }
25.
26.     while (head)
27.         {
28.                 if (table[head -> value])
29.                 {
30.                         printf("There is an element that appears in
                            the fixed list!\n");
31.                         return;
32.                 }
33.                 head = head -> next;
34.         }
35.
36.     printf("There is no element that appears in the fixed
        list!\n");
37. }
38.
39. void insert(list* &head, int value)
40. {
41.     list *element = new list;
42.     element -> value = value;
43.     element -> next = head;
44.     head = element;
45. }
46.
47. int main()
48. {
49.     // our list - initially empty
50.     list *fixed = NULL;
51.     insert(fixed, 42); insert(fixed, 2); insert(fixed, 23);
        insert(fixed, 7); insert(fixed, 23);
52.
53.     list *head = NULL;
54.     insert(head, 10); insert(head,7); insert(head, 44);
        insert(head, 11);
55.
56.     element_in_fixed(head, fixed);
57.
58.     return 0;
59. }
```

There is an element that appears in the fixed list!

Q: What is the complexity of the function? What is the complexity of the naïve approach?

A: A naïve approach would iterate through the given list and then one more time through the fixed list, having complexity O(M*N), where M and N are the lengths of the two lists. Our algorithm, on the other hand, runs in O(M+N).

Q: What if the list contained numbers that are too big, or negative integers?

A: If the list contained negative integers or numbers that are too large to be used as an index to an array, we would have at least two options:

Generate the index of each element in the fixed list using a hash function which produces an index that matches our algorithm. For example, the function hash(x) = abs(x) % 10000 would produce only positive values, smaller than 10,000.

Choose another type of data structure. A binary search tree would be a good approach, as it enables searching for an element on O(log N), where N is the total number of elements in the fixed list.

LISTS: IF AT ANY POINT THESE LINK LIST ARE MERGING TOGETHER?

Given Two Singly Link List, You have to find out If at any point these link list are merging together?

SOLUTION: First of all, here is the struct we will use to represent the list:

```
1.   typedef struct node{
2.       int data;
3.       node *next;
4.   } *pnode
```

As usual, a node contains some data (an integer in this case) and a pointer to another memory location. The idea of the algorithm will be the following:

1. We firstly compute the length of the first list and the store the value of the last node.

2. We repeat step one for the second list.

3. If the last nodes of the two lists are different, this means there is no join in the lists, so we return NULL.

4. Else, we 'align' the two lists by incrementing the head of the longer list by the difference between the length of the two lists. You will see this point better in the example below.

5. Iterate through the two lists at the same time, as long as the elements at the current index are different.

6. Stop when we have encountered the first equal element. This is the point where the join starts.

Let's consider an example, so you can understand this concept better. Suppose the two lists are l1={0, 1, 2, 3, 4} and l2={5, 25, 3, 4}. The steps above can be applied to this example in the following way:

1. l1.length = 5, l1.last = 4, l2.length=4, l2.last = 4.

2. l1.last = l2.last, so a join must have occurred at some point.

3. We align the two lists by incrementing the head of the longer list (l1) by 5-4 = 1. The two lists are now {1,2,3,4} and {5,25,3,4}.

4. We iterate from the beginning of the two new lists until we find an equal element.

   a) 1!=5, 2!=25, but 3=3, so in this case 3 is the point where the two lists are joined.

What is the maximum value for the size of the lists?

ASSUMPTION/LIMITATION:

- We will assume a reasonable value for the size of the lists, so as not to obtain any segmentation fault.

MAJOR DATA STRUCTURES:

Singly linked lists

UNIT TESTS:	
POSTIVE FUNCTIONAL TEST CASES	
INPUT	EXPECTED OUTPUT
L1={0,1,2,3,4,5}, L2={3,4,5}	3
L1={0,1,2,3,4,5}, L2={9,4,5}	4
NEGATIVE FUNCTIONAL TEST CASES	
List size < 0	Invalid input

Here is a sample answer:

```
1.   /*Data-structure for the nodetypedef struct Node */
2.   typedef struct node{
3.       int data;
4.       node *next;
5.   } *pnode;
6.
7.   /*IMPORTANT FUNCTIONS */
8.   void insert_link_list(node ** ,int );
9.   void print_link_list(node ** llist);
10.  pnode insert_joined_node(pnode list1, pnode list2,int val);
11.  pnode find_joined_node(pnode list1, pnode list2);
12.  void insert_together(pnode t1,pnode t2,int val);
13.  void increment_node_by(pnode t, int val);
14.
15.  /* FUNCTION : test_program() */
16.  test_program()
17.  {
18.      node *llist1 = NULL;
19.      node *llist2 = NULL;
20.      pnode tnode = NULL;
21.      int element,no_of_element,count;
22.      printf("\n*** Creation of first link list *** \n");
23.      printf("\nHow many elements you want to enter\n");
24.      scanf("%d",&no_of_element);
25.      for(count=0;count<no_of_element;count++)
```

```
26.    {
27.            printf("\n Enter the [%d] element : ",count);
28.            scanf("%d",&element);
29.            insert_link_list(&llist1,element);
30.    }
31.    printf("\n*** Creation of second link list ***\n");
32.    printf("\nHow many elements you want to enter\n");
33.    scanf("%d",&no_of_element);
34.    for(count=0;count<no_of_element;count++)
35.    {
36.            printf("\n Enter the [%d] element : ",count);
37.            scanf("%d",&element);
38.            insert_link_list(&llist2,element);
39.    }
40.    printf("\n=Printing the elements if first link list=\n");
41.    print_link_list(&llist1);
42.    printf("\n=Printing the elements if second link list=\n");
43.    print_link_list(&llist2);
44.    printf("\nHow many element you want to
45.    join at the end of above linked list\n");
46.    scanf("%d",&no_of_element);
47.    for(count=0;count<no_of_element;count++)
48.    {
49.            printf("\n Enter the [%d] element with value :=
               %d:
50.            ",count,count);
51.            insert_joined_node(llist1 ,llist2,element);
52.    }
53.    printf("\n Finding out whether join is available or not
       \n");
54.    if (find_joined_node(llist1,llist2) == NULL)
55.    {
56.            printf("\nThere is no joined node on this given
57.            two Linked List\n");
58.    }
59.    else
60.    {
61.            tnode = find_joined_node(llist1,llist2);
62.            printf("\nJoined node is starting
63.            from the following node \n");
64.            print_link_list(&tnode);
65.    }
66.    printf("\n *** End of the Program *** \n");
67. }
68.
69. /* FUNCTION : insert_joined_node */
70. pnode insert_joined_node(pnode list1, pnode list2,int val)
71. {
72.    int len1 = 1, len2 = 1;
73.    pnode t1,t2;
74.    // If any one of the list value is null, then return NULL
```

```
75.     if(list1 == NULL || list2 == NULL) return NULL;
76.     t1 = list1;
77.     t2 = list2;
78.
79.     // Compute length of first link list and it's last node
80.     for(;t1->next != NULL; t1 = t1->next)
81.             ++len1;
82.
83.     // Compute length of first link list and it's last node
84.     for(;t2->next != NULL; t2 = t2->next)
85.             ++len2;
86.     insert_together(t1,t2,val);
87. }
88.
89. /* Function : insert_together */
90. void insert_together(pnode list1, pnode list2,int val)
91. {
92.     node *temp;
93.     temp = (node *)malloc(sizeof(node));
94.     temp->data = val;
95.     temp->next = NULL;
96.     list1->next = temp;
97.     list1->next = temp;
98. }
99.
100. /* FUNCTION : find_joined_node */
101. pnode find_joined_node(pnode list1, pnode list2)
102. {
103.     int len1 = 1, len2 = 1;
104.     pnode t1,t2,t;
105.
106.     // If any one of the list value is null, then return NULL
107.     if(list1 == NULL || list2 == NULL) return NULL;
108.     t1 = list1;
109.     t2 = list2;
110.
111.     // Compute length of first link list and it's last node
112.     for(;t1->next != NULL; t1 = t1->next)
113.             ++len1;
114.
115.     // Compute length of first link list and it's last node
116.     for(;t2->next != NULL; t2 = t2->next)
117.             ++len2;
118.
119.     // Compare last node of the first link list with last node
        of second
120.     if (t1 != t2) return NULL;
121.
122.     // increment the longer list by the difference in length
        so that
123.     // the pointers are equidistant from the join
```

```
124.    t = len1 > len2 ? list1 : list2;
125.    increment_node_by(t, abs(len1 - len2));
126.
127.    // last pass to find the join.
128.    for(;list1 != list2; list1 = list1->next, list2 = list2-
        >next);
129.
130.    return list1;
131. }
132.
133. /* FUNCTION : increment_node_by */
134. void increment_node_by(pnode node, int val)
135. {
136.    for(int i = 0; i < val; ++i)
137.            (node) = (node)->next;
138. }
139.
140. /*FUNCTION : print_link_list*/
141. void print_link_list(node ** llist)
142. {
143.    node *temp;
144.    temp = *llist;
145.    while((temp)!= NULL)
146.    {
147.            printf(" [%d]-->> ",(temp)->data);
148.    (temp) = (temp)->next;
149.    }
150. }
151.
152. /*FUNCTION : insert_link_list*/
153. void insert_link_list(node ** llist,int element)
154. {
155.    node *temp;
156.    node *pTemp;
157.    if (*llist == NULL)
158.    {
159.    (*llist)= (node *)malloc(sizeof(node));
160.    (*llist)->data = element;
161.    (*llist)->next = NULL;
162.    }
163.    else
164.    {
165.            pTemp = *llist;
166.            while((pTemp)->next != NULL)
167.            {
168.            (pTemp) = (pTemp)->next;
169.            }
170.            temp = (node *)malloc(sizeof(node));
171.            temp->data = element;
172.            temp->next = NULL;
173.            (pTemp)->next = temp;
```

```
174.    }
175. }
```

LISTS: REMOVE ALL NODES WITH EVEN VALUES

Given a singly linked list of integers, write a function to remove all nodes with even values.

SOLUTION: The lists will be represented in the usually way, with nodes that contain some data (integers, in this example) and pointers to another memory location. The algorithm that we will be using considers all the cases of deleting items from a singly linked list. The steps are the following:

1. Initiate two pointers, current and prev, since when deleting from a singly linked list we will often need to know the previous element of the one deleted. Suppose the name of our list is 'list'. We then initialize prev with NULL and current with list.

2. Iterate through the list and when encountering an even element, delete it as follows:

    a) If the element is at the head of the list then just set current to point to the next element, and keep prev to NULL.

       i. For example, if list={2,1,4, 3}, current=list and prev=NULL, the new list will become {1,4,3}, current will still point to its head and prev will still point to NULL.

    b) If the element is at the tail of the list, then just set the previous element to point to null.

       i. For example, if the current list is {1,3,4} and current is point to 4 and prev is pointing to 3, then we just make prev to point to NULL, meaning the list is now {1,3}.

    c) If the element is in the middle of the list, then we set prev to point to current -> next.

       i. For example, if we are trying to delete '2' from list={1,3,2,4}, when current is pointing to '2' and prev is pointing to '3', then we just make prev to point to 4 (skip over the '2').

3. If the element is even, we just ignore it, by increasing both current and prev.

4. The algorithm stops when we have reached the end of the list.

CLARIFICATION POINT-1:

What is the maximum value for the length of the list?

ASSUMPTION/LIMITATION:

- We will assume a reasonable value for the size of the lists, so as not to obtain any segmentation fault.

MAJOR DATA STRUCTURES:

Array of integers

UNIT TESTS:	
POSTIVE FUNCTIONAL TEST CASES	
INPUT	EXPECTED OUTPUT
{0,1,2}	{1}
{1,0} {8,1,3,6}	{1} {1,3}
NEGATIVE FUNCTIONAL TEST CASES	
Empty list	Invalid input

Here is a sample answer:

```
1.   BOOL removeAllNodesWithEvenValues(node ** llist)
2.   {
3.       node *prevP,*currP; // Maintian two pointers
4.       prevP = NULL; // prev pointer
5.       currP = *llist; // next pointer
6.
7.       //It received singly linked
8.       list's head pointer as Input.
9.
10.      if(*llist == NULL)
11.      {
12.             printf("Invalid Parameter");
13.             return FALSE;
14.      }
15.
16.      //Traverse Singly Link list, check Its Integer Value,
17.      If it's even, remove that node from the linked list.
18.
19.      while((currP)!= NULL)
20.      {
21.             printf("[0x%u] [%d]-->> ",currP,(currP)->data);
22.             if(0 == currP->data%2)
23.             {
24.      //Case-1: If this is head node;
25.                     if(currP == *llist)
26.                     {
27.                             *llist = (*llist)->next;
28.                             free(currP);
```

```
29.                              prevP = NULL;
30.                              currP = *llist;
31.                  }
32.
33.     //Case-2: If this is last node
34.                      else if (currP->next == NULL)
35.                      {
36.                              prevP->next = NULL;
37.                              free(currP);
38.                              /* Case-3 list has been traversed */
39.                              return TRUE;
40.                      }
41.
42.     //Case-3 if this is a middle element
43.                      else if(prevP!=NULL && currP->next != NULL)
44.                      {
45.                              prevP->next = currP->next;
46.                              free(currP);
47.                              currP = prevP->next;
48.                      }
49.              }
50.
51.          else
52.          { //Case-4 odd item - do not delete
53.                      prevP = currP;
54.                      currP = currP->next;
55.              }
56.      }
57.      return TRUE;
58. }
```

FURTHER EXERCISE:

Q: Is the implementation of this task using singly linked lists
   better than using arrays of integers?

A: Yes, in the case of array of integers, deleting an element
   could take up to O(N) time because we need to move all the
   elements to the right of the value deleted one step to the
   left. With singly linked lists, deletion is done in constant
   time.

LISTS: DETECTS WHETHER A LINKED LIST HAS CIRCULAR REFERENCE OR NOT

Write a function that detects whether a linked list has circular reference or not.

SOLUTION: There are several cases to consider for the purpose of this problem. These are the following:

1. The list only has one element
   a) If the element points to itself then the list has a circular reference and our algorithm will handle this.
   b) If the element does not point to itself this must mean no circular reference is present.

2. If the list has two elements
   a) If these two elements are pointing to each other, this means a circular reference is present in the list.
   b) If these two elements are not pointing to each other, no circular reference is present.

3. Finally, if the list has multiple elements, the steps we will perform are the following:
   a) Create a 'slow' pointer and a 'fast' pointer. Initially, the fast pointer is the second element in the list and the slow pointer is the first element in the list.
   b) At each iteration we increase the fast pointer by 2 units and the slow pointer by 1.
   c) If the fast pointer 'catches' the slow pointer before the fast pointer reaches NULL then this must mean the list has a circular reference. If not, then the answer is negative.

Consider the following example:

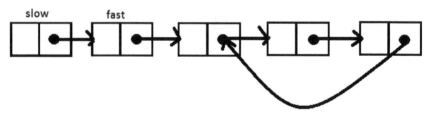

After the first step, fast would take the value of the fourth element, while slow will take the value of the second. After one more step, they will both take the value of the third element. Slow == Fast, which means that our list has a circular reference.

CLARIFICATION POINT-1:

How many elements will the list store?

ASSUMPTION/LIMITATION:

- We will assume a reasonable value for the size of the list, so as not to obtain any segmentation fault.

MAJOR DATA STRUCTURES:

Singly linked list

Here is a sample answer:

```
1.    BOOL CircularReferenceOrNot(Node *psargList)
2.    {
3.    // Declare one slow pointer and another Fast Pointer
4.        Node *psSlow;
5.        Node *psFast;
6.
7.    // Link List head pointer should not be NULL
8.        if(psargList == NULL)
9.        {
10.               printf("Error : Head Node point No Where");
11.               return FALSE;
12.        }
13.
14.     // Case-1 :If the list has one node
15.        psSlow = psargList;
16.        if(psargList->Next)
17.               psFast = psargList->Next;
18.        else
19.               return FALSE;
20.
21.    // Case-2 if the list has just one element,
22.    and Its next pointer pointing to itself.
23.
24.        if(psSlow == psFast)
25.               return TRUE;
26.
27.    // Traverse the list until Slow Pointer doesn't meet with
       Fast Pointer.
28.        while(psSlow!=psFast)
29.        {
30.    // Move Slow pointer to next node
31.               psSlow = psSlow->Next;
32.               if(psFast->Next)
33.               {
34.    // Move Fast pointer to next to next node
35.                       psFast = psFast->Next;
```

```
36.                     if(psFast->Next)
37.                             psFast = psFast->Next;
38.                     else
39.                             psFast = NULL;
40.             }
41.             else
42.             {
43.                     psFast = NULL;
44.             }
45.
46.             // Case-3: If slow or fast whoever approaching to
                 NULL node, means no Circular Reference Detected.
47.             if(psSlow == NULL || psFast == NULL)
48.                     return FALSE;
49.
50.             // Case-4: If slow or fast are meeting, means
                 Circular Reference detected
51.             if(psSlow == psFast)
52.                     return TRUE;
53.     }
54. }
```

FURTHER EXERCISE:

Q: What if the list had unique elements?

A: If this was the case, then we could have used a look-up
   table to store the values that were encountered in the list
   along the way. If we ever reach a value that had previously
   been traversed then this means that the list has a circular
   reference.

TREE: N-ARY TREE

How do you represent an n-ary tree? Write a program to print the nodes of such a tree in breadth first order.

SOLUTION: Let's consider the following n-ary tree:

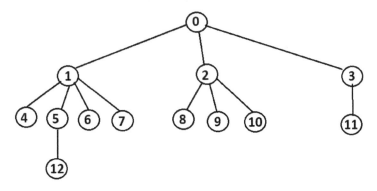

The way we can represent this in the memory of our program is by using an array of singly linked lists. Each list stores the children of a node. For example, tree[0] would store the list {1, 2, 3}, tree[1] would store the list {4, 5, 6, 7} and so on.

A breadth-first search traversal is in fact a level traversal of the tree and will the nodes in the order of their levels (first 0, then 1,2,3 in any order, then the nodes on level 2 in any order etc.). We will use a queue for this algorithm, as described in the data structure section of the book. The steps are as follows:

- Start with an empty queue
- Add the root of the tree to the queue
- While there are elements to be processed in the root
    - ▷ Current element = dequeue(queue)
    - ▷ Add all the children of current element to the queue and print them

For the tree given above, these steps are as follows:

- Add 0 to the queue
- Current element = 0, so add 1,2,3 to the queue and print them
- Current element = 1, so add 4,5,6 and 7 to the queue and print them
- Current element = 2, so add 8, 9, and 10 to the queue and print them, and so on.

```
1.   Print_Tree(tree):
2.       Add root of tree to queue
3.       While (head of queue < tail of queue)
4.               Current_node = dequeue(queue)
5.               Add all children of Current_node to queue
6.               Print all children of Current_node
7.               head of queue = head of queue + 1
```

CLARIFICATION POINT-1:

What is the maximum number of nodes for the tree?

ASSUMPTION/LIMITATION:

- We will use the tree drawn above for our example which has 12 nodes.

MAJOR DATA STRUCTURES:

n-ary tree, array of singly linked lists

Here is a sample solution that implements the steps described above:

```
1.   #include <cstdio>
2.
3.   using namespace std;
4.
5.   struct list
6.   {
7.       list *next;
8.       int value;
9.   };
10.
11.  void print_tree(list *tree[])
12.  {
13.      if (tree == NULL)
14.      {
15.              printf("Invalid input!\n");
16.              return;
17.      }
18.
19.      int queue[20];
20.      int qHead = 0, qTail = 0;
21.
22.      // start with root - we assume the root is always tree[0]
23.      // add root to queue
24.      queue[qTail++] = 0;
25.      printf("0 ");
26.
27.      // while there are more nodes to be expanded
```

```
28.    while(qHead < qTail)
29.    {
30.            // add all childs of current node to the root
31.            for (list *iterator = tree[queue[qHead]]; iterator;
               iterator = iterator -> next)
32.            {
33.                    queue[qTail++] = iterator -> value;
34.                    printf("%d ", iterator -> value);
35.            }
36.            qHead++;
37.    }
38. }
39.
40. void insert(list* &head, int value)
41. {
42.    list *element = new list;
43.    element -> value = value;
44.    element -> next = head;
45.    head = element;
46. }
47.
48. int main()
49. {
50.    // our tree - initially empty
51.    list *tree[13];
52.    for (int i = 0; i <= 12; i++)
53.            tree[i] = NULL;
54.
55.    printf("The BFS traversal of the n-ary tree:\n");
56.
57.    insert(tree[0], 1); insert(tree[0], 2); insert(tree[0],
       3);
58.    insert(tree[1], 4); insert(tree[1], 5); insert(tree[1],
       6); insert(tree[1], 7);
59.    insert(tree[2], 8); insert(tree[2], 9); insert(tree[2],
       10);
60.    insert(tree[3], 11); insert(tree[5], 12);
61.
62.    print_tree(tree);
63.
64.    return 0;
65. }
```

OUTPUT:	FURTHER EXERCISE:
The BFS traversal of the n-ary tree:	Q: Can you think of an alternative implementation?
0 3 2 1 11 10 9 8 7 6 5 4 12	A: A BFS traversal of the tree can also be performed recursively, but due to the large number of calls to the function this approach is more inefficient.
	Q: What if the number of nodes is unknown?
	A: If the number of nodes in the initial tree is unknown we would need to allocate the queue dynamically. For example, we could use a singly linked list with two pointers, one for the head and one for the tail of the queue.

TREE: FRINGE, WHICH TAKES A TREE AND RETURNS ITS FRINGE

Write a function to return the fringe of an n-ary tree taken as an argument. The fringe of a tree is the set of leaf nodes in the tree.

SOLUTION: Let's work on the n-ary tree we have used for our previous task:

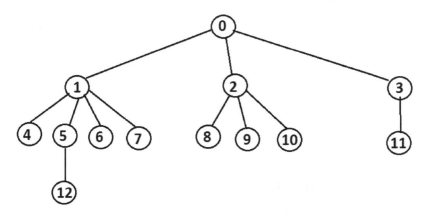

Based on the definition given above, the fringe of this tree is the list {4, 12, 6, 7, 8, 9, 10, 11}. A good, non-recursive, algorithm for performing this task is to use the BFS traversal we have seen in the previous task and adding an extra condition to it whenever we process a node. This condition is as follows: if the list of children of the current node is empty, then this must mean that the current node is a leaf, so add it to the fringe of the tree.

PSEUDO CODE:

```
1.    Print_Tree(tree):
2.        Fringe={}
3.        Add root of tree to queue
4.        While (head of queue < tail of queue)
5.                Current_node = dequeue(queue)
6.                Add all children of Current_node to queue
7.                Add those children that are leaves to Fringe
8.                head of queue = head of queue + 1
9.        return Fringe
```

CLARIFICATION POINT-1:

What is the maximum number of nodes for the tree?

ASSUMPTION/LIMITATION:

- We will use the tree drawn above for our example which has 12 nodes.

MAJOR DATA STRUCTURES:

n-ary tree, singly-linked lists

Here is a sample solution that implements the steps described above:

```
1.    #include <cstdio>
2.
3.    using namespace std;
4.
5.    struct list
6.    {
7.        list *next;
8.        int value;
9.    };
10.
11.   list* get_fringe(list *tree[])
12.   {
13.       // the set of leaves; initially empty
14.       list *fringe = NULL;
15.
16.       // leaves are nodes with no children, so we will just traverse the tree
17.       // and add to the list those that have no children
18.       int queue[20];
19.       int qHead = 0, qTail = 0;
20.
21.       // start with root - we assume the root is always tree[0]
22.       // add root to queue
23.       queue[qTail++] = 0;
24.
25.       // while there are more nodes to be expanded
26.       while(qHead < qTail)
27.       {
28.           // add all childs of current node to the root
29.           for (list *iterator = tree[queue[qHead]]; iterator;
                iterator = iterator -> next)
30.           {
31.               queue[qTail++] = iterator -> value;
32.
33.               // if node iterator->value is a leaf add to
                  tree
34.               if (tree[iterator->value] == NULL)
35.               {
36.                   list *element = new list;
```

```
37.                                    element -> value = iterator ->
                                       value;
38.                                    element -> next = fringe;
39.                                    fringe = element;
40.                        }
41.                }
42.            qHead++;
43.        }
44.
45.    return fringe;
46.  }
47.
48.  void insert(list* &head, int value)
49.  {
50.      list *element = new list;
51.      element -> value = value;
52.      element -> next = head;
53.      head = element;
54.  }
55.
56.  int main()
57.  {
58.      // our tree - initially empty
59.      list *tree[13];
60.      for (int i = 0; i <= 12; i++)
61.              tree[i] = NULL;
62.
63.      insert(tree[0], 1); insert(tree[0], 2); insert(tree[0],
         3);
64.      insert(tree[1], 4); insert(tree[1], 5); insert(tree[1],
         6); insert(tree[1], 7);
65.      insert(tree[2], 8); insert(tree[2], 9); insert(tree[2],
         10);
66.      insert(tree[3], 11); insert(tree[5], 12);
67.
68.      list *fringe = get_fringe(tree);
69.
70.      // print fringe
71.      printf("The fringe of the tree: ");
72.      for (list * iterator = fringe; iterator; iterator =
         iterator -> next)
73.              printf("%d ", iterator -> value);
74.
75.      return 0;
76.  }
```

OUTPUT:	FURTHER EXERCISE:
The fringe of the tree: 12 4 6 7 8 9 10 11	Q: What if the number of nodes is unknown?
	A: If the number of nodes in the initial tree is unknown we would need to allocate the queue dynamically. For example, we could use a singly linked list with two pointers, one for the head and one for the tail of the queue.

TREE: BINARY TREE LEVEL BY LEVEL, LEFT TO WRITE

Write a function that that a Binary Tree as a parameter and outputs a breadth first traversal of the tree (i.e. writes out the tree level by level, left to right). The function header to be used is

void Print (node* tree) {}

'node' is a struct that defines the standard implementation of binary trees, with a value, and two pointers, one for left and one for right.

SOLUTION: We will be working on the following example:

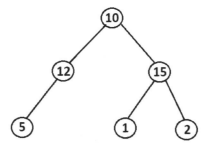

Note that the tree passed as an argument to the function is a general binary tree, not necessarily a binary search tree. The BFS traversal of a binary tree is similar to that we have seen before, but at each step we consider the left and right child of the current node, if they exist, instead of considering all children like we did with the n-ary tree. The steps are as follows:

- Start with an empty queue
- Append the root to the queue (in our case the root is 15, so Q={15})
- While there are nodes to be processed in the queue
    - ▷ Perform a dequeue() operation on Q (in our example, the current node would be 15).
    - ▷ Print the current node.
    - ▷ Add the left and right child to the queue, in this order (Q = {12, 15})
- In our example, the configuration of the queue throughout the program would be Q={15,12,15,5,1,2}, which is exactly what we need for this task.

We stop when there are no more elements to be processed (in our example, at node 2).

PSEUDO CODE:

```
1.   Print(tree):
2.       Q={}
3.       Add root to queue
4.       While there are nodes to be processed in Q
5.               Current node = dequeue(Q)
6.               Print current node
7.               If current node has left child
8.                       Add left child to Q
9.               If current node has right child
10.                      Add right child to Q
```

CLARIFICATION POINT-1:

What is the maximum number of nodes in the tree?

CLARIFICATION POINT-2:

Is the tree a binary search tree?

ASSUMPTION/LIMITATION:

• We will assume the tree is not a binary search tree.

• Furthermore, in our example, for simplicity, the tree will only hold 6 nodes.

MAJOR DATA STRUCTURES:

Binary tree

Here is a sample solution that implements the steps described above:

```
1.   #include <cstdio>
2.
3.   using namespace std;
4.
5.   struct node
6.   {
7.     node *left, *right;
8.     int value;
9.   };
10.
11.  void insert(node *&tree, int value)
12.  {
13.     tree = new node;
14.     tree -> value = value;
15.     tree -> left = tree -> right = NULL;
```

```
16.  }
17.
18.  void print(node *tree)
19.  {
20.      if (tree == NULL)
21.      {
22.              printf("Invalid input!\n");
23.              return;
24.      }
25.
26.      node* queue[20];
27.      int qHead = 0, qTail = 0;
28.
29.      // add root to queue
30.      queue[qTail++] = tree;
31.
32.      // while there are elements to be processed in the queue
33.      while (qHead < qTail)
34.      {
35.              printf ("%d ", queue[qHead] -> value);
36.
37.              // add left and / or right node
38.              if (queue[qHead] -> left)
39.                      queue[qTail++] = queue[qHead] -> left;
40.
41.              if (queue[qHead] -> right)
42.                      queue[qTail++] = queue[qHead] -> right;
43.
44.              qHead++;
45.      }
46.  }
47.
48.  int main()
49.  {
50.      // our tree - initially empty
51.      node *tree = NULL;
52.
53.      // insert some values into the tree
54.      insert(tree, 10);
55.      insert(tree->left, 12); insert(tree->right, 15);
56.      insert(tree->left->left, 5);
57.      insert(tree->right->left, 1); insert(tree->right->right,
         2);
58.
59.      printf("Level-by-level traversal of the tree:\n");
60.      print(tree);
61.
62.      return 0;
63.  }
```

OUTPUT:	FURTHER EXERCISE:
Level-by-level traversal of the tree:	Q: Can you think of another more naïve approach?
10 12 15 5 1 2	A: An alternative approach to this task is an algorithm that includes an extra integer in the struct used to define the node, which gives the level of the node. The algorithm would then call the function with an extra parameter and perform D traversals of the tree, where D is its depth, checking whether the nodes are located at the corresponding level. This is extremely inefficient and not recommended.

TREE: COPY OF AN EXISTING BINARY TREE

Write a function to create a copy of an existing binary tree

SOLUTION: We will be working on the following binary tree, which we have seen in some of the previous tasks:

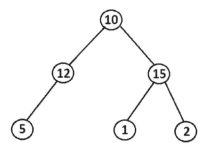

The task of copying a binary tree can easily be performed with a single traversal of the tree. This can be either a pre-order, post-order or in-order traversal. For the purpose of this example we will use a method with two parameters, a source tree and a destination tree, which performs a pre-order traversal of the initial tree and, as each node is traversed, copies it into the destination tree.

The steps of the algorithm can be explained on our example tree as follows:

- Start with the root, copy the root in the destination tree;
- Go left, copy the node holding the '12' into the destination tree;
- Go left, copy the node holding the '5' into the destination tree;
- Go back to the root, as all the other nodes along the way do not have a right sub-tree;
- Copy the node holding the '15' to the destination tree, and so on.

Finally, in order to check the correctness of our function we will perform an in-order traversal of both trees and check these are the same.

PSEUDO CODE:

```
1.   Copy(sourceTree, destinationTree):
2.       If sourceTree = NULL)
3.               destinationTree = NULL
4.               return
5.       copy current node in sourceTree to destinationTree
6.       copy (sourceTree.left, destinationTree)
7.       copy (sourceTree.right, destinationTree)
```

CLARIFICATION POINT-1:

What is the maximum number of nodes in the tree?

CLARIFICATION POINT-2:

Is the tree a binary search tree?

ASSUMPTION/LIMITATION:

- We will assume the tree can be any binary tree, not necessarily a binary search tree.

- Furthermore, in our example, for simplicity, the tree will only hold 6 nodes.

MAJOR DATA STRUCTURES:

Binary trees

Here is a sample solution that implements the steps described above:

```
1.   #include <cstdio>
2.
3.   using namespace std;
4.
5.   struct node
6.   {
7.      node *left, *right;
8.      int value;
9.   };
10.
11.  void insert(node *&tree, int value)
12.  {
13.     tree = new node;
14.     tree -> value = value;
15.     tree -> left = tree -> right = NULL;
16.  }
17.
18.  void inorder(node *tree)
19.  {
20.     if (tree == NULL) return;
21.
22.     // process left subtree
23.     inorder(tree -> left);
24.     // process current node
25.     printf("%d ", tree -> value);
26.     // process right subtree
27.     inorder(tree -> right);
28.  }
29.
30.  void copy(node* &sourceTree, node* &destinationTree)
```

```
31.  {
32.      // if we have reached a null pointer
33.      // just make destination null as well
34.      if (sourceTree == NULL)
35.      {
36.              destinationTree = NULL;
37.              return;
38.      }
39.
40.      // copy current node, then left and right nodes
41.      destinationTree = sourceTree;
42.      copy(sourceTree->left, destinationTree -> left);
43.      copy(sourceTree->right, destinationTree -> right);
44.  }
45.
46.  int main()
47.  {
48.      // our trees - initially empty
49.      node *sourceTree = NULL;
50.      node *destinationTree = NULL;
51.
52.      // insert some values into the source tree
53.      insert(sourceTree, 10);
54.      insert(sourceTree->left, 12); insert(sourceTree->right,
         15);
55.      insert(sourceTree->left->left, 5);
56.      insert(sourceTree->right->left, 1); insert(sourceTree-
         >right->right, 2);
57.
58.      // copy source into destination
59.      copy (sourceTree, destinationTree);
60.
61.      printf("Inorder traversal of the source tree:\n");
62.      inorder(sourceTree);
63.      printf("\nInorder traversal of the destination tree:\n");
64.      inorder(destinationTree);
65.
66.      return 0;
67.  }
```

OUTPUT:	FURTHER EXERCISE:
Inorder traversal of the source tree: 5 12 10 1 15 2 Inorder traversal of the destination tree: 5 12 10 1 15 2	Q: Is there a non-recursive approach to this task? A: Yes, any traversal of the tree can be done with the use of a stack, as we will see in one of the next tasks. As we add the elements to the stack, we can also copy them to the destination tree, eventually achieving the same result.

TREE: TRAVERSALS OF BINARY TREE WITHOUT RECURSION

Write functions to produce the Inorder, Preorder and Postorder traversals of a binary tree without recursion.

SOLUTION: Again, we will be working on the following example binary tree:

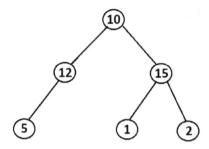

The first thing to mention is that we will be using a stack for all three algorithms. This will enable us to store each node at every step and hence avoid using when traversing the tree. For these examples, our stack will be implemented as a singly linked list and each entry will hold the node of a tree, rather than the value stored in the node. The structure of the stack is as follows:

```
1.   struct stack
2.   {
3.       stack *next;
4.       node *treeNode;
5.   };
```

Let's explain how the in-order traversal (left subtree – current node – right sub-tree) works first:

- We start with an empty stack and the root of the tree
- While the stack is not empty or the current node is not NULL

    a) If the current node exists (is not NULL) add it to the stack and then work with the left sub-tree of the current node (remember, the in-order traversal always starts with the left sub-tree)

    b) Else (the stack is not empty)

        i.   Output the value of the top of the stack

        ii. Pop the stack

        iii. Set current node to be the right sub-tree of the current node.

Let's check these steps and their effects with our example binary tree:

- We start with currentNode = root and the stack s={} (initially empty)
- The stack is empty, but currentNode is not NULL, so we enter the loop
- Add currentNode to the stack, and set currentNode to its left sub-tree (s={10} currentNode = 12)
- Repeat the step above (s={10, 12}, currentNode = 5)
- Repeat again (s = {10, 12, 5}, currentNode = NULL)
- This time currentNode is NULL, so we pop the stack, print the elements (output 5, 12, 10) and set currentNode to the right subtree of the root
- We repeat the same steps for the right subtree

Next, let's look at the pre-order traversal (current node -> left -> right) of a binary tree without using recursion. The steps are as follows:

- Start with an empty stack and push the root of the binary tree to the stack (remember, with pre-order traversal the root is always printed first).
- While there are still elements to be processed in the stack;
    - ▷ Process the top of the stack and pop it;
    - ▷ Add the right child of the current node to the stack;
    - ▷ Add the left child of the current node to the stack.
- We are adding the right child first because in this way the left child will be pushed over the right child in the stack and therefore processed before it.

Let's see how this algorithm works with our example:

- We start with an empty stack s ={} and currentNode = 10 (the root);
- We push 10 to the stack, so s={10}
- There are elements to be processed in the stack, so we pop the stack, output 10 and push the right and left children of 10 to the stack. S={15, 12}.
- We pop the stack again, output 12 and push 5 to the stack. S={15, 5}.
- Output 5 and add nothing to the stack, as 5 has no left or right child.
- Output 15 and push 2 and 1 to the stack s={2,1}
- Output 1; there is nothing to push to the stack.
- Output 2; there is nothing to push to the stack.
- The algorithm now stops.

Finally, the post-order traversal of a binary tree without the use of recursion requires to know whether any of the nodes had previously been visited, so in order to achieve this effect we will add an extra value to our struct, used to represent the tree, as follow:

```
1.   struct node
2.   {
3.       node *left, *right;
4.       int value;
5.       bool visited;
6.   };
```

The Boolean variable 'visited' will be set to true whenever we visit a node along the way in our post-order traversal. This field is needed because we are only allowed to push to the stack an element whose left and right children were already processed (remember, the post order traversal order is left sub-tree -> right sub-tree -> current node). So we will use the flag 'visited' in order to mark whether both children were already pushed to the stack or not.

Let's see how this traversal really works:

- Start with an empty stack and the current node set to the root of the binary tree;
- Push the root to the stack
- While there are elements to be processed in the stack
    - ▷ Set the current node to the top of the stack
    - ▷ If the current node has a non-visited left child add it to the stack
    - ▷ Else If the current node has a non-visited right child add it to the stack
    - ▷ Else process the current node, mark it as visited and also pop the stack.

Let's see how this works with our example:

- Again we start with s={} and currentNode = root of the binary tree;
- We push the root to the stack, so s={10}.
- The top of the stack (10) has a non-visited left child, so we push it s={10, 12}.
- Again, the top of the stack (12) has a non-visited left child, so we push this too s={10,12,5}
- 5 has neither a left nor a right child, so we output it and pop the stack s={10,12}
- The same is valid for 12, as 5 was already visited, so we output 12. S={10}.
- 10 has a non-visited right, child so we add 15 to the stack s={10, 15}.
- 15 has a non-visited left child, so we add 1 to the stack s={10,15,1}.
- 1 has no children, so we output it and pop the stack s={10,15}
- 15 has a non-visited right child, so we pop it to the stack s={10,15,2}.

- 2 has no children, so we output 2 and pop the stack
- 15 has no more non-visited children, so we output 15 and pop the stack
- We finally output 10 and the algorithm stops.

Because recursion is not used, all these algorithms use O(N) space, where N is the number of nodes in the binary tree. This is because we are only using stacks of N elements and do not make any recursive calls.

The time complexity is also linear, O(N), because our algorithms do not backtrack (visit each node multiple times by making 'steps back' for each path in the tree), as the recursive approaches do. What we do instead is process an element from the stack at each step.

PSEUDO CODE:

As shown

CLARIFICATION POINT-1:

What is the maximum number of nodes in the tree?

CLARIFICATION POINT-2:

Is the tree a binary search tree?

ASSUMPTION/LIMITATION:

- We will assume the tree is not a binary search tree.

- Furthermore, in our example, for simplicity, the tree will only hold 6 nodes.

MAJOR DATA STRUCTURES:

Binary tree

Here is a sample solution that implements the steps described above:

```
1.    #include <cstdio>
2.
3.    using namespace std;
4.
5.    struct node
6.    {
7.       node *left, *right;
8.       int value;
9.       bool visited;
10.   };
11.
12.   struct stack
13.   {
```

```
65.    element -> next = s;
66.    s = element;
67.
68.    // while stack is not empty
69.    // process all the items one by one
70.    // and then process their left and right child
71.    while (s != NULL)
72.    {
73.            node *currentNode = s -> treeNode;
74.            printf ("%d ", currentNode -> value);
75.            // pop stack
76.            s = s -> next;
77.
78.            // push right and left child
79.            if (currentNode -> right)
80.            {
81.                    stack *element = new stack;
82.                    element -> treeNode = currentNode -> right;
83.                    element -> next = s;
84.                    s = element;
85.            }
86.
87.            if (currentNode -> left)
88.            {
89.                    stack *element = new stack;
90.                    element -> treeNode = currentNode -> left;
91.                    element -> next = s;
92.                    s = element;
93.            }
94.    }
95. }
96.
97. void postorder(node *tree)
98. {
99.    // start with an empty stack
100.   stack *s = NULL;
101.
102.   // push root to stack
103.   stack *element = new stack;
104.   element -> treeNode = tree;
105.   element -> next = s;
106.   s = element;
107.
108.   // while there are elements to be processed in the stack
109.   while (s != NULL)
110.   {
111.           node *currentNode = s -> treeNode;
112.
113.           // if left child exists and was not visited before
114.           if (currentNode -> left && !currentNode -> left ->
               visited)
```

```
14.      stack *next;
15.      node *treeNode;
16.  };
17.
18.  void insert(node *&tree, int value, bool visited)
19.  {
20.      tree = new node;
21.      tree -> value = value;
22.      tree -> visited = visited;
23.      tree -> left = tree -> right = NULL;
24.  }
25.
26.  void inorder(node *tree)
27.  {
28.      // start with an empty stack
29.      stack *s = NULL;
30.
31.      while (s != NULL || tree != NULL)
32.      {
33.              // if current node is not null
34.              // push it to the stack and go left
35.              if (tree != NULL)
36.              {
37.                      stack *element = new stack;
38.                      element -> treeNode = tree;
39.                      element -> next = s;
40.                      s = element;
41.                      tree = tree -> left;
42.              }
43.              else
44.              {
45.                      // pop from the stack and print value
46.                      printf("%d ", s -> treeNode -> value);
47.                      tree = s -> treeNode -> right;
48.                      s = s -> next;
49.              }
50.      }
51.  }
52.
53.  void preorder(node * tree)
54.  {
55.      if (tree == NULL)
56.      {
57.              printf("Invalid input!\n");
58.              return;
59.      }
60.
61.      // start with an empty stack and push the root to it
62.      stack *s = NULL;
63.      stack *element = new stack;
64.      element -> treeNode = tree;
```

```
115.            {
116.                    // push it to the stack
117.                    stack *element = new stack;
118.                    element -> treeNode = currentNode -> left;
119.                    element -> next = s;
120.                    s = element;
121.            }
122.
123.            // do the same for right child
124.            else if (currentNode -> right && !currentNode ->
                right -> visited)
125.            {
126.                    stack *element = new stack;
127.                    element -> treeNode = currentNode -> right;
128.                    element -> next = s;
129.                    s = element;
130.            }
131.
132.            else
133.            {
134.                    // if no left or right child to be added
135.                    // print value and mark as visited
136.                    printf ("%d ", s -> treeNode -> value);
137.                    s -> treeNode -> visited = true;
138.                    s = s -> next;
139.            }
140.    }
141. }
142.
143.
144. int main()
145. {
146.    // our tree - initially empty
147.    node *tree = NULL;
148.
149.    // insert some values into the source tree
150.    // mark them ass as unvisited first (which is why we use
         false)
151.    insert(tree, 10, false);
152.    insert(tree->left, 12, false); insert(tree->right, 15,
         false);
153.    insert(tree->left->left, 5, false);
154.    insert(tree->right->left, 1, false); insert(tree->right-
         >right, 2, false);
155.
156.    // inorder traversal
157.    printf("Inorder traversal:\n");
158.    inorder(tree);
159.
160.    // preorder traversal
161.    printf("\nPreorder traversal:\n");
```

```
162.    preorder(tree);
163.
164.    // postorder traversal
165.    printf("\nPostorder traversal:\n");
166.    postorder(tree);
167.
168.    return 0;
169. }
```

OUTPUT:

Inorder traversal:

5 12 10 1 15 2

Preorder traversal:

10 12 5 15 1 2

Postorder traversal:

5 12 1 2 15 10

TREE: LEAST COMMON ANCESTOR IN A REVERSED BINARY TREE

Find the lowest common ancestor in a reversed binary tree.

SOLUTION: As you might have guessed, a reversed binary tree is a binary tree in which every node points to its parent node instead of its children. Consider the following binary tree, which we will be working with for the purpose of this example:

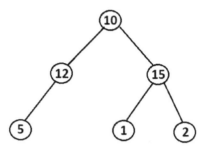

The node storing the key '10' points to NULL, as it is the root of the tree and does not have a parent. Next, the nodes storing the keys '12' and '15' point to 10, and so on.

Now, the lowest common ancestor (commonly abbreviated as LCA) is the task of finding the first node encountered on the path to the root of the tree. For example, take the nodes 1 and 2. The path from 1 to 10 is 1-15-10. Next, the path from 2 to 10 is 2-15-10. The first common node in this path is 15. Following the same logic, the LCA of 5 and 2 is the root of the tree itself, as there is no other common node in this path.

Since we are using a reversed binary tree, the task of finding the LCA of two nodes is fairly straightforward. The algorithm we will be using requires us to know if a node has been visited on the way to the root or not, so we will be using an extra variable in the structure representing the binary tree, as we did for the postfix traversal of the tree without recursion in the previous task.

The algorithm is based on the idea that if we start from both nodes and move along the path to the root, the LCA of the two nodes will be the first node that was visited twice. For example, if we are trying to find the LCA of 1 and 2 in the tree above, we would mark '15' as visited when we proceed from 1, and also encounter it on our way from '2' to the root. This means '15' is the LCA of the tree.

The steps are as follows:

- While any of the two given nodes are not null
  - a) If node 1 is not null
    - i. If it was already visited then this must be the LCA, so return it
    - ii. Else mark it as visited and set its value to its parent
  - b) Do the same for node 2

PSEUDO CODE:

```
1.  Find_lca(node1, node2):
2.      While node1 is not null or not 2 is not null
3.          If node 1 is not null
4.              If node 1 was visited previously
5.                  Return it
6.              Else node1 = node1.parent
7.          If node 2 is not null
8.              If node 2 was visited previously
9.                  Return it
10.             Else node2 = node2.parent
```

CLARIFICATION POINT-1:

What is the maximum number of nodes in the tree?

CLARIFICATION POINT-2:

Is the tree a binary search tree?

ASSUMPTION/LIMITATION:

- We will assume the tree is not a binary search tree.

- Furthermore, in our example, for simplicity, the tree will only hold 6 nodes.

MAJOR DATA STRUCTURES:

Binary tree

Here is a sample solution that implements the steps described above:

```
1.  #include <cstdio>
2.
3.  using namespace std;
4.
5.  struct node
6.  {
7.      node *parent;
8.      int value;
9.      bool visited;
```

```
10.  };
11.
12.  node *insert(node *parent, int value, bool visited)
13.  {
14.      node *tree = new node;
15.      tree -> value = value;
16.      tree -> parent = parent;
17.      tree -> visited = visited;
18.      return tree;
19.  }
20.
21.  node *find_lca(node* node1, node *node2)
22.  {
23.      // while the two nodes are non-NULL
24.      while (node1 || node2)
25.      {
26.              // if node 1 still exists
27.              if (node1)
28.              {
29.                      // if it is visited for the second time
                         then
30.                      // it must mean that this is the LCA
31.                      if (node1 -> visited == true)
32.                              return node1;
33.                      // mark as visited go up in the tree
34.                      node1 -> visited = true;
35.                      node1 = node1 -> parent;
36.              }
37.
38.              // repeat for node 2
39.              if (node2)
40.              {
41.                      if (node2 -> visited == true)
42.                              return node2;
43.                      node2 -> visited = true;
44.                      node2 = node2 -> parent;
45.              }
46.      }
47.
48.      // if no common element in the path return NULL
49.      return NULL;
50.  }
51.
52.  int main()
53.  {
54.      // our tree - initially empty
55.      node *root = NULL;
56.
57.      // insert the root first; no parent
58.      root = new node;
59.      root -> value = 10;
```

```
60.     root -> visited = false;
61.     root -> parent = NULL;
62.
63.     // add the other elements
64.     node *rootLeft = insert(root, 12, false);
65.     node *rootRight = insert (root, 15, false);
66.     node *rootLeftLeft = insert(rootLeft, 5, false);
67.     node *rootRightLeft = insert(rootRight, 1, false);
68.     node *rootRightRight = insert(rootRight, 2, false);
69.
70.     // LCA of of 5 and 16, for example
71.     node *lca = find_lca(rootLeftLeft, rootRight);
72.     if (lca)
73.             printf("The LCA for %d and %d is %d\n",
74.                     rootLeftLeft -> value, rootRight -> value,
                        lca -> value);
75.
76.     // mark all as unvisited again for second lca
77.     root -> visited = false;
78.     rootLeft -> visited = false; rootRight -> visited = false;
79.     rootLeftLeft -> visited = false;
80.     rootRightLeft -> visited = false; rootRightRight ->
        visited = false;
81.
82.     lca = find_lca(rootRightLeft, rootRightRight);
83.     if (lca)
84.             printf("The LCA for %d and %d is %d\n",
85.                     rootRightLeft -> value, rootRightRight ->
                        value, lca -> value);
86.
87.     return 0;
88.  }
```

OUTPUT:	FURTHER EXERCISE:
The LCA for 5 and 15 is 10	Q: How would you find the LCA of two nodes in a regular binary tree (not a reversed one)?
The LCA for 1 and 2 is 15	A: If the binary tree given was not a reversed one (with each node pointing to its left and right child instead) we would have had to start from the root and find the path to each of the two given nodes, and remember the elements encountered along the way. Next, we would start from the end of both paths and look for the first node that appears in both. This approach is more inefficient in terms of space and memory than the one we have just seen.

TREE: NEXT LARGER VALUE IN A BINARY TREE

Given a binary search tree, and a value that may or may not be in it, write a function to find the next larger value.

SOLUTION: We will be working with the following binary search tree for this task:

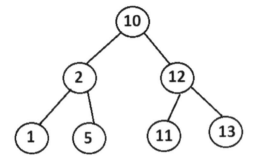

Basically, what this task tells us is, given an integer value, return the smallest value in the tree larger than the integer. For example, given 9 we would have to return 10, and given 10 we would return 11.

The algorithm we will show uses an optimized traversal of the tree and performs the following steps:

- For each node visited:
    - ▷ If the value given is bigger than or equal the one of the node, then go right, as we need to look for a bigger value and all the bigger values are in the right sub-tree of the current node
        - this step is what makes the traversal optimal, as we do not need to visit the left sub-tree of the current node in this case;
    - ▷ Otherwise, we traverse the left sub-tree, as we are perhaps looking for a smaller value.
- The final result will be the minimum value larger than the given value encountered along the way on our traversal.

Beause of the optimization step we have seen above, the compelxity of our algorithm is O(log N), where N is the number of nodes in the tree, as at every step we visit either the left or right sub-tree of the current node.

PSEUDO CODE:

```
1.  Largest_value(node, value, result):
2.      If node is NULL
```

```
3.              Return
4.      If (node.value – value > 0)
5.              If node.value is better than result
6.                      Result = node.value
7.      If value >= node.value
8.              Largest_value(node.right, value, result)
9.      Else
10.             Largest_value(node.left, value, result)
```

CLARIFICATION POINT-1:

What is the maximum number of nodes in the tree?

CLARIFICATION POINT-2:

Is the tree a binary search tree?

ASSUMPTION/LIMITATION:

- We will assume the tree is a binary search tree.

- Furthermore, in our example, for simplicity, the tree will only hold 7 nodes.

MAJOR DATA STRUCTURES:

Binary search tree

Here is a sample solution that implements the steps described above:

```
1.    #include <cstdio>
2.
3.    using namespace std;
4.
5.    struct node
6.    {
7.       node *left, *right;
8.       int value;
9.    };
10.
11.   void insert(node* &tree, int value)
12.   {
13.      // if position is empty then insert
14.      if (tree == NULL)
15.      {
16.              tree = new node;
17.              tree -> value = value;
18.              tree -> left = tree -> right = NULL;
19.              return;
20.      }
21.
```

```
22.    // if given value is smaller than or equal to the current
       one
23.    // go left
24.    if (value <= tree -> value)
25.          insert(tree -> left, value);
26.    // else go right
27.    else
28.          insert(tree -> right, value);
29. }
30.
31. void largest_value(node *bst, int value, int &result)
32. {
33.    // if null then no value has been found
34.    if (bst == NULL) return;
35.
36.    // if current value is greater than the given one
37.    if (bst->value - value > 0)
38.          // if first time or better solution than what we
              have so far
39.          // update result
40.          if(result == -1 || bst->value-value < result-
              value)
41.                result = bst -> value;
42.
43.    // if current value is smaller than or equal to given
       value
44.    // then we are definitely looking for a larger value in the
       tree
45.    // so we go right
46.    if (bst -> value  - value <= 0)
47.          largest_value(bst -> right, value, result);
48.
49.    // else traverse left
50.    else
51.          largest_value(bst->left, value, result);
52. }
53.
54. int main()
55. {
56.    // our binary tree - initially empty;
57.    node *bst = NULL;
58.
59.    // add elements to it
60.    insert(bst, 10); insert(bst, 2); insert(bst, 1);
       insert(bst, 5);
61.    insert(bst, 12); insert(bst, 11); insert(bst, 13);
62.
63.    int result = -1;
64.
65.    largest_value(bst, 2, result);
66.    if (result == -1)
```

```
67.                    printf("No value larger than 2 exists in the
                       tree!\n");
68.     else
69.                    printf("The next value larger than 2 is %d\n",
                       result);
70.
71.     result = -1;
72.     largest_value(bst, 11, result);
73.     if (result == -1)
74.                    printf("No value larger than 11 exists in the
                       tree!\n");
75.     else
76.                    printf("The next value larger than 11 is %d\n",
                       result);
77.
78.     result = -1;
79.     largest_value(bst, 15, result);
80.     if (result == -1)
81.                    printf("No value larger than 15 exists in the
                       tree!\n");
82.     else
83.                    printf("The next value larger than 15 is %d\n",
                       result);
84.
85.
86.     return 0;
87. }
```

OUTPUT:	FURTHER EXERCISE:
The next value larger than 2 is 5 .	Q: Can you think of a naïve approach to this task? What is its complexity?
The next value larger than 11 is 12	A: A more naïve approach to this task performs a regular traversal of the tree and checks all the elements in it in order to find the best one that fits in the description of the task. Depending on the approach (recursive of iterative), the complexity of this naïve solution could be linear or exponential.
No value larger than 15 exists in the tree!	

TREE: SENDING/RECEIVING BINARY TREE OVER THE NETWORK

Given a binary search tree, write a function that will send this over the network and write another function that will read it from the network and create the tree back again.

SOLUTION: For this task we will work with the same binary tree we have seen in the previous task, as follows:

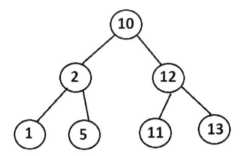

It is clear that we need to find a way to encode the binary search tree before sending it in order for the receiver to be able to reconstruct it correctly. An in-order or post-order traversal of the tree would not help, as the root needs to be the first element we add in the tree at re-construction. But what about pre-order traversal? Let's see how this would work on our example.

The pre-order traversal of the tree above is 10 2 1 5 12 11 13. We can see that the root is the first element and we can also check that this order is favorable for the reconstruction of the tree (i.e. we would obtain a binary search tree with the same shape if we inserted the elements in this order).

Our algorithm includes two functions, one that simulates the behavior of the sender, creating the pre-order traversal of the tree and passing it to another function. This other function is the receiver, which, taken the pre-order traversal array will re-construct the tree. In the end, we will perform an in-order traversal of both trees, in order to check whether they are equal.

PSEUDO CODE:

```
1.   send_and_receive_bst(tree):
2.       preorder[] = pre-order traversal of the tree
3.       receive_and_decode_bst(preorder)
4.
5.   receive_and_decode_bst(preorder[])
```

```
6.          reconstructedTree = empty bst
7.          for each element in preorder
8.                  insert element into reconstructedTree
```

CLARIFICATION POINT-1:

What is the maximum number of nodes in the tree?

ASSUMPTION/LIMITATION:

- In our example, for simplicity, the tree will only hold 6 nodes.

- We will also assume our tree is a binary search tree

MAJOR DATA STRUCTURES:

Binary search tree

Here is a sample solution that implements the steps described above:

```
1.   #include <cstdio>
2.
3.   using namespace std;
4.
5.   struct node
6.   {
7.      node *left, *right;
8.      int value;
9.   };
10.
11.  void insert(node* &tree, int value)
12.  {
13.     // if position is empty then insert
14.     if (tree == NULL)
15.     {
16.             tree = new node;
17.             tree -> value = value;
18.             tree -> left = tree -> right = NULL;
19.             return;
20.     }
21.
22.     // if given value is smaller than or equal to the current
        one
23.     // go left
24.     if (value <= tree -> value)
25.             insert(tree -> left, value);
26.     // else go right
27.     else
28.             insert(tree -> right, value);
29.  }
30.
31.  void preorder(node* bst, int preOrder[])
```

```
32.  {
33.      if (bst == NULL) return;
34.
35.      // add current node value to preOrder array
36.      preOrder[++preOrder[0]] = bst -> value;
37.
38.      // go left and right
39.      preorder(bst -> left, preOrder);
40.      preorder(bst -> right, preOrder);
41.  }
42.
43.  void inorder(node* bst)
44.  {
45.      if (bst == NULL)
46.              return;
47.
48.      // process left subtree
49.      inorder(bst -> left);
50.
51.      // process current node
52.      printf("%d ", bst -> value);
53.
54.      // process right subtree
55.      inorder(bst -> right);
56.  }
57.
58.  void receive_and_reconstruct_bst(int preOrder[])
59.  {
60.      // if empty tree => invalid
61.      if (preOrder[0] == 0)
62.      {
63.              printf("Empty tree!\n");
64.              return;
65.      }
66.
67.      // reconstruct the tree
68.      node *reconstructedTree = NULL;
69.
70.      // add each element to the new tree
71.      for (int index = 1; index <= preOrder[0]; index++)
72.              insert(reconstructedTree, preOrder[index]);
73.
74.      // print the tree
75.      printf("The inorder traversal of the reconstructed
             tree:\n");
76.      inorder(reconstructedTree);
77.  }
78.
79.  void send_and_receive_bst(node* bst)
80.  {
81.      if (bst == NULL)
```

```
82.     {
83.             printf("Invalid input!\n");
84.             return;
85.     }
86.
87.     // the pre-order representation
88.     // preOrder[0] will store the number of elements
89.     int preOrder[20] = {0};
90.
91.     // build the preorder representation of the tree
92.     preorder(bst, preOrder);
93.
94.     // send the preorder representation to the other function
95.     receive_and_reconstruct_bst(preOrder);
96. }
97.
98. int main()
99. {
100.    // our binary tree - initially empty;
101.    node *bst = NULL;
102.
103.    // add elements to it
104.    insert(bst, 10); insert(bst, 2); insert(bst, 1);
        insert(bst, 5);
105.    insert(bst, 12); insert(bst, 11); insert(bst, 13);
106.
107.    send_and_receive_bst(bst);
108.
109.    return 0;
110. }
```

OUTPUT:	FURTHER EXERCISE:
The inorder traversal of the reconstructed tree: 1 2 5 10 11 12 13	Q: What if the tree was not a binary search tree? A: If the tree was not a binary search tree, we could send it to the receiver function as an array of lists. The list associated with each node would store the children of the given node. (In our example, list[10]={2,12} and so on). This would make it possible for the receiver to reconstruct the initial tree.

TREE: BINARY SEARCH TREE – MIN/MAX/INSERT/DEL/...

Implement the following functions for a binary search tree:
- **A function to return the minimum element of a tree;**
- **A function to return the maximum element of a tree;**
- **A function to return the successor of a node;**
- **A function to return the predecessor of a node;**
- **A function to insert a node into the tree;**
- **A function to delete a node from the tree;**
- **A function to print the tree;**

SOLUTION: For this task we will work with the same binary tree used in some of the previous tasks, as follows:

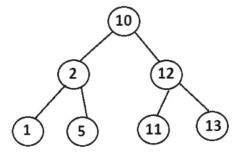

First of all, we have already seen insertion functions and printing functions plenty of times. However, what we have not discussed so far is how to remove a node from a binary search tree. There are three main situations that arise:

- If the node has no children, then just delete it;
- If the node has only one child then the child replaces the node; for example, if we removed the 1 from the tree above and then wanted to remove the 2, then it would be enough to replace the node storing '2' with the one holding '5'.
- Finally, if the node has both children then the steps are as follows:
    - ▷ Find the smallest value in the right sub-tree;
    - ▷ Set the value of the node to this value;
    - ▷ Delete the duplicate value from the right sub-tree;
- For example, if we wanted to delete the root of the tree above (10), we would replace 10 with 11 (the smallest value in the right sub-tree), and

then delete the 11. The key thing to remember is that the smallest value in the right sub-tree is obtained by going as deep to the left as possible, starting from the root of the right sub-tree (which in our case is 12).

Next, the methods for finding the minimum or maximum element in a binary search tree are trivial. From the properties of a binary search tree, we know that every element to the left of a node is smaller than the node, while every element to the right is larger. Considering this, all we need to do to find the minimum / maximum elements of a tree is go as much to the left (or right, for maximum) as possible and return the corresponding value. In our example, starting from the root, the leftmost value is 1, which is the minimum in this case, and the rightmost value is 13, which is the maximum.

Finally, we will consider the problem of finding the successor or predecessor of a node in a binary search tree (i.e. the node that contains the next smallest / largest key). The first idea would be to perform an in-order traversal of the tree, storing the whole representation of the tree in an array, and then returning the element that follows / preceeds the value for which we are trying to compute the predecessor or successor. This approach is inefficient, requires $O(N)$ space and does not use all the properties of a binary search tree.

Alternatively, here is how to tackle the successor problem for a given node in a more efficient way:

- If the node has a right child, then its successor is the node in the right sub-tree which contains the smallest key. This is the same concept we have previously used (for the deletion part). Take for example the root of our example tree, 10. The smallest value in the right sub-tree is 11, which is the successor of 10.

- On the other hand, if the node does not have a right child, then its successor is the ancestor that contains the next larger key. For example, given 5 in our tree, as we go up to the root, we encounter 2 and 10. 2 is smaller than 5, so we do not consider it. 10 is the first value bigger than 5, which makes it the successor of the node containing 5.

- If the node has no ancestors and no right child then the node has no successors. This can only happen in case of the root node with no right child.

The predecessor of a node is basically the opposite of the successor problem and is defined as follows:

- If the node has a left child, then its predecessor is the largest value in the left sub-tree; for example, given 10 in the binary search tree above, this value is 5;

- If the node does not have a right child, then its predecessor is the ancestor that contains the next smaller key; Given 11, for example, this value is 10, as 12 > 11.

The implementation of the successor / predecessor methods would be easier if we stored a pointer to the parent of every node, but this is a rather uncommon practice. We will therefore work with a binary search tree represented in the more common way, with pointers to the left and right child. As we traverse the tree from the root to the bottom, we will retain the last node that matches the condition discussed above.

For example, let's say we are trying to determine the predecessor of 11. As we advance from the root, the path towards 11 is 10-12-11. We will use a variable to store the value of the last node in the path smaller than 11. In our case, this is 10.

PSEUDO CODE:

```
1.   Minimum(bst):
2.       While bst.left
3.               bst = bst.left
4.       return bst.value
5.   Maximum(bst):
6.       Analogous to minimum
7.
8.   Successor(root, node):
9.       If node has a right child
10.              Return smallest value in right sub-tree
11.      Succ = null;
12.      While(root != null)
13.              If (node. value < root. value)
14.                      Succ = root
15.                      Root = root.left
16.              Else
17.                      Root = root.right
18.      Return succ
19.
20.  Predecessor(root, node):
21.      Analogous to successor
```

CLARIFICATION POINT-1:

What is the maximum number of nodes in the tree?

ASSUMPTION/LIMITATION:

- In our example, for simplicity, the tree will only hold 6 nodes.

- We will also assume our tree is a binary search tree

MAJOR DATA STRUCTURES:

Binary search tree

Here is a sample solution that implements the steps described above:

```cpp
1.    #include <cstdio>
2.
3.    using namespace std;
4.
5.    struct node
6.    {
7.       node *left, *right;
8.       int value;
9.    };
10.
11.   void insert(node* &tree, int value)
12.   {
13.      // if position is empty then insert
14.      if (tree == NULL)
15.      {
16.              tree = new node;
17.              tree -> value = value;
18.              tree -> left = tree -> right = NULL;
19.              return;
20.      }
21.
22.      // if given value is smaller than or equal to the current one
23.      // go left
24.      if (value <= tree -> value)
25.              insert(tree -> left, value);
26.      // else go right
27.      else
28.              insert(tree -> right, value);
29.   }
30.
31.   void inorder(node* bst)
32.   {
33.      if (bst == NULL)
34.              return;
35.
36.      // process left subtree
37.      inorder(bst -> left);
38.
39.      // process current node
40.      printf("%d ", bst -> value);
41.
42.      // process right subtree
43.      inorder(bst -> right);
44.   }
45.
46.   int minimum(node* bst)
47.   {
48.      // go as much to the left as possible
```

```
49.      while (bst -> left)
50.              bst = bst -> left;
51.
52.      return bst -> value;
53.  }
54.
55.  int maximum(node* bst)
56.  {
57.      // go as much to the right as possible
58.      while (bst -> right)
59.              bst = bst -> right;
60.
61.      return bst -> value;
62.  }
63.
64.  node* successor(node *bst, node *currentNode)
65.  {
66.      // if right child then go right and then
67.      // as far as possible to the left
68.      // return the successor
69.      if(currentNode -> right != NULL)
70.      {
71.              currentNode = currentNode -> right;
72.              while (currentNode -> left)
73.                      currentNode = currentNode -> left;
74.              return currentNode;
75.      }
76.
77.      // if no right subtree we start and search for the
         successor
78.      // from root
79.      node *succ = NULL;
80.      while (bst != NULL)
81.      {
82.              if (currentNode -> value < bst -> value)
83.              {
84.                      succ = bst;
85.                      bst = bst -> left;
86.              }
87.              else if (currentNode -> value > bst -> value)
88.                      bst = bst -> right;
89.              else
90.                  break;
91.      }
92.
93.      return succ;
94.  }
95.
96.  node* predecessor(node *bst, node *currentNode)
97.  {
98.      // if left child then go left and then
```

```
99.     // as far as possible to the right
100.    // return the predecessor
101.    if(currentNode -> left != NULL)
102.    {
103.            currentNode = currentNode -> left;
104.            while (currentNode -> right)
105.                    currentNode = currentNode -> right;
106.            return currentNode;
107.    }
108.
109.    // if no left subtree we start and search for the
        successor
110.    // from root
111.    node *pred = NULL;
112.    while (bst != NULL)
113.    {
114.            if (currentNode -> value < bst -> value)
115.            {
116.
117.                    bst = bst -> left;
118.            }
119.            else if (currentNode -> value > bst -> value)
120.            {
121.                    pred = bst;
122.                    bst = bst -> right;
123.            }
124.            else
125.                break;
126.    }
127.
128.    return pred;
129. }
130.
131. void remove(node* &bst, int value)
132. {
133.    // if current node is null return
134.    if (bst == NULL) return;
135.
136.    // if the value to be deleted then delete it
137.    if (bst -> value == value)
138.    {
139.            // if leaf then just mark is as NULL
140.            if (!bst -> left && !bst -> right)
141.            {
142.                    bst = NULL;
143.                    return;
144.            }
145.
146.            // else if only one child the child becomes the
                new node
147.            if (!bst -> left)
```

```
148.                    bst = bst -> right;
149.
150.            else if (!bst -> right)
151.                    bst = bst -> left;
152.
153.            // if both children are there
154.            // find smallest value in right subtree
155.            node * smallest = bst -> right;
156.            while (smallest -> left) smallest = smallest ->
                left;
157.
158.            // set the value accordingly
159.            bst -> value = smallest -> value;
160.
161.            // delete the duplicate
162.            remove (bst -> right, smallest -> value);
163.    }
164.
165.    // if we haven't found the value yet
166.    // keep looking for it
167.    remove (bst -> left, value);
168.    remove (bst -> right, value);
169. }
170.
171. int main()
172. {
173.    // our binary tree - initially empty;
174.    node *bst = NULL;
175.
176.    // add elements to it
177.    insert(bst, 10); insert(bst, 2); insert(bst, 1);
        insert(bst, 5);
178.    insert(bst, 12); insert(bst, 11); insert(bst, 13);
179.
180.    // print the tree
181.    printf("The tree in in-order traversal: ");
182.    inorder(bst);
183.    printf("\n");
184.
185.    // compute the minimum element -- initialize with value of
        root
186.    int min = minimum(bst);
187.    printf ("The minimum element in the tree is %d\n", min);
188.
189.     // compute the maximum element -- initialize with value
         of root
190.    int max = maximum(bst);
191.    printf ("The maximum element in the tree is %d\n", max);
192.
193.    // compute the successor of 5
194.    int value = 5;
```

```
195.    node *succ = successor(bst, bst -> left -> right);
196.    if (succ == NULL)
197.            printf("%d has no successor!\n", value);
198.    else
199.            printf("The successor of %d is %d\n", value, succ
                -> value);
200.
201.    // compute the predecessor of 11
202.    value = 11;
203.    node *pred = predecessor(bst, bst -> right -> left);
204.    if (pred == NULL)
205.            printf("%d has no predecessor!\n", value);
206.    else
207.            printf("The predecessor of %d is %d\n", value,
                 pred -> value);
208.
209.    // delete root
210.    remove(bst, 10);
211.
212.    // print node after deletion
213.    printf("Tree after deletion of root:");
214.    inorder(bst);
215.    printf("\n");
216.
217.    return 0;
218. }
```

OUTPUT:	FURTHER EXERCISE:
The tree in in-order traversal: 1 2 5 10 11 12 13 The minimum element in the tree is 1 The maximum element in the tree is 13 The successor of 5 is 10 The predecessor of 11 is 10 Tree after deletion of root:1 2 5 11 12 13	Q: What are the complexities of these functions, compared to their naïve approaches? A: All these functions (finding the min, max, successor / predecessor of a node in a binary search tree) can be performed with a naïve approach, by traversing the tree and storing it into an array, which is processed afterwards. The time and space complexity for this is O(N), while all our functions run in O(log N), which is a major improvement.

TREE: DISTANCE BETWEEN 2 VALUES IN A BINARY SEARCH TREE.

Find the distance between two values in a binary search tree. The header of the function should be int distance(node *root, int val1, int val2) and you are not allowed to use recursion.

SOLUTION: Let's work for one last time with the following binary search tree:

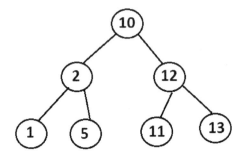

A first idea would be to find the LCA of the two nodes (lowest common ancestor) and compute the distance between each node and the lowest common ancestor. Considering the way our tree will be represented in memory(with pointers to the left and right children, rather than the parent), this approach would be very inefficient and we need to find a way to start from the root of the tree.

The algorithm we will use performs the following steps:

- Start from the root;
- If both values we are looking for are located to the left or to the right of the current node, descend into the corresponding sub-tree;
- The length of the path between the two nodes will be the sum of the depth of the nodes in the sub-tree we have descended.

Consider, for example, that we want to compute the distance between 11 and 13. We start from the root and, since both values are located in the right sub-tree descend in it. The distance between the two nodes is equal to the sum of their depths in the right sub-tree (1 + 1 = 2).

If we want to compute the distance between 5 and 11, for example, we do not descend into any sub-tree, as one of the values is at the left of the root and the other one at the right. In this case the distance is the sum of the depths in the initial tree (2 + 2 = 4).

```
PSEUDO CODE:

1.  Find distance(root, val1, val2):
2.      If val1=val2 return 0
3.      While both values are in the left or right subtree
4.              If they are in the left subtree
5.                      root = root.left
6.              else
7.                      root = root.right
8.      return depth(root, val1) + depth(root, val2)
```

CLARIFICATION POINT-1:

What is the maximum number of nodes in the tree?

ASSUMPTION/LIMITATION:

• In our example, for simplicity, the tree will only hold 6 nodes.

• We will also assume our tree is a binary search tree

MAJOR DATA STRUCTURES:8

Binary search tree

Here is a sample solution that implements the steps described above:

```
1.  #include <cstdio>
2.
3.  using namespace std;
4.
5.  struct node
6.  {
7.      node *left, *right;
8.      int value;
9.  };
10.
11. void insert(node* &tree, int value)
12. {
13.     // if position is empty then insert
14.     if (tree == NULL)
15.     {
16.             tree = new node;
17.             tree -> value = value;
18.             tree -> left = tree -> right = NULL;
19.             return;
20.     }
21.
22.     // if given value is smaller than or equal to the current
        one
23.     // go left
24.     if (value <= tree -> value)
```

```
25.              insert(tree -> left, value);
26.      // else go right
27.      else
28.              insert(tree -> right, value);
29.  }
30.
31.  int depthInBST(node *bst, int val, int currentLevel)
32.  {
33.      // if current node is not null
34.      if (bst != NULL)
35.      {
36.              // if we reached the value return current level
37.              if (bst -> value == val)
38.                      return currentLevel;
39.
40.              // else if val is smaller go left
41.              if (val <= bst -> value)
42.                      return depthInBST(bst -> left, val,
                        currentLevel + 1);
43.              else
44.                      return depthInBST(bst -> right, val,
                        currentLevel + 1);
45.      }
46.  }
47.
48.  int find_distance(node* bst, int val1, int val2)
49.  {
50.      if (bst == NULL)
51.      {
52.              printf("Invalid input!\n");
53.              return 0;
54.      }
55.
56.      // if the two values are equal return 0
57.      if (val1 == val2)
58.              return 0;
59.
60.      // while both values are in the left or right subtree
         descend into that subtree
61.      while((bst -> value < val1 && bst -> value <val2) || (bst
         -> value >val1 && bst->value >val2))
62.      {
63.              // if left subtree
64.              if(val1 < bst -> value)
65.                      bst = bst -> left;
66.              // if right subtree
67.              else
68.                      bst = bst -> right;
69.      }
70.
71.      return depthInBST(bst, val1, 0) + depthInBST(bst, val2, 0);
```

```
72.  }
73.
74.  int main()
75.  {
76.      // our binary tree - initially empty;
77.      node *bst = NULL;
78.
79.      // add elements to it
80.      insert(bst, 10); insert(bst, 2); insert(bst, 1);
         insert(bst, 5);
81.      insert(bst, 12); insert(bst, 11); insert(bst, 13);
82.
83.      int val1 = 5, val2 = 11;
84.      int distance = find_distance(bst, val1, val2);
85.      printf("The distance between %d and %d is %d\n", val1,
         val2, distance);
86.
87.      return 0;
88.  }
```

OUTPUT:	FURTHER EXERCISE:
The distance between 5 and 11 is 4	Q: Can we compute the depth of an element in a tree iteratively?
	A: Yes, the depth of a node in a tree can be computed iteratively. We start with the root and we descend into either the left subtree or the right subtree, depending on where the value we are looking for is. The depth of the node is equal to the number of descents we have made.

GRAPH: GRAPH'S BREADTH FIRST TRAVERSAL

Write a function that performs the breadth-first search traversal of a graph.

SOLUTION: Let's work on the following undirected graph:

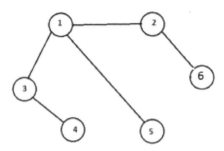

We will use an array of lists of adjacent vertices in order to achieve an efficient representation of our graph. For example, graph[1] is a list containing the elements {2,3,5} for the graph above.

In terms of the actual traversal, this has been discussed in more detail in the section corresponding to graph algorithms. The main idea is that at each step we list all the neighbors of the current node and then start expanding them one by one. Our program will start from node 1, so the BFS traversal will look like:

1 5 3 2 4 6 (5 comes after 2, for example, because we are using single linked lists to represent the graph, and we insert 5 after the 2 at the head of the list). Whenever we expand a node, we need to know whether it had been previously traversed or not, in order to avoid listing the same node twice.

PSEUDO CODE:

```
1.   Bfs(graph):
2.       Queue={}
3.       Add node 1 to Queue
4.       While there are elements to be processed in Queue
5.               Current = dequeue(Queue)
6.               alreadyTraversed[Current] = true
7.               For all neighbors of Current
8.                       If alreadyTraversed[neighbor] = false
9.                               Add neighbor to queue
```

CLARIFICATION POINT-1:

What is the maximum number of nodes in the graph?

Is the graph directed?

ASSUMPTION/LIMITATION:

- For the purpose of our example, we will use an undirected graph with only 6 nodes.

MAJOR DATA STRUCTURES:

Undirected graph

Here is a sample solution that implements the steps described above:

```
1.    #include <cstdio>
2.    #define maxNumberOfNodes 1000
3.
4.    using namespace std;
5.
6.    struct node
7.    {
8.       node *next;
9.       int value;
10.   };
11.
12.   void insert(node* graph[], int source, int destination)
13.   {
14.      // add destination to graph[source]
15.      node *element = new node;
16.      element -> value = destination;
17.      element -> next = graph[source];
18.      graph[source] = element;
19.   }
20.
21.   void bfs(node* graph[], int numberOfNodes)
22.   {
23.      if (numberOfNodes == 0)
24.      {
25.              printf("Invalid input!\n");
26.              return;
27.      }
28.
29.      // have a table for storing whether a node was already
         traversed or not
30.      // initially false
31.      bool alreadyTraversed[numberOfNodes + 1];
32.      for (int index = 0; index <= numberOfNodes; index++)
33.              alreadyTraversed[index] = false;
34.
35.      // the queue for storing the nodes
```

```
36.        int queue[numberOfNodes];
37.        int qHead = 0, qTail = 0;
38.
39.        // start with node 1
40.        queue[qTail++] = 1;
41.
42.        // while there are elemnets to be processed in the queue
43.        while (qHead < qTail)
44.        {
45.                // dequeue and expand
46.                int currentNode = queue[qHead];
47.                qHead++;
48.                printf ("%d ", currentNode);
49.
50.                // mark current node as visited
51.                alreadyTraversed[currentNode] = true;
52.
53.                for (node *neighbor = graph[currentNode]; neighbor;
                        neighbor = neighbor -> next)
54.                        if (!alreadyTraversed[neighbor -> value])
55.                                queue[qTail++] = neighbor -> value;
56.        }
57. }
58.
59. int main()
60. {
61.    // our graph, represented as a list of neighbors,
       initially empty
62.    int numberOfNodes = 6;
63.    node *graph[maxNumberOfNodes + 1];
64.    for (int index = 0; index <= numberOfNodes; index++)
65.            graph[index] = NULL;
66.
67.    // populate the graph
68.    insert(graph,1,2); insert(graph,2,1); insert(graph,1,3);
       insert(graph,3,1);        insert(graph,1,5);
       insert(graph,5,1);
69.    insert(graph,2,6); insert(graph,6,2); insert(graph,3,4);
       insert(graph,4,3);
70.
71.    printf("The BFS traversal of the graph:\n");
72.    bfs(graph, numberOfNodes);
73.
74.    return 0;
75. }
```

OUTPUT:

The BFS traversal of the graph:

1 5 3 2 4 6

GRAPH: GRAPH'S DEPTH FIRST TRAVERSAL

Write a function to perform a depth-first search traversal of a given graph.

SOLUTION: We will work with the same undirected graph as in the previous example, as follows:

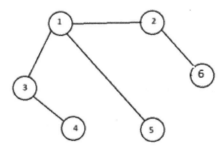

As opposed to BFS, with a DFS traversal we expand a vertex as soon as we list it. For example, if we start from 1, a valid DFS traversal is 1 5 3 4 2 6. This is obtained as follows:

- We output 1 and traverse all its neighbors;
- Let's say the first one encountered is 5; output it and go back to 1, as this has no other neighbors.
- The next neighbor is 3. Output it and visit its neighbors.
- The first and only neighbor of 3 is 4, so we output it, and so on.

Again, we will need a look-up table to tell us whether a node had been traversed previously or not.

The following program implements two versions of the DFS traversal of graphs, a recursive and a non-recursive one. With the recursive method, once we find the first unvisited neighbor of a node we make a recursive call to the traversal function, as we can see in the pseudo-code below.

The iterative approach is trickier and is based on the use of a stack. Whenever we visit a node, we add its first unvisited neighbor to the stack and traverse it. If a node has no unvisited neighbors, then we pop the stack and continue working with its top. We stop when all the elements have been added to the stack, which means they have all been traversed.

PSEUDO CODE:

```
1.    Dfs(graph, numberOfNodes, node, alreadyTraversed):
2.        Print node
```

```
3.      alreadyTraversed[node] = true
4.      for all neighbors of node
5.              if (alreadyTraversed[neighbor] = false)
6.                      dfs(graph, numberOfNodes, neighbor,
                        alreadyTraversed)
```

CLARIFICATION POINT-1:

What is the maximum number of nodes in the graph?

CLARIFICATION POINT-2:

Is the graph directed?

ASSUMPTION/LIMITATION:

• For the purpose of our example, we will use an undirected graph with only 6 nodes.

MAJOR DATA STRUCTURES:

Undirected graph

Here is a sample solution that implements the steps described above:

```
1.   #include <cstdio>
2.   #define maxNumberOfNodes 1000
3.
4.   using namespace std;
5.
6.   struct node
7.   {
8.      node *next;
9.      int value;
10.  };
11.
12.  void insert(node* graph[], int source, int destination)
13.  {
14.     // add destination to graph[source]
15.     node *element = new node;
16.     element -> value = destination;
17.     element -> next = graph[source];
18.     graph[source] = element;
19.  }
20.
21.  void dfs(node* graph[], int numberOfNodes, int currentNode,
         bool alreadyTraversed[])
22.  {
23.     // print current node and mark as visited
24.     printf ("%d ", currentNode);
25.
26.     alreadyTraversed[currentNode] = true;
```

```
27.
28.    // expand on current node
29.    for (node *neighbor = graph[currentNode]; neighbor;
       neighbor = neighbor -> next)
30.            if (!alreadyTraversed[neighbor -> value])
31.                    dfs(graph, numberOfNodes, neighbor ->
                       value, alreadyTraversed);
32. }
33.
34. int main()
35. {
36.    // our graph, represented as a list of neighbors,
       initially empty
37.    int numberOfNodes = 6;
38.    node *graph[maxNumberOfNodes + 1];
39.    for (int index = 0; index <= numberOfNodes; index++)
40.            graph[index] = NULL;
41.
42.    // again, we need to know whether any of the nodes has
       been visited before
43.    bool alreadyTraversed[numberOfNodes + 1];
44.    for (int index = 0; index <= numberOfNodes; index++)
45.            alreadyTraversed[index] = false;
46.
47.    // populate the graph
48.    insert(graph,1,2); insert(graph,2,1); insert(graph,1,3);
       insert(graph,3,1); insert(graph,1,5); insert(graph,5,1);
49.    insert(graph,2,6); insert(graph,6,2); insert(graph,3,4);
       insert(graph,4,3);
50.
51.    // DFS; start with node 1
52.    printf("The DFS traversal of the graph:\n");
53.    dfs(graph, numberOfNodes, 1, alreadyTraversed);
54.
55.    return 0;
56. }
```

OUTPUT:	FURTHER EXERCISE:
The DFS traversal of the graph: 1 5 3 4 2 6	Q: Is there an iterative approach to DFS? A: Yes, DFS can also be achieved with the use of a stack. Whenever we visit a node, we add all its unvisited neighbors to the stack. The next element to be visited will be the top of the stack. Because of its memory inefficiency, the iterative approach for DFS is not as commonly used as the recursive version.

GRAPH: TOPOLOGICAL SORT PROBLEM

Write a function that displays a topological sort of the nodes of a graph.

SOLUTION: First, it should be clear from the beginning that topological sort can only be computed on directed graphs. We will use the following as an example to our problem:

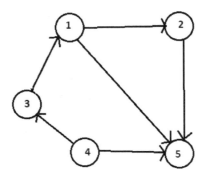

Let's remember the task scheduling problem, which is a classical example for the applicability of the topological sort algorithm. Suppose we are given N tasks to perform and some of these tasks depend on the outcome of others, which need to be performed before them. Such kind of problems can be solved by building a graph and applying the topological sorting algorithm.

For example, the graph above can be interpreted as a graph for topological sorting. The 5 nodes are the tasks that need to be performed, while the edges tell us the following:

- Task 1 depends on task 5, so task 5 needs to be performed before it (edge 1->5)

- Task 3 depends on task 1, so task 1 needs to be performed before it (edge 3->1), and so on.

A valid topological sort would therefore be as follows: 5 2 1 3 4. Note that usually the topological sorting problem has more than one solution.

The algorithm we will be using uses a depth first search traversal of the graph with some slight modifications. The major difference is that we will only output a vertex (a task) when all the other vertices it depends on had been already outputted (all the tasks the execution of the current task depends on were completed).

In order to achieve this effect, we will modify the 'alreadyTraversed' look-up table we have used in regular DFS. The table will now store one of three states for every vertex, as follows:

- alreadyTraversed[vertex] = 0 if vertex has not been traversed yet;
- alreadyTraversed[vertex] = 1 if vertex has been traversed and outputted;
- alreadyTraversed[vertex] = 2 if vertex has been traversed, but it was not outputted yet, which means there are some other vertices that need to be outputted first.

We will perform the following steps when we traverse a node:

- if alreadyTraversed[node] = 2 (i.e. we have already traversed it, but there may be other nodes that need to be outputted before node can be outputted) we skip it;
- else if node has not been traversed yet (alreadyTraversed[node] = 2)
  - ▷ we mark it as temporarily traversed, as we cannot know at this point whether there may be other nodes that need to be outputted before it;
  - ▷ we traverse all its neighbors recursively, as in DFS;
  - ▷ we mark node as permanently visited (alreadyTraversed[node]=1) and output it
- we repeat for all nodes, as long as there are mode of them which were not traversed.

Take our example graph. If we start from 1, we perform the following steps:

- 1 was not visited, so we mark it as temporarily visited and traverse all its neighbors; we start with 2;
- 2 has not been visited, so we mark it as temporarily visited; we traverse its neighbor again, which is 5;
- 5 has no neighbor, so we mark it as permanently visited and output it;
- We go back to 2, for which we have traversed all the neighbors, so we output 2;
- We go back to 1, for which we have traversed all the neighbors, so we output 1;
- There are more nodes to be traversed; the next one is 3, which does not have any unvisited neighbor, so we mark it as permanently visited and output it; we do the same for 4.

PSEUDO CODE:

```
1.    Topsort(graph,numberOfNodes,currentNode,traversed[]):
2.       While there are nodes for which traversed[node]=0
```

```
3.                Select one such node and call traverse(node)
4.
5.    Traverse(graph,numberOfNodes,currentNode,traversed[]):
6.         If traversed [currentNode] = 2 return
7.         Else If traversed [currentNode] = 0
8.          Traversed[currentNode] = 2;
9.          For all neighbors of currentNode
10.               Traverse(graph,numberOfNodes,neighbor,traversed[])
11.         Traversed[currentNode] = 1
```

CLARIFICATION POINT-1:

What is the maximum number of vertices in the graph?

CLARIFICATION POINT-2:

Is the graph directed?

ASSUMPTION/LIMITATION:

- For the purpose of this example we will use a directed graph
  with 5 nodes.

MAJOR DATA STRUCTURES:

Directed graph

Here is a sample solution that implements the steps described above:

```
1.    #include <cstdio>
2.    #define maxNumberOfNodes 1000
3.
4.    using namespace std;
5.
6.    struct node
7.    {
8.        node *next;
9.        int value;
10.   };
11.
12.   void insert(node* graph[], int source, int destination)
13.   {
14.       // add destination to graph[source]
15.       node *element = new node;
16.       element -> value = destination;
17.       element -> next = graph[source];
18.       graph[source] = element;
19.   }
20.
21.   void traverse(node* graph[], int numberOfNodes, int
      currentNode, int alreadyTraversed[])
22.   {
```

```
23.     // if currentNode is temporary then stop
24.     if (alreadyTraversed[currentNode] == 2)
25.             return;
26.
27.     // if current Node was not visited
28.     if (alreadyTraversed[currentNode] == 0)
29.     {
30.             // mark it as temporarily visited
31.             alreadyTraversed[currentNode] = 2;
32.
33.             // expand on it;
34.             for (node *neighbor = graph[currentNode]; neighbor;
                neighbor = neighbor -> next)
35.                     traverse(graph, numberOfNodes, neighbor ->
                        value, alreadyTraversed);
36.
37.             // mark current node as permanent
38.             alreadyTraversed[currentNode] = 1;
39.             printf("%d ", currentNode);
40.     }
41. }
42.
43. void topsort(node* graph[], int numberOfNodes, int
    currentNode, int alreadyTraversed[])
44. {
45.     // while there are nodes that were not traversed traverse
        them
46.     bool allNodesTraversed = false;
47.     while(!allNodesTraversed)
48.     {
49.             allNodesTraversed = true;
50.             for (int nodeIndex = 1; nodeIndex <= numberOfNodes;
                nodeIndex++)
51.                     if (alreadyTraversed[nodeIndex] == 0)
52.                     {
53.                             traverse(graph, numberOfNodes,
                                nodeIndex, alreadyTraversed);
54.                             allNodesTraversed = false;
55.                     }
56.     }
57. }
58.
59. int main()
60. {
61.     // our graph, represented as a list of neighbors,
        initially empty
62.     int numberOfNodes = 5;
63.     node *graph[maxNumberOfNodes + 1];
64.     for (int index = 0; index <= numberOfNodes; index++)
65.             graph[index] = NULL;
66.
```

```
67.     // again, we need to know whether any of the nodes has
        been visited before
68.     // alreadyTraversed[x] = 0 -> not visited
69.     // alreadyTraversed[x] = 1 -> visited
70.     // alreadyTraversed[x] = 2 -> temporarily visited (there
        are other nodes to be traversed)
71.     int alreadyTraversed[numberOfNodes + 1];
72.     for (int index = 0; index <= numberOfNodes; index++)
73.             alreadyTraversed[index] = 0;
74.
75.     // populate the graph
76.     insert(graph,1,2); insert(graph,1,5); insert(graph,2,5);
77.     insert(graph,3,1); insert(graph,4,3); insert(graph,4,5);
78.
79.     // DFS; start with node 1
80.     printf("The topological sort is:\n");
81.     topsort(graph, numberOfNodes, 1, alreadyTraversed);
82.
83.     return 0;
84. }
```

OUTPUT:	FURTHER EXERCISE:
The topological sort is: 5 2 1 3 4	Q: Is there any alternative algorithm for topological sort? A: Another algorithm for topological sort was created by Kahn back in 1962 and uses the list of all nodes with no incoming edges to achieve the result. It is not widely used because graphs are normally represented with adjacency lists, which makes it hard to maintain a list of the nodes with no incoming edges.

MIX: WRITE A MEMORY MANAGER

Write a memory manager: init, malloc and free given a fixed size of memory.

SOLUTION: Managing computer memory properly has always been an important aspect in programming and in computer science in general. A good memory manager allocates a block of memory efficiently to all processes that require it and also ensures that once the block is not used it can be freed and passed to another process / variable that can reuse it later on.

But what do we actually mean by allocating memory efficiently?

Suppose we have 128 KB of memory available, composed of adjacent blocks of 1 byte each. This is equal to 131,072 bytes. An integer is normally stored on 32 bits, or 4 bytes, so this is enough to store 32,768 integers. If we know in advance how much memory each process (or variable) requires (for example, when we allocate the memory statically at compile time) then we would know exactly how to allocate adjacent memory blocks to each process.

Suppose we have 3 arrays, of 10,000 integers each. In this case, the first 40,000 bytes would be allocated to the first array, the next 40,000 to the second, and so on. This is an efficient allocation of memory because when an iteration through any of the arrays is performed, only adjacent blocks of memory are accessed. If, on the other hand, we would allocate the first block to the first array, the second block of memory to the second one, the third to the third array, the fourth to the first array, and so on, iterating through the arrays would be done by accessing blocks located at a distance of 3 from each other, which would make the program slower.

Just as there are functions that allocate memory, there are also functions that free it up. We won't get into too much detail on how memory allocation takes place, because this process is based on using libraries from the operating system, so it is different for Windows, Linux, Mac OS, and so on. What we will do is write a program to simulate the allocation of a fixed block of memory.

Normally, operating systems make use of the so-called buddy memory allocation technique. This divides memory into partitions, which are usually in the form of linked lists. In order to keep things simple, instead of using a list of hundreds of thousands of elements, we will just store the total number of blocks in an integer variable, and then store the intervals [start, end] of free memory in an array of elements of data type 'interval', defined as follows:

```
1.   struct interval
2.   {
3.       int start, end;
4.   };
```

For example, if our array would store {[0,50000], [55000, 75000], [100000-120000]}, this means blocks 0 to 50,000, 55,000 to 75,000 and 100,000 – 120,000 are available and can be allocated for the variables of our program. Every time a request to allocate / free up some memory is made, these intervals will be updated. For example, if the initial free memory is defined by the interval [0,2000] and we allocate the first 100 blocks of memory to a variable, the remaining free memory will be [0,2000] – [0,100] = [0, 1900], generally the difference of 2 intervals a and b can be expressed as:

```
1.   [a.start a.end] - [b.start b.end] = [max(a.start, b.end),
     max(a.end, b.start)];
```

For example, [1000, 6000] – [1000, 2000] = [2000, 6000].

Suppose we have the following scenario:

- We have 128 KB of memory available;

- We initialize 3 arrays of integers, a[25000], b[500] and c[692], so 29768 integers in total. This leaves us with enough space to store 3000 more integers.

- At this point the most efficient way to allocate memory would be to allocate blocks 0 – 100,000 to a, 100,001 to 102,000 to b and 102,001 to 104,769 to c.

- At some point, the program does not need array b anymore, so makes a call to free up the space allocated to it.

- Then, the program needs another array d, of 3000 integers. Our memory looks like this:

- The first space is the one initially allocated to b, but this is, however, not enough for variable d.

- If we allocate the first free space to d, then we would need to add more blocks from the last chunk of free memory. On the other hand, if we allocate the last chunk of memory to d, this would be more efficient, as d will be a contiguous array, stored on adjacent memory blocks.

Based on our discussions, we can deduce the following:

- We need an efficient data structure to tell us what memory blocks are available at whenever the program makes a request for memory allocation our function needs to do its best to allocate adjacent blocks to the new variable.

- In order to achieve this effect we will use the concept of interval arithmetic, as examplained above.

- At first we will start with an interval defining the whole memory (i.e. for 128 KB, this would be [0, 131072] (128 KB = 131072 B).
- As we allocate memory, we perform the difference between intervals. For example, when we allocate a:
  ▷ [0, 131,072] – [0, 100,000] = [100,001 – 131,072], which is our remaining free space.
- Whenever we free memory we perform interval addition.
- When we have to allocate memory again, we would check each free interval and allocate memory efficiently.

Here is a sample solution that implements the steps described above:

```
1.   #include <cstdio>
2.
3.   using namespace std;
4.
5.   struct interval
6.   {
7.       int start, end;
8.   };
9.
10.  // our intervals of free memory
11.  // initially one interval defining the entire memory block
12.  int number_of_intervals = 1;
13.  interval free[100];
14.
15.  int min(int a, int b)
16.  {
17.      return a < b ? a:b;
18.  }
19.
20.  int max(int a, int b)
21.  {
22.      return a > b ? a:b;
23.  }
24.
25.  interval subtract(interval a, interval b)
26.  {
27.      interval result;
28.      result.start = max(a.start, b.end);
29.      result.end = max(a.end, b.start);
30.      return result;
31.  }
32.
33.  void my_malloc(interval &interv, int number_of_bytes)
34.  {
35.      // find the first interval of free memory that fits
```

```
36.     for (int intervalIndex = 0; intervalIndex < number_of_
        intervals; intervalIndex++)
37.     {
38.             // if enough space allocate it
39.             if (free[intervalIndex].end - free[intervalIndex].
                start > number_of_bytes)
40.             {
41.                     interv.start = free[intervalIndex].start;
42.                     interv.end = interv.start + number_of_
                        bytes;
43.                     break;
44.             }
45.     }
46.
47.     // mark memroy as used by interval subtraction
48.     free[0] = subtract(free[0], interv);
49. }
50.
51. void my_free(interval interv)
52. {
53.     // add the memory interval to the free memory interval
        array
54.     free[number_of_intervals].start = interv.start;
55.     free[number_of_intervals].end = interv.end;
56.     number_of_intervals++;
57. }
58.
59. int main()
60. {
61.     // memory size in KB
62.     int memory_size = 128;
63.     free[0].start = 0;
64.     free[0].end = memory_size * 1024; // from KB to B
65.
66.     // simulate the scenario discussed in the lesson
67.     // we will store each array as the start and end of the
68.     // memory space used for the purpose of this example
69.     interval a;
70.     my_malloc(a, 100000); // for array a
71.     printf("a was allocated blocks %d to %d\n", a.start, a.end);
72.
73.     interval b;
74.     my_malloc(b, 2000); // for b
75.     printf("b was allocated blocks %d to %d\n", b.start, b.end);
76.
77.     interval c;
78.     my_malloc(c, 2768); // for c
79.     printf("c was allocated blocks %d to %d\n", c.start, c.end);
80.
81.     // free up b
82.     my_free(b);
```

```
83.
84.    // allocate memory for d
85.    interval d;
86.    my_malloc(d, 3000);
87.    printf("d was allocated blocks %d to %d\n", d.start, d.end);
88.  }
```

OUTPUT:	FURTHER DISCUSSIONS:
a was allocated blocks 0 to 100000	If a program makes repeated calls to malloc or free, then this may actually slow down the performance of the program. As a consequence, a programmer may choose to write their own 'memory pool', in which case only one call would be made to malloc / free. Memory would then be allocated from this memory pool.
b was allocated blocks 100000 to 102000	
c was allocated blocks 102000 to 104768	
d was allocated blocks 104768 to 107768	

MIX: ANGLE BETWEEN HOUR AND MINUTE NEEDLE

Given the time in hour and minutes, find the angle between the hour needle and the minute needle, on a round clock.

SOLUTION: Suppose we have the following clock:

As you already know, the two needles have the origin in the same point (the center of the circle that defines the clock). It is common to represent the minute needle as the longer of the two. Hence the clock above shows the hour 12:15.

Now, because the two needles have a common origin, they will always define an angle between them. Here are a couple of facts that will help us devise an algorithm:

- A circle has 360 degrees in total;
- This means that with every hour the hour needle moves 360 / 12 = 30 degrees, and every minute the minute needle moves 360 / 60 = 6 degrees.
- However, the tricky part to consider is to calculate how many degrees the hour needle moves in a minute, so we can have a way to correlate the two.
- Since we have already established that an hour is worth 30 degrees and since there 60 minutes in an hour, we can conclude that every minute the hour needle moves 30/60 = 0.5 degrees.

Another aspect to consider is that the angle we are looking for will always have a value between 0 and 180 degrees. For example, in the picture below, the angle we are looking for is the one marked in red, not the one in blue:

We can start by computing how far from the hour '12' each needle is. This can be done in the following way:

- We know that with every hour the hour needle moves 30 degrees and with each minute it moves an additional 0.5 degrees. Therefore, the hour needle will be at 30 * hour + minutes / 2 from its straight position (hour 12). Let's call this variable degrees_hour;

- Every minute the minute needle moves by 6 degrees, so it will be at an angle of 6 * minute from its straight position (where it shows 0 minutes). We will call this variable degrees_minute;

- Now, the angle between the two can be computed as abs(degrees_hour – degrees_minute).

- Let's consider the example 12:40. We perform the following steps:

    ▷ degrees_hour = 30 * 0 (we convert 12 to 0, as well as 60 to 0 in case of minutes) + 40 / 2 = 0 + 20 = 20 degrees.

    ▷ degrees_minute = 40 * 6 = 240.

    ▷ The number we are looking for is abs(20-240) = 220.

    ▷ However, this is the angle showed in blue in the picture above. In order to find the red angle (which will always be between 0 and 180 degrees), we will subtract 360 from the value we compute. So in this case 360-220 = 140 is the value we are looking for.

PSEUDO CODE:

```
1.    angle(hour, minute):
2.        degrees_hour = hour * 30 + minute / 2
3.        degrees_minute = minute * 6;
4.        angle_value = abs(degrees_minute - degrees_hour)
5.        if (angle_value > 180)
6.                angle_value = 360 - angle_value;
7.        return angle_value
```

CLARIFICATION POINT-1:

What values for hour / minute will the program accept?

ASSUMPTION/LIMITATION:

- Our program will accept hour as an int between 0 and 12 and minute between 0 and 60.

MAJOR DATA STRUCTURES:

Integers

UNIT TESTS:

POSTIVE FUNCTIONAL TEST CASES

INPUT	EXPECTED OUTPUT
H=12, M=40	140
H=12, M=0	0
H=3, M=30	75

NEGATIVE FUNCTIONAL TEST CASES

H<0 or H>12	Input invalid
M<0 or M>60	Input invalid

Here is a sample solution that implements the steps described above:

```
1.   #include <cstdio>
2.   #include <cmath>
3.
4.   using namespace std;
5.
6.   float angle(int hour, int minute)
7.   {
8.      if (hour < 0 || hour > 12 || minute < 0 || minute > 60)
9.      {
10.             printf("Invalid input!\n");
11.             return 0;
12.     }
13.
14.     // if hour == 12 or minute == 60 convert these to 0
15.     if (hour == 12) hour = 0;
16.     if (minute == 60) minute = 0;
17.
18.     // compute degrees_hour and degrees_minute
19.     float degrees_hour = 30 * hour + minute / 2;
20.     float degrees_minute = minute * 6;
21.
22.     float angle_value = abs(degrees_hour - degrees_minute);
23.
24.     // convert from "blue angle" to "red angle"
25.     if (angle_value > 180)
26.             angle_value = 360 - angle_value;
27.
28.     return angle_value;
29.  }
30.
31.  int main()
32.  {
33.     int hour = 12;
34.     int minute = 40;
35.     float angle_value = angle(hour, minute);
```

```
36.      printf("The angle between the needles at %d:%d is %g\n",
         hour, minute, angle_value);
37.
38.      hour = 12;
39.      minute = 0;
40.      angle_value = angle(hour, minute);
41.      printf("The angle between the needles at %d:%d is %g\n",
         hour, minute, angle_value);
42.
43.      hour = 3;
44.      minute = 30;
45.      angle_value = angle(hour, minute);
46.      printf("The angle between the needles at %d:%d is %g\n",
         hour, minute, angle_value);
47.
48.      return 0;
49. }
```

OUTPUT:

```
The angle between the needles at 12:40 is 140

The angle between the needles at 12:0 is 0

The angle between the needles at 3:30 is 75
```

MIX: ALL SUBSETS OF LENGTH K.

Given a set {1,2,3,4,5...n} of n elements, write code that outputs all subsets of length k. For example, if n = 4 and k = 2, the output would be {1, 2}, {1, 3}, {1, 4}, {2, 3}, {2, 4}, {3, 4}

SOLUTION: We will also use a backtracking approach for this task, but with some optimizations. Notice that all the subsets are sorted, so when we are building a subset it is no longer needed to check whether we can fit all elements at the current position in the subset. It is enough to start from the value of the previous element, increased by 1. For example, if our current subset is {1}, we know for sure that the next element we will be adding has a value between 2 and n.

Our algorithm uses a backtracking approach, since we are asked to generate all subsets, and performs the following steps:

- Initialize an array subset[], which will hold the subset as we create it. We will store our elements at indexes between 1 and k. Because at each step we are starting from the previous value stored in the subset, increased by 1, we need to explicitly set subset[0] = 0; in this way, when we are trying to add an element to subset[1] this will have a value between 1 and n.

- Iterate through all the elements that can be added to the current position and add them one by one.

- Make a recursive call to the function. This function will stop when we have successfully built a complete subset (i.e. when there are k elements in the subset, or when the function is recursively called with position k+1).

Let's discuss the pseudo-code below on an example. Suppose we have n=5 and k=3 (we are asked to build subsets of length 3 of the set {1,2,3,4,5}). The steps our algorithm will perform are as follows:

- We iterate from 1 to N and add 1 to the current subset; subset={1}.

- We iterate from 2 to N and add 2 to the current subset; subset={1,2}.

- We iterate from 3 to N and add 3 to the current subset; subset={1,2,3}.

- At this point, we have a complete subset, so we print (1,2,3) and go back to the previous step.

- We continue with level = 3, and build the subset {1,2,4}.

- This subset is also complete, so we output it and we go back again, where we build and output(1,2,5).

- After this step, there are no more elements to iterate through at level 3, so we go back to level2.

- We replace '2' with the next element, '3', so subset={1,3}.
- At level 3, we iterate from 4 to 5 and build (1,3,4) and (1,3,5), and so on.

PSEUDO CODE:

```
1.  Output_subset(n,k,level,subset[]):
2.      if level = k + 1
3.              print complete subset
4.              return
5.      for value from subset[level - 1] to n
6.              subset[level] = value
7.              output_subset(n,k,level+1,subset)
```

CLARIFICATION POINT-1:

What is the maximum number for n?

CLARIFICATION POINT-2:

Is (x,y) the same subset as (y,x)?

ASSUMPTION/LIMITATION:

- Our program will assume a maximum value of 100 for n

- We will also generate subsets without repetition (e.g. (1,2) is the same as (2,1), etc.).

MAJOR DATA STRUCTURES:

Array of integers

UNIT TESTS:

POSTIVE FUNCTIONAL TEST CASES

INPUT	EXPECTED OUTPUT
n=1,k=1	(1)
n=5,k=5	(1,2,3,4,5)
n=3,k=2	(1,2),(1,3),(1,4),(2,3), (2,4),(3,4)

NEGATIVE FUNCTIONAL TEST CASES

k>n	Input invalid
n=0	Input invalid
k=0	Input invalid

Here is a sample solution that implements the steps described above:

```
8.      #include <cstdio>
9.      #define maxNumberOfElements 100
10.
```

```
11.  void output_subsets(int n, int k, int level, int subset[])
12.  {
13.      if (k > n || n == 0 || k == 0)
14.      {
15.              printf("Invalid input!\n");
16.              return;
17.      }
18.
19.      if (level == k + 1)
20.      {
21.              // output current subset
22.              for (int subsetIndex = 1; subsetIndex <= k;
                 subsetIndex++)
23.                      printf("%d ", subset[subsetIndex]);
24.              printf("\n");
25.              return;
26.      }
27.
28.      // iterate through all the elements that can be added to
         the subset
29.      // i.e. previous element + 1 to n
30.      for (int elementIndex = subset[level - 1] + 1;
         elementIndex <= n; elementIndex++)
31.      {
32.              subset[level] = elementIndex;
33.              output_subsets(n,k,level + 1, subset);
34.      }
35.  }
36.
37.  int main()
38.  {
39.      int n = 5;
40.      int k = 3;
41.
42.      // our subset array, initially empty
43.      int subset[maxNumberOfElements] = {};
44.
45.      printf("The subsets are as follows:\n");
46.      output_subsets(n, k, 1, subset);
47.
48.      return 0;
49.  }
```

OUTPUT:	FURTHER EXERCISE:
The subsets are as follows: 1 2 3 1 2 4 1 2 5 1 3 4 1 3 5 1 4 5 2 3 4 2 3 5 2 4 5 3 4 5	Q: What if we were trying to generate the subsets of length k of a set of N random elements? A: If we did not know what elements the set contains, then we would have to mark which elements we have used during a generated subset. This can be done with the use of a look-up table, as we have seen in some of the previous tasks that we tackled with a backtracking approach (e.g. an alreadyVisited[] array of Boolean values). This solution would not hold if the set contained duplicates (for example, the set {1,2,2,3,4,4}. In this case, a workaround would be to count the frequency of the elements and only mark an item as already visited of we have included it multiple times in the subset. (e.g. alreadyVisited[2] = true if we have used 2 two times in our current generated subset).

MIX: IF TWO RECTANGLES OVERLAP

Write a function to check if two rectangles defined as below overlap or not.

struct rect {int top, bot, left, right;} r1, r2;

SOLUTION: First of all, let's discuss the representation of the two rectangles. The four integer values in the struct have the following meaning:

- Top – the y coordinate of the top 2 points;
- Bottom – the y coordinate of the 2 points at the bottom;
- Left – the x coordinate of the two points to the left;
- Right – the x coordinate of the two rightmost points.

The following picture shows the (x,y) coordinates of the four points as expressed above and will help you visualize and understand this representation better:

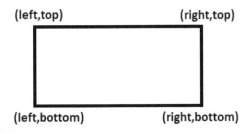

Now, let's consider an example from which we can deduce the condition under which two rectangles r1 and r2 intersect. Suppose r1 and r2 are placed in a Cartesian coordinate system, as follows:

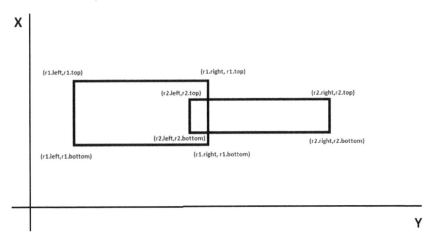

Let's think about this problem the other way round for a moment and consider the cases when two rectangles do not intersect, as shown in the following picture:

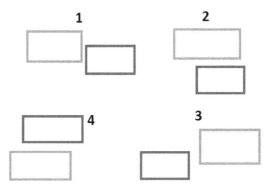

From the four cases above, we can deduce that two rectangles do not intersect in the following situations:

1. The right edge of the green rectangle is closer to the left then the left edge of the blue rectangle. (or green.right < blue.left).

2. The bottom edge of the green rectangle is above the top edge of the blue rectangle (or green.bottom > blue.top).

3. The left edge of the green rectangle is closer to the right then the right edge of the blue rectangle (or green.left > blue.right).

4. The top edge of the green rectangle is below the bottom edge of the blue rectangle (or green.top < blue.bottom).

All we need to do at this point to obtain the condition under which two rectangles intersect is to negate the four statements above. Therefore, two rectangles r1 and r2 intersect if and only if the following four conditions occur at the same time:

1. r1.right > r2.left
2. r1.bottom < r2.top
3. r1.left < r2.right
4. r1.top > r2.bottom

It does not matter which of the two rectangles r1 or r2 is the blue or green one in the figure above, as if you read the conditions backwards (i.e. r2.left < r1.right for the first condition, and so on), you will obtain the same relations, but with r2 to the left side of the sign.

PSEUDO CODE:

```
1.   Overlap(r1,r2)
2.       If r1.left < r2.right and r1.right > r2.left
3.                   and r1.top > r2.bot and r1.bot < r2.top
```

```
4.              return true
5.      return false
```

CLARIFICATION POINT-1:

What is the maximum value for the coordinates of the two rectangles?

ASSUMPTION/LIMITATION:

*   We will assume all the coordinates of a rectangle fit in the in-
    teger data type

MAJOR DATA STRUCTURES:

Rectangles represented as a structure of four integers

UNIT TESTS:	
POSTIVE FUNCTIONAL TEST CASES	
INPUT	EXPECTED OUTPUT

r1.left = 2; r2.left = 5;
r1.right = 6; r2.right = 9;
r1.top = 7; r2.top = 8;
r1.bot = 2; r2.bot = 3;
	The two rectangles overlap!

NEGATIVE FUNCTIONAL TEST CASES	
r1.left >= r1.right	Input invalid
r2.left >= r2.right	Input invalid
r1.top <= r1.bottom	Input invalid
r2.top <= r2.bottom	Input invalid

Here is a sample solution that implements the steps described above:

```
1.   #include <cstdio>
2.
3.   using namespace std;
4.
5.   struct rect
6.   {
7.      int top, bot, left, right;
8.   } r1, r2;
9.
10.  int overlap(rect r1, rect r2)
11.  {
12.     // check input validity
13.     if (r1.left >= r1.right || r1.bot >= r1.top
14.      || r2.left >= r2.right || r2.bot >= r2.top)
15.     {
16.             printf("Invalid input!\n");
17.             return -1;
```

```
18.        }
19.
20.     // condition for overlapping
21.     if (r1.left < r2.right && r1.right > r2.left &&
22.             r1.top > r2.bot && r1.bot < r2.top)
23.             return 1;
24.
25.     else
26.             return 0;
27. }
28.
29. int main()
30. {
31.     // set some coordinates for rectangle
32.
33.     // left = x coordinate of left boundary
34.     r1.left = 2; r2.left = 5;
35.     // right = x coordinate of right boundary
36.     r1.right = 6; r2.right = 9;
37.     // top = y coordinate of top boundary
38.     r1.top = 7; r2.top = 8;
39.     // bottom = y coordinate of bottom boundary
40.     r1.bot = 2; r2.bot = 3;
41.
42.     if(overlap(r1, r2))
43.             printf("The two rectangles overlap!");
44.     else
45.             printf("The two rectangles do not overlap!");
46.
47.     return 0;
48. }
```

OUTPUT:

The two rectangles overlap!

BITS: REVERSE THE BITS OF A NUMBER

How would you reverse the bits of a number with log N arithmetic operations, where N is the number of bits in the integer (eg 32,64..)?

SOLUTION: The first approach to this task would perform N/2 steps and is based on starting from both ends of the number in binary and swapping pairs of bits. For example, given the number 10010110 we would swap the following pairs of indexes: (0,7),(1,6),(2,5),(3,4) in order to obtain 01101001.

There is, however, a more efficient algorithm to achieve this. The main idea is that we will start by swapping adjacent bits, then adjacent pairs of bits, then adjacent pairs of pairs of bits, and so on. Let's consider another example. Given the number 11011100, we will firstly swap the following pairs (0,1), (2,3), (4,5) and (6,7). At this step, the number will be 11101100.

We will then continue to swap pairs of adjacent bits ('11' and '10', and '11' and '00', respectively) and we will achieve 10110011. Finally, we swap the 2 groups of 4 numbers and obtain 00111011, which is the reverse representation of the initial number. It can be proven that this effect is achieved on all numbers. If we can find a way to do the swapping in constant time, then we will obtain an algorithm that reverses the order of bits in an integer in O(log N).

There is a trick discovered by Edwin Freed in 1983, in an article titled 'Binary Magic Numbers', which we will be using to bring our idea further and implement the algorithm at a later point. This trick is based on using a number called a 'mask' each time we do the swapping and applying the following formula:

value = ((value >> x) & mask) | ((value & mask) << x), where:

- Value is the number whose bits we are trying to reverse in logarithmic time;
- x is the number of adjacent bits we are reversing (x=1 if we are reversing single adjacent bits, x=2 if we are reversing pairs of adjacent bits, x=4 if we are reversing groups of 4 adjacent bits, etc.)
- the '>>' is the right shift operator; shifting basically means moving the bits of a number to the left or to the right
  - ▷ for example, the sequence 101101, right shifted with one bit gives 010110
  - ▷ the sequence 1100101, right shifted with 2 bits gives 0011001
  - ▷ notice that we add leading 0s in order to compensate for losing the least significant bit.

- '<<' is the left shift operator and is analogous to the right shift; note that when we shift to the left we need to add 0s at the end of the number;
- finally, mask is a constant number that can be best visualized in its hexadecimal representation and, depending on the value of x can take the following values:
  - $\triangleright$ x = 1 - > mask = 0x55555555 = 01010101010101010101010 1010101$_2$
  - $\triangleright$ x = 2 - > mask = 0x33333333 = 00110011001100110011001 10 0110011$_2$
  - $\triangleright$ x = 4 - > mask = 0x0F0F0F0F= 0000111100001111000011110 0001111$_2$
  - $\triangleright$ x = 8 - > mask = 0x00FF00FF= 000000001111111100000000 1 1111111$_2$
  - $\triangleright$ x = 16 - > mask = 0x0000FFFF= 000000000000000011111111 11111111$_2$
  - $\triangleright$ we can start seeing a pattern on these masks already; every pattern is a repeated sequence of 2^{x-1} 1s, followed by 2^{x-1} 0s.
- & and | and the bitwise 'and' and 'or' operators, respectively.

Let's consider an example. Suppose we are given value = 10110110 and we want to reverse the 2 groups of four bits in it, '1011' and '0110', so x=4. We choose the mask '0x0F0F0F0F'. Let's apply the formula:

value>>x = 10110110 >> 4 = 00001011

(value>>x) & mask = 00001011& 00001111000011110000111100001111 = 000001011

value & mask = 10110110 & 00001111000011110000111100001111 = 00000110

(value & mask) << x = 00000110 << 4 = 01100000

((value >> x) & mask) | ((value & mask) << x) = 000001011 | 01100000= 01101011, which is the result of the swap.

So, let's summarize all these steps of the algorithm. Given an n-bit number, where n is a power of 2, we can reverse its bits by swapping groups of 1, 2, 4, 8,..., n/2 bits using the formula described above. This algorithm runs in O(log N). We will look at an implementation in the following task, where we will use these steps to reverse a 32 bit number.

Let, start with a quick overview of what we have discussed for the previous task. Given an n-bit number, where n is a power of 2, we can reverse its bits by swapping groups of 1, 2, 4, 8,..., n/2 bits using the following formula:

value = ((value >> x) & mask) | ((value & mask) << x), where x is the size of the group that we will swap.

Let's take the following example: n=00000000000000001111111111111111 (16 0s followed by 16 1s), or 65535 in decimal. We want our program to output 11111111111111110000000000000000 (16 1s followed by 16 0s).

This can be achieved by groups of 1,2,4,8 and 16 bits, obtaining the following intermediate results:

1. 00000000000000001111111111111111 (no visible result when swapping adjacent bits, as there are 16 0s and 16 1s);

2. 00000000000000001111111111111111

3. 00000000000000001111111111111111 (the groups in red are swapped with those in blue)

4. 00000000000000001111111111111111 (again, we are about to swap red with blue)

5. 11111111111111110000000000000000

The output of the program can be interpreted in 2 ways:

- If we consider the number is unsigned, then the value of 11111111111111110000000000000000 in decimal will be 4294901760 ($2^{31} + 2^{30} + .. + 2^{16}$).

- If we are using signed numbers, the most significant bit (the first '1') denotes a negative number, which in decimal would be translated to -65536.

PSEUDO CODE:

```
1.   Reverse_bits(value):
2.       Swap adjacent bits one by one
3.       Swap groups of 2 adjacent bits
4.       Swap groups of 4 adjacent bits
5.       Swap groups of 8 adjacent bits
6.       Swap groups of 16 adjacent bits
```

CLARIFICATION POINT-1:

Is the number a signed or an unsigned integer?

ASSUMPTION/LIMITATION:

- We will consider both situations, when a number is a signed or an unsigned integer.

MAJOR DATA STRUCTURES:

Integers represented in binary / hex

Here is a sample solution that implements the steps described above:

```
1.   #include <cstdio>
2.
3.   using namespace std;
4.
5.   int reverse_bits(unsigned int value)
6.   {
7.       // swap odd and even bits
8.       value = ((value >> 1) & 0x55555555) | ((value &
         0x55555555) << 1);
9.       // swap consecutive pairs
10.      value = ((value >> 2) & 0x33333333) | ((value &
         0x33333333) << 2);
11.      // swap nibbles ...
12.      value = ((value >> 4) & 0x0F0F0F0F) | ((value &
         0x0F0F0F0F) << 4);
13.      // swap bytes
14.      value = ((value >> 8) & 0x00FF00FF) | ((value &
         0x00FF00FF) << 8);
15.      // swap 2-byte long pairs
16.      value = ((value >> 16)   ) | ( value << 16);
17.
18.      return value;
19.  }
20.
21.  int main()
22.  {
23.      // value 00000000000000001111111111111111 in binary
24.      unsigned int value = 65535;
25.
26.      // should expect to get 11111111111111110000000000000000
27.      // or 4294901760
28.      int reversed = reverse_bits(value);
29.
30.      // output unsigned
31.      printf ("The number formed by the reversed bits (unsigned)
         is %u\n", reversed);
32.
33.      // output signed
34.      printf ("The number formed by the reversed bits (signed)
         is %d\n", reversed);
35.
36.      return 0;
37.  }
```

```
OUTPUT:
The number formed by the reversed bits (unsigned) is 4294901760

The number formed by the reversed bits (signed) is -65536
```

HASH: NOTE THAT IS CONSTRUCTED USING WORDS

Imagine a note that is constructed using words cut out from a book (e.g. If the book was "I am a very short and useless book" then "very useless" and "I am a book" can be constructed using words from the book while "and books" cannot). Implement the following function in C# (if you know it, C/C++ otherwise):

bool CanConstructNote(string note, string book)

SOLUTION: The first thing to notice is that the requirements of this task do not mention anything about the grammar or the alphabet used for the book, so we will firstly need to validate the input. Next, the algorithm we will be using uses a hash table. The concept of hashing was discussed in detail at an earlier point in the book.

The idea is that if we add all words in the book into a hash table then we would be able to efficiently tell whether a word in the note is present in the hash table or not and hence in the book. Our algorithm performs the following steps:

- Build a hash table with all the words in book;
- Iterate through all the words in note. If any word is not present in the hash table then this means the note cannot be reconstructed from book words, so we stop.

For example, given the book "I am a good book" and the note "good book", we add "I", "am", "a", "good" and "book" to the hash table and we can easily check that the two words in the note, "good" and "book" are already present there.

PSEUDO CODE:

```
1.    CanConstructNote(note,book):
2.            hashTable = {}
3.            for each word in book
4.                    add word to hashTable
5.            canConstructNote = true
6.            for each word in note
7.                    if (word is not in hashTable)
8.                            canConstructNote = false
9.            return canConstructNote
```

CLARIFICATION POINT-1:

What kind of grammar alphabet will be used for the book?

What is the maximum length of the book?

ASSUMPTION/LIMITATION:

- We will assume the grammar / alphabet of the book only comprises English letters and punctuation marks, which will not be considered as part of a word.

- At the same time, we will also assume the size of the book will fit the type string in C#.

MAJOR DATA STRUCTURES:

Strings

```
1.    bool CanConstructNote(string note, string book)
2.    {
3.        /* Separate book words */
4.        /* \W+ one or more non-word characters together */
5.        string[] bookArray = Regex.Split(book, @"\W+");
6.
7.        /* Create a Hashtable to store book's words */
8.        Hashtable bookHT = new Hashtable();
9.        /* Key Value for Book's word values */
10.       short keyIndex = 0;
11.
12.       /* Validate Input */
13.       if (String.IsNullOrEmpty(note) || String.
          IsNullOrEmpty(book))
14.       {
15.           return false;
16.       }
17.
18.       /*Add Each Keyword to book's word's hashtable */
19.       foreach (string eachWord in bookArray)
20.       {
21.           bookHT.Add(keyIndex, eachWord);
22.           keyIndex++;
23.       }
24.
25.       /*Separate note words*/
26.       string[] noteArray = Regex.Split(note, @"\W+");
27.       bool CanConstructNoteFlag = true;
28.
29.       /* Check Each word of note into to book's word's hashtable
          */
30.       foreach (string cutword in noteArray)
31.       {
32.           if (!bookHT.ContainsValue(cutword))
33.           /*Set CanConstructNoteFlag to false if note's word
```

```
34.            not available in book's word's hashtable
35.            */
36.                    CanConstructNoteFlag = false;
37.      }
38.    return CanConstructNoteFlag;
39.  }
```

HASH: PRIME NUMBERS TO REPRESENT
THE SIZE OF A HASH TABLE

What is a hash, and why do we usually choose prime numbers to represent the size of a hash table? Use a mathematical explanation for this purpose.

SOLUTION: When we have to store many numbers in a data structure, usually more than a statically allocated structure would allow, it is common to use the technique referred to as hashing. A hash is a key / value data structures that assigns a key to each value we have to store with the use of a special function, commonly referred to as a hash function.

In order to get a clear picture, you can think of a hash just like a person's first name, which is basically a short way to remember that person, even though there will surely be other people around with the same name. In this way, when you are referring to a friend name John, for example, you will reduce your 'search space' to only those people with this name.

The same principle can be applied to numbers. Just as remembering people is easier by their name then by their passport number or national ID number, remembering any value by its hash code is easier than by the value itself.

Hashing is done with the use of a hash table, which is basically a data structure in which every index is a key (a first name, if we take the analogy above) and has a value associated with it (a person in the same example). In order to achieve an even distribution of the elements in the table it is common to use a prime number as the size of this hash table.

So far there hasn't been too much mathematical work that can prove the link between prime numbers and random number generators. However, it was repeatedly demonstrated that the use of a prime number will always result in a more even distribution in the hash table.

A possible explanation could be that when we multiply a set of random numbers and analyze the results obtained at a bit-level, we will obtain numbers that are more different from each other. Take, for example, the set {12, 5, 3, 10}. When we multiply each of these numbers by 4 we will notice that they tend to follow a common pattern. In base 2, the results of the multiplications would be {110000, 10100, 1100, 101000}. We can see that all the numbers end with the bit 0. On the other hand, if we multiply by a prime (such as 7) it would be harder to find such a pattern. Even though there is no concrete mathematical proof that this is only valid for prime numbers, it seems that this idea has been adopted by most professionals in the field.

This property is not only valid for multiplication, but for any other operation a hashing function may use. This is the main reason why prime numbers have been used for a long time for this purpose.

SEQUENCE: LENGTH OF A PATTERN

You are given a sequence of numbers and you know that at, some point in this sequence, a pattern will start and repeat until the end of the sequence. For example, in the following sequence

0 1 3 4 -2 43 5 2 10 4 -2 43 5 2 10 4 -2 43 5 2 10 4

The pattern is "-2 43 5 2 10 4".

Write a function to compute the length of this pattern.

SOLUTION: Perhaps the easiest approach to this task is the naïve solution, which starts from the end of an array, and checks whether patterns of length 1, 2, 3, and so on. Depending on the techniques used, this type of algorithm can run in O(N2) or even in exponential complexity. In the following lines, however, we will present an approach to this task in O(N).

First of all, we can extract some very useful information from the requirements of the task. For example, we know exactly that the pattern we are looking for ends at the last index in the sequence. In the example above, the array ends with '4', so we know that the repeating pattern must also end with '4'. Following this principle, if we reverse the initial array, the pattern would start with 4, making it easier for us to find it. In the array above, we would need to find the pattern "4 10 2 5 43 -2".

Based on this idea, we can perform the following steps:

1. Reverse the initial array. Now the problem reduces to finding a pattern that starts with the first character of the array and repeats throughout the sequence. In our example, the reversed array would be 4 10 2 5 43 -2 4 10 2 5 43 -24 10 2 5 43 -2 4 3 1 0 and we need to look for a pattern that starts with 4 and repeats at least once.

2. Find the next index of the first character in the sequence (e.g., the '4' in the example above) and store this in a variable. Let's call this variable 'position'.

   a) If the sub-array defined by the indexes [0, position - 1] repeats twice at the beginning of the array, then this is the pattern we are looking for;

      i. For example, in our reversed array, 4 10 2 5 43 -2 4 10 2 5 43 -24 10 2 5 43 -2 4 3 1 0, the next 4 is at index 6 and we can easily see that the sub-array defined by [0,5] (4 10 2 5 43 -2) appears twice, which means it is a pattern at the beginning of the reversed array (the end of the non-reversed array), so we stop.

b) Otherwise, search for the next occurrence of the initial number and repeat step a.

    i.   For example, given the reversed array 4 1 4 2 4 1 4 2 4 1 4 2 0 3, the next occurrence of 4 is at index 2, but "41" is not a pattern in the array (does not appear at least twice). The next occurrence is at index 4. The sub-array 4 1 4 2 appears twice at the beginning of the array, so this is the pattern we are looking for.

PSEUDO CODE:

```
1.   Length_of_sequence(array)
2.       array = reversed array
3.       for i = 1 to array.length
4.           if (array[i] == array[0])
5.               if the sub-sequence (0,i) is valid
6.                   return i
```

CLARIFICATION POINT-1:

What is the maximum length of the sequence?

ASSUMPTION/LIMITATION:

• We will assume the maximum length of the sequence is 1000.

MAJOR DATA STRUCTURES:

Array of integers

UNIT TESTS:

POSTIVE FUNCTIONAL TEST CASES

INPUT	EXPECTED OUTPUT
0 1 2 3 9 8 3 3 3 3 3	1
0 1 2 1 3 3 2 1 3 3 2 1 3 3 2	4
0 5 6 4 3 2 2 3 2 3 2 3 2 3 2 3	2

NEGATIVE FUNCTIONAL TEST CASES

Length of sequence <= 2	Input invalid

Here is a sample solution that implements the steps described above:

```
1.   #include <cstdio>
2.   #include <cstring>
3.   #define maxNumberOfElements 1000
4.
5.   using namespace std;
6.
```

```
7.    int length_of_repeating_sequence(int array[], int
      numberOfElements)
8.    {
9.        if (numberOfElements < 2)
10.       {
11.               printf("Invalid input!\n");
12.               return 0;
13.       }
14.
15.       // reverse array
16.       for (int arrayIndex = 0; arrayIndex < numberOfElements /
          2; arrayIndex++)
17.       {
18.               // do a swap
19.               int temp = array[arrayIndex];
20.               array[arrayIndex] = array[numberOfElements -
                  arrayIndex - 1];
21.               array[numberOfElements - arrayIndex - 1] = temp;
22.       }
23.
24.       // find the next position of the starting number in the
          pattern
25.       for (int arrayIndex = 1; arrayIndex < numberOfElements;
          arrayIndex++)
26.               if (array[arrayIndex] == array[0])
27.               {
28.                       // check whether 0-arrayIndex is a valid
                          pattern
29.                       bool validPattern = true;
30.                       for (int patternIndex = 0; patternIndex <
                          arrayIndex; patternIndex++)
31.                               if (array[patternIndex] !=
                                  array[arrayIndex + patternIndex])
32.                                       validPattern = false;
33.                       if (validPattern == true)
34.                               // return its length
35.                               return arrayIndex;
36.               }
37.   }
38.
39.   int main()
40.   {
41.       int numberOfElements = 22;
42.       int numberOfElements2 = 12;
43.       int numberOfElements3 = 15;
44.       int array[maxNumberOfElements] = {0,1,3,4,-2,43,5,2,10,4,-
          2,43,5,2,10,4,-2,43,5,2,10,4};
45.       int array2[maxNumberOfElements] =
          {0,1,2,3,9,8,3,3,3,3,3,3};
46.       int array3[maxNumberOfElements] = {0,1,2,1,3,3,2,1,3,3,2,1
          ,3,3,2};
```

```
47.
48.    int length = length_of_repeating_sequence(array,
       numberOfElements);
49.    printf("The length of the repeating sequence for array 1
       is %d\n", length);
50.
51.    length = length_of_repeating_sequence(array2,
       numberOfElements2);
52.    printf("The length of the repeating sequence for array 2
       is %d\n", length);
53.
54.    length = length_of_repeating_sequence(array3,
       numberOfElements3);
55.    printf("The length of the repeating sequence for array 3
       is %d\n", length);
56.
57.    return 0;
58. }
```

OUTPUT:

```
The length of the repeating sequence for array 1 is 6

The length of the repeating sequence for array 2 is 1

The length of the repeating sequence for array 3 is 4
```

DIGITS: REVERSE THE DIGITS OF A GIVEN INTEGER

Write a program which reverses the digits of a given integer.

SOLUTION: This program can be done in a straightforward way, with the following steps:

- Extract the digits from the end of the given number, one by one.
- Append these at the end of an integer (this can be done by repeatedly multiplying the integer by 10 and adding the digits).
- If the original number was negative, restore the sign.
- Return the integer built with these steps.

Consider we are given the number -123. We need to remember that the number was negative, so we use a Boolean variable at the beginning of our program. We then perform the following steps:

- Extract 3 from the end of '123'. (this can be done by using the % - mod – operator).
- Append 3 to an integer that will store the reversed number. This integer is 3 at this step.
- Extract 2 from the end of the number and append it to the integer (3 * 10 + 2 = 32).
- Extract 1 and append one more time (32 * 10 + 1 = 321).
- Restore the sign, so our integer now holds -321.
- The algorithm now terminates.

PSEUDO CODE:

```
1.   reverse(number)
2.       reversed_number = 0
3.       while number > 0
4.               reversed_number = reversed_number*10 + number%10
5.               number = number / 10
6.       if number was negative
7.               reversed_number = reversed_number * -1
8.       return reversed_number
```

CLARIFICATION POINT-1:

Can the number be negative?

CLARIFICATION POINT-2:

Can the number end with a 0?

ASSUMPTION/LIMITATION:

- Our program will also work on negative integers.

- We will regard numbers that end with 0 as invalid for the purpose of this program.

MAJOR DATA STRUCTURES:

Integers

UNIT TESTS:	
POSTIVE FUNCTIONAL TEST CASES	
INPUT	EXPECTED OUTPUT
100421 -318953151	124001 -151359813
NEGATIVE FUNCTIONAL TEST CASES	
100	Input invalid

Here is a sample solution that implements the steps described above:

```
1.    #include <cstdio>
2.
3.    int reverse(int number)
4.    {
5.       if (number % 10 == 0)
6.       {
7.              printf("Invalid input!\n");
8.              return 0;
9.       }
10.
11.      // if number is negative make it positive and remember it
         was negative
12.      bool isNegative = false;
13.      if (number < 0)
14.      {
15.             isNegative = true;
16.             number *= -1;
17.      }
18.
19.      // add each digit one by one
20.      int reversed_number = 0;
21.      while (number)
22.      {
```

```
23.                 reversed_number = reversed_number * 10 + number %
                    10;
24.                 number = number / 10;
25.     }
26.
27.     // restore sign
28.     if (isNegative)
29.             reversed_number *= -1;
30.
31.     return reversed_number;
32. }
33.
34. int main()
35. {
36.     int number1 = 100421; int number2 = -318953151;
37.
38.     int reversed_number = reverse(number1);
39.     printf("%d reversed is %d\n", number1, reversed_number);
40.
41.     reversed_number = reverse(number2);
42.     printf("%d reversed is %d\n", number2, reversed_number);
43.
44.     return 0;
45. }
```

OUTPUT:

100421 reversed is 124001

-318953151 reversed is -151359813

BITS: COUNT THE NUMBER OF 1S IN A 32 BIT INTEGER

Give an efficient algorithm to count the number of 1s in a 32 bit integer.

SOLUTION: The first naïve approach would be to convert the 32 bit number into binary and then iterate through each bit, counting those that are set to '1'. Even though this algorithm can run in constant time (32 steps), there is an even more efficient approach to this task, which may save us plenty of time when we integrate this algorithm into a bigger task.

The algorithm we will be using is based on the following ideas:

- Any number that is a power of 2 has only one '1' bit in its binary representation (e.g. 1, 10, 100, etc.).
- An efficient way to check whether a number is a power of 2 or not is to perform a bitwise AND operation between the number and number − 1.

  - ▷ Take, for example, 16, which is represented as 10000 in binary. 16 − 1 = 15, which is 1111. So we notice that for every power of 2, subtracting 1 makes the 1 at the front disappear and all the 0 bits turn into 1 bits. This means that performing a bitwise end operation between n and n-1, where n is a power of 2, will always produce 0.

  - ▷ Let's see what this kind of operation does for numbers that are not powers of 2. For example, $19_{10} = 10011_2$. 18 in base 10 is 10010 in base 2. 10011 AND 10010 = 10010. It may not be clear from only one example, but it appears that this trick clears the rightmost 1 bit from the binary representation of the integer.

  - ▷ Let's consider one extra number, 14, which is 1110. 14-1 = 13 = 1101. We can see that, again, AND-ing the two values removes the rightmost bit in '1110'.

Because of the properties discussed above, we can easily build the following simple algoritm:

- Count = 0;
- While the number is not a power of 2

  - ▷ Count = count + 1;
  - ▷ Remove the rightmost 1-bit from the number using the formula above.

PSEUDO CODE:

```
1.    Number_of_ones(number)
2.        Count = 0;
3.        While number != 0
4.                Number = number AND (number - 1)
5.                Count++;
6.        Return count
```

MAJOR DATA STRUCTURES:

Integers

Here is a sample solution that implements the steps described above:

```
1.    #include <cstdio>
2.
3.    int number_of_ones(int number)
4.    {
5.        int count = 0;
6.
7.        // perform an AND operation applied to
8.        // number and number - 1
9.        while (number)
10.       {
11.               number = number & (number - 1);
12.               count++;
13.       }
14.
15.       return count;
16.   }
17.
18.   int main()
19.   {
20.       int number1 = 7; int number2 = 16; int number3 = 255;
21.
22.       int count = number_of_ones(number1);
23.       printf("The number of 1 bits in the binary representation
          of %d is %d\n", number1, count);
24.
25.       count = number_of_ones(number2);
```

```
26.     printf("The number of 1 bits in the binary representation
        of %d is %d\n", number2, count);
27.
28.     count = number_of_ones(number3);
29.     printf("The number of 1 bits in the binary representation
        of %d is %d\n", number3, count);
30.
31.     return 0;
32. }
```

OUTPUT:

The number of 1 bits in the binary representation of 7 is 3

The number of 1 bits in the binary representation of 16 is 1

The number of 1 bits in the binary representation of 255 is 8

CIRCLE: ROUTINE TO DRAW A CIRCLE

Write a routine to draw a circle (x ** 2 + y ** 2 = r ** 2) without making use of any floating point computations at all.

SOLUTION: First, let's start with the idea of an algorithm. Consider the following circle, with the center in (0,0):

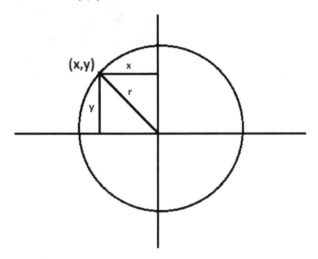

As we can see from the figure, using Pythagoras's theorem, we can deduce that a point with coordinates (X,Y) is located on the surface of the circle if and only if $X^2 + Y^2 = R^2$. We will use this idea to draw our circle. Notice that we do not need to perform any kind of floating computation in our algorithm. The steps are as follows:

- Iterate through all the possible points that can belong to the circle (y-r to y+r for the y axis and x-r to x+r for the x axis);
- If the point belongs to the circle choose a color for it and draw it.

Now, for the drawing part we will use the windows.h library. In order to make this work at its full capacity, an IDE such as Microsoft Visual Studio is recommended. As you can see from the code below, windows.h comes with certain useful functions, such as GetConsoleWindow(), which returns an instance of the terminal that appears on the screen after a program in C++ is run. We can then manipulate this terminal to draw pixels at the coordinates we specify using the SetPixel() method, as you can see from the program above.

Notice that if we use the $x^2 + y^2 = r^2$ relation, the program would only draw the exterior of the circle, as follows:

However, in order to make our circles look better, we will use the condition $x^2 + y^2 < r^2$, which draws the whole interior of a circle, as you can see in the 'Output' section below.

PSEUDO CODE:

```
1.    Draw_circle(x,y,r)
2.        Console = get console window
3.        Context = context(console)
4.
5.        For j = y-r to y+r
6.                For i = x-r to x+r
7.                        If ((i-x)² + (j-y)² < r²)
8.                                Draw pixel at (i,j) in console
```

MAJOR DATA STRUCTURES:

Integers, console window

Here is a sample solution that implements the steps described above:

```
1.    #include "stdafx.h"
2.    #include <windows.h>
3.    #include <iostream>
4.    #include <cmath>
5.
6.    using namespace std;
7.
8.    #define PI 3.14
9.
10.   void draw_circle(int x, int y, int r)
11.   {
12.      //console handle
13.      HWND console = GetConsoleWindow();
```

```
14.     //get context
15.     HDC context = GetDC(console);
16.
17.     //Choose any color
18.     COLORREF yellow= RGB(255,255,0);
19.
20.     for(int yCoord = y - r; yCoord <= y + r; yCoord++)
21.     {
22.             for (int xCoord = x - r; xCoord <= x + r; xCoord++)
23.             {
24.                     if (((xCoord - x)*(xCoord - x)+(yCoord -
                        y)*(yCoord - y)) < r * r)
25.                     SetPixel(context, xCoord, yCoord, yellow);
26.             }
27.     }
28.
29.     // make the console wait
30.     cin.ignore();
31. }
32.
33. int main()
34. {
35.     draw_circle(100, 100, 50);
36.     draw_circle(250, 100, 50);
37.     return 0;
38. }
```

Output:

ARDS: SHUFFLING A DECK OF CARDS

This module solves a coding problem that involves shuffling a deck of cards. The problem Description is as follows:

- **You are given a deck containing n cards. While holding the deck:**
- **Take the top card off the deck and set it on the table**
- **Take the next card off the top and put it on the bottom of the deck in your hand.**
- **Continue steps 1 and 2 until all cards are on the table. This is a round.**
- **Pick up the deck from the table and repeat steps 1-3 until the deck is in the original order.**

Write a program to determine how many rounds it will take to put a deck back into the original order. This will involve creating a data structure to represent the order of the cards. This Program should be written in C or C++. Do not use STL. It should take a number of cards in the deck as a command line argument and write the result to stdout.

SOLUTION: Our program will be written in Visual C++ and will consist of a simulation of the actual game. The steps we will be performing are the following:

1. Remove the top card from the deck;
2. Set the card just removed on the table;
3. Take the next card off the top and place it at the bottom of the deck;
4. Repeat until all cards are on the table. A round has ended at this point.
5. Compare the original order with the current order
   a) If they are qual, then the game has finished;
   b) If not, we need to continue;
6. Pick up the deck from the table and repeat first four steps.

```
CLARIFICATION POINT-1:
```

```
What is the specific value of the number of cards?
```

CLARIFICATION POINT-2:

What kind of environment does the program need to be developed in?

ASSUMPTION/LIMITATION:

- We will assume the number of cards is between 1 and 52, as there are 52 cards in a standard pack. At the same time, we will use Visual Studio C++ as a development environment.

MAJOR DATA STRUCTURES:

Array of integers

Here is a sample answer, running in O(N):

```
1.    #include "stdafx.h"
2.    #include <stdio.h>
3.    #include <stdlib.h>
4.    #include <string.h>
5.    #include <common.h>
6.    #include <HandFunctions.h>
7.    #include <TableFunctions.h>
8.
9.    int _tmain(int argc, char* argv[])
10.   {
11.       CARD *psTopCardInHand = NULL;                  /* Top Card
                                                             Node In Hand
                                                             */
12.       CARD *psBottomCardInHand = NULL;               /* Bottom Card
                                                             Node In Hand
                                                             */
13.
14.       CARD *pOriginalTopCardInHand = NULL;           /* Original
                                                             Top Card Node
                                                             In Hand */
15.       CARD *psOriginalBottomCardInHand = NULL;       /* Original
                                                             Bottom Card
                                                             Node In Hand
                                                             */
16.
17.       CARD *psTopCardOnTable = NULL;                 /* Top Card
                                                             Node In Table
                                                             */
18.       unsigned short uiTotalCardOnTable = 0;         /* At a Time
                                                             Total Card in
                                                             Table */
19.       unsigned short uiCardIndex = 0;                /* Card Index
                                                             */
20.       unsigned short uiCardVal = 0;                  /* Card Value
                                                             */
```

```
21.    unsigned short uiTotalCard = 0;              /* Total Card
                                                    to Shuffle */
22.    unsigned short LOG = 0;
23.    unsigned short argIndex =  0;                /* Argument
                                                    Index */
24.    unsigned short OriginalOrder =  0;           /* Flag to
                                                    test the Order
                                                    */
25.    unsigned short iResult =  0;                 /* Flag to
                                                    test the
                                                    Function
                                                    Result */
26.
27.
28.    /////////////////////////////Command Line Argument Handling
       - Begin //////////////////////////////////
29.    if( argc != 2 ) // argc should be 2 for correct execution
30.    {
31.     Usage();
32.    }
33.
34.    argIndex = argc;
35.
36.    if(argv[--argIndex])
37.    {
38.       uiTotalCard = atoi((const char *)argv[argIndex]);
39.       /*
40.       On success, atoi function returns the converted integral
          number as an int value.
41.       If no valid conversion could be performed, a zero value
          is returned.
42.       If the correct value is out of the range of
          representable values, INT_MAX or INT_MIN is returned.
43.       */
44.       if (CheckRange(uiTotalCard))   /* Maximum Value of Card -
          52 */
45.       {
46.              Usage();
47.       }
48.       if(argc == 3)
49.       {
50.              if(strcmp((const char *)argv[--argIndex],"-l")
                 == 0)
51.              {
52.                   LOG = TRUE;
53.              }
54.
55.              else
56.              {
57.                   Usage();
58.              }
```

```
59.        }
60.
61.    }
62.    //////Command Line Argument Handling - End//////  //
       Intialize Index of each card
63.    if(TRUE != PickUpTheDeckFromTheTable(&psTopCardInHand,
64.    &psBottomCardInHand,
65.     uiTotalCard))
66.    {
67.        printf(" PickUpTheDeckFromTheTable :Intilization of
           Cards Failed");
68.        exit(0);
69.    }
70.
71.    // To Preserve Original Order
72.    if(TRUE !=PickUpTheDeckFromTheTable(&pOriginalTopCardInHa
       nd,
73.    &psOriginalBottomCardInHand,
74.    uiTotalCard))
75.    {
76.        printf(" PickUpTheDeckFromTheTable : Intilization of
           Cards Failed");
77.        exit(0);
78.    }
79.
80.    // Maximum number of round for given number of card
81.    // = Given No of Card * Given No of Card;
82.    // For Card 1 to 52 it shows number of pass not more than
       Given number of Card.
83.    // Complexity up to 52 cards is Order-N (In terms of
       Number of Full Rounds)
84.    // Once Count Increases from 52, e.g - 54 it shows Total
       number of Rounds = 1680
85.    // However on small number it shows rounds like this :
86.    // Number of Cards = 1--->>Number of Rounds = 1
87.    // Number of Cards = 2--->>Number of Rounds = 2
88.    // Number of Cards = 3--->>Number of Rounds = 3
89.    // Number of Cards = 4--->>Number of Rounds = 2
90.    // Number of Cards = 5--->>Number of Rounds = 5
91.    // Number of Cards = 6--->>Number of Rounds = 6
92.    // Number of Cards = 15--->>Number of Rounds = 15
93.    //.
94.    //.
95.    //.
96.    //Number of Cards = 52--->>Number of Rounds = 510
97.    //.
98.    //.
99.    //.
100.   //Number of Cards = 101--->>Number of Rounds = 3360
101.   //.
102.   //.
```

```
103.    //.
104.    //Number of Cards = 120--->>Number of Rounds = 120
105.    for(uiCardIndex = 1;uiCardIndex <=
        (uiTotalCard*uiTotalCard) ; uiCardIndex++)
106.    {
107.       uiCardVal = 0;
108.       /* No More Card On Hand */
109.       while(!IsNoMoreCardOnHand(psBottomCardInHand))
110.       {
111.        /* Take The Top Card Off The Deck Step-1*/
112.        iResult = TakeTheTopCardOffTheDeck(&psTopCardInHand,
113.        &psBottomCardInHand,
114.        &uiCardVal);
115.            if(iResult != TRUE)
116.            {
117.                    printf("TakeTheTopCardOffTheDeck Error");
118.                    exit(0);
119.            }
120.            /* Set it On the Table Step-1*/
121.            iResult = SetItOnTheTable(&psTopCardOnTable,&uiTot
            alCardOnTable,uiCardVal);
122.            if(iResult != TRUE)
123.            {
124.                    printf("print appropriate error");
125.                    exit(0);
126.            }
127.             /* Take the next card off the top Step-2*/
128.            iResult = TakeTheTopCardOffTheDeck(&psTopCardInHa
            nd,
129.               &psBottomCardInHand,
130.            .  &uiCardVal);
131.            if(iResult != TRUE)
132.            {
133.                    if(iResult == CARDS_FINISHED_FROM_DECK)
134.                    {
135.                            break;
136.                    }else
137.                    {
138.                            printf("TakeTheTopCardOffTheDeck
                            error");
139.                            exit(0);
140.                    }
141.            }
142.
143.            /* put it on the bottom of the deck in your hand.
            Step-2*/
144.            iResult = PutItOnTheBottomOfTheDeckInYourHand(&psT
            opCardInHand,
145.            &psBottomCardInHand,
146.            uiCardVal);
147.            if(iResult != TRUE)
```

```
148.                    {
149.                            printf("PutItOnTheBottomOfTheDeckInYourHand
                               error");
150.                            exit(0);
151.                    }
152.
153.            /*
154.                Continue steps 1 and 2 until all cards are on
                    the table.
155.                This is a round.
156.                Step -3
157.            */
158.        } // end While(!IsNoMoreCardOnHand(psBottomCardInHand))
159.
160.        if(LOG)
161.        {
162.                printf("\n\t\t-Current Order - Round : %d\t\t\
                    n",uiCardIndex);
163.                iResult = Print(psTopCardOnTable,uiTotalCard);
164.                if(iResult != TRUE)
165.                {
166.                    printf("Print Error");
167.                    exit(0);
168.                }
169.                printf("\n\t\t-----------------\t\t\n");
170.        }
171.
172.        /* Compare Originial Order with Current Order */
173.        if((psTopCardOnTable->uiCardIndex ==
           pOriginalTopCardInHand->uiCardIndex))
174.        {
175.            if (CompareOrder(psTopCardOnTable,pOriginalTopCard
               InHand,uiTotalCard))
176.            {
177.                    OriginalOrder = TRUE;  /* if Equal -
                    Success */
178.            }
179.        }else
180.        {
181.                    OriginalOrder = FALSE;   /* else - Continue
                    */
182.        }
183.
184.        /* if Equal - Success */
185.        if(OriginalOrder)
186.        {
187.                printf("\n\nNumber of Rounds put this deck
                    back into the original order.\n\n");
188.                printf("\t\t\t-- %d --\n",uiCardIndex);
189.                break;
190.        }
```

```
191.
192.            uiTotalCardOnTable = uiTotalCard;
193.
194.            while(!IsNoMoreCardOnTable(uiTotalCardOnTable))
195.            {
196.                    /* Pick up the deck from the table - Step-4
                       */
197.                    if(TRUE == PickUpTheCardFromTheTable(&psTop
                       CardOnTable,
198.                    &uiTotalCardOnTable ,
199.                    &uiCardVal))
200.                    {
201.                            iResult = PutItOnTheBottomOfTheDeckI
                               nYourHand(&psTopCardInHand,
202.
               &psBottomCardInHand,
203.
               uiCardVal);
204.                            if(iResult != TRUE)
205.                            {
206.                                    printf("PickUpTheCardFromTheT
                                       able Error");
207.                                    exit(0);
208.                            }
209.
210.                    }else {
211.                        exit(0);
212.                    }
213.        }// End while(IsNoMoreCardOnTable(uiTotalCardOnTable))
214.            /*repeat steps 1-3 until the deck is in the
                   original order.Step-4 */
215.    }// End for
216.
217. }// End Main
```

```
DeckOfCards.exe -l 3

Usage    :    DeckOfCards -l DeckOfCards

(Mandatory)NumberOfCards : Deck of Cards<1..52>

(OPTIONAL) -l                : Show Full Sequence while putting
deck back in Original Order

             -Current Order - Round : 1

- 2 - - 3 - - 1 -

             ------------------

             -Current Order - Round : 2

- 3 - - 1 - - 2 -

             ------------------

             -Current Order - Round : 3

- 1 - - 2 - - 3 -

             ------------------

Number of Rounds put this deck back into the original order.

                  -- 3 -

…>DeckOfCards.exe 52

Number of Rounds put this deck back into the original order.

     -- 510 --
```

SERIES: MISSING INTEGER

You have a tape with all but one of the integers between 1 and 1,000,000. No duplicates. You can read it once, after which it will self-destruct.

- **Implement the code to find the missing integer**
- **Outline why you selected your approach to solving the problem**
- **Document any assumptions that you make**

SOLUTION: There are two main approaches that can be taken into account for solving this task. We will start with the most inefficient of the two which uses a hash table. The steps of this algorithm are the following:

1. Create an initially empty look-up table (hash table) of 1,000,000 Boolean values with the following meaning:

   ▷ Table[i] = true if and only if element i was found in the tape.

2. Iterate through the tape (represented as an array of integers) and mark the position of each element found in the hash table with true.

3. Iterate through the hash table, with an index from 1 to 1,000,000 and check which of the index has the value false. This is the element missing from the array.

There is, however, a much more efficient approach in terms of memory, which does not even need a hash table to achieve the task. Instead, this approach will be based on a formula from mathematics. This formula is often used in arithmetic progressions and can be expressed in the following way:

- $1 + 2 + 3 + \ldots + n = n*(n + 1) / 2$;

Now that we have a formula to compute the sum of the 1,000,000 numbers given in this problem, we can develop the following algorithm:

1. Let nSum be the sum of the complete tape (the sum of the numbers between 1 and 1,000,000).

2. Compute the sum of the numbers that are actually in the tape (our array of integers). Call this variable tapeSum.

3. The element we are looking for will always be given by nSum – tapeSum.

For example, suppose our tape contains numbers from 1 to 5. Given the initial configuration {1,2,4,5} we can check 3 is the element missing by performing the following subtraction:

- $(1 + 2 + 3 + 4 + 5) - (1 + 2 + 4 + 5) = 3$.

Because the sum of the numbers between 1 and 1,000,000 can get quite large, we will use variables of type 'unsigned long long', rather than int.

PSEUDO CODE:

```
1.   FindMissingInteger(arr, n):
2.              tapeSum = 0 nSum = 0
3.              nSum = n*(n+1)/2
4.              for tapeIndex from 0 to n
5.                    tapeSum = tapeSum + arr[tapeIndex]
6.              return nSum - tapeSum
```

CLARIFICATION POINT-1:

Which of the two algorithms described above will we use?

ASSUMPTION/LIMITATION:

- We will use the second algorithm from those described, as this is more efficient in terms of space and time.

MAJOR DATA STRUCTURES:

Array of integers

UNIT TESTS:	
POSTIVE FUNCTIONAL TEST CASES	
INPUT	EXPECTED OUTPUT
{0,1,2,4,5,6,7,…,1000000}	3
NEGATIVE FUNCTIONAL TEST CASES	
Array size < 0	Invalid input

Here is a sample answer:

```
1.   unsigned int FindMissingInteger(unsigned int arr[],unsigned
     int arrlen)
2.   {
3.   unsigned long nSum = 0;
4.   unsigned long tapeSum = 0;
5.   unsigned long tapeIndex;
6.   // Sum from integer 1 to n is n*(n+1)/2
7.   nSum = (N * (N + 1))<< 1;
8.   for(tapeIndex = 0; tapeIndex < N ;tapeIndex++)
9.   {
10.  tapeSum += tapeSum + arr[tapeIndex];
11.  }
12.  return (nSum - tapeSum);
13.  }
```

Further reads for Coding and Algorithms

CODING:

C++ Primer Plus (6th Edition) (Developer's Library)	Stephen Prata
The C++ Programming Language, 4th Edition	Bjarne Stroustrup
Effective C++: 55 Specific Ways to Improve Your Programs and Designs (3rd Edition)	Scott Meyers
C++ Concurrency in Action: Practical Multithreading	Anthony Williams
Modern C++ Design: Generic Programming and Design Patterns Applied	Elisabeth Freeman, Eric Freeman, Bert Bates, Kathy Sierra, Elisabeth Robson

ALGORITHMS:

Introduction to Algorithms	Thomas H. Cormen, Charles E. Leiserson, Ronald L. Rivest, Clifford Stein
An Introduction to the Analysis of Algorithms (2nd Edition)	Robert Sedgewick, Philippe Flajolet
Foundations of Algorithms, Fourth Edition	Richard Neapolitan, Kumarss Naimipour
Concrete Mathematics: A Foundation for Computer Science (2nd Edition)	Ronald L. Graham, Donald E. Knuth, Oren Patashnik
Data Structures and Algorithms	Alfred V. Aho, Jeffrey D. Ullman, John E. Hopcroft

Test Areas

Software Quality and Testing requires the ability to programmatically/non-programmatically test the product, measure test coverage, develop the best automation, and drive testability and diagnostic ability into the product, while promoting the best practices in quality areas.

TEST LABS, TEST A HTML PAGE, TEST A DATA CENTER, TEST A CONTENT DELIVERY NETWORK, SETUP TO TEST CLOUD COMPUTING LABS, TEST MOBILE APPLICATIONS, TEST SERVER APPLICATIONS, TEST CONNECTIVITY, TEST OPERATING SYSTEM, TEST VOICE OVER BASED SOLUTIONS, TEST 3G NETWORK, TEST MOBILE CALL, TEST REAL TIME SYSTEMS, TEST A LOGGING FRAMEWORK, TEST A LIBRARY, TEST A IDE, TEST BUILD SYSTEM, TEST A GUI

Software Development Engineer, Test (SDET), Test / Quality Assurance (QA) Engineer (Computer Software), Test / Quality Assurance (QA) Engineer (Integrated Circuit), **Test / Quality Assurance (QA) Engineer**, (Computer Networking), Test Analyst, Test Engineer (Automation), Test Engineer, Automation, Test Engineer, Computer Hardware, Test Engineer, **Test Engineering Manager**, Test Manager, **Software Lead Tester**, Software Quality Analyst, Software Quality Assurance (SQA) Analyst, **Software Quality Assurance (SQA) Engineer**, Software Quality Assurance (SQA) Lead, **Software Quality Assurance (SQA) Lead Tester,** Software Quality Assurance (SQA) Manager, Software Quality Assurance (SQA) Specialist, **Software Quality Assurance (SQA) Supervisor**, Software Quality Control (QC) Analyst, Software Quality Control (QC) Manager, **Software Quality Engineer Manager, Software Quality Tester,**, Software Team Leader, **Software Technical Training Coordinator**, Software Test Analyst, Software Test Associate, **Software Test Engineer (STE)**

TEST CONCEPTS/ FREQUENTLY USED TERMS	**TOOLS/SCRIPT/ LANGUAGES**	**TEST STRATEGIES/ STANDARDS**

Bug Reports, Test Plan, **Test Area Breakdown**, Test Environments, **Equivalence classing, Release Testing**, System **Integration Testing**, Subsystem Integration Testing, Automation **Testing**, Development of Automated Test Tool, **Writing Test Scripts**, Module Testing, **Test Cases Development**, Test Plan, Test Execution, **White/Black box** Testing, API Testing, Full Test Life cycle, **Acceptance Testing**, Regression Testing, **Feature Testing…**

Cucumber,
Fitnesse,
HP QuickTest Professional,
IBM Rational Functional Tester,
LabVIEW,
Maveryx,
Oracle Application Testing Suite,
QF-Test Quality,
Ranorex Ranorex GmbH,
Rational robot,
Robot Framework,
Selenium,
SilkTest,
eggPlant,
EiffelStudio AutoTest,
SOAtest,
TestComplete,
Testing Anywhere,
TestPartner,
Time Partition Testing (TPT),
TOSCA Test suite,
Visual Studio Test Professional,
Watir,
Telerik, WinCE, 3G Test tools, Database test tools, Bad Boy, HP Load Runner
C++, C#, Tᴄʟ, Exᴘᴇᴄᴛ, Jᴀᴠᴀ, PHP, Pᴇʀʟ, Pᴏᴡᴇʀsʜᴇʟʟ, Pʏᴛʜᴏɴ, ᴏʀ Rᴜʙʏ…

Pᴇʀғᴏʀᴍᴀɴᴄᴇ Tᴇsᴛ Cᴀsᴇs: Test the performance of this function, when data in note or book is fairly large or note has fewer words but the book has very large data or vice versa. Rᴇɢʀᴇssɪᴏɴ Tᴇsᴛɪɴɢ: If this function gets updated because of some reason or requirement change, then regression test cases required. Sᴄᴇɴᴀʀɪᴏ Tᴇsᴛɪɴɢ: Various use cases need to explore based on its actual use, and then its test cases could be written. **Globalization test cases:** If this function supports multiple languages, as its string supports char in Unicode format, so similar test needs to perform on different languages. Mᴜʟᴛɪᴘʟᴇ Tʜʀᴇᴀᴅs: If this function will be used in Multithreading environment, Tᴇsᴛ Lᴀʙs, Dᴇᴠᴇʟᴏᴘᴍᴇɴᴛ ᴏғ ᴠᴀʀɪᴏᴜs ᴄᴜsᴛᴏᴍɪᴢᴇᴅ ᴛᴇsᴛ ᴛᴏᴏʟs, ʟᴏɢ ᴘᴀʀsɪɴɢ ᴛᴏᴏʟs, ʙᴜɪʟᴅ ᴠᴇʀɪғɪᴄᴀᴛɪᴏɴ ᴛᴏᴏʟs…
Test Driven development, efficiency of software system,
KAIZEN,
Quality Assurance Plan,
Quality Control,
Reliability of a software system,
Software Quality Attributes,
Testability of a software system…

TEST INTERVIEWS

Apple, Microsoft, Amazon, Google, Adobe and many other companies have specific test positions:

- Software Development engineer in test
- Software Quality Engineer in Test
- Software Engineer in Test
- Software Test Engineer
- Software Quality Engineers
- …

It's not straightforward to measure the test activity, as there are a lot of things to do in terms of testing, and this is an incremental activity.

You may be assigned a project that requires testing an HTML page or testing a GUI or desktop or mobile application or set up the test lab or the content delivery network or the data center or the security test or GPS system or the real-time system or the battery power or anything.

And if somehow you are interested to apply a job for test profile, then definitely the interviewer would like to talk with you and discuss with you various test related things to see:

- Whether you are comfortable testing tools and products
- If you really understand the real meaning of test
- How you can make the product solid
- …

WHAT TYPE OF JOB INTERVIEW DISCUSSION ONE MAY EXPECT FOR TESTING POSITIONS ?

It all depends on the level of position example:

If the hiring is happening for a test manager position, if yes, then it require to interview or to ask or to discuss the set of core points, so that the interviewee can prove his capabilities to handle or manage the product for test.

But most interviews discuss following things for sure e.g. if we talk about the software test engineers or any positions related to the test profile Test concepts

- Test tools and scripting languages
- Test standards and strategies
- Past experience in testing

- Attitude towards testing
- Current learning about testing
- Behaviour towards the next level career on testing
- Accomplishment made on testing e.g. development of a test tool

You must understand the actual test task could be anything, example:

Testing the Google maps or Microsoft Internet Explorer or MS office or Facebook's timeline feature or Facebook data center or Amazon cloud computing solutions or Apple iPhone related features, applications, device drivers, GUI and many other things.

That again consist various modules, and then again there will be a set of people who will be responsible for a single module, and by having the complete team-work, all people working to deliver the stable product or the test task for what they responsible for.

Such test related job profile require to use test concepts, test tools, programming languages, development of various strategies, standards and then preparing the best strategy/approach to test the business solution. This is a continuous activity it's huge.

But on interviews the questions are small (e.g. usual duration of single interview is from 45 minutes to 60 minutes, it can have single to multiple rounds). The questions are made on such a way, so that required job profile's skills and expertise can be tested based on the individual's test related offerings (as defined on his CV).

This chapter explains the set of sample question/ answers related to the test interviews, so that an interviewee can prepare himself based on the offering he would be going to make for the employer.

What are the elements of a good bug report?

RATIONALE: *One of the basic activity for a software test professional is to discover the bugs and log it.*

SAMPLE ANSWER FROM A PROFESSIONAL POINT OF VIEW

Bug reports depend on case by case. Few bugs are straightforward, which might not require to fill every single field.

- X module is not running, and to execute a test case 'A' require 'X' to run. So it's a show stopper, and straight forward (make sure to check whether such bug already exist)

- By filling a specific web form for a particular functionality on a web application. It's not inserting various other data fields into the database. This bug requires to provide all inputs, e.g. regarding the data connections, may be the table name where value didn't fill up, get values based on some rules from other data tables, information about those tables, process followed, what environment was settled up. Maybe, there was a requirement to set some default values before executing this test case, many things, so this test case requires detailed information then just as usual.

Altogether following are the common fields to fill up for such a bug –report, yes its required to write the description, but it should be narrow down to concerned module than an open-ended bug description.

- Bug heading
- Detailed bug descriptions, (including logs location if any, dump files if any, screen shots if any, reference to any design or requirement document),
- The scenario when this bug was found
- Reason why this is bug?
- Category of this bug, severe or mild
- Various other dependent parameters e.g.; module it's found, or feature name, version of this release,
- Priority of this bug e.g.; P0, P1, P2 or show stopper etc.
- Very important thing is its reproducibility information

TEST PLAN: GOOD TEST PLAN

What are the elements that make a good test plan?

RATIONALE: *Test plan is the organized approach for the testing of a product/feature/module in question.*

SAMPLE ANSWER FROM A PROFESSIONAL POINT OF VIEW

Writing a test plan it's not straight forward and has pre-defined set of items to write. Its all depends on what kind of testing it is and various other parameters, e.g.; clearing requirement, test environment, timeline, project phase, role, resources, dependency, targeted customer, end user(different age group, or different profession), targeted industry, interoperability, conformance product specification, requirement use cases.

If this were an Operating System, subsequent test plan elements would be different, and if it would be web application, then test plan items would be different. on the network protocols testing, there might be a component to consider the rfc standards, interoperability and data centric web application will have more concerns with database functionality.

Altogether following test plan elements must be available in a test plan, but again, its description would be different based on the type of project and may be some other additional items.

- Measured coverage of test
- What to test what not to be test
- References to various other artifacts, e.g.; requirements considered
- Test area breakdown, if that is a module or integrations of various modules
- What kind of testing going to perform
- Possible functional testing – which again divided in positive and negative testing
- Non-functional testing – e.g.; performance, stress
- Globalization testing
- Accessibility testing
- Open points if any
- Timeline
- List of test cases
- Automation criteria

- Test case classifications with priorities
- Test time line
- Test environments

TYPE OF TESTING: EQUIVALENCE CLASSIFYING

What is equivalence classifying?

RATIONALE: *Various test related theoretical technical words exist, and a interviewer would like to understand the interviewee's practical comments on that.*

SAMPLE ANSWER FROM A PROFESSIONAL **POINT OF VIEW**

However in broad term if we see that we always do the equivalence class testing, as we have a full project to test and it has several modules, which have already divided in equivalence groups, and then such modules again divided to its sub modules and so on, this what is also a practice of equivalence classing.

TYPE OF TESTING: FUNCTIONAL VERSUS INTEGRATION TESTING

What is the difference between functional and integration testing?

RATIONALE: *Various test related theoretical technical words exist, and a interviewer would like to understand the interviewee's practical comments on that.*

SAMPLE ANSWER FROM A PROFESSIONAL POINT OF VIEW

Following is the generic difference between the functional testing and integration testing,

However, on functional testing, the more concentration into the operational aspects of the individual application or may be whole system. The integration testing more concern into the unification, to check whether the integration across modules happened correctly (which might lead to regression testing to check that).

TYPE OF TESTING: BLACK AND WHITE BOX TESTING

What is the difference between black and white box testing?

RATIONALE: *One of the standard question which is known to every software professional. But here the interviewer would like to understand interviewee's practical comment on this.*

SAMPLE ANSWER FROM A PROFESSIONAL **POINT OF VIEW**

Black Box – When a functional item to be tested based on the given input and received output, without indulging the internal implementation of that functional item as an individual or whole system.

White Box – When a functional item to be tested based on the given input and received output, with indulging the internal implementation of that functional item as an individual or whole system.

It all depends what on the view of a professional to say what is black and white e.g.

- An API can be treated as a black box testing: A test objective is required to test an API (application programming interface) for given set of input values and in return expect corresponding values.

- An API can be treated as a white box testing: A test objective is required to test a API (application programming interface) for given set of input values and to test internal flow of that API e.g. how implemented logic has been exercised based on the given input values, all logic paths are exercised from the given input values.

TYPE OF TESTING: KINDS OF TESTING HAVE YOU DONE

What kinds of testing have you done in the past?

RATIONALE: *Interviewer would like to understand the interviewee's test related experience.*

SAMPLE ANSWER FROM A PROFESSIONAL POINT OF VIEW

Type of testing can have standard name or a project specific names e.g. testing of 'A' module in project 'XYZ', release testing of a software product 'XYZ'.

In my experience, I was involved in several projects and performed distinct type of testing based on the project needs, and that could be called with diverse types of names, e.g. Release Testing, System Integration Testing, Subsystem Integration Testing, Automation Testing, Development of Automated Test Tool, Writing Test Scripts, Module Testing, Test Cases Development, Test Plan, Test Execution, White/Black box Testing, API Testing, Full Test Life cycle, Acceptance Testing, Regression Testing, Feature Testing

TEST TOOL:
YOUR UNDERSTANDING RELATED TO A TEST TOOL

May you please define your understanding related to a test tool?

RATIONALE: *A software test and quality professional performs diverse types of testing by having clear test-objectives and several other test related parameters. Various functional/non-functional testing could be achieved via Test-Tools, as more automation will happen, it will take less time to test especially in regression and incremental release of that software product. Several test-tools might be used out of the box, but on many work situations, it requires to write a test tool from scratch.*

Interviewer wants to understand whether the interviewee has ever written any test tool from scratch or what type of thought-process he or she keeps relating to a test tool.

SAMPLE ANSWER FROM A PROFESSIONAL POINT OF VIEW

The test-tool is something, which facilitates the test process by automating the set of manual actions required to test functional/non-functional item.

EXAMPLE -1

In software, where a functional item requires receiving user's input, process it and provide a feedback to a user, e.g. successful and non-successful cases.

Rather, a test professional prepares a set of inputs, and manually enters those inputs to the software to test successful/non-successful test cases. It's better to write a test automation, which can generate all possible types of input and generates a test report.

EXAMPLE -2

A test tool can be a library of a set of functions, which are developed to generate relevant input for the developed APIs under test.

EXAMPLE -3

A test tool can be to ease the access of test results: In a situation, various test cases of different-2 modules have been tested, and their logs have been separately stored on a pre-configured/default location. So rather than user digging to particular location and finding out the details of any specific test cases, a test- tool can provide provides a summary report of all the executed test cases and linked towards their detailed log.

SAMPLE ANSWER FROM A PROFESSIONAL POINT OF VIEW

As a software test professionals I analyze automation based on measured test coverage, test activities and test tool automates testability, e.g. I might need to test same test multiple times, because an incremental release of X.

Developing or using any existing test tool is not a straight-forward activity. It all depends on test requirements.

- Test tools or test stub might need to develop from scratch; e.g. development of a device driver might require automation for its API exposed to system applications.
- Customization of existing test tool; e.g. based on the load requirement, it required to perform some configuration at Apache Jmeter Test Tool.

In my experience, I wrote several test tools e.g.

* Wrote a tool which parses log files, prepare a summary report and e-mail to set of people.

* Test cases automation for various features of the software product Xs, e.g.; audit every user action by using record and playback frameworks

* Wrote a test tool which automates various SIP calls signalling flow.

TEST CASES: TEST A SODA MACHINE

How Would You Test a Soda Machine?

RATIONALE: *Its very common for a interviewer to put some open-ended questions and observe the interviewee's thought process.*

SAMPLE ANSWER FROM A PROFESSIONAL POINT OF VIEW

Test a Soda Machine, It's just a word, It doesn't provide full information for testing, some of my ideas related to this open ended question e.g.

MEASURING TEST COVERAGE

- In terms of a feature; Test the tap function while serving the soda, Measure the iciness of soda, measure the size of a soda container while filling and then measure the size of soda while getting from tap
- In terms of part; iciness module, cooling engine, soda tapped functions, tank functions.

TEST ENVIRONMENT

- Test the coolness of soda machine on certain weather condition,
- Test the freshness of soda while serving to customer on different-2 conditions,
- Test the taste of soda by preserving soda n number of days on different temperature,
- Test the soda machine on certain simulated environment

WHEN TO TEST

- Test while manufacturing the soda machine, e.g. test the solidness of a cabinet, test the leakage of the tank.
- Test on time to time on different-2 phases of manufacturing of soda machine
- Test the usability of machine
- Test the machine after assembly

If you please let me know some specific/exact information about soda machine then the above approach can be made specific.

TEST CASES:
NOTE THAT IS CONSTRUCTED USING WORDS

Imagine a note that is constructed using words cut out from a book (e.g. If the book was "I am a very short and useless book" then "very useless" and "I am a book" can be constructed using words from the book while "and books" cannot). Implement the following function [the function header is intentionally given in pseudo-code]

/* bool CanConstructNote(string note, string book) */

The function returns true if the note can be constructed using words from the book and false otherwise.

Provide as few test cases as you need to completely test the sanity of the function. For each test case state specifically what condition it tests.

RATIONALE: *Interviewer would like to observe interviewee's approach while deducing the test cases of a sample problem.*

SAMPLE ANSWER FROM A PROFESSIONAL POINT OF VIEW

TEST REQUIREMENT

Imagine a note that is constructed using words cut out from a book (e.g. If the book was "I am a very short and useless book" then "very useless" and "I am a book" can be constructed using words from the book while "and books" cannot).

```
bool CanConstructNote( string note, string book)
```

TEST ENVIRONMENT

Tools Used: Microsoft Visual Studio 2005, Version 8.0.50727.762

Operating System: Microsoft Windows Vista Home Premium Service Pack 1

Hardware: Intel(R) Core(TM)2 Duo CPU, T7250 @ 2.00 Ghz, 2 GB Of RAM

SANITY TEST CASES

<Functional Positive Tests>

CASE-1: When note has been constructed from Book by taking fewer words.

Input :

Book "I am a very short and useless book"

Note "useless book"

Expected output : TRUE

CASE-2 : When note has been constructed from Book, and note has been constructed by taking all words from Book

Input :

Book "I am a very short and useless book"

Note "I am a very short and useless book"

Expected output : TRUE

CASE-3: When note and book have special characters

Input :

Book "~!@$#%^#@%$^&$^#@%$^"

Note "~@!#$%#@!~# !~@#$^%#@%$ ~!@#$%"

Expected output : TRUE

CASE-4: When note and book have digits

Input :

Book "Sumit has wrote test cases 6 and 12"

Note "Sumit has 6 and 12"

Expected output : TRUE

<Functional Negative Tests>

CASE-1: When Book is empty have no words.

Input :

Book ""

Note "I am a very short and useless book"

Expected output : FALSE

CASE-2: When note is empty have no words.

Input :

Book "I am a very short and useless book"

Note ""

Expected output : FALSE

CASE-3 When note and book both are empty have no words

Input :

Book ""

Note ""

Expected output : FALSE

(Its assumed that book or note can note consider the empty value)

CASE-4: When note and book are not empty but note cannot be constructed from book

Input :

Book "I am a very short and useless book"

Note "and books"

Expected output : FALSE

SPECIAL TEST CASES

- Performance test cases: Test the performance of this function, when data in note or book is fairly large or note has fewer words but the book has very large data or vice versa.
- Regression testing: If this function gets updated because of some reason or requirement change, then regression test cases required.
- Scenario testing: Various use cases need to explore based on its actual use, and then its test cases could be written.

- Globalization test cases: If this function supports multiple languages, as its string supports char in unicode format, so similar test needs to perform on different languages.

- Multiple Threads: If this function will be used in Multithreading environment

- Test Harness: Its automation also possible, when test cases randomly generate book values and note values to test consistency for all positive, negative, special test cases.

TEST CASES: TEST TO REMOVE ALL NODES WITH EVEN VALUES

Given a function as "removeAllNodesWithEvenValues" to remove all nodes with even values

Provide a set of test cases to test this function.

Function Signature : BOOL removeAllNodesWithEvenValues(node ** llist)

llist – Head node singly linked list of integers

BOOL – enum BOOL {TRUE,FALSE};

node – typedef struct node{ int data; node *next} *pnode;

RATIONALE: *Interviewer would like to observe interviewee's approach while deducing the test cases of a sample problem.*

SAMPLE ANSWER FROM A PROFESSIONAL **POINT OF VIEW**

TEST ENVIRONMENT

API Name: BOOL removeAllNodesWithEvenValues(node ** llist)

OS: Windows-Vista

Target Platform: MachineX86 (/MACHINE: X86)/32-bit

Language Used: C Language/ Visual C++ 2005 (Compiler)

Integers range on 32 bit machine: 2147483647 to -2147483648

TEST CASES

<Error Test Cases>

    PARAMETER CHECKS

    INPUT: Passing head node of the linked as NULL

    Expected OUTPUT: Function should print the message:" Invalid Parameter" and return False as result

INPUT: Link list with Out-of-the-range integers value e.g.(If +ive then > 2147483647 and if –ive then < -2147483648).

Expected OUTPUT: If value will be given as 2147483649, then it will be rollover to count 2 in –ive side, which will be as -2147483649

UNIT TEST CASES

Number of Node = 1

INPUT: 1->NULL

EXPECTED OUTPUT: 1->NULL

Number of Node = 2

INPUT: 2->4->NULL

EXPECTED OUTPUT: NULL

Number of Node = 4

INPUT: 1->2->4->6->NULL

EXPECTED OUTPUT: 1->NULL

Number of Node = 4

INPUT: 2->4->6->8->10->12->1->3->5->NULL

EXPECTED OUTPUT: 1->3->5->NULL

Number of Node = 6

INPUT: 1->3->6->8->10->1->3->5->NULL

EXPECTED OUTPUT: 1-3->1->3->5->NULL

Number of Node = 4

INPUT: 2->2->2->2->NULL

EXPECTED OUTPUT: NULL

Number of Node = 4

INPUT: 1->1->1->1->NULL

EXPECTED OUTPUT: 1->1->1->1->NULL

SPECIAL TEST CASES

Automation of the test cases: run a script, which is automatically creating a link list have random number of elements (1 to n), with possible integer range, later this script showing the input linked list and output link list.

Stress Test: running the above script for certain number of hours.

Performance Test: test the performance of this API based on the given linked list (number of elements) and time require to process to remove the even values.

TEST CASES: TEST TO REMOVE THE NTH NODE

**Write test cases in the form of [Input , Expected Output]
To test the function:**

**// This functions removes the Nth node from a single
link list.
ReturnValue RemoveNthNodeFromLinkedList(Node**
Head , unsigned short int NthNode)
Where : Head – Head node of linked list , NthNode –
Node no. to delete
typedef struct Node
{ void *data;   struct Node *next; } Node;
enum ReturnValue
{ FALSE = -1; TRUE = 1; INVALID_PARAMETER; }**

RATIONALE: *Interviewer would like to observe interviewee's approach while deducing the test cases of a sample problem.*

SAMPLE ANSWER FROM A PROFESSIONAL **POINT OF VIEW**

This task require to write test cases to test API

APPROACH

My high level approach to write test cases starts from –

- Analysis for test items
- Factorize test items and narrow down to sub groups if require,
- Afterwards go for functional test cases which again divided in positive
  functional test cases and negative functional test case
- Start from basic tests to advanced test cases
- Then non-functional test cases, where one can consider about perfor-
  mance, stress, globalization, integration or some other aspects of testing.

POSITIVE FUNCTIONAL TESTS

TEST CASE-1

- Pre-Condition: Linked List which have 6 elements: 1->2->3->4->5->6->Null
- Input: Head Node of Linked List | 6th Node to Delete
- Expected Output: Remove API will return TRUE
- Linked List has now 5 elements 1->2->3->4->5->Null

TEST CASE-2

- Pre-Condition: Linked List which have 5 elements: 1->2->3->4->5->Null
- Input: Head Node of Linked List: 1th Node to Delete
- Expected Output: Remove API will return TRUE
- Linked list have now 4 elements: 2->3->4->5->Null

TEST CASE-3

- Pre-Condition: Linked List which has 4 elements: 2->3->4->5->Null
- Input: Head Node of Linked List: 2nd Node to Delete
- Expected Output: Remove API will return TRUE
- Linked List has now 3 elements: 2->4->5->Null

TEST CASE-4

- Pre-Condition: Linked List which have 6 elements: 1->2->3->4->5->6->Null
- Input: Head Node of Linked List: 7th Node to Delete
- Expected Output: Remove API will return FALSE:
- Linked List have now 6 elements :1->2->3->4->5->6->Null

TEST CASE-5

- Pre-Condition: Linked List which have 6 elements: 1->2->3->4->5->6->Null
- Input: Head Node of Linked List :0th Node to Delete
- Expected Output: Linked List have now 6 elements
- 1->2->3->4->5->6->Null

- CASE: Test the case when linked list have just one element, and input has given to remove this one element
  - ▷ Expected Output: Remove API will return TRUE, And Linked list will have no element left
- CASE: Test Case when linked list have none element and given Nth Node value is greater than 0 and head node value is correct
  - ▷ Expected Output: Remove API will return INVALID_PARAMETER
- CASE: Test Case when linked list have none element and given Nth Node value is greater than 0 and head node value is Null
  - ▷ Expected Output: Remove API will return INVALID_PARAMETER
- CASE: Test Case when linked list have several element and given Nth Node value is equal to 0
  - ▷ Expected Output: Remove API will return INVALID_PARAMETER
- CASE: Test Case when linked list have several element and given Nth Node value is several number greater than the number of elements in the linked list
  - ▷ Expected Output: Remove API will return FALSE
- CASE: Test Case when linked list have several element and given Nth Node value is just one number greater than the number of elements in the linked list
  - ▷ Expected Output: Remove API will return FALSE
- CASE: Test case when linked list have 65535 elements Give input to remove first, last or middle, item
  - ▷ Expected Output: Test the output of this Remove API based on given input, It should returned TRUE
- CASE: Test case when linked list have 65535 elements
  - ▷ Give the input value greater than 65535
  - ▷ [In this case the greater value will be rolled back, consider this fact while executing this test case]
  - ▷ Expected Output: Test the output of this Remove API based on given input, It should returned TRUE
- CASE: Test the case when linked list will be circular, test it should not come into any infinite loop

NON-FUNCTIONAL TEST CASES

- Compute the performance of this function to remove one element from a linked list, e.g.; last element, first element or any random middle element, Output: performance measure

- Perform stress testing by calling this function when there are low memory or CPU utilization is low, Out Put: stress measure

If require write the automation of above test cases by using any available test framework e.g.; write test case automation, which create a random list for a random size in between 0 to 65535, and reads the given input from a given input file, and expected output value, and log the results.

Agile Testing: A Practical Guide for Testers and Agile Teams	By Lisa Crispin and Janet Gregory (Jan 9, 2009)
How Google Tests Software	James A. Whittaker (Author), Jason Arbon (Author), Jeff Carollo (Author)
Software Testing (2nd Edition)	Ron Patton
Managing the Testing Process: Practical Tools and Techniques for Managing Hardware and Software Testing	Rex Black
Implementing Automated Software Testing: How to Save Time and Lower Costs While Raising Quality	Bernie Gauf (Author), Elfriede Dustin, Thom Garrett (Author)
Lessons Learned in Software Testing	by Cem Kaner, James Bach and Bret Pettichord
How We Test Software at Microsoft [Paperback]	Alan Page (Author), Ken Johnston (Author), Bj Rollison (Author)

Thought Process

To understand the interviewee's thought process, an interviewer may present some scenarios e.g. design a highly scalable client/server solution to locate the presence of mobile devices, optimize an existing traffic light systems or design a mobile operating system for disabled users or senior citizens.

OPEN ENDED: DESIGN A NEW OPERATING SYSTEM

If you are asked to design a new Operating System, what would be your key design requirements?

THOUGHT PROCESS: It is worth mentioning from the start that this question is about high-level concepts of a new operating system, so a right answer should not include any implementation details. At the same time, most of the aspects related to performance should also be avoided when providing an answer. After all, performance is about engineering and the focus of this question should be on more general design principles, such as security or robustness.

First of all, a good question to ask the interviewer would be 'What kind of operating system do these design requirements apply to?'. There are various classifications of operating systems. A first classification arises from the platform the operating system is written for. There are two main categories:

- Mobile operating systems – this is the kind of operating system that runs on mobile devices (mobile phones, tablets, other similar gadgets). The focus of such an operating system should be reducing power consumption, as most devices that will use it run on battery.

- Desktop operating systems – this is the operating system that runs on devices that are normally attached to a power source (desktop PCs, laptops). The focus of such an OS would be performance, rather than saving power.

Other types of operating systems include:

- Single-tasking / Multi-tasking operating systems – single-tasking operating systems can only execute one program at a time, while a multitasking OS can run multiple programs at any given moment.

- Single-user / Multi-user operating system – single-user operating systems can be used by one user at a time, while a multi-use OS enables multiple connections to the same machine (for example, remote connections using the SSH command from other computers).

- Distributed / non-distributed operating systems – a distributed operating system manages a group of computers, rather than a single one, and makes these computers appear as a single more powerful machine. The advantage is that computations can be carried out on multiple computers at the same time.

Our model answer will focus on designing a single-user, multi-tasking, non-distributed operating system for desktop computers (PC, Mac, laptop). Here is a list of design principles you may wish to discuss with the interviewer when asked this question, along with some important points for each:

- **Security** - in terms of the security of a new operating system, perhaps the most important aspect to mention is that users should not have the right to access files that are not meant to be accessed by them. In this sense, the separation between processes that belong to the operation system (those initiated by system calls, for example) and those initiated by the action of users is crucial and should not be missed.

- **Simplicity** - the simplicity of an operating system is usually defined by how easy it is for the user to find exactly what they are looking for. An example is choosing the right name for file managers ('My computer' and 'Computer' are good examples that are already used by the world's biggest OS manufacturers)

- **Robustness** – the design of an operating system is robust if the addition of new features does not cause any unexpected problems with the ones that are already implemented.

- **Extensibility** – Generally, an operating system that can be easily extended is regarded as a good operating system. Take, for example, Linux. The fact that made this operating system so popular is its customizability. Experienced users can build their own features or even write their own Linux distributions using the libraries provided.

- **Uniformity** – A uniform design for a new operating system is a design in which most components of the operating system are consistent. This may include choosing an appropriate color scheme and similar graphics for components with the same functionality.

- **Predictability** - This principle is about how easily a user can predict where bits of functionality of the operating system are located. For example, considering the trends that are already established, we can predict our users would expect to find the properties of a file by right-clicking on it.

- **Reversibility** – It may sometimes happen that the users of an operating system perform an operation that they want to cancel or undo. In this sense, a good design for a new operating system should be reversible, allowing this to happen easily.

- **Support for multiple platforms** - Last but not least, we live in a world where mobile platforms have become an absolute necessity. Therefore, any operating system that can be extended to such devices, or at least offer support for remotely logging in from these has a clear advantage.

To sum up, the key thing to remember is that open ended questions will always be open-ended and there are perhaps an infinite number of answers for them. As long as you keep asking questions and clearly establish the kind of operating system the interviewer is looking for, you will eventually be able to produce a good answer. Mobile operating systems differ greatly from desktop ones, for example, so it is important not to miss this step.

OPEN ENDED:
HOW WOULD YOU TEST A CD-ROM DRIVE?

How would you test a CD-ROM drive?

THOUGHT PROCESS: The first important aspect you will need to discuss with the interviewer is what kind of role you are assigned when testing a CD-ROM drive. This is a big task and this aspect needs to be clearly defined before you can start thinking about the steps that you need to carry out. When talking about your role in assessing the quality of such a device, make sure you ask the interviewer under which of the following categories you fall:

Consumer	Obviously, as a consumer you wouldn't have any technical background so you are most likely to assess the general functionality. A sensible approach would be making sure the CD-ROM reads and writes the type of media permitted at the right speed and in accordance to the capacity of the optical media.
Member of the design team	Since every company has its own trademark and logo, a design team will be asked to come up with an original sketch of the product. They would have to distinguish between a design for laptops and PCs and make it as original and visually appealing as possible.
Quality Engineer	If you are working in the quality assurance department, you ensure the product is suitable for the large audiences. Your task would be to determine whether the device is easily accessible and intuitive enough to be operated. For example, people with disabilities such as blindness should be able to clearly access the eject tray button. Also, a good point of discussion is health and safety; the case has to be sturdy enough and avoid sharp edges.
Member of manufacturing team	As a member of the manufacturing team, your main role would be to check that all the components used are in a good state and conform to the general standards an ideal product should adhere to. At the same time you will also be responsible for handling the automated mechanics meant to put together the CD-ROM drive.
Tester	As a tester, you will most likely be asked to verify the functional requirements of the device once this is manufactured. This implies rigorous testing under various parameters. The model answer below will tackle this category in more detail.

There are various aspects that make some CD/DVD drives better than others. In the following lines we will discuss some of these, along with some proper ways of testing them.

First, we must separate the concepts of reading and writing when it comes to CD-ROM/DVD-ROM drives. If the device also has writing capabilities then we must test these two concepts separately. Let's start with some notions on data reading from an optical storage disk (CD, DVD, Blu-Ray media, etc):

- The reading speed of a drive, as you may have noticed, is expressed as an integer value, followed by X (e.g. 52X). But what does this X actually mean?

- An X is equal to 0.1536 MB/s, so a CD-ROM that is capable of reading data at 52X would actually transfer it at a rate of 7.98 MB/s. This is quite slow compared to most hard disks nowadays, especially SSDs or the external drives with support for USB 3.0.

- Older drives used to support speeds of 2X or 4X, but nowadays 56X has been achieved.

- In addition to the reading speed of the device, the data transfer rate is also influenced by the system cache. The cache is a very fast memory section used by the operating system to temporarily store data. For example, if a 2-3MB file is copied from a CD/DVD drive, it is likely for the operating system to store it in the cache, in the event that it may be needed again soon.

- If the same file is requested shortly after, then the OS will fetch it from the cache rather than from the optical media disk. This aspect should also be taken into account when testing an optical drive. Not reading the same file twice in a short time interval will lead to more accurate estimations of the drive's speed.

The writing speed is not influenced by the cache, so all the points above except for the last one apply to writing to an optical disk. Usually, the writing speed is slower than the reading speed because this operating is more 'expensive' and consumes more resources.

Some further aspects that we may wish to consider when testing a CD-ROM drives are as follows:

- The load time – the time it takes for the device to actually load the disk (time between the insertion of the disk and the moment when its contents actually show up in the file manager).

- The seek time – the user often needs to access files stored at random locations on the disk (non-contiguous blocks of memory). If this is the case, then the time it takes for the head of the CD-ROM to move from one location to another is called the seek time.

- Spinup and spindown times – the spinup time is similar to the load time and it is the interval between the moment when the disk was placed in the proper position for reading and the moment data is actually accessible to the user (in simpler terms, this is how much rotation time the disk needs before data can be accessed). The spindown time is the opposite of spinup and is the time it takes for the drive to 'stop' a rotating disk.

There are already many pieces of software that can test all these performance criteria of an optical drive. An example is Nero DiscSpeed.

To sum up, you need to keep in mind that whenever you are confronted with these types of open-ended questions you have to think outside the box and not limit yourself to one specific answer. The interviewer will most likely look for your ability to cover all the aspects involved and make the right links in any situation. Asking more questions in order to clarify the problem is a typical process called requirements gathering which takes place at the beginning of every complex project in order to establish exactly what the customer has in mind.

OPEN ENDED:
WHEN A USER TYPES A CHARACTER ON A KEYBOARD

What actually happens when a user types a character on a keyboard? What is the process before the character appears in a text editor such as Microsoft Word, for example?

THOUGHT PROCESS: From an abstract point of view, operating systems are just pieces of software whose main goal is to hide hardware details from users. A good example is that when we type a character on a keyboard, it is automatically detected and processed for us by the operating system. Then, text editors or any other applications receive this input and, from this point, how the input is used is up to the software.

For example, the function scanf() in C++ tells the operating system that it needs to fetch a character or a combination of characters from the keyboard (or whatever the standard input is) for further processing. But how is this input actually fetched? This is what we will discuss in the following lines.

We will assume a standard keyboard, connected to the motherboard of the computer is used, along with any operating system.

First of all, it is good to know that all operating systems come with the so-called **kernel**. A kernel is a bit of functionality that manages resources provided by the hardware, such as the RAM memory, CPU and peripherals. Because this question is related to the use of a keyboard, we will focus on the kernel's peripheral manager.

With most operating systems, each peripheral has a separate manager, often called a **device driver**. This is a piece of software that controls the peripheral and creates the link between the operating system and the keyboard, mouse, printer, or any other such device. The device driver is necessary because the OS needs to identify the peripheral correctly (i.e. know whether the device plugged in the motherboard is a mouse, a keyboard, a printer, etc.) and also know how to operate it properly (e.g. how to move information from the keyboard to the program that requires it). In Windows, the drivers of the various devices connected to the PC can be accessed via the Device Manager application.

This occurs mainly because some sort of control over peripherals is required. If programs were able to interact with the peripherals directly this could lead to hazardous situations (for example, if multiple programs try to access information from a peripheral at the same time). This is where the need of an intermediate entity arises (in this case, this entity is the operating system and its kernel).

So what are the actual steps when the user types a character, before it appears in a text editor or word processor?

- When a key is hit, an interrupt signal is transmitted from the keyboard. This signal is defined by a number.

- The keyboard device driver uses this number to execute the correct interrupt handler and process the input from the keyboard buffer.

- Note that if multiple keys are pressed at the same time, (or a key is pressed before the previous key is released), the interrupt handler is only executed after all the characters have been stored in the keyboard buffer.

- The interrupt handler lets the peripheral know it is ready for more data after the interrupt handler routine is executed.

- In the meantime, the information is passed on successively to the next functions of the kernel, until it reaches the application layer.

- At the application layer level, the information is picked up by the display driver.

- The display driver needs to know which application requested the information initially, so it performs a check on the current running applications.

- The text editor / word processor (e.g. Microsoft Word) tells the display driver this is the application the information needs to be directed to.

- The information is directed to the text editor / word processor.

Further discussions, such as using various types of keyboards (connection via PS/2 or USB, international keyboards) can continue with the interviewer at this point, based on to what extent the job is focused on the hardware part of computer science. Even if it's not, it is always useful for a programmer to have a general idea about how peripherals work.

OPEN ENDED: DESIGN A NEW TRAFFIC LIGHT SYSTEM

If you are asked to design a new traffic light system, what would be your key design requirements?

THOUGHT PROCESS: First of all, the key point to establish when being confronted with open ended questions like this one is to think about all the possible scenarios where you would normally be asked to design and implement such a system. You will have to ask further questions in order to clarify your role. If the interview is not face to face you are obviously unable to ask for further clarifications so you will need to make your own assumptions. When talking about traffic lights in general their main purpose is to draw attention on something or signal the occurrence of some event. Here are some examples where such a mechanism would be required.

- Road traffic
- Airport traffic
- Rockets
- Maritime signaling

Traffic lights tend to differ when it comes to the number and variety of colors. For example, pedestrian traffic lights only have red and green signaling stop and go, whereas vehicle traffic adds the color yellow to emphasize the transition between stop and go, forcing the driver to take measures in advance. Other examples would be Formula 1 traffic lights, indicating the countdown to the start of the race or a sports stadium lighting system meant to direct fans to the exit gates after the match has ended.

In our model answer given below we will assume that we are asked to design a traffic lights model meant to fluidize the traffic in a busy intersection. We will need to take into account two design categories.

Firstly, let's consider the principal design requirements:

- **Fuel consumption minimization** - Reducing the waiting time for traffic participants automatically reduces fuel consumption as well, mainly because an idling engine consumes plenty of fuel and also emits pollutants in the air, so this step would automatically come with benefits for the environment as well.

- **The sequence of signals** – The sequence of signals is actually a more complex process then most people think. For example, in addition to ensuring the right order of colors (red – amber/ yellow – green), a good system should also consider the time the yellow light stays active, for example. This needs to be computed according to the size of the intersection and the average speed of traffic participants. Cars and pedestrians should have enough time to finish crossing the intersection before the 'red' light appears.

- **The type of controller**

  ▷ The controller of a traffic light system can be pre-timed (allow a number of seconds for each light), or can be adjusted according to the needs of the traffic participants. For example, we have all seen the pedestrian traffic lights triggered by the push of a button. In this case the controller needs to dynamically adjust the time period during which a light is active.

  ▷ This idea can be brought even further, to traffic controllers that work with sensors, for example, and adjust the time allowed for each light based on how busy an intersection is. There are various types of sensors that can be used. Using movement sensors would perhaps be complicated and risky because of the potentially high error rate, but the detectors placed in the pavement turn out to work quite well. These can measure the frequency of vehicles / pedestrian for each direction of the intersection and therefore tell the controller to adjust the time each light is active.

Optionally, the design of a traffic light system could also include exchanging information between traffic lights at different intersections. It is often unpleasant for participants in traffic to stop at all consecutive lights, so it would be ideal to achieve some synchronization between these.

Secondly, the other category to mention is the functional requirements. By these, we are referring to the actual purpose of the system – to direct traffic. Some of these requirements are as follows:

- In the case of road traffic lights, apart from the sequence of colors should ideally display the direction which is made available or unavailable to the drivers. This is marked by an arrow of the corresponding color. For example, if you see a green arrow pointing to the right it means you are free to go right.

- When it comes to pedestrian crossings in the intersection, the arrows would be replaced by a green walking man if allowed to proceed or a red stationary man if required to stand.

- In case of a timed controller, an idea would be to also include a countdown timer accompanied by the red or green color, symbolizing the time left to wait in the intersection or proceed.

Again, you need to remember that this is an open ended question which can be approached in various ways. The idea is to keep asking questions until you find out what kind of scenario the interviewer had in mind. A sensible idea would be not to omit aspects such as non-functional requirements. For example, how would you rate the performance of your system? Or under what parameters would you ideally test it? For the sports stadium example, stress testing would be a point worth mentioning. You would want to fill the stadium up with the maximum number of people allowed in order to assess the performance of the traffic lights.

OPEN ENDED: SOFTWARE PURCHASE APPLICATION

Consider the scenario : You have been asked to work on the testing of a new 'Software Purchase' application. This application will allow users to buy software products online. Full details of the application are unclear at the moment, but the following details are provided to you:

- The new website will be based on a client/server architecture.
- Customers will also be able to access the website via a mobile device or a pc based internet browser.
- The company has a database system which tracks customer data after a purchase is made.
- This data may be updated by customers (e.g. a customer may change their address or phone number).

(A). Please provide a detailed list of the additional information that you would need, in order to start working on the testing of this application.

(B).Please provide a detailed list of the specific security considerations that you need to take into account for this application.

(C). Please provide a detailed list of the potential performance issues likely to arise in a system like this and outline what you would test for them.

(D). Assuming you have provided the additional information to you, design a detailed test plan for this application. You will need to test both normal mode operation as well as corner cases and unusual conditions.

THOUGHT PROCESS: Professionals receives unclear or the detailed available up to very high level for the given tasks e.g.

- Please compare the following software monitoring solution for xyz purpose e.g hyperic hq (from vmware) and nagios (from nagios)
- P2P Based Solutions prefers SIP or XMPP (Jingle) for Signaling
- Is zlib useful to improve data transfer performance for BSD Socket based client/server application?
- Ideal window scale factor for mobile client/server file transfer app?
- Simulated NAT Traversal environment on a Virtual Box
- and then professionl uses a defined approach to implement the given task by considering various parameters e.g. use cases, requirements, targetted users, reources, time, professional's role, budget and many others.

A

1. What are the detailed requirement and specifications of this MSP application?
2. What is the time line of the testing?
3. How many resources do I have to test it?
4. Who are the targeted customers?
5. What are the deliverables of test execution?
6. What process we are using to develop the test automation?
7. What is the application development plan, and on which phase of the development plan, such test assignment has handed over to me.
8. Is it to be tested for physically challenged people (example: blind)?
9. Is it to be tested on different localizations or only to USA? Applicable geography to access this application?
10. At what stage I will get the resources e.g.; different mobile devices, PCs and other accessories
11. Architecture of this application and other design documents
12. Is this application ban to use by specific set of users?

B

1. Protects the user privacy e.g.; customer details, credit card number etc
2. In client server architecture, every client is known; every request received by server will have information on who originated this request. In web, users are anonymous thus pose a greater security risk.
3. Clients are much more controlled in client-server. Which OS they will use, which platform they will run on, what browser will be used everything can be controlled. In comparison to that, nothing can be controlled in web.

4. Number of clients that can be connected to the server is predictable and can be controlled in the traditional client server, but it cannot be controlled in the Web so sclaing need to be considerd.

5. Web gives more opportunity to malicious users to tamper data at the client side as well as at the network level. Chances of data being tampered in the traditional client server architecture are much lesser as compare to web.

6. Credit card information gateway should be encrypted.

7. Rollback/Cancel on unsuccessful transactions.

C

1. Behaviour of application of different browsers. (Test case will be based on supported browser for this application, their user friendly rendering of pages, security constraints provided by browsers)

2. Behaviour of application on different devices, network bandwidth, different platforms. (Test cases based on different -2 network speeds / different devices/ different platforms)

3. When the load increases how to handle it.

4. What are the key performance parameters.

5. Turnaround time of the application, e. g.; if before initiate this application on client, if it install any security plug-in.

6. How application behaves on multiple sessions initiated by same user on different/same devices.

7. How this application behaves on stress.

8. Application behaves user friendly while navigate via using keyboard, mouse, different device keypad

D

Test Plan:

1. Test objective

2. Test environment

3. est harness design

4. User(client side) access feature of MSP **Functional/ Non-Functional testing of user access feature

5. Server side feature of MSP

6. Security features of MSP

7. Installation features of MSP

8. Integration testing of MSP

9. System integration testing

10. Build verification testing

11. Deployment testing

12. Localization testing (testing based on different geographical location e.g.; china, japan, france)

13. Testing with third part application e.g. this application will integrate some other plugins and if interact with banks

OPEN ENDED:
TIME PASSES AND A PROGRAM HEARS NOTHING

First Question: Suppose Program A, (a client program, because it makes a request) asks Program B, a server program, to update some fields in a database. Program B is on another computer. Program A expects Program B to report that either: (1) the operation was successfully completed, or (2) the operation was unsuccessful (for example, because the requested record was locked.) However, time passes and A hears nothing. What should A do?

THOUGHT PROCESS: It happens in professional daily life, when he or she encounters work related issues with limited or almost no information.

May be the Interviewer would like to understand Interviewee's thought process to tackle such kind of situation.

ANALYSIS

It depends on my situation, whether I am solving this problem as an administrator, or developer or Tester.

I might need to analyze problem behavior e.g. whether this is happening first time, it's happened earlier as well. Also I need to analyze the situations when database record got locked e.g. What client was doing as a program logic, server situation.

SOLUTION AREAS

After analysis I will find solutions areas e.g. perform analysis at client program 'A or perform analysis at server program 'B'

SOLUTION ANALYSIS AT CLIENT 'A' SIDE

'A' makes a request from 'B', and hears nothing; in that case, 'A' may perform one of the following action to remind 'B' for the sent request:

A should maintain a response timer; if that timers expire then 'A' should again inquire his message status from B.

If B is still unresponsive, then it should resend the request by keeping the surety (or adding a flag which tells this is resend data) e.g. before inserting the same data to the database it will check for duplicacy.

'A' might check whether connection is still up with B or not? because 'A' hasn't receive any answer from 'B'.

Understand the client business logic, if that has created the problem.

SOLUTION ANALYSIS AT SERVER 'B' SIDE

Immediate solution is to restart the server program

Kill another program which locked this record.

MISC

Perform some database action to debug this situation

It might be possible that this is a known problem, and somebody else has dependency on it,

WHAT ARE THE POSSIBILITIES?

There could be several things may wrong, Its hard to tell just because of this scenario,

Because other request might made this database busy so 'A' was unable to answer the request

It might possible that such situation happens just once in millions or once in thousands

May be server sent the reply, but client didn't interpret that

May be because of network congestion that packet was dropped e.g. one need to check whether it was TCP connection or UDP connection

MAY BE RECENTLY SOME PATCH WAS ADDED THAT BROUGHT SOME PROBLEM

May be this is already existing issue and bug has logged already

May be some update has n't been installed on server side

May be X service is not running who actually manages such issue.

So there could be several issues.

HOW 'A' CONCLUDE WHICH THING GO WRONG?

Do Step-By-Step analysis of this issue

Reproduce this Issue again and again based on what was performed when this issue came

Check everything including client logic A and server logic B

That will return what went wrong

This would be one of the approaches

HOW TO CONFIRM 'A' WORKS RIGHT.

If A Works right, then apply similar communication with other server, and see whether its possible do duplicate

See the format of the sent request from A

Send other request than this request,

Debug the A's code

Send some other request from A's To C (some other server)

OPEN ENDED:
DESIGN SECURITY AND PERFORMANCE TEST

What do you care about when you design security tests and performance tests?

THOUGHT PROCESS: Most of the product can be differnetiate because of its performance based on the use cases, for what its implemented e.g. how web app 'A' works on xyz load vs web app 'B', how web app 'A' securly works on xyz conditions.

I may care following while designing security and performance tests:

- Security and Performance tests are non-functional tests, which should be done when functionality of system is stable.
- Measure the coverage of performance tests e.g. performance parameters, performance scenarios
- Measure the coverage of security tests e.g. security parameters, security scenarios

EXAMPLE TO MEASURE THE COVERAGE FOR SECURITY AND PERFORMANCE TESTS

A feature of a server program allows clients to download the files, and client/server program work with following major scenarios and logic e.g.

1. Clients request multiple files to download and then Client queue the multiple-files-requests, and for each download: Client creates the connection with server, Client downloads one file, and Client closes the connection.

2. Clients request multiple files to download, and then Client sends single multiple-files-requests to server, and for this download: Client creates single connection with server, Client downloads all files, and Client closes the connection.

Measure the coverage for performance tests, e.g. file downloaded-time with above scenarios [1] and [2]Measure the coverage for Security tests, e.g. encrypted file-contents, authorization to download the files.

Test Coverage will help to define next steps e.g. various test-vectors, associated test environment, test automation.

OPEN ENDED: WHEN YOU MANAGE YOUR TEST TEAM

What is the most troublesome aspect when you manage a test team with 10 people and a dev team with 8 people? How can you resolve it?

THOUGHT PROCESS: This is a kind of open ended question; different professionals may refer to different types of problems, based on their experience and views.

May be the Interviewer wanted to understand interviewee's thought process, if he or she will be the lead of such a type of team.

Here I am assuming trouble means the situations, and such types of situations are common and understandable; these are not a problem at all.

SOME OF THE TROUBLES OR SITUATIONS

- Test team says "this is a bug", but development team says "this is not a bug" e.g. developer developed the system in their development environment and tester tested the system in real test environment

- Changes in design and requirements may introduce conflicting between developers and test teams e.g. over the time more requirement understood, and analysis made the changes in requirement which reflected design as well.

RESOLVING TROUBLES OR SITUATIONS

Each type of problem or trouble requires a different type of strategy; as a lead I may follow this approach:

- Understand the situation

- Discussion with dependent people, to analyze and totally understand the situation

- Work with development and test team to resolve the trouble, e.g. discussion with both teams or with an individual and prepare a strategy which works well for both dev and test team, common discussion with all team dependent team members

Based on the project, team type and situation, resolving first trouble might give some challenges, but subsequent troubles or situation may require less efforts.

OPEN ENDED: TYPE A URL INTO THE ADDRESS BAR

What happens when a user types a URL into the address bar of an Internet browser e.g. Netscape, Chrome. Perform a hit to fetch the webpage and after a while the corresponding webpage displayed.

THOUGHT PROCESS: Some of the frequently used computer's application might turn into the scenarios, which look very general, but it carries a lot of technical information e.g. browsing internet.

Interviewer would like to understand Interviewees basics, thought process, approach to provide summarize answer for the given open ended scenario related to data communication.

This scenario involves several types of technologies related to Client/Server architecture for data communication.

It talks about the overall flow of request/response, which includes various types of technical concepts e.g.

Protocols: DNS, HTTP, TCP/IP, ARP, Routing Protocols

Functional processing: Packaging a HTTP request, adding certain Protocol headers and writing it to lowest ethernet adapter to travel to destination.

In high level:

Client as an internet browser sends this webpage request to a web server by typing the URL at address bar and perform hit button.

- Certain processing happens inside the browser application e.g. browser application verifies the correctness of types URL, browser approaches to appropriate DNS server to receive the IP address of typed URL as DNS response, browser prepare a HTTP get request and send to the web server.

- Certain processing happens in the TCP/IP stack e.g. to send a get request to web server, client initiate a TCP connection to the Web server, IP protocol adds its header, ARP protocol find MAC address for corresponding next hope

Travelling this request from client machine to web werver (assuming it's located in other network), uses the depth of routing technologies e.g. if client machine located in korea and server located in United States, then this require to travel from various routers.

On arrival of this request at web server, It processed by the TCP/IP stack of that machine where web server is running. web-server prepares a response back to the client, which travels back to the client machine from where this request was originated.

I have explained this scenario in a high level flow; please let me know any specific step which I can explain detail e.g. step: How Internet browser issues a DNS query request and get a DNS response?, step: How doles the ARP get the corresponding MAC address ?, Step: How web-server parses received HTTP get request?, step: what happens if web-server send a reply and client didn't received it ?

It also depends on the type of interview e.g. telephonic vs face-to-face, if it's a face-to-face then it's a good practice that a professional explains its answer while drawing a diagram on white-board or paper.

Technical Areas

The Computer Science Industry is dispersed in diversified areas, and its professionals are characterized by specialized knowledge and skills.

If a professional applies for a job which is related to a specific domain and technical skills, then it's obvious that an Interviewer will test Interviewee's technical skills e.g. embedded domain and device driver's development skills, web domain and CSS/JavaScript skills, banking domain and network security skills.

PROFILE_SUMITARORA.DOCX
OR
PROFILE_SUMITARORA.PDF
OR
RESUME_SUMITARORA.PPT
OR
CV_SUMITARORA.TXT

TECHNICAL AREAS

INVOLVEMENT IN THE SOFTWARE ENGINEERING AND DEVELOPMENT OF:

AllShare Platform, Samsung South Korea, V2OIP/Windows-CE/Linux Board Support Packages (Freescale, Shanghai, China), **VOIP (OKI Japan – Acme Technologies, India)**, CTI (Computer Telephony Integration – NETWORK PROGRAMS – INDIA), **TCP/IP(NEC-JAPAN), SS7 (Tecklec Eagle-Signal Transfer Point – Aricent, India)**, GSM (Alcatel-MxBSC – Aricent, France, China, India), Routers (NEC-UXSS-Router), **Microsoft Windows CE's BSP**, Amalga, Samsung's Cloud Infrastucture, **Samsung's Remote Access Solutions**

SKILLS

Languages: C, C++, (C#, Java)

Libraries: Boost(C++), Sockets (libJingle), Multithreading (LibJingle), Events(Libjingle)

APIs: Windows/Mac/Linux File System, Sockets, Events, Multithreading

Platforms: Windows/Linux/(WinCE/MS-Auto/Mac/Android)

TECHNOLOGIES USED

Open Source: Apache Solr, Google's libJingle, OpenVPN, libupnp, Linux Kernel, Netty, Node. Js, MongoDB

Embedded/Device Drivers: CD-ROM, Storage, FM-Radio, i.MX Series Freescale Processors, Board Support Packages

Protocols: Telecom SS7(Layer-4, SCCP, Layer-3, MTP3) and datacom protocols(Layer-2 ARP, Layer-3 IPV4/IPV6, ICMP, IGMP, Layer-4 – UDP, TCP), Signalling Protocol(SIP, SDP) IP-Protocol (STUN, TURN), Application Protocol (TFTP, FTP, DNS), Communication Protocol(HTTP), Network Management (SNMP), Wireless Protocol(Bluetooth), XMPP

Web/Databases : wordpress/php/css/ javascript/mysql/lamp

Tools : Code optimization to testing, packets captures, simulators, wrote customized tools.

Documentation: MS-Office/Latex/Adobe Tools/Nuance Dictator/Whitesmoke

Cloud : Amazon, Xen Server, Nagios, Software Monitoring, Data Center

Most of the technical interviews on technical areas depend on the contents defined in the resume.

- It depends on what type of professionals you are e.g. an IT professional worked on the domain of banking, healthcare, telecommunications, data communication, cloud infrastructure.

- You may be a standard engineer who are worked on different projects with different technologies used but skills was same e.g. C++ programming language and Linux OS.

- You may be a professional who worked on similar projects and similar technologies e.g. VOIP based solutions by using xyz skill set.

- You may be a professional who worked on different projects, technologies, skills e.g. voip area, web area, telecom area and then cloud infrastructure area with dissimilar skills (C++, Java, PHP, .NET).

- It might be possible that you are a fresh engineer or just passed out from the college, but again it all depends on how you are presenting your key learnings/projects/accomplishment you made during your graduation/post-graduation.

Because the resume will tells to the interviewer, about what an interviewee going to offer as his technical skills to the company or this job position.

See this common objective defined in a CV:

- Looking forward to build a progressive career in a challenging environment and to present myself with best of my innovative ideas and technical skills.

See this specific objective defined in a CV:

- A professional has opted his career towards the electrical design related job opportunities :
    - ▷ Challenging electrical design engineer position that offers advancement potential with interest in electrical product designing, customizing power solutions, electrical products drawings, industrial automation, power systems and electrical standards.

- A professional has opted his career towards the teaching job opportunities in computer science and mathematics:
    - ▷ Challenging full-time post graduate teacher position in mathematics that offers advancement potential with interests in Calculus, Algebra, Vectors, Statics, Dynamics, Statistics and Computer Science.

- A professional has opted his career towards the research related job opportunities:

▷ Challenging development/research position that offers advancement potential with interests in Nanochemistry, Liposome based gene delivery, Fabrication of nano / microstructures, cellular assays, organic synthesis and protein purification domains.

See below different career summary :

- See the below career summary defined in the CV (defined by a 0-1 years of experience person (a b.tech in electrical engineering)):

  ▷ Commissioning experience in the steel Industry for Industrial Installation and commissioning of PLC & DRIVE Panels, SCADA & HMI for steel making process lines

  ▷ Maintenance experience while working with SCADA: RTU (make – Areva/Alstom-S900) for controlling and monitoring substations

- See the below career summary defined in the CV (defined by a 2-3 years of experience person in iPhone app development area):

  ▷ I started working on iPhone app development with Cocoa Touch and Objective-c just after Apple opened the SDK for public in early 2008 and continuing till now. Instead of going with jail break sdk I started with all authenticated tools and followed best practices. My expertise are in building utilities, life style application, client-server apps with http REST interface over JSON/XML data, views and view controller programming, sqlite persistence, location based service development etc.

- See the below career summary defined in the CV (defined by a 4-5 years in the field of designing:

  ▷ X years of experience in design industry by executing end-to-end extensive visual design, UI/UE design, and illustration projects for many leading-edge clients in the field of graphics design, multimedia, interaction design, visual identity, motion graphics and Illustration.

  ▷ Developed unique shadow play, an interactive installation based on "Little Red Riding Hood" by means of narrative design

  ▷ Versatile in terms of design, production and integration fully utilizing the potentials of new media

  ▷ Masters (interactive digital media) from university of x, new media design from y, bachelors (information design z university

  ▷ Creative thinker and quick study with the ability to adapt to rapidly changing business situations and tight deadlines. Strong communications skills, multilingual (english, french, japanese) ability facilitate a high level of collaboration among co-workers in a team-oriented environment.

- See the below career summary defined in the CV (defined by a 5+ years in the field of enterprise business application development:

  ▷ A seasoned hands-on Technical Lead with 5+ years of experience in designing, developing enterprise scale business applications for financial industry. A strong team player, adept at providing solutions, guiding and motivating team members towards achieving maximum productivity.

See below job description vs job description and achievements:

- A professional has defined his job description with the achievement as well:

  <Job Description>

  ▷ Responsible for reviewing business requirements, writing functional specification and creating detail technical design document for Java enterprise business applications.

  ▷ Responsible for leading seven member development team in designing and developing Equity Research distribution system.

  ▷ Responsible for deploying, testing, troubleshooting, and performance tuning Java applications module, Database and Application servers.

  ▷ Responsible for communicating and working with cross-functional teams spread globally on various aspects of the application.

  ▷ Responsible for supporting business users by enhancing systems and helping them resolve their concerns and queries, thereby maintaining a smooth day-to-day business operation.

  <Achievements>

  ▷ Developed a low latency, highly scalable large scale distributed business enterprise application using Oracle Coherence and weblogic application server; this service helped significantly to Analysts and other applications to retrieve, manipulate huge Company, Industry and Sector information in reliable and faster way.

- A professional has only defined his job description but just responsibilities no achievements :

  ▷ Execution/Development/Automation/Maintenance of System BSP Modules on different hardware platforms e.g.; File System Tests, Interrupt Tests, OCTL Tests, Timer Tests, Storage Device Tests

- ▷ Development of Various BSP Development Test Tool In C#/ C++/.NET/Visual Studio- 2005 e.g.; Log Parsing Tool, Test Configurations Tools

- ▷ Porting/Automation of System BSP test cases from one hardware platform to another.

- ▷ Wrote various XML configurations files and C# Utilities, which reads config from file for some specific purpose of test.

- ▷ Writing shims which are used with conjunction of application Verify tool that can be used for detecting memory leaks and resource leaks in native code e.g.; File I/O APIs CreateFileW, ReadFile, CloseHandle, Fault Injection.

- ▷ CD-ROM/Storage Device Driver: Test Design, Test Design Specification Creation, Reliability testing Tool for low memory, high CPU Utilization conditions, Automation of Various CDROM IOCTL Test cases, Use Case Scenarios, CD-ROM File System.

If you see all above then you may notice that an interviewer changes his approach to interview a candidate based on the the defined career summary or objective or past exeprience related thing or any thing as your CV/resume offer. You may have worked on various projects and then you may have used the various technologies or maybe part of the technology, so words can make difference e.g. skills versus skills used, technologies versus technologies used.

The more narrow you down the skills offerings and more clear you define what you're going to offer that will be more easier for an interviewer to understand your capabilities e.g. C++ (rating : 5, 3+ yrs of experience), C++ (rating :7, 5+ years of exepreince). It also let the interviewer to ask the relevant questions as defined the offerings in your CV/Resume.

SAMPLE QUESTIONS: C++'S OBJECT SLICING

C++ related questions e.g.; what is Object Slicing in C++?

RATIONALE: *Interviewer saw candidate's 3+ years of C++ experience from his CV, so he asked a question related with C++.*

SAMPLE ANSWER FROM A PROFESSIONAL POINT OF VIEW

Object slicing may happen when derived class object assigned by value to base class object. Object slicing bug may create memory corruption, It depends on case by case but by defining pure virtual functions in base class so that base instance will not be allowed or assigning derived class object by reference to base class may prevent object slicing issue (**and the discussion continued**)

SAMPLE QUESTIONS: DESIGN PATTERNS

Design patterns: explain types of design patterns and your experience using them in past

RATIONALE: *Interviewer read interviewee's CV, and found that he has worked on various C++ projects e.g. designed/implemented work items in C++.*

SAMPLE ANSWER FROM A PROFESSIONAL POINT OF VIEW

Once someone applying OOPS to design the solution of his project, then it could be great idea to have understanding of design patterns which are already experienced and provide a reference for a designer to design the coding architecture of OOPS based projects.

I have just studied design patterns types from books especially which talks about: creational, structural, behavioural, concurrency kind of design patterns, but in my understanding these are all available for reference these may not be a direct fit to your requirement.

On some situation I have used singleton design pattern, where my task require creating only object and it should be accessible from various functions, usually while getting global values. (**and the discussion continued ...**)

Why go for OOPS ?

RATIONALE: *Experience professional may provide the technical concepts on more practical ways.*

SAMPLE ANSWER FROM A PROFESSIONAL POINT OF VIEW

Definitely it depends from situation to situation and case by case

- While writing programs the important things is data, which flow from function to function for processing, received in a form of input, and goes for processing to series of functions.
- Language like C etc have series of functions and a programmer has to use his programming concepts to makes code reliable, stable organized.
- OOPS are some of the standard concepts which can make data belong to individual object, and provide inbuilt ways for data access.
- Inheritance to reuse existing data, and polymorphism, all together maps programming to real words.
- Most of the high level programming languages provide OOPS capabilities **(and the discussion continued ...)**

SAMPLE QUESTIONS: INHERITANCE, ISA, HASA TYPES

Discussion on inheritance, ISA, HASA types

RATIONALE: *While working on a project, which require to design the set of classes, and then relationship between the designed classes. Such relationship surely require to use the inheritance e.g. isa, hasa, and many others (aggregation, compose, generalization, realization).*

SAMPLE ANSWER FROM A PROFESSIONAL **POINT OF VIEW**

Common answer about inheritance: types of inheritance and meanings of private, public, protected inheritance

- While using inheritance concepts, ISA and HASA keeps a high importance, e.g.; HASA denotes those relationships like one class say CAR has his subclasses e.g.; engine, body
- Car class has engine or Car HAS A engine.
- Apple is a Fruit or Sparrow is a Bird - so Apple inheriting the Fruit class, and Sparrow inheriting Bird Class (**and the discussion continued …**)

SAMPLE QUESTIONS: POLYMORPHISM

Please explain your understanding related with polymorphism?

RATIONALE: *Experience professional may provide the technical concepts on more practical ways.*

SAMPLE ANSWER FROM A PROFESSIONAL POINT OF VIEW

Polymorphism (one name multiple forms) is product/programming (if refer to software development and engineering) design technique, its goal to provide single/similar/common/look-alike interface to the external world.

Means logically organized features, and related functions can provide similar interface.

Ex: Rotate (Object, Angle) -> Object can be Triangle, Rectangle, Square

Here Rotate is one function, which receive object name and angle two parameters, and capable to do handle different shapes to rotate.

This polymorphism term more commonly used in object oriented programming. Polymorphism concepts and how effectively it could be practiced, has been clearly defined in OOPS concepts, where means are available to understand/practice and implement it.

e.g.; in C++ - There are meanings/concepts/when to use/difference are available for static polymorphism (operator/function overloading) and dynamic (run-time) polymorphism **(and the discussion continued ...)**

SAMPLE QUESTIONS: INHERITANCE, ISA, HASA TYPES

Describe a specific example where you used polymorphism and inheritance related to object oriented methodology and c++ in one of your projects?

RATIONALE: *Interviewer read interviewee's CV, and found that he has worked on various C++ projects e.g. designed/implemented work items in C++.*

SAMPLE ANSWER FROM A PROFESSIONAL POINT OF VIEW

In one of my project which was the implementation of V2OIP (Video and Voice Over IP) middleware, there I implemented module name Call Manager.

Call Manager: The call manager manages call-connections. This lets the application easily make or receive calls, control events and implement call features e.g. call transfer, call hold, conference call.

Basically Call Manager in V2OIP provides the abstract interface to the application, which can pass possible events received from the user application e.g.; Make Call, Call hold to the Call-Manager, and call manager can do rest of the processing for this Call operation.

Call Manager also separate the call managing functionality from the Call signaling Stack, and it perform most of the call operations from the high level view. In another way, it reduces the complexity of the V2OIP to handle the high level call control operation and it also provide the ongoing call operations updates to the application.

Call Manager provided the abstract interface to the Call/V2oip Application. A Call/V2oIP application can initialize and start the Call Manager. It also provide a list of call events, which can be passed from Call/V2oIP application to the Call Manager as downstream events and Call Manager can also pass some call events to the Call application as upstream events.

For the same I wrote Call Control Adapter Classes, which Implements runtime polymorphism using virtual functions. This Call Control adapter class either call the functionality of H.323 or SIP signaling stack for various call operations.

And Call Manager inherits this Call control Adapter Class to implement call applications. (**and the discussion continued ...**)

SAMPLE QUESTIONS: AN ABSTRACT CLASS

As a Developer, why would one want to use an abstract class? Describe a specific example of when you have used this in the past?

RATIONALE: *Interviewer read interviewee's CV, and found that he has worked on various C++ projects e.g. designed/implemented work items in C++.*

SAMPLE ANSWER FROM A PROFESSIONAL **POINT OF VIEW**

Abstract class basically defines whenever it requires to keep the top interface same across the modules, and that required implementation of these modules by using of these abstract classes.

In other terms abstract class provides the summary of the intended implemention of a project, which have explicitly unimplemented methods, and based on the requirement those could be implemented.

Recently I developed a tool which is based on factory design patters of OOA/D.

On this tool, the top interface is test abstract class, which defined init(), execute(), setup(), exit() kind of methods, so anybody who want to write his test suits, he can inherit test suits abstract class and implement its methods (**and the discussion continued …**)

SAMPLE QUESTIONS:
DYNAMIC MEMORY IN EMBEDDED SYSTEMS

Describe a specific example of when you used dynamic memory in an embedded system

RATIONALE: *Interviewer read interviewee's CV, and found that he has worked on various embedded projects e.g. designed/implemented work items in the embedded domain.*

SAMPLE ANSWER FROM A PROFESSIONAL **POINT OF VIEW**

To Allocate the dynamic memory in embedded systems I have used following memory management functions :

GetSystemInfo, HeapAlloc, HeapCreate, HeapDestroy, HeapFree, HeapReAlloc, HeapSize, VirtualAlloc, LocalAlloc, VirtualFree, VirtualProtect, VirtualQuery

These all functions provide the facility to make memory pools, also called fixed-size-blocks allocation, allow dynamic memory allocation comparable to malloc or C++'s operator new. As those implementations suffer from fragmentation because of variable block sizes, it can be impossible to use them in a real time system due to performance. A more efficient solution is pre allocating a number of memory blocks with the same size called the memory pool. The application can allocate, access, and free blocks represented by handles at runtime (**and the discussion continued ...**)

SAMPLE QUESTIONS: LINUX

What are the directories on Linux, why are these directories used for, explain the file system, directory structure, etc.

RATIONALE: *Interviewer saw candidate's Linux experience from his CV, so he asked a basic question related with Linux operating system.*

SAMPLE ANSWER FROM A PROFESSIONAL **POINT OF VIEW**

Following types of directories (used to group the files) exist by default in ububtu(Linux):

/(root), /bin(contains utilities like cp, cat),/boot(contains Boot-Loader),/dev(for device drivers),/etc(system configuration files e.g.; resolv.conf, nsswitch.conf),/home,/lib(libraries files for /bin and /sbin),/media(generic mount point for removable devices),/mnt(mount point for temporary file system),/opt(for optional packages),/sbin(system Binaries,/srv,/sys(kernel system related files),/tmp(temporary contents),/usr(user specific),/Var(variable contents like logs etc)

* File system: File system is a major component in operating system, that provide a abstract interface to users by hiding file storage/retrieval management in/from hard-disk, cd-rom etc

* There are different types of file system exist e.g.; windows 7 use NTFS [new technology file system] and Mac uses HFS (hierarchical file system) Plus file system for hard-drive (**and the discussion continued ...**)

SAMPLE QUESTIONS:
INTER PROCESS COMMUNICATION IN LINUX

What happens when you type "PS –A" as a command in a Linux command shell?

RATIONALE: *Interviewer saw candidate's Linux experience from his CV, so he asked a basic question related with Linux Operating system:*

PS command means process command, from which one can see all active process related information e.g.; which process are running, corresponding process ID.

SAMPLE ANSWER FROM A PROFESSIONAL POINT OF VIEW

*ps command used to show the active number of process running in system, while giving switch as -e (it shows all process running in the system), other than that it provides several switch option which helps to see anything to everything related to process information at Linux/Unix flavoured system (**and the discussion continued ...**)

SAMPLE QUESTIONS:
INTER PROCESS COMMUNICATION IN LINUX

Did you use IPC before? Can you explain it? What about shared memory and messages queues?

RATIONALE: *Interviewer saw candidate's Linux Experience from his C V, so he asked a question related with Linux operating system.*

SAMPLE ANSWER FROM A PROFESSIONAL POINT OF VIEW

IPC stands for interposes communications. A program in run state used to be a process. It happens when different process runs around (process got forked or threaded and created it's another copy/thread). So communication across process happens via means of sockets, shared memory, pipes, semaphores, signals.

Threading is an another way to divide your executable task in small component for efficiency e.g.; an application is running with two threads, one thread showing UI in front and another thread waiting for the input to get. Another thread got activated once it receive the Input from UI and which later connect to any other process located on other computer or network to transfer this received Input.

e.g.; on this case (second thread) - socket could be used as network endpoint (binded with port/ip) to connect with another network resource.

Discussion about shared memory, message queues etc:

If someone is using threads, then its beneficial to use shared memory. Because then shared memory will be on same address space, and you will be using locks to manage that memory , and everything will be on same place, so you can maintain the synchronization.

However if there are processes, and then you are using the shared memory, then synchronization will cost you a lot. you need to maintain the synchronization. Another things, if processes are running in same processor its, okay, but if they are running on different machine, then again you need to do the memory transfer from one processor address space to another address space, while on message queue, you need not to do the synchronization stuff.

* Shared memory.

Advantage: Fast

Disadvantage: additional burden of keeping synchronisation.

* Message queues.

Advantage: synchronisation is taken care

Disadvantage: relatively slower than shared memory (**and the discussion continued ...**)

SAMPLE QUESTIONS: MULTITHREADING

Explain the use of the pthread condition variable

RATIONALE: *Multithreading is one of the very common programming method-ology, which used on most of the projects. POSIX (Portable operat-ing system interfaces) is a IEEE standard, which has provided posix threads(pthread_xxx) interfaces and those are used on windows/ linux for system programming e.g. threads, mutexes, condition vari-ables, cancellation, thread specific data.*

Interviewer saw candidate's multithreading experience from his CV, so he asked a question related with pthread multithreading.

SAMPLE ANSWER FROM A PROFESSIONAL POINT OF VIEW

Pthread or POSIX threads is a API standard, pthread condition variable type of pthread_cond_t used by threads in a situation e.g.; thread suspend its execution until it meets with a condition on pthread condition variable.

To have its exact use, it require pthread_cond_signal and pthread_cond_wait kind of pthread functions, one sample use case e.g.; two threads got created by a pro-gram, and both are playing with a pthread condition variable say "COUNT", so both can work together based on the situation of count variable e.g., If COUNT has even values thread A will work and on odd values thread B will work (**and the discussion continued ...**)

SAMPLE QUESTIONS: RTOS PRIORITY OF TASKS

RTOS: Describe a specific example of a situation when you determined the priority of tasks. what technique(s) did you use?

RATIONALE: *Most operating system carries following type of OS concepts :*

- *Major design goals, history, release system, design principles*
- *High level idea of kernel, system libraries, system utilities*
- *High level idea of kernel modules*
- *Interesting OS related concepts e.g. how kernel's module management works e.g. insmod, how driver registration works, how conflict resolution works e.g. multiple driver accessing same h/w resource*
- *Process management in OS e.g. process identity, process context, scheduling context, virtual memory context*
- *Process, thread, proorities with OS*
- *Scheduling algorithms with OS e.g. preemptive, priority based algorithm*
- *Kernel synchronization e.g. prior to version x kernel was non –preemptive kernel (meaning running in kernel mode could not be preëmpted)*
- *Spinlocks and semaphore*
- *Critical section, processor's interrupt control h/w*
- *Memory management e.g. pages, virtual memory, management of physical memory, swapping and paging, execution and loading of user programs*
- *File System*
- *Input/Output : block drivers, character devices, network devices*
- *Socket interface, protocol drivers, network device drivers*
- *Security e.g. authentication and access drivers*

Interviewer saw candidate's RTOS(real time operating system) related experience from his CV, so he asked a question related with RTOS.

SAMPLE ANSWER FROM A PROFESSIONAL POINT OF VIEW

Recently I have worked with WinCE threads, which supports 256 thread priorities (zero is the highest priority and 255 is the lowest).

High priority task prevent lower priority task to run, so all tasks need to be written so that they do not use excessive CPU time or overall system may suffer.

Example of when I determined the priority of tasks.

For an example, I wrote one application which interacts to system with three threads. The threads are a GUI thread, a data collection thread and a touch driver interrupt thread.

1. The GUI thread needs to update data and be responsive to the user. Users are important and their impression of the system is important to selling product, so when the user wants to interact with the system one need to be responsive. The priority of the GUI thread can actually be low if the other threads in the system give it time to run once in a while.

2. The application was designed to collect data. Missing data will be perceived as worse than not responding to the user. This thread priority needs to be high, but because data collection can be CPU intensive this thread needs share the CPU.

3. The user interacts with the system through the touch panel. If application don't detect when the user touches the panel, the GUI will certainly not respond. This thread priority also needs to be high, but processing touch panel input is not very CPU intensive. Setting this priority higher than the data collection thread will probably not cause data to be missed.

There was another situation, in which various threads were running in its own normal priority, but all threads are supposed to filter data based on receive data from serial port, So I made high priority of serial Port thread.

Techniques Used

CeSetThreadPriority

This function sets the priority for a real-time thread on a thread by thread basis and it takes two parameter one thread Id and another is thread priority from zero to 255. **(and the discussion continued ...)**

SAMPLE QUESTIONS:
INTERACTION OF TASKS AT DIFFERENT PRIORITIES

RTOS: Describe a specific example of the interaction of tasks at different priorities within the RTOSs you have used?

RATIONALE: *Interviewer saw candidate's RTOS related experience from his CV, so he asked a question related with RTOS.*

SAMPLE ANSWER FROM A PROFESSIONAL **POINT OF VIEW**

Wince 6.0 board support package which is almost provides the RTOS services runs various tasks e.g. NK.EXE (OAL), GWES.EXE (touch, display, keyboard), FileSys.Exe(object store, rom fs, storage manager), Device.EXE(block device, serial, custom), Services.exe (ftp, httpd, telnetd) threads which interacts with hardware devices.

These all thread priorities are defined based on following priorities: 0-19 (open real time above drivers), 2 0(graphics vertical drivers), 99 (power management resume thread), 100-108 (usb ohci uhci, serial), 109-129 (irsir1, ndis, touch), 130 (kitl), 131 (vmini), 132 (cxport), 145 (ps2 keyboard), 148 (ircomm), 150 (tapi), 248 (power management), 249 (wavedev, mouse, pnp, power), 250 (waveapi), 251 (normal), 252-255 (open applications)

Defining the priority of the thread/task is to carefully understand the order of the execution of tasks, it's also depends that all tasks are running on same priority and on some specific situation the priority of task changes because of the task order, e.g.; in some situation one task receive data and then another task filter that data and then another display in gui. So task which display data to gui could be in low priority, and some time could be in high priority when it changes from idle mode(running screen savers) to active mode.

Priority inversion also happens when higher priority thread blocks lower priority thread to run and those are specific scenario, which can be analyzed carefully and on that time one can perform priority inversion to avoid deadlock. Its also possible when a thread is waiting for a asynchronous I/O and its blocks other threads, on that scenario one might need to perform priority inversion (**and the discussion continued ...**)

SAMPLE QUESTIONS: SECURITY LEVELS

Explain a few security levels you are familiar with.

RATIONALE: *Interviewer saw candidate's security related experience from his CV, so he asked a basic question related with security.*

SAMPLE ANSWER FROM A PROFESSIONAL **POINT OF VIEW**

- SQL Security:
    - ▷ SQL injection
    - ▷ SQL authentication
    - ▷ Restriction to scripts and regular expression

- Web based Security
    - ▷ Application Pool
    - ▷ Web.config authentication and authorisation
    - ▷ Windows based authentication
    - ▷ Kerberos Authentication
    - ▷ SSL - Security Certificates
    - ▷ Digest Authentication - Auth Token
    - ▷ Impersonation

- Security at File System and registry level
    - ▷ ACL –Access Control Lists
    - ▷ CACL –Modify Access Control Lists

- Security at Firewall level
- Security at transport Layer e.g. Secure Socket Layer
- Site to Site tunnel via Virtual Private Network e.g. OpenVPN
- Cryptographic protocols for encryption, decryption (**and the discussion continued …**

SAMPLE QUESTIONS: SIP METHODS

What are different SIP methods?

RATIONALE: *Interviewer viewed candidate CV and found candidate past experience in SIP(session initiation protocol), and asked about it.*

SAMPLE ANSWER FROM A PROFESSIONAL **POINT OF VIEW**

Discussion about REGISTER, INVITE, ACK, CANCEL, BYE, OPTIONS as defined in rfc-3261

- REGISTER for registering contact information,
- INVITE, ACK, and CANCEL for setting up sessions,
- BYE for terminating sessions,
- OPTIONS for querying servers about their capabilities.
- There is some SIP extension which defines extra methods e.g.; SIP extensions, documented in standards track RFCs, may define additional methods e.g.; NOTIFY defined in rfc-3265

For a Cloud Infrastructure professional's

Citrix XenServer 6.0 Administration Essential Guide	Daniele Tosatto
Web Operations: Keeping the Data On Time	By John Allspaw /Jesse Robbins
Building a Monitoring Infrastructure By Nagios	By David Josephsen
Data Center Fundamentals	Mauricio Arregoces, Maurizio Portolani

For a Linux os professional's

Linux Kernel Development (3rd Edition)	Robert Love
Understanding the Linux Kernel, Third Edition	Daniel P. Bovet, Marco Cesati Ph.D. (Author)
The Linux Programming Interface: A Linux and UNIX System Programming Handbook	Michael Kerrisk
Professional Linux Kernel Architecture	Wolfgang Mauerer

for a ... professional's

....	

How To's

On this How To section you will be explained some of the standard situations where candidate can prepare better or cross check better Or he already knows what to do on those situation but still if he/she want to refer someone guidelines e.g.; prepare a strategy for effective job search

JOB SEARCH: STRATEGY FOR JOB SEARCH

How do you prepare a strategy for job search?

RATIONALE: *It happens that professionals gets their first placement from the campus, but still that also require a strategy e.g. as that also require to prepare the career profile, prepare to get ready for discussion.*

Professional may prepare a strategy by writing their technical blog or develop an application or answers on stack overflow or contribution on the open source or anything else. Different professionals will have different approach to prepare their career profile and different way to present to the prospective employer.

SAMPLE ANSWER FROM A PROFESSIONAL **POINT OF VIEW**

DEFINE MYSELF

I may write a small write-up approximately (15 to 25 Lines), which can minimum cover following:

- My Specifics: highlights career summary, current/past job role, skills.
- What I am looking: possible job roles, types of industry and how my capabilities could be a great fit.

Later I forward this write-up to prospective recruiters.

PROSPECTIVE RECRUITERS

- General recruiters who works for recruitment company e.g. XYZ recruitment services
- Specific recruiters who works for a specific company e.g. Microsoft, Google, Cisco

TYPES OF CVS

- General CVs for general or specific recruiters to let them understand my background, skills and interest if actual job position unknown to me.
- Specific CVs for general recruiters or specific recruiters to let them understand my background, skills and interest if actual job position known to me.

*Known: because of job advertisements at company's job site, or any other job site

*Unknown: enquired possible job opportunities via friends, network, acquaintances and recruiters.

PROPER PLANNING

- I might plan to do a proper planning for my job search e.g. understand practical concepts of industry, projects etc.

FINALIZE MY LIST OF COMPANIES

- Min -10
  - ▷ Microsoft, Google, Adobe, NetApp, Ciena, ST Microelectronics, Yahoo, Facebook, FreeScale, Broadcom | [Read these companies website and understand their requirements based on the job-section, product and also see my interest and I will find a match]

FINALIZE LOCATIONS

- Min -4
  - ▷ A, B, C, D

FINALIZE TYPES OF DOMAIN

- Min -3
  - ▷ Project consulting for J2EE based services and products,
  - ▷ J2EE ERP Technical Architect,
  - ▷ Business/Market/Product Development for J2EE based services and Products

FINALIZE INDIVIDUAL SET OF TECHNOLOGIES

Min -3 e.g. Java and related frameworks, Database, JPA in Linux, Windows and Mobile Platform

More specifically

1. JBOSS and other Application Server: Concept of Application Server, Administration, Deployment as well as Auto deployment e.g. starting stopping server.

   Concept of web container, EJB container, JSP Engine, Servlet Engine, Server›s load balancing, Clustering, Heap Size...

2. Middle-ware Java component and various Frameworks: Java, EJB3 (Stateful/Stateless Session Bean, Entity Bean), Connection Pooling, Instance

Pooling, Transactions, J2EE Design Patterns. JBoss Seam Framework, ORM (object relational mapping)

3. Presentation Layer: (Web Development) HTML, XML, JSP, JSF(Java Server Faces), Servlet, JDBC

4. MySQL, Database Layer: PL/SQL, Database architecture, ER-Diagram, creating database, table, schema, Store-procedure, view

Start connecting with anyone e.g. friends, recruiters, websites, anything and hunt until the day I do not get perfect or semi-perfect or ideal job.

It may take 6 to 12 weeks to land.

TIME PLANNING

Plan it - Two weeks to understand the domain of all companies, their products, and try to make a list of people, recruiters, acquaintances who work there.

Two Weeks - prepare myself, and CV

Three Weeks - Start applying and preparing my self

Three Weeks - Get a right Job

CAREER PATH: YOUR CAREER

May you explain which career path you chose while joining to job market and how?

RATIONALE: *At some point of time individuals feels the urge to choose a career based on their certain career oriented parameters e.g. educational background, experiences, interest, beliefs, technologies trends, job opportunities specifics, suggestions from certain type of professionals, growth in short term vs. long-term.*

Individuals also study and observe happenings in the related industry e.g. by networking with similar types of professionals, visiting company's websites, joining tech events, trend of hiring.

SAMPLE ANSWER FROM A PROFESSIONAL **POINT OF VIEW**

During my academic I concentrated in the field of Information Retrieval and spent three years to explore this area e.g. studied books to learn IR basics, studied basics of Apache Hadoop, studied basics of Apache Solr, developed small application to exercise the capabilities of technologies and my creativity, participated in university technical events, networked with similar types of professionals and made myself as a professional for text search based technologies.

So I searched job opportunities in similar area and since then I am working into the field Information retrieval.

SAMPLE ANSWER FROM A PROFESSIONAL **POINT OF VIEW**

During my academic I concentrated in the field of Network Tools Development and spent three years to explore this area e.g. studied socket programming, studied networking internals of Linux operating systems, studied rfcs for TCP/IP protocols, studied rfcs related with routing protocols, practically exercised Network related tools (ping, nslookup, whois, traceroute, monitoring tools), practically analyzed ethernet packet capture tools (tcpdump, ethreal, Net analyzer), practically analyzed Wi-Fi Packet Capture Tool-AiroPeek (Wild Packets) wireless network traffic and protocol analyzer from WildPackets for 802.11(a, b, g), understood wireless LAN (WLAN) network troubleshooting and monitoring challenges, Written small network tools to understand my capabilities and creativity.

So I searched job opportunities in similar area and since then I am working into the field networks tools development.

CAREER PATH: YOUR CV

How do you organize and frame your professional details into a CV for job opportunities?

RATIONALE: *Individual organize their professionals details into a CV based on their focus areas and it also depends then on prospective CV readers.*

May be professional preparing these details for finding the entry level jobs which would be seen by only HR recruiters or next level or it may be possible that this CV would be seen by Project Leaders, or Project Managers, it all depends.

Because people organize their details based on their to fit to their purpose.

SAMPLE ANSWER FROM A PROFESSIONAL POINT OF VIEW

I defined my professional details based on the specific job role in my mind, it could have 2-3 variations, based on my interests or trend such as following roles are more or less same :

- software developer in test, software quality engineer, software engineer in test

- software project manager, software engineering manager, program manager

Misc

Misc FAQ related to this Book:

FAQ: THIS BOOK

A.1   **What kind of Q/A does EXECUTE THE JOB INTERVIEW-Book Provide?**

A A.1:   EXECUTE THE JOB INTERVIEW book provides a prevalent combination of Job-Interviews questions/answer related to Information Technologies industry.

A.2   **Why read EXECUTE THE JOB INTERVIEW-Book If it's easily possible to get various question and answers from the Internet?**

A A.2:   Attending a job interview requires considerable planning, and a job interview usually involves discussion, and that discussion involves a set of questions/answers.

Based on a professional experience and belief a professional usually refers to various sources to plan his or her job -discussion e.g. Internet, friends, self-prepared notes etc.

In a common case – this book provides an extra option to plan a job-Interview discussion in advance.

In Practice:

    ▷   EXECUTE THE JOB INTERVIEW is a digital/physical companion in a form of a printed book to let its reader to get focused in one flow.

    ▷   EXECUTE THE JOB INTERVIEW 's readers gets contiguous and effective thoughts to plan his or her job-interview.

    ▷   EXECUTE THE JOB INTERVIEW contains organized notes for a job interview discussion, which invokes a professional to organize his or her thoughts.

All together, EXECUTE THE JOB INTERVIEW has organized the most prevalent discussion topics of the job interview and it has been built up in the philosophy of well organized, fair and effective thoughts related to the planning for a interview-discussion.

A.3   **Why are only a few coding questions/answers explained ? why aren't all technical areas covered?**

A A.3:   EXECUTE THE JOB INTERVIEW doesn't concentrate on technical or a specific type of knowledge, It explains prevalent combination of job-Interviews questions and its answers from a professional point of view.

EXECUTE THE JOB INTERVIEW 's objective is to let readers prepare well for interviews, be organized and make effective thoughts related to his or her planning for a job-interview-discussion.

A.4 I found an error on a Question/Answer/anywhere in the book?

A A.4: To make EXECUTE THE JOB INTERVIEW better please report any issue at: errata@thecareertools.com, and we will try to fix it on the next release version.

A.5 May I prepare my job-interview from these Q/A only? And is this good enough?

A A.5: Please refer to DISCLAIMER. This book is just a reference, not a complete guide, It may help you little or a lot, it all depends.

Example: General Areas, Past Project Area Q/A are most standard onces, a professional may refer those Q/A and prepare his own thoughts, which best suits and fit to his or her situation.

A.6 May I know how did you find all of these Q/A ?

A A.6: All these Q/A aren't copied from anywhere, If any answer or Q happened to be same from some other place, then it's purely coincidence. These are written based on self experience e.g. author mentored candidates, author interviewed by set of companies, author interviewing candidates, author working in 2 different geographical locations.

A.7 Can I provide some of my comments related to thebok ?

A A.7: Please contact: suggestions@thecareertools.com

A.8 I found some questions that may be suitable for this book

A A.8: Please Contact errata@thecareertools.com

Subject line must start from: EXECUTE THE JOB INTERVIEW or EIJ

A.9 Will you have a next version of this book?

A A.9: Please keep visiting www.thecareertools.com or send us an e-mail at : contact@thecareertools.com

Subject line must start from: EXECUTE THE JOB INTERVIEW or EIJ

A.10 **I would like to talk with the author and arrange a consultancy interview**

A A.10: Please do following :

Send an e-mail at : sumit@thecareertools.com

Subject line must start from: EXECUTE THE JOB INTERVIEW or EIJ

A.11 **I have some suggestions with respect to the content of the book. Can I report them?**

A A.11: Please get in touch with: suggestions@thecareertools.com

Subject line must start from: EXECUTE THE JOB INTERVIEW or EIJ

A.12 **I tried to run the code given in xyz question, but it gave a error. Why is this happening?**

A A.12: Read Disclaimer

A.13 **How can I get an update when the next version of this book is released?**

A A.13: Please send an e-mail at : contact@thecareertools.com

Subject line must start from: EXECUTE THE JOB INTERVIEW or EIJ / Next Release

A.14 **I was not convinced by the various Questions, and the questions do not fit my thought process.**

A A.14: Please send your feedback at: feedback@thecareertools.com and also read the disclaimer.

Appendix

WHAT IS YOUR SKILL TABLE?

1. Browser Side (programming)	2. Server Side (programming)	3. Server Software	4. Compiler Suits	5. Browser Technologies
HTML	Java Server Pages	apache web server	GNU gcc/g++	layout
CSS	Servlets	apache tomcat	Borland's Turbo C++	rendering
Java Script	PHP	jetty	Microsoft's Visual studio	graphics (2D/3D)
NPAPI	Perl(optional)	node.js	LLVM	media layer
google native client	Ruby (optional)	lightpd	CLANG	javascript engines (v8, spider monkey)
activeX plugin (	Python	netty	JDK (java compiler)	networking (libuv, curl etc)
COM)	erlang (optional)	web sphere	NDK (android native compiler)	parsing (http, html)
mozilla xp com	Google Go	microsoft IIS	gc (google go compiler)	font config, free type
w3c		JBOSS	rustc (mozilla rust compiler)	threading and thread pools
			code generation concepts	Webkit technology
			lexical analysis	
			Abstract syntax tree	
			Intermediate code	

6. Desktop application	7. Mobile application	8. Operating systems	9. Computer networking	10. Cloud computing
Qt gtk java (SWT etc) MFC, win32 programming	Objective-C, Cocoa for iphone Android SDK, eclipse, java Qt /Qt creator webos (HP or Palm) Windos mobile sdk	Linux (complete administration) Windows (must know) Android Haiku/BeOS (optional, good to know) Mac OSX (must know) webinos tizen meego/ Jolla black berry os	TCP/IP xml-rpc web rtc web sockets distributed hash table (DHT) socket programming xmpp, http, smtp, ftp, vnc, afp, nfs ping, finger, gopher etc protocols middleware (RPC/RMI/Corba) Distributed Hash tables NAT ARP	Content networking, CDNs proxy, load balancing virtualization Platform as a Service Software as a Service Storage as a Service clustering and super computing Amezon S3 etc fundamentals

11. Game Programming	12. Computing	13. Tools/ editors/ IDEs	14. Computer architecture	15. Programming languages
open gl	multi threading	vi (for every thing)	x86 (must know)	C++ / C / C#
SDL	open mp	komodo	arm (must know)	Java
mozilla azure	parallel	GIT version control (github)	concept of followings:	Java Script
skia	programming	SVN, perforce, Hg (murcurial)	stack	Go
micro soft direct	open CL	CVS, bugzilla, jira, confluence	heap	rust
X	event based	code collaborator	stack pointer	regular
open AL	models/	doxygen, source forge	program counter	expression
webkit	asnycronous	google code, eclipse	DS, CS, SS, Fence register	shell
transitions	programming	web storm (for java script)	etc	programming
cairo	Algorithms and	virtual box or vm ware	free variables	xml, json
core animation	data structures	office suit (ms office or open office)	closures	html
(apple)	crypto graphy	ebook writing tool like iBook	memory allocation of	other optional :
physics engine		Author, Tex/ Latex	various variables	ruby
(chipmunk)		dependency checker	process control block	python
cocos 2d (		team viewer	thread local storage	perl
iphone)		vlc (player + video convertor)	thread control block	lua
		audacity, filezilla	processor registers	erlang
		phone gap	offsets in dynamic libraries	coffe script
			static vs dynamic libraries	

16. Database	17. Design Patterns, Anti patterns, Methodologies	18. Simulation/ Emulation	19. Testing/Automation/ Build tools	20. Embedded Tools
mysql	Singleton, decorator, adapter,	busybox	apache jmeter	21. Telecom Standards
oracle	wrapper, proxy, aggregation,	qemu	QTP	22. IETF Standards
couch db (no sql data base)	iterator, MVC ..... etc		load runner	
mongo db	UML		selenium IDE	23. Standradizations
memcached	HLD, LLD, SDLC, agile		ant	24. Healthcare ....
hibernate (persistance layer)	scrum		cmake	25. Banking
spring JDBC	exception handling anti patterns		gyp	
DB2			hudson	...

Table 1: Skills

ON WHICH TYPE OF INDUSTRY CENTRIC SOLUTIONS ARE YOU INVOLVED OR WOULD LIKE TO BE INVOLVED?

Industry Centric Solutions
Banking and Financial Services
Insurance
Healthcare
Pharmaceuticals and Life
Science
Retail & Logistics
Education and E-learning
Gaming
Utilities
Construction
Telecom
Misc Professional, Scientific, and Technical Solutions
....

Table-2: Industry Centric solutions

WHICH JOB TITLE CLOSELY DEFINES THE TYPE OF PROFESSIONAL YOU ARE OR EXPECT TO BE?

Most common job titles are Software engineers, Software developers or Software testers ?

C# Developer	Search Engine Marketing (SEM) Associate	Senior Storage Engineer	Software Quality Assurance (SQA) Supervisor
C/C++/Java/Python/Php Software Engineer	Search Engine Marketing (SEM) Consultant	Senior Storage Specialist, (Computer Information Technology)	Software Quality Control (QC) Analyst
Data Warehouse Analyst	Search Engine Marketing (SEM) Coordinator	Senior Strategy Analyst	Software Quality Control (QC) Manager
Data Warehouse Developer	Search Engine Marketing (SEM) Manager	Senior Strategy Manager	Software Quality Engineer Manager
Data Warehouse Manager	Search Engine Marketing (SEM) Specialist	Senior Supplier Quality Engineer (SQE)	Software Quality Tester
Database Administration (DBA) Manager	Search Engine Marketing (SEM) Strategist	Senior Support Services Technician	Software Specialist
Database Administrator (DBA)	Search Engine Optimization (SEO) Account Manager	Senior Systems Administrator	Software Team Leader

Database Analyst	Search Engine Optimization (SEO) Analyst	Senior Systems Analyst	Software Technical Training Coordinator
Database Analyst/ Programmer	Search Engine Optimization (SEO) Director	Senior Systems Developer	Software Test Analyst
Database Design Administrator	Search Engine Optimization (SEO) Expert	Senior Systems Engineer	Software Test Associate
Database Design Analyst	Search Engine Optimization (SEO) Guru	Senior Systems Engineer (Computer Networking / IT)	Software Test Engineer (STE)
Database Engineer	Search Engine Optimization (SEO) Lead	Software Applications Program Manager	Software Test Lead
Database Manager	Search Engine Optimization (SEO) Manager	Software Architect	Software Test Technician
Information Assurance Engineer	Search Engine Optimization (SEO) Marketing Strategist	Software Architect, Applications	Software Trainer
Information Assurance Manager	Search Engine Optimization (SEO) Professional	Software Architect, Operating Systems	Sr. Software Engineer / Developer / Programmer
Information Assurance Officer	Search Engine Optimization (SEO) Researcher	Software Design Director	System Administrator, Computer / Network

Information Center Representative	Search Engine Optimization (SEO) Specialist	Software Design Engineer (SDE)	System Administrator, PC
Information Systems (IS) Analyst	Search Engine Optimization (SEO) Team Manager	Software Design Engineer in Test (SDET)	System Administrator, Server
Information Systems (IS) Manager	Security Administrator, Computer Network	Software Design Manager	System Administrator, Unix Server
Information Systems (IS) Supervisor	Security Administrator, IT	Software Developer	System Administrator, Web
Information Systems Audit Manager	Security Aide	Software Developer / Business Analyst, Client Applications	System Administrator, Windows Server
Information Systems Auditor	Security Architect, IT	Software Developer / Business Analyst, Database	System Certifications & Compliance Auditor
Information Systems Coordinator, Medical	Security Consultant, (Computing / Networking / Information Technology)	Software Developer / Business Analyst, Web Applications	System Certifications & Compliance Engineer
Information Technology (IT) Architect	Security Consultant, IT	Software Developer, Client / Server	System Integration Engineer

Information Technology (IT) Consultant	Security Coordinator, Bank (Physical / Personnel / Grounds Security)	Software Developer, Client Applications	System Support Administrator
Information Technology (IT) Director	Security Director, Computing / Networking / Information Technology	Software Developer, Data Warehouse	System Support Administrator (Computer)
Information Technology (IT) Intern	Senior Data Mining Analyst	Software Developer, Database	Systems & Programming Director
Information Technology (IT) Manager	Senior Data Quality Analyst	Software Developer, Embedded Devices	Systems & Programming Manager
Information Technology (IT) Supervisor	Senior Database Administrator (DBA)	Software Developer, Games	Systems Administrator
Information Technology (IT) Trainer	Senior Database Engineer	Software Developer, Operating Systems	Systems Analysis Manager
Information Technology Specialist	Senior Network Administrator, IT	Software Developer, SAP	Systems Analysis Supervisor
Network & Computer Systems Administrator Assistant	Senior Network Coordinator	Software Developer, Server	Systems Developer

Network / System Administrator, General Office	Senior Network Coordinator, IT	Software Developer, Web Applications	Systems Engineer
Network Administrator, Data Center	Senior Search Engine Optimization (SEO) Expert	Software Development Engineer (SDE)	Systems Engineer (Computer Networking / IT)
Network Administrator, IT	Senior Search Engine Optimization (SEO) Manager	Software Development Engineer, Test (SDET)	Systems Engineer, IT
Network Administrator, LAN	Senior Search Engine Optimization (SEO) Specialist	Software Development Manager	Systems Engineer, Messaging
Network Administrator, LAN / WAN	Senior Search Marketing Analyst	Software Engineer	Systems Integrator (Computer / Networking)
Network and Computer Systems Director	Senior Shipping Manager	Software Engineer / Developer / Programmer	Systems Intern
Network Control Operator	Senior Software Architect	Software Engineering / Development Director	Systems Manager, IT
Network Control Supervisor	Senior Software Development Engineer (SDE)	Software Engineering Group Manager	Systems Programmer Analyst

Network Engineer	Senior Software Development Engineer, Test (SDET)	Software Engineering Manager	Systems Technician (Computer)
Network Engineer, IT	Senior Software Engineer	Software Lead Tester	Test / Quality Assurance (QA) Engineer (Computer Software)
Network Engineer, Wireless RF	Senior Software Engineering / Development Director	Software Quality Analyst	Test / Quality Assurance (QA) Engineer (Integrated Circuit)
Network Operations Center (NOC) Technician	Senior Software Development Engineer (SDE)	Software Quality Assurance (SQA) Analyst	Test / Quality Assurance (QA) Engineer, (Computer Networking)
Network Support Engineer	Senior Software Development Engineer, Test (SDET)	Software Quality Assurance (SQA) Engineer	Test Analyst
Network Systems / Data Communications Analyst	Senior Software Engineer	Software Quality Assurance (SQA) Lead	Test Engineer (Automation, Computer Hardware, Semiconductor)
Network Technician, IT	Senior Software Engineering / Development Director	Software Quality Assurance (SQA) Lead Tester	Test Engineer, Automation

Network/Data Communications Manager	Senior Sous Chef	Software Quality Assurance (SQA) Manager	Test Engineer, Computer Hardware
Search Engine Marketing (SEM) Analyst	Senior Staff Counsel	Software Quality Assurance (SQA) Specialist	Test Engineer, Semiconductor , Test Engineering Manager, Test Manager

Table-3 : Job Titles

INDEX

A

About yourself 8, 29–30, 32
Academic background 32, 35
Adding two n-bit binary integers 285
Algorithm 4, 13, 171, 195–204, 206,
    211–212, 214, 216–221, 223–226,
    233–234, 246, 248–251, 253–254,
    261, 264–265, 267, 269–271, 273,
    276, 291, 293–294, 302, 307–308,
    313, 317, 321, 325, 329, 336, 339,
    342, 348, 352, 360, 363, 365, 367,
    370, 374–375, 382, 385, 388–389,
    391, 393, 396, 399, 402, 406,
    410–411, 418, 426, 436, 447, 455,
    461, 464, 467, 471, 479, 484, 486,
    491, 496, 500, 512, 523, 533, 537,
    545–546, 550, 555, 559, 562, 565,
    576–577, 646
Algorithmic solution 271
Algorithms complexities
    examples 198
Algorithms during interviews 261
Algorithms walk through 195–196,
    198–199, 204, 206, 209–210, 215,
    220, 224
Algorithm to do wild card string
    matching 370
All subsets of length k 537
Amazon 9, 11, 14, 21, 24–25, 93,
    581–582
An abstract class 639
Anagrams 259, 374–378
Angle between hour and minute
    needle 533
Apple 9, 11, 14, 107, 191, 261, 581–
    582, 630, 636
Appraisal 142
Approach while designing the x 118
Architecture, specifications 123
Areas for improvement 17, 55
Array 22, 197–204, 207–208, 210, 212,
    214–219, 221, 226–229, 232, 234–

235, 239–240, 252–254, 258, 261,
    267, 269–274, 276–282, 285–286,
    290–296, 298–300, 302–303, 307–
    309, 311–314, 317–319, 321–327,
    329–334, 336–339, 343–345, 349,
    363–364, 367, 371, 374, 379, 383,
    388, 391, 393, 399–400, 403, 422,
    462, 467–468, 500, 502, 505, 516,
    528–529, 531, 537–539, 555–558,
    569, 576–577
Array or linked list 270
Associative arrays 194, 258–260
A well designed product 131

B

Best practices 70, 77–78, 139, 189,
    579, 630
Best/worst 198
Binary search trees 204–205, 241,
    246–247, 255, 261, 377
Binary tree level by level, left to
    write 475
Bits 213–214, 258, 288, 403, 528,
    545–548, 562–564, 607
Brute-force approach 206–208
B-trees 247
Bubble sort 199–201
Bucket sort 202–203
Bug report 583
Business line 102
Business requirements of xyz
    project 145

C

Career aspirations 37, 39, 41, 43–44,
    46, 79–80, 82, 86, 127, 140–141
Career cautious 84
Career change 86
Career movement 88, 90, 92
Career negotiation 93
Career objectives 94

R

Rabin-karp algorithm 223
Radix sort 202
Recently studied or researched? 46
Recommendation 39, 114, 152, 154
Red-black trees 244–247, 261, 377
Remove all nodes with even values 17, 461, 597
Removing duplicates 329
Returns the number of times any character in string 399
Reverse a singly linked list 436
Reverse the bits of a number 545
Reverse the digits of a given integer 19, 559
Reverse the order of words 388
Reversing a double linked list 238
Role on xyz project 101
Rooted trees 194, 240–241, 244, 247
Routine to draw a circle 565
Rtos priority of tasks 646

S

Sample interview loop 14, 17, 21, 24
Sample questions 17, 21, 633–643, 645–646, 648–650
Sample sde interview 21
Sample sdet interview 17
Sample sqet interview 24
Scale from 1-to-10 159, 180
Searching approaches 204–206
Searching in arrays and linked lists 204
Security levels 649
Selection sort 200
Sending 94, 500
Sequence of the form 012345678910111213141 5 313
Sets and multi-sets 255–257
Share your experience 129
Shuffling a deck of cards 568
Simulating check-out lines 235
Sip methods 24, 650
Software development life cycle 155
Software purchase application 135, 615

Software testing 27–28, 33, 157–158
Sorted array rotation 336
Sorting approaches 199–203
Spending non-work hours 84
Split the array in odd and even 321
Stacks 92, 118, 232–234, 262, 267, 298–300, 406–408, 410, 412, 486
Stack using two queues 418
Stage of the current work item 109
Strategy for job search 654
String algorithms 220–221, 223–224, 367
String representation of the integer 342
Strings 46, 194, 220, 223–224, 229–231, 267, 339, 342, 345, 348, 352, 356–357, 360–361, 363, 367, 370–371, 374, 377–379, 382–383, 385–386, 388, 391–392, 395–396, 399–400, 402, 551
String search 206, 224
String to see if it contains palindromes 345
Strong technical skills 159
Strtok function 352
Suggestion 80, 116–117, 179, 184
Supervisor's comments about you 152
Surrounding work items 184

T

Task management 251
Task scheduling algorithm 212
Team collaboration 161, 189
Team leading 137
Team matching 72, 163, 165, 167
Team members' comments about you 154
Team size information 112
Team work 79, 163, 182
Technical areas 15, 627, 629, 660
Technical skills 15, 26, 53, 86, 159, 169, 171, 173, 175, 177, 187, 627, 629
Technologies domain 173
Technology differences 175
Test areas 15, 24, 61, 127, 579
Test a soda machine 592